CHOICES FOR A HEALTHY HEART

by Joseph C. Piscatella

Recipes by Bernie Piscatella

WORKMAN PUBLISHING, NEW YORK

ACKNOWLEDGMENTS

This book has become a reality thanks to the support and cooperation of many people. In particular, we are grateful to the many medical professionals who gave of their time and expertise, providing valuable appraisals of and suggestions concerning the manuscript. These include Dr. Denton Cooley, Dr. Victor Froelicher, Dr. Barry Franklin, Dr. Evette Hackman, Amy Harkey (R.D.), Diane Gallagher (R.N.), Jean Macy (R.D.), Mary Prather (R.D.), Patricia Lewis (R.N.) and Lynn McInerny (R.N.). In addition, Joan Imhof, Patti Brutskern, Peggy Paradise, Kathy Anderson and Bonnie Nelson were very helpful in providing editorial comment and suggestions for change. Anne Piscatella and Joe Piscatella played an instrumental role in proofing the manuscript. And finally, our thanks to Peter Workman for his faith in our work, and to Sally Kovalchick and Lynn Strong for their fine editorial hand.

Library of Congress Cataloging-in-Publication Data
Piscatella, Joseph C.
   Choices for a healthy heart.

   Bibliography: p.
   Includes indexes
   1. Heart—Diseases—Popular works.   2. Heart—Diseases—Prevention.   3. Low-calorie diet—Recipes.
I. Piscatella, Bernie.   II. Title.
RC672.P55 1987   616.1'205   87-10439
ISBN 0-89480-138-4 (pbk.)

Workman Publishing Company
1 West 39 Street
New York, New York 10018

First printing October 1987
10 9 8 7 6 5 4 3

*To our mothers,
who taught us to find
the positive even in
adversity.*

FOREWORD

by Denton A. Cooley, M.D.

en years ago, when Joseph Piscatella learned at age 32 that he must undergo surgery for life-threatening coronary artery disease, he had no idea what a blessing his experience would prove to be—both for himself and for others like him. Until serious illness struck, Piscatella, like most other Americans, had been complacent about good health. His brush with coronary artery disease made him realize that, although surgery could correct the immediate problem, it could not provide a permanent solution. Piscatella's efforts to adopt a healthier lifestyle resulted in his first book, *Don't Eat Your Heart Out,* which has enjoyed outstanding success. Now its companion volume, *Choices for a Healthy Heart,* focuses on critical aspects of modern lifestyle that influence quality of health and length of life.

Researchers no longer doubt that certain basic lifestyle factors such as diet, exercise, alcohol, smoking and stress are key determinants of an individual's susceptibility not only to coronary artery disease but also to other fatal disorders. One of the most highly publicized life-threatening diseases in recent years—acquired immune deficiency syndrome (AIDS)—is associated with a specific lifestyle that many in society find unacceptable. The fear that AIDS may become a national epidemic has reached panic proportions in some areas. Yet coronary artery disease, which is already a national epidemic that causes death and disability on a vastly broader scale than AIDS, is associated with a lifestyle that, if not actually glorified, is at least accepted as the American way.

As this foreword is being written, our country has just celebrated its 211th birthday. American citizens have more freedom of choice, particularly with regard to individual lifestyle, than any other people in the world. Although our way of life has come to symbolize freedom from want, from hunger and from limitation, many of our modern conveniences have proved to be mixed blessings: the automobile frees us from geographical constraints but condemns us to a sedentary existence; television expands our mental horizons but imprisons us within four walls; fast food adds minutes to our days but may subtract years from our lives.

Despite the recent national craze for exercise and physical fitness (at least in certain portions of our society) and the growing number of persons who are becoming health-food conscious, the mainstay of our national diet is still sugar, salt and fat. Most of us probably celebrated our nation's birthday with a distinctively American diet: indeed, what would a Fourth of July picnic be without steaks, hot dogs, cheeseburgers, potato chips, beer, soft drinks, apple pie and ice cream? Of course, there is nothing better for the heart and soul than a relaxing, fun-filled holiday. But for how many Americans is the "national diet" a daily affair?

Suppose a person could see into the future and know that, unless preventive measures were taken, one year—or two or ten—from now he or she would become the victim of a murderer or an automobile accident. Moreover, suppose the necessary preventive steps were clearly defined and were well within the potential victim's ability to perform. If such a person refused to take these steps, his or her sanity would be seriously questioned. The average American's chance of being murdered or becoming an accident victim is vastly more remote than the chance of death from cardiovascular disease. Nevertheless, most Americans continue to indulge in the very habits and behavior patterns that have been overwhelmingly linked with such disease.

The good news is that, although a few risk factors (notably gender and heredity) are beyond human control, cardiovascular disease is not an inevitable phenomenon. The growing emphasis on the role of individual responsibility in preventing such disease is an immense sign of hope. *Choices for a Healthy Heart* provides a thoughtful, sensible, scientifically valid standard against which concerned readers of any age—whether or not they already have heart disease—can measure their own lifestyles. Because Joseph Piscatella has suffered from heart disease and has demonstrated these principles in his own life, his words may be more effective than the warnings of the medical profession. If this book becomes as widely read as it deserves to be, and if its suggestions are implemented on a broad enough scale, cardiovascular surgeons may see fewer patients with coronary artery disease.

Dr. Cooley is Surgeon-in-Chief at the Texas Heart Institute in Houston. He has recently published a guide to healthful eating entitled *Eat Smart for a Healthy Heart Cookbook*.

CONTENTS

COOKBOOK

*"The phenomenon of health is a
living activity, not a product. It is
not something to have, but
something to be. It is a procession,
not a possession."*

Dr. Robert Hoke

INTRODUCTION

I n 1977, at age 32, I had open-heart bypass surgery to correct a 95% blockage of the left main coronary artery. That was how I learned about good health, lifestyle and the concept of choice.

Discovering good health while being ill might seem contradictory on the surface, but in reality this is the way most people come to practical terms with the subject. Good health is usually not a true concern until it's threatened. As long as physical problems or ailments are not evident, most of us take our health for granted and treat it as if it were a permanent state. We forget that many diseases take a long time to manifest themselves in pain or other symptoms. We don't understand that well-being isn't automatic—that it comes about as the result of positive lifestyle choices.

That's the way it was with me. For most of my life, good health was not a high priority. I wanted to be healthy, but not enough to work at it. There were other, seemingly more important things that took my time and interest: family, career, finances. Besides, I'd always been healthy. There were no major illnesses or conditions in my life, and no reason for that to change. Ominous diseases like cancer and heart disease were things that happened to other people. For me, they simply weren't real.

Not that everything was perfect, of course. From time to time, I'd tell myself to take better care: "I really should lose some weight" or "I ought to get more exercise" or "I should ease up on the stress at work." But very little was ever done. Healthy habits were a good topic for cocktail conversation, but to execute them in real life—that was always a project for tomorrow.

"Tomorrow" for me came with the open-heart surgery. Completely unexpected, the need for surgery in itself was traumatic, but it became doubly so when I learned that it would provide no long-term solution. It would correct the immediate problem—the threat of blood supply being cut off from the heart—by creating a new arterial channel around the blockage. It would take away the chest pain. But it wouldn't change the basic situation: at 32 years of age I had coronary heart disease, the number one killer in the United States.

Suddenly "good health" vaulted into a priority position in my life. My perspective instantly changed. For the first time, I became seriously interested in my physical health, particularly my cardiovascular health.

I had reached what the health professionals call a "teachable moment," a time when a person is ready to listen, to learn, and to take action to foster health. Unfortunately, most people don't experience such moments until their physical condition is threatened. Once high blood pressure is detected, they become serious about salt in the diet. Once a heart attack takes place, they find time to exercise. Once emphysema is evident, they stop smoking. In my case, it took a brush with death to get my attention. Now I was anxious to learn about heart disease. I was concerned about my future. If one blockage could grow, couldn't others? And I was concerned for my children.

With their father a cardiac patient, they were statistically more at risk for the disease. What I needed to know for rehabilitation, they needed to know for prevention.

One of the first things I learned was that I wasn't the only one with a heart problem, although it had felt that way while I was recovering in the hospital. There were times when I would say to myself, "Out of the whole country, why me?" But once I looked into the problem, it was evident that so many Americans suffer from coronary heart disease that it's now considered a national epidemic.

Every minute of the day three Americans have a heart attack, producing about 1.5 million each year. These yield some 600,000 to 800,000 deaths. Perhaps, like the national debt, these numbers are too large for us to comprehend in real-life terms. A graphic illustration better makes the point: *American heart attack deaths in one year equal the American deaths in 10 Vietnam wars.* In other words, if 10 Vietnam veterans' monuments were stacked one on top of the other, the result would constitute a monument to heart attack victims for a single year.

The scope of the problem is incredible. According to the Framingham Study, which since 1948 has continuously monitored heart disease in Americans, by age 60 every fifth man and every seventeenth woman in the United States suffers a heart attack.

Before surgery, I knew that heart disease was a serious problem; afterwards, I learned it was a modern plague. Over half of all Americans (51%) die from cardiovascular disease. This means that the total deaths in any given year from all other causes—cancer, auto accidents, leukemia, airplane tragedies—are still fewer than the deaths from heart and blood vessel disease.

Perhaps because the problem is so widespread, this is accepted as a part of our culture and generally ignored by the population. If six fully loaded 747s were to crash on one day, the headlines would shout about the 2,200 people killed. Yet that is the number lost every day—365 days a year—to heart attack. Indeed, judging from the headlines, one would get the impression that most Americans die from one of three causes: AIDS, murder or auto accidents. These are all serious problems, but their impact on American mortality pales by comparison with heart and blood vessel disease. To put it into perspective:

Your chance of contracting AIDS (assuming you are heterosexual and not an intravenous drug user):	1 in 1,000,000
Your chance of being murdered:	1 in 10,000
Your chance of dying in an auto accident:	1 in 5,000
Your chance of dying of heart and blood vessel disease:	1 in 2

The essential question—why are Americans prone to heart disease?—led me to an understanding that there is a relationship between lifestyle, the way we choose to live, and cardiac health. This was not the historical view. For many years coronary heart disease and heart attacks were regarded as a natural part of the degenerative process, the inevitable consequences of aging and genetics. Now, after 35 years of sustained investigation beginning with the Framingham Study, certain controllable factors that contribute to the risk of heart disease have been identified. These "cardiac risk factors" include high blood pressure, elevated cholesterol, cigarette smoking, overweight, lack of exercise and chronic stress. They are not endemic to the human condition; rather, they are the result of choices. We often assume that our lifestyle is healthy, that we're doing the "right thing," when in fact we're on the road to coronary disaster. We often live as if our habits don't matter. They do. The fact is that at least 90% of premature strokes and heart attacks are preventable. They are caused not by genetics or age but by the ill effects of poor diet, lack of exercise, too much stress, and cigarette smoking. The individual impacts of these lifestyle choices are cumulative and interconnected.

I had not understood this in the past partly because of a misconception concerning health status. I thought there were just two categories: "ill" and "well." When I had signs or symptoms—a congested chest or an upset stomach, for example—I was ill. But without any signs or symptoms, I was well. Indeed, this misconception was reinforced by the doctor in my annual physical exams. If everything looked fine, I was told: "You are well."

Four months before my surgery, I had a physical exam that declared me "well." Did I grow a 95% blockage in four months? No, of course not. The truth is that I wasn't "well" at the time of the exam. Nor was I "ill." Instead, I occupied a middle position, one in which most Americans find themselves: "not sick."

There's a difference between being "well" and being "not sick." When good health is taken for granted and is not promoted by conscious lifestyle choices and actions, "not sick" is the best that one can hope for. An overweight, smoking, sedentary 30-year-old man may feel great, but he is not "well." In order to achieve a high degree of well-being, he must make positive choices about how to live healthfully. Those decisions would be to lose weight, stop smoking and start exercising. Then, and only then, would he have a chance at really being "well."

Unfortunately, the American way of life fosters cardiac risk factors. In its 1982 report "Health and Behavior," the National Academy of Sciences concluded that half of the 10 leading causes of death in the United States are primarily related to lifestyle. It doesn't have to be that way. Lifestyle habits are a two-edged sword. They can work for good health—or against it. The choice is ours to make.

The impact of lifestyle was demonstrated recently by a study concerning coronary mortality rates. Heart attack deaths peaked in the 1960s at about 1.2 million per year. Today, the mortality rate is down by about 500,000 lives each year. Some have attributed fewer heart attack deaths to medical progress; others have credited changes made in the American lifestyle. The study, conducted by Drs. Lee

Goldman and E. Francis Cook at the Harvard Medical School, analyzed reasons for the drop in coronary deaths from 1963 to 1982 in terms of medical vs. lifestyle factors. Their findings were:

Impact on Lives Saved

Medical Factors

1. Pre-hospital resuscitation and care (CPR)	4.0%
2. Coronary care units	13.5
3. Coronary bypass surgery	3.5
4. Drug therapy	10.0
5. Treatment for high blood pressure	8.5
Total impact of medical factors	**39.5%**

Lifestyle Factors

1. Reduction of fat/cholesterol in the diet	30.0%
2. Reduction in cigarette smoking	24.0
Total impact of lifestyle factors	**54.0%**

This study illustrated that 39.5% of the lives saved could be attributed to medical intervention such as bypass surgery, better treatment for high blood pressure, and more hospitals with coronary care units. But 54% of the lives saved came as the result of just two positive changes in the American lifestyle—a reduction in cigarette smoking and a diet designed to reduce cholesterol. (Exercise and stress management were not included in this study.) The conclusion: positive lifestyle changes clearly have had more of an impact on heart attack mortality rates than has sophisticated medicine. Syndicated columnist George Will sums up nicely the result of such findings: "For the past few decades science has been coming to a thumping conclusion: Grandma was right! Research shows that longevity is indeed enhanced by not smoking, drinking only moderately, eating three proper meals a day, not eating between meals, keeping weight down, exercising, and sleeping eight hours a night. Once upon a time we believed Grandma because she was Grandma. Today we believe Grandma because UCLA or MIT says what she had said all along.''

It was evident in retrospect that my lifestyle—a diet heavy on meat, milk and fast food, little time for aerobic exercise, excessive stress at work—had fostered my coronary heart disease. I was moved to institute positive lifestyle changes. I wanted my lifestyle to work for my health, not against it.

One of the results of this new outlook was research into a healthy, practical diet pattern. That research culminated in my first book, *Don't Eat Your Heart Out*. My main concern in that book was to educate the reader about the relationship of coronary heart disease to a diet rich in fat, cholesterol, salt, sugar and total calories, and to provide practical knowledge and tools—the "how-to"—for permanently changing eating habits. The Positive Diet presented in *Don't Eat Your Heart Out* clearly illustrates that eating well and eating healthfully are not in opposition. The use of the book by over 4,500 hospitals as a teaching tool testifies to the value of its practical information and realistic approach.

Choices for a Healthy Heart, a natural extension of *Don't Eat Your Heart Out*, builds on the Positive Diet concept of low-fat eating with current information based on scientific research, practical cooking tips and meal plans, and over 200 tested recipes. It is a companion to *Don't Eat Your Heart Out* and goes further in three dietary areas:

1. Changing unhealthy recipes into healthy ones. This technique allows you to analyze your own favorite recipes in order to identify negative elements and to substitute more healthful ingredients. The results are recipes which are both heart-healthy and tasty.

2. Lowering the fat content of an entire meal. A "low-fat" food is generally defined as one with 25% or less of the calories derived from fat. This definition, while positive from a health standpoint, precludes many favorite

American foods from a low-fat diet. When measured individually against this low-fat criterion, certain foods—such as red meat and cheese—cannot be included. This is a problem for many people, even those highly motivated to eat healthfully: if all foods over 25% fat are eliminated, what's left?

This book teaches how to look at the whole meal so that the fat content *for the meal* is in line. It shows how to balance a high-fat food—roast pork, for example—with low-fat foods to result in a meal in which 25% or less of the calories come from fat. This technique opens up many opportunities for making meals that conform to low-fat guidelines yet use familiar, favorite foods. For this reason, all the recipes in this book have been analyzed for caloric and fat content by Dr. Evette Hackman, R.D., a registered dietitian.

3. The 500-Calorie Solution. This is a realistic method for losing weight and keeping it off permanently. Indeed, permanent weight control is a major concern of the book, for three reasons. First, excessive weight is a cardiac risk, so health is enhanced by shedding pounds and controlling weight. Second, what a person does to control weight permanently—a positive lifestyle regimen of diet and exercise—is exactly what is needed to promote cardiac health. Eating and exercising for weight control result in a lowering of LDL ("bad") cholesterol, an increase in HDL ("good") cholesterol, a reduction in blood pressure and an improvement in cardiac strength. And third, a keen interest in weight and appearance may be the essential element in moving Americans to take action for good cardiac health. Despite the magnitude of the problem, most people continue to be unmoved by the risk of coronary heart disease in their lives. They do not react well to threatening medical statistics and believe that if anything bad is to happen, it will happen to "the other guy." As a result, most are not motivated by "good health" to eat well and exercise. Losing weight for appearance, however, *is* a motivator (witness the connection between successful weight loss and high school reunions). Indeed, it may be the best motivator for adopting healthy habits. If people are stimulated to institute a positive lifestyle that results in better cardiac health, who cares if the motivation for change is how they look in a bathing suit?

Choices for a Healthy Heart also covers the other critical aspects of lifestyle that impact health and longevity: exercise, stress, smoking and attitude. It illustrates that these key areas are interrelated and work together to produce a lifestyle that promotes good health—or illness. Most important, this book not only identifies the healthy lifestyle choices to be made but provides "how-to" information for implementing healthy choices. It shows that choices and actions *can* positively influence the quality of health and the length of life.

This book completes what *Don't Eat Your Heart Out* started by providing an understanding of how to make healthy habits a reality. It, too, is based on scientific data and personal experience, and reflects common sense in putting good health principles into action. As a cardiologist friend of mine, Dr. Steve Yarnall, says: "You don't have to be a nutritionist to understand that simple foods without added fats, sugars, sodiums, dyes and preservatives are generally preferable. You don't have to be a scientist to understand that the grease you sandblast from your oven and soak off your dishes isn't something you want inside your arteries. You don't have to be a physiologist to understand that regular, moderate exercise is preferable to no exercise. And you don't have to be a genius to figure out that setting fire to tobacco leaves and inhaling the smoke doesn't make a whole lot of sense."

Choices for a Healthy Heart provides information, incentive and understanding to choose and implement a healthier lifestyle. It is designed to be used by cardiac patients in rehabilitation and by healthy people interested in prevention. It is my hope that it will provide "a teachable moment" for many readers.

During the years since my open-heart surgery, I have

learned many lessons. One of the most important is also one of the simplest. It is a premise upon which a positive lifestyle can be built:

If you do not take time today for health,
you will have to make time tomorrow for illness.

Joseph C. Piscatella
1987

CHAPTER 1

THE ROLE OF LIFESTYLE

L ifestyle is essentially the way we choose to live. On the surface level, it is a social commentary on contemporary life—styles, mores, entertainment, values and work ethic. Indeed, much attention has been paid to this aspect of lifestyle within the last few years. Both *Time* and *Newsweek,* for example, now offer ''Lifestyle'' sections, as do numerous other publications throughout the country. *Life, People, US, Town & Country* and other such magazines are devoted exclusively to the way we live today. Even the electronic media serve up a smorgasbord of lifestyle programs, ranging from radio-dispensed psychological counseling to television glimpses of famous and wealthy people.

So much attention has been paid to this side of lifestyle, however, that a far more important aspect has been overlooked—the relationship between the way we choose to live on one hand and our health and longevity on the other.

We Americans tend to assume that our lifestyle is healthy and that the way we live is normal, when the truth is that our lifestyle leads us down a road toward illness. In fact, the two major causes of death for Americans, heart disease and cancer, are products of lifestyle choices and habits. Some people don't understand the link between health and the way we choose to live. Others understand the link and yet continue along the same course as if they led a charmed existence—as if they were immune to illness and only "the other guy" will be struck by disaster.

The fact is that certain fundamental lifestyle choices ultimately dictate health and longevity for each of us. These choices include.

- Diet: what and how much to eat
- Exercise: whether or not to be physically active on a regular basis
- Stress: whether to manage or ignore it
- Smoking: whether or not to start, continue or break the habit

These are the controllable aspects of lifestyle that count, either for or against good health. The ill effects of bad diet, lack of exercise, stress and smoking are cumulative and interconnected. In the final analysis, ill health is not an isolated event but the result of an accumulation of abuses, each a seemingly inconsequential lifestyle decision. This is particularly apparent in the development of the American lifestyle since World War II.

Diet

The modern American diet pattern has changed dramatically from prewar days. One of the most striking differences is the frequency of restaurant meals today. The American Restaurant Association estimates that 50% of all meals presently are eaten outside the home and predicts that this figure will rise to 75% by 1995. Of particular concern is the fact that almost 8 out of 10 of these meals consist of fast foods. Just how much fast food is consumed in this country is reflected by a study done at Columbia University, which calculated that the average length of time

Americans spend eating a restaurant meal is seven minutes! Indeed, every day about 20% of the population eats at a fast-food restaurant. High in fat, salt and calories, low in fiber and nutrition, fast foods contribute notably to coronary heart disease.

Another significant dietary change is the modern reliance on processed foods, which, like their fast-food counterparts, are rich in fat, salt and calories, and low in fiber. Canned vegetables and tinned meat were available before the war, but packaged foods generally took a back seat to fresh foods. In modern society, however, food from boxes and cans has become the norm.

In many parts of the country, red meat consumption also went sky-high after the war. Red meat was affordable, and for the first time it became a staple. While consumption is down from the 1950s, many Americans continue to eat red meat at well over half their meals. It is the principal source of fat on the American diet.

The same is true for whole-milk dairy products. Postwar mothers fed their children copious amounts of milk, cheese, ice cream and other whole-milk foods for protein and calcium. This habit continues today, particularly because of concern over osteoporosis. What isn't realized, however, is how much artery-blocking fat comes with the calcium.

And finally, gourmet cooking. Many returned from France after the war wanting gourmet meals made with butter, cream and cheese. Simple dishes were dressed up with fatty sauces to become "sinfully rich." Although lighter, healthier meals have become popular recently, many Americans still consider rich sauces to be the ultimate mark of civilized eating.

As Dr. Mark Hegsted, director of the federal government's Human Nutrition Center, has commented: "I think we ought to recognize that the menu we happen to eat today was never planned. It just grew, like Topsy, as the result of our affluence and the efficiency of the American farmer, and the fact that we consume it today is obviously no indication that it is desirable."

Exercise

Prior to World War II much of America was a blue-collar society, working with its hands and burning up substantial calories. After the war, automation eased the physical workload in fields and factories, as did labor-saving devices in the home. In addition, the country progressively became a white-collar society. The age of industrialization gave way to the age of information. Work became more sedentary—and so did workers.

Two other postwar factors have had a great influence on physical activity: the automobile and the television set. Postwar America moved to the suburbs, which meant riding to work in automobiles, sitting all day, then riding home. After a tough day of riding and sitting, what's done for relaxation? Sitting again to watch television! According to George Gallup, a television set is on 7.1 hours a day in the average home. TV watching has become America's favorite leisure-time activity.

Smoking

The growth of smoking can also be traced to the war years. During World War II, GI's were given free cigarettes to calm their nerves before going into combat, and the habit stayed with many of them. This was also the point in time when it became socially acceptable for women to smoke in public. As a result the number of smokers increased, reaching a high in the late 1950s of one out of every two adults.

Stress

It's difficult to state with certainty that life before World War II was less stressful, but many experts believe this to be so. Modern life moves at a quicker pace. More information is available today, and faster decisions are needed. Divorce rate, juvenile delinquency, changing male/female roles—these are but a few of the problems facing contemporary society. In addition, many people premise their desires and goals on media advertising. "Life would be perfect," they say to themselves, "if only I had (fill in the blank)." There is much stress in the modern lifestyle, and for many people this stress is chronic.

THE IMPACT OF LIFESTYLE ON CORONARY HEART DISEASE

Our lifestyle habits directly affect our health and longevity, particularly where coronary heart disease is concerned, yet many Americans live as if these habits don't count. Over 1.5 million heart attacks each year, however, give testimony to the fact that lifestyle *does* count. Indeed, an examination of heart disease in the United States reveals two points that invariably link disease with the way we choose to live.

1. Coronary heart disease is a modern phenomenon. Americans die today in great numbers from heart and blood vessel disease, but it hasn't always been that way. As a matter of historic fact, heart disease occurred infrequently until after World War II. Americans in 1900 could expect to die from infectious diseases, mainly pneumonia, influenza or tuberculosis. Death from heart attack was a rarity. Dr. Paul Dudley White, considered the father of modern-day cardiology, drives home this reality: "When I graduated from medical school in 1911," he notes, "I had never heard of coronary thrombosis, which is one of the chief threats to life in the United States and Canada today—an astounding development in one's own lifetime."

American mortality today stems not from infections but from lifestyle choices. As stated by Dr. John Farquhar, director of the Stanford Heart Disease Prevention Program: "The American way of life may be hazardous to your health." Put another way, the American way of life has come to dictate the American way of death.

The impact of modern lifestyle on mortality is reinforced by longevity data. In 1911, a benchmark year for health statistics in the United States, the average length of life was 52 years. By 1984, the average had risen to 72 years. On the surface this appears to represent a 20-year gain in life expectancy, which naturally leads to a questioning of the premise that American lifestyle choices have hurt the nation's health. After all, if we're living 20 years longer than our forefathers, we must be doing something right. A deeper look into the 1911 figures, however, reveals that infant mortality was a factor. A lot of babies died in the early 1900s, and their numbers influenced the longevity averages.

A comparison of two adults gives a much clearer picture of the true relationship. Comparing the statistical length of life for a 45-year-old man in 1984 with that of a 45-year-old man in 1911 shows that the 1984 man outlives his 1911 counterpart not by 20 years but by only 2.2 years! This is incredible in light of the many medical advances made since the turn of the century: more and better-equipped hospitals, ambulance service, penicillin, 911 emergency numbers, chemotherapy, bypass surgery—the list goes on. Americans today have many more medical advantages than did Americans in 1911. Yet the gain in life span has not been tremendous, because these advantages have been offset by poor lifestyle choices.

2. *Coronary heart disease does not occur throughout the world.* Three-quarters of the world's population does not suffer heart attacks. There are entire areas of the globe where coronary heart disease is virtually unknown. There is no problem in Asia, South America, Africa or even southern Europe—except in the cities where people have been "westernized." Heart disease exists in the United States, Canada, the British Isles, Scandinavia and northern Germany. The respective lifestyles in these areas parallel one another.

The preponderance of heart disease is not genetic but cultural. This can be seen in a comparison of fatherland to immigrant groups: Italians, Greeks and Japanese, for example, do not die of heart attack. Italian-Americans, Greek-Americans and Japanese-Americans do.

A good example of the direct effect of lifestyle habits can be shown in health data from Scandinavia and Great Britain during and after World War II. Wartime rationing of food and luxury items in these countries produced radical changes, including reduced intake of fat, principally because of rationed meat, eggs and dairy products; reduced intake of sugar; decreased cigarette consumption; increased intake of complex carbohydrates (potatoes, vegetables, greens); and increased physical activity. The data show that these lifestyle changes were responsible for a significant drop in heart disease deaths (67% in Finland) as compared with prewar days. After the war, however, people returned to their old habits and a corresponding rise in heart attack deaths took place.

Western, "civilized" lifestyle as practiced in the United States has produced a culture that induces coronary heart disease. As long as poor decisions regarding key lifestyle questions are made, heart disease will continue to be an American plague.

HOW THE HEART WORKS

In order to appreciate the relationship between fundamental lifestyle decisions and cardiovascular health, it's important to have some understanding of the cardiovascular system. At the center is the heart, a small but powerful organ responsible for pumping blood throughout the body. The heart is not large—it's about the size of a clenched fist and weighs 7 to 12 ounces—but its performance is superhuman. Each day the heart beats over 100,000 times and pumps about 1,800 gallons of blood, which circulates continuously to the trillions of cells that make up the human body. In an average lifetime, this amazing organ will beat over two and a half billion times and pump enough blood to fill 13 supertankers each with a capacity of one million barrels. The continuous circulation of blood is necessary because each cell has a need for oxygen and nutrients. The arteries carry oxygen-rich blood from the heart to the cells. Once oxygen and nutrients have been deposited with the cells, the blood becomes oxygen-poor and returns to the heart via the veins.

Like the rest of the body, the cells of the heart need a constant supply of nutrient-rich, oxygenated blood in order to function. Although gallons of blood flow through its chambers to be pumped to the body, the heart cannot use this blood for its own needs. The only way that oxygenated blood can reach the heart is through the coronary arteries. Each time the heart beats, a portion of the blood pumped is siphoned through these arteries back to the heart itself.

The most serious weakness in the design of the cardiovascular system is the size of the coronary arteries. They are very small—about an eighth of an inch in diameter, the

THE CORONARY ARTERIES

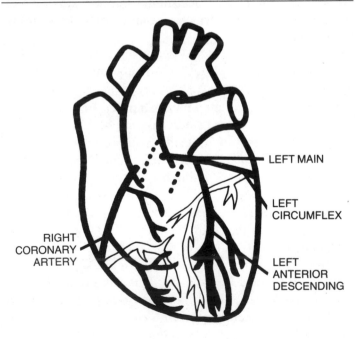

RIGHT CORONARY ARTERY

LEFT MAIN

LEFT CIRCUMFLEX

LEFT ANTERIOR DESCENDING

same size as a piece of cooked spaghetti—and it doesn't take much for them to become clogged. The most common obstruction is a "fatty streak," a layer of fatty, fibrous cholesterol-laden deposits on the interior walls of the coronary arteries, characteristic of the disease atherosclerosis. The deposits thicken the artery wall, thus narrowing the channel through which blood reaches the heart. This condition was aptly described in 1705 by physiologist William Cowper, who observed an artery that "very much resembled a bit of the stem of a tobacco pipe, its sides were so thick, and its bore consequently much lessened." Although cholesterol is not the sole ingredient in an arterial blockage, it is certainly the most important. The rate at which the fatty streak develops depends primarily on how much cholesterol is in the blood, available to be deposited. Most cardiologists believe that the disease starts early in life in Western societies where the diet is rich in animal fat. Year after year, the fatty streak continues to grow, making the arteries hard and inelastic, and obstructing more and more of the channel, much as rust clogs an old water pipe.

For most people, the development of atherosclerosis takes 30 to 40 years, during which time there may be no symptoms. Then, quite suddenly, symptoms of clogged arteries appear. One of the first may be chest pain, or angina

THE DEVELOPMENT OF ATHEROSCLEROSIS

No
atherosclerosis

Only
moderate
atherosclerosis

Severe
atherosclerosis

pectoris, usually experienced upon exertion and indicating that the artery is clogged to the point where blood flow to the heart is inadequate. If the blockage (or a combination of blockage and blood clot) cuts off blood supply to the heart completely, the result is a heart attack. In this situation, the heart can quit beating (cardiac arrest) or it can "panic" and beat uncontrollably. The latter condition, called fibrillation, may cause the heart to beat itself to death.

The insidiousness of atherosclerosis lies in the fact that a person with severe coronary artery blockages may have no symptoms at all—until the moment when a "sudden" heart attack takes place. Indeed, for many people, the first symptom is the last.

HOW LIFESTYLE DECISIONS AFFECT THE HEART

The effect of poor lifestyle decisions is to promote heart disease by injuring the coronary arteries, causing strain on the heart and elevating the levels of cholesterol and other fats to produce an imbalance in the blood chemistry.

Coronary Artery Damage

Since the coronary arteries are the sole pipeline for blood to reach the heart, the importance of their health cannot be minimized. Cholesterol in the bloodstream does little harm until it collects on a coronary artery wall, where it becomes an impediment to blood flow and can clog the artery to produce a heart attack. Cholesterol tends to collect at points in the artery wall where cells have been damaged. When damage occurs, blood is rushed to the site to create a healing "patch," much as a scab will form over a skinned knee. But if the blood contains excessive cholesterol, the site becomes a nest where the cholesterol can collect to start a fatty streak. Obviously, the more wounds, the more potential deposit sites. Some wounds occur quite naturally. The coronary arteries, sitting on the outside of the cardiac muscle, are forced to twist and turn each time the heart beats—over 100,000 times a day. This movement can cause small tears on the inner wall. Such wounds are a product of the human condition, and everyone has a number of them.

Certain aspects of lifestyle, however, significantly increase arterial wounds. Carbon monoxide, a powerful byproduct of cigarette smoke, enters the bloodstream from the lungs and passes through the coronary arteries; in doing so, it irritates the lining of the artery wall and produces wounds where cholesterol can collect. Excessive stress works much the same way. When a person is under stress, extremely powerful potent hormones race through the bloodstream and cause injury to the artery walls. Chronic stress is a particularly significant problem. Then the hormones are constantly circulating through the bloodstream, producing a continual risk of injury for the arteries. In addition, the coronary artery itself can harden and become brittle as a result of high blood pressure. When this occurs, its ability to expand and contract—movements needed to push blood to the heart—is impaired. According to research from the Harvard Medical School, high blood pressure is triggered in many people by an excess of salt in the diet. With the average American consuming about 15 pounds of salt per year, it's no wonder that 37 million Americans suffer from this condition.

These three lifestyle factors—smoking, stress, diet—can produce serious physiological results. But lifestyle is not predetermined; it's a choice. If better decisions are made, enhanced cardiovascular health and increased longevity can result.

Strain on the Heart

The heart is an amazing muscle, with a truly awesome work capacity, but still it requires a constant supply of oxygen and nutrients via the bloodstream. The efficiency of its operation is found in the balance between workload and oxygen supply. When the workload is moderate and the supply of oxygen is regular, the heart beats without a problem. But should the workload become too heavy, or the oxygen supply too little, the cardiac muscle can be strained to the point of heart attack.

Aspects of lifestyle that strain the heart include smoking, diet, stress and lack of exercise. The two chief by-products of cigarette smoke—nicotine and carbon monoxide—work together to increase strain on the heart. Nicotine, a stimulant, causes the heart to beat faster. The heart, therefore, needs more oxygen to support its higher rate of activity. But carbon monoxide absorbs oxygen in the blood, thus reducing the amount available for the heart. The greater workload demand (nicotine) and less oxygen available (carbon monoxide) combine to place tremendous strain on the cardiac muscle. Indeed, the strain of smoking one pack of cigarettes a day is equal to being 100 pounds overweight.

High blood pressure also produces strain by requiring the heart to pump harder to deliver needed blood. Two factors that promote this condition are a high-salt diet and chronic stress. Salt, or sodium, causes the fluid level of the blood to increase; in order to move the additional fluid, the heart must work harder, producing strain. Chronic stress causes blood pressure to be increased for short periods. Studies indicate that if blood pressure is raised often enough, the condition may become permanent.

One of the most significant causes of high blood pressure and cardiac strain is excess weight. Being overweight is an American characteristic rooted in two aspects of lifestyle: a high-fat, high-calorie diet and a lack of exercise. When caloric intake consistently exceeds caloric use, body fat piles up—and since each pound of fat contains about three-quarters of a mile of blood vessels, every excess pound of fat causes the heart to work harder.

Smoking, stress, diet, lack of exercise—these are the lifestyle factors that produce strain on the heart. And yet each of these factors represents a choice.

Blood Chemistry Imbalance

In the opinion of many health professionals, the most critical link between poor lifestyle and coronary heart disease is the negative impact on blood cholesterol and other blood fats. Without the buildup of fatty streaks and blockages—the result of elevated cholesterol in the blood—coronary heart disease would not take place. Smoking, stress and high blood pressure are associated with high rates of heart attack only in populations where elevated cholesterol levels are common. As stated by Dr. Robert Wissler of the University of Chicago, "Cigarette smoking or hypertension or emotional stress . . . has very little influence on heart disease except as added factors. In other words, the primary problem is what is happening in terms of cholesterol." Blood chemistry—particularly the level of cholesterol in the blood—acts independently and as a catalyst with other risk factors to cause coronary heart disease and heart attack.

Numerous studies have shown a link between cholesterol levels and risk for heart attack. Indeed, the more cholesterol in the blood, the greater the risk for heart attack. The principal type involved in coronary heart disease is LDL (low-density lipoprotein), or "bad" cholesterol, as distinguished from HDL (high-density lipoprotein), or "good" cholesterol. LDL cholesterol, which clogs arterial channels, is a product of a diet high in saturated fat. The American diet—rich in red meat, whole-milk dairy products, fast foods, processed foods and commercially baked goods—is heavy in saturated fat and bears much of the responsibility for elevated LDL cholesterol levels in the population.

A second blood fat of importance is triglycerides. Like cholesterol, this fat also clogs the coronary arteries. Elevated triglyceride levels are often a result of overweight and excessive sugar in the diet. With more than half of all adults considered overweight, and with a diet that provides 128 pounds of sugar annually for each adult American, it's easy to understand why elevated triglycerides are a problem.

Blood chemistry, then, can be significantly affected by lifestyle choices. To be sure, some people have a genetic makeup that promotes elevated cholesterol/triglycerides. But for most of us, decisions and habits regarding diet, exercise, stress and smoking ultimately dictate balanced or unhealthy blood makeup.

HOW CHILDREN ARE AFFECTED BY LIFESTYLE

The Greek scholar Demosthenes never hit his students when they made a mistake; instead, he struck their parents. His theory was that children learn by example and are therefore blameless if they do wrong. Never has this been more applicable than in the lifestyles and the health of children today.

It's nice to believe that children do what adults say. They do not. They do what adults do. In following adult role models, many children pick up unhealthy lifestyle habits at an early age. They smoke, experience stress, avoid exercise and overeat. The result is that many children today are well on their way to coronary heart disease and heart attack. As University of Michigan researcher Guy Reiff has observed, "Cardiovascular disease starts in the first grade." Consider the following:

- A study of elementary children in Michigan found that 98% showed at least one major risk factor for heart disease. Twenty-eight percent had high blood pressure; 42% had abnormally high levels of cholesterol in the blood. More than half had a combination of three or more risk factors.

- A similar study in New York City found that 1 out of 3 children had one significant risk factor for heart attack by age 14.

■ Autopsies of young children who died in auto accidents in Los Angeles and Cincinnati showed artery blockages greater than 50% in children as young as age 7.

■ A Health and Human Services Department study found that the proportion of overweight American children had increased more than 50% over two decades.

■ A similar study at Louisiana State University found over 15% of children and adolescents aged 7 to 17 to be clinically obese.

"Kids are less fit now than at any other time data has been taken," says Dan Haydon, executive director of the Governor's Commission on Physical Fitness in Texas. In fact, the President's Council on Physical Fitness and Sports found that current fitness levels declined from levels measured in 1967 and 1977. This trend is especially worrisome because poor physical fitness increases the likelihood of heart attacks and other ailments in adulthood.

America's young people are becoming unhealthy adults before they know it. Many do not participate in physical education classes daily. Television—which some watch over 50 hours a week—and video games keep them out of physical activity. They have easy access to high-calorie fast foods and junk foods, rich in harmful fat and cholesterol. Many feel pressure to perform in the classroom and on the playing field. To make it all worse, teenagers—especially females driven by the desire to be thin—are smoking in record numbers.

These are all important factors, but the underlying cause is that children adopt lifestyles parallel to those of their parents. "There is no doubt about it," says Dr. Donald Benson. "We see the same factors that increase the risk of heart attacks and strokes in adulthood developing in children and causing the beginnings of heart disease." But lifestyle does not *have* to be harmful to the health of children. If we as adults are concerned about proper diet, regular exercise, stress control and not smoking, so will our children be concerned. If we lead an active, healthy life, the chances are good that our children will also. When we make positive lifestyle choices, we improve not only our own well-being but that of our children as well.

KEY LIFESTYLE CHOICES WORK TOGETHER

Lifestyle habits work in concert to impact cardiovascular health. For this reason, choosing a single healthier option—to stop smoking cigarettes, for example—provides no panacea. The chart on the facing page demonstrates that the greater the number of risk factors present, the greater the likelihood of a heart attack. The chart shows how the risk increases for a 45-year-old man who smokes cigarettes, for one who smokes and has a blood cholesterol level of 310, and for one who smokes, has the same high cholesterol level and has a systolic blood pressure of 180. Thus cardiovascular well-being is not attained with one-dimensional solutions.

This is not always understood, even by people who are interested in good health. Some runners and endurance athletes mistakenly believe that exercise can offset a high-fat diet, cigarette smoking or other poor lifestyle habits. Even Jim Fixx, author of *The Complete Book of Running*, may not have understood this connection. In an interview with a London newspaper, Mr. Fixx declared that he was not very concerned with diet. A running program of 10 miles a day, he said, sufficiently stoked his "furnace" to "burn up" whatever was eaten. In fact, according to the interview, he took no precaution in his breakfast choices that morning: fried eggs, sausage, fried potatoes, butter, cream—a cardiac disaster!

On the other extreme are people who watch diet religiously but who rarely are physically active. They eat grains, fruits and vegetables, and, as New York *Times* health columnist Jane Brody once commented, "sprinkle on wheat germ like it was holy water." But they don't

CUMULATIVE IMPACT OF HEART ATTACK RISK FACTORS

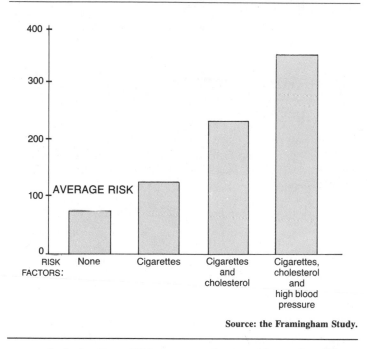

Source: the Framingham Study.

move their bodies. This approach doesn't work, either. There is simply no magic in being a sedentary vegetarian.

What *does* work is a balance of healthy choices in all the critical lifestyle areas. This interrelationship is shown in the Cardiovascular Health Risk Self-Assessment on pages 28–31. By taking the test, you will be able to determine your present level of cardiovascular protection. More important, if you are not pleased with your score, you can immediately identify the factors that penalized you. With the exception of a few areas, such as family history, most of the factors are within your power to control. Once the penalizing factors are identified, you have established the areas in your life where change is necessary. Then you can use *Choices for a Healthy Heart* as a self-help guide for information about those areas and for learning skills to make healthy changes. Just as poor decisions can damage health, positive ones can support good health. A high risk of heart attack does not have to be a necessary consequence of living in the United States.

After all, good health is a choice.

TESTING YOUR CARDIOVASCULAR RISK

What effect does your lifestyle have on your risk for heart disease? The following self-assessment, developed by Dr. Shirley H. Hazlett of the California State Department of Education, will give you a good idea. For a more detailed and accurate assessment, check with your physician.

Cardiovascular Health Risk Self-Assessment

This test measures 10 risk categories. In each one, find the statement that best decribes you. Each statement carries a number of points. At the end of the test, add up your points and compare the total with the self-assessment chart to determine your approximate cardiovascular risk.

CATEGORIES   **POINTS**

1. Age

10 to 20	80
21 to 30	70
31 to 40	60
41 to 50	50
51 to 60	20
61 and over	10

YOUR SCORE:

2. Gender

Female, under 40	70
Female, 40 to 50	60
Female, over 50	50
Male	30
Male, stocky	20
Male, bald and stocky	10

YOUR SCORE:

3. Family History

This section applies only to immediate blood relatives, i.e., parents, grandparents, brothers, sisters, aunts and uncles. "Heart disease" means angina, heart attack, bypass surgery, high blood pressure or stroke. If you find that more than one statement applies, use the one that carries the least points.

No known family history of heart disease	70
One relative (over 60) with heart disease	60
Two relatives (over 60) with heart disease	50
One relative (under 60) with heart disease	40
Two relatives (under 60) with heart disease	20
Three relatives (under 60) with heart disease	10

YOUR SCORE:

4. Systolic Blood Pressure

Blood pressure is expressed as two numbers, e.g., 120/85. The first number is the systolic pressure, which indicates the greatest pressure the blood vessels encounter. (Systolic pressure should ideally be below 140.) If you don't know your blood pressure, use the statement "121 to 140" (60 points); if you're on blood pressure medication, use the statement that describes your blood pressure *without* medication.

Up to 100	80
101 to 120	70
121 to 140	60
141 to 160	50
161 to 180	30
181 to 200	20
Over 200	10

YOUR SCORE:

5. Aerobic Exercise

This must include a minimum of 20 minutes' nonstop exercise done at an aerobic pace.

5 to 7 times weekly	80
3 to 4 times weekly	70
2 times weekly	60
Once weekly	40
Once monthly	30
Complete lack of exercise	10

YOUR SCORE:

6. Use of Tobacco

Non-tobacco user	100
Former tobacco user (4 months or more tobacco-free)	80
1 to 10 cigarettes daily; pipe and/or cigar smoker	50
11 to 19 cigarettes daily or chew tobacco infrequently	40
20 to 29 cigarettes daily or chew tobacco infrequently	30
30 to 39 cigarettes daily or chew tobacco frequently	20
40 or more cigarettes daily or chew tobacco very frequently	10

YOUR SCORE:

7. Salt (Sodium)

Read food labels. Avoid all foods with sodium. Add no salt at the table or in cooking.	70
Read food labels. Avoid most foods with sodium. Add no salt at the table. Use ¼ amount when cooking.	60
Read food labels. Avoid most foods with sodium. Add no salt at the table. Use salt in cooking.	40
Avoid most foods with sodium. Add limited salt at the table. Use salt when cooking.	30
Avoid some foods with sodium. Add salt at the table. Use salt in cooking.	20
Eat foods with sodium. Add salt at the table. Use salt in cooking.	10

YOUR SCORE:

8. Blood Cholesterol

If you don't know your cholesterol level, use the statement "231 to 255 mg" (40 points).

Below 180 mg	70
181 to 205 mg	60
206 to 230 mg	50
231 to 255 mg	40
256 to 280 mg	30
281+ mg	10

YOUR SCORE:

9. Weight Control

Use the following formula to find your ideal weight: for men, 105 pounds for the first 5 feet of height and 6 pounds for each additional

inch; for women, 100 pounds for the first 5 feet of height and 5
pounds for each additional inch.

More than 5 pounds below ideal weight	70
Ideal weight plus or minus 5 pounds	60
6 to 20 pounds overweight	50
21 to 35 pounds overweight	40
36 to 50 pounds overweight	20
51 to 65 pounds overweight	10

YOUR SCORE:

10. Stress Management

Identify personal stress and practice stress management daily	70
Identify personal stress and practice stress management 5 to 6 days a week	60
Identify personal stress and practice stress management 3 to 4 days a week	50
Identify personal stress and practice stress management 1 to 2 days a week	30
Identify personal stress but never practice stress management	20
Cannot identify sources of personal stress and never practice stress management	10

YOUR SCORE:

YOUR TOTAL SCORE:

Approximate Protection Against Heart Disease

High	650 to 760
Moderate to high	530 to 649
Moderate	420 to 529
Low to moderate	270 to 419
Low	90 to 269

Obviously, such a self-assessment is not infallible. By assigning
numerical values to certain lifestyle habits, however, we can set a
relationship between those habits on one hand and cardiovascular
risk on the other.

Remember, *your* score is reflective of *your* lifestyle. If you don't
like your score, find out where you were penalized and change that
habit. With the exception of the first three categories, all are determined by your choices and actions.

CHAPTER 2

THE AMERICAN DIET

An Unhealthy Choice

Until modern times, most dietary problems were caused by an insufficiency of food. Cyclical food shortages—frequently the result of crop failures, bad weather and wars—were a way of life. People often didn't get enough to eat, became undernourished, and suffered disease and death.

In America, this is no longer the primary problem. Although shortages do exist, in general our nation has a sufficient food supply. As a result, rickets, scurvy and the other diseases caused by insufficient nutrition have disappeared. For these reasons, most Americans consider their diet to be healthy. This is a gross misconception. Abundant food does not equate to a healthy diet.

The fact is that what Americans choose to eat is hazardous to their health. Far too rich in fat, salt, sugar, cholesterol and total calories, the contemporary national diet has produced an entirely new genre of food-induced diseases. As characterized by John Kenneth Galbraith, we are one of the "most overfed and undernourished" populations in the world. Six of the 10 leading causes of death in the United States are linked to diet: coronary heart disease, cancers of the colon and breast, high blood pressure, stroke, and cirrhosis of the liver. Other ailments associated with diet include gout, diabetes, osteoarthritis and gall bladder disease. These are the internal manifestations of poor diet; the external manifestation is a population severely overweight.

The devastating effect of the modern American diet on health and longevity is not a new concept to health professionals. Since 1958, at least 17 major health organizations (including the American Heart Association, the National Cancer Institute, the National Institutes of Health and the U.S. Surgeon General) have called for sweeping changes in the way America eats. Even Congress got involved when the U.S. Senate Select Committee on Nutrition and Human Needs issued new dietary guidelines in 1977 to counteract the health effects of the national diet pattern. The committee called for a decrease in the excessive consumption of harmful elements—fat (especially saturated fat), cholesterol, sugar, salt, alcohol and calories—and an increase in the more healthful complex carbohydrates (fresh fruit, vegetables, legumes and whole grains). The recommendations specifically included:

- A reduction in fat from 42% to 30% of total calories
- A reduction in saturated fat from 16% to 10% of total calories
- A reduction in cholesterol from 600 to 300 milligrams per day
- A reduction in sodium from 8,000 to 3,300 milligrams per day

The committee also recommended a diet with less red meat and whole milk, fewer processed and fast foods, and fewer non-nutritive foods such as candy, soft drinks and alcoholic beverages.

Unfortunately, most Americans have not responded to the suggested dietary changes. This seems strange given the body of knowledge connecting the modern diet to over-weight and to a plethora of diseases and unhealthy conditions. After all, if what we choose to eat can make us fat or can kill us, it seems only reasonable to make better, more positive choices. Yet, as a nation, our diet continues to be negative. Dietary decisions continue to be based on convenience, economics, status, taste, impulse—on influences other than good health.

Of course, there is no one American diet. Anyone who has eaten a hot dog on Long Island, a taco in Los Angeles or a prime rib in Kansas City knows that favorite foods differ from one end of the country to the other, reflecting ethnic heritage and regional preferences. While individual foods may differ, however, there is a commonality that produces a distinctly American diet pattern—one that is uniformly excessive in fat, cholesterol, salt, sugar and total calories. From Boston to San Diego, Seattle to Miami, the basic national diet is the same—sweet and salty fat! Consider what Americans eat in just one day:

      13 pizzas the size of the Roman Colosseum
      47 million hot dogs
   2,250 head of cattle as fast-food hamburgers
       3 million gallons of ice cream
     1.2 million gallons of hard liquor
     5.8 million pounds of chocolate

Some two-thirds of all calories in the average American diet have little nutritional value—42% come from fat, 24% from sugar, 5% from alcohol. In effect, the rest of the calories are asked to meet all our major nutritional needs. This is a poor management ratio. What business or sports team could succeed with only a third of its people pulling the oars for everyone?

The chief problems with the American diet—excessive fat, sugar and salt—are responsible for a number of diseases and debilitating conditions. No condition is more serious than coronary heart disease. More specifically, the American diet produces three major conditions that promote heart disease: elevated blood cholesterol, high blood pressure and overweight. Each of these is a potential killer, a natural result of the American diet pattern.

ELEVATED CHOLESTEROL

Though designated as a principal culprit, in truth cholesterol is not all bad. Essential for cell wall construction, the transmission of nerve impulses and the synthesis of important hormones, it has a legitimate role in the healthy functioning of the body and poses no problem when present in the correct amount. When the levels in the blood are excessive, however, cholesterol can accumulate on the coronary artery walls, clog the channel and prevent blood from reaching the heart. Blood flow is generally impacted when 75% of the channel has been blocked. It is for this reason that elevated blood cholesterol is considered the chief risk factor for a heart attack.

Blood cholesterol is made up of cholesterol from foods eaten and from cholesterol produced by the body. If a person ate no cholesterol at all, the body would manufacture enough for its needs. Dietary cholesterol is not the chief reason for high levels of cholesterol in the blood. The more important factor is saturated fat in the diet, which causes the body to produce excessive cholesterol.

CHOLESTEROL LEVELS

As Dr. Robert Levy, director of the National Heart, Lung and Blood Institute, observes, "There is no controversy that blood cholesterol is a risk factor for heart attack." The body of research linking blood cholesterol to incidence of heart attacks is substantial. Early studies done on test animals, usually monkeys, showed that a diet rich in fat and dietary cholesterol increased the blood cholesterol levels—along with the incidence of heart attacks. Epidemiological studies on population groups show the same results. In his Seven Country Study, Dr. Ancel Keys found that populations whose diet included a lot of saturated fat also had uniformly high levels of blood cholesterol—which closely matched their heart attack rates. Research also reveals that the relationship between blood cholesterol and the chance of coronary heart disease is a continuous one, with the risk of the disease rising as the cholesterol level in the blood increases.

It is an acknowledged axiom that the higher the level of blood cholesterol, the greater the risk of heart attack. Indeed, numerous studies show that different cholesterol levels can be equated with statistical levels of risk. According to the National Institutes of Health, a level under 200 substantially reduces the risk of heart disease. Conversely, as the level increases, so does the risk. The Framingham Study illustrates that the risk of heart attack for a person with a cholesterol level of 260 is four times higher than that for a person with a level of 200. As blood cholesterol increases, it seems to be deposited somewhat uniformly throughout the coronary artery system. Harvard pathologists have found that once a single artery is 50% blocked, virtually no segment of the other coronary arteries is free of the disease.

Just as increased blood cholesterol levels will cause the incidence of heart attack to rise, decreased levels have been shown to cause heart attack incidence to drop. In 1984 the results of a 10-year study by the National Institutes of Health, which involved thousands of middle-aged men, revealed that lowering blood cholesterol prevented heart attacks. The men in this study, called the Coronary Primary Prevention Trial, were divided into two groups. One group took a cholesterol-lowering drug; the other did not. The results were astonishing. The group who used the drug showed an average drop in cholesterol of a mere 8.5% yet suffered 19% fewer heart attacks and 24% fewer cardiac deaths than the group who did not use the drug. This study illustrated that for every 1% reduction in cholesterol, there was a 2% decrease in cardiac risk.

THE RELATIONSHIP OF BLOOD CHOLESTEROL LEVELS AND THE FIRST CORONARY EVENT

(Men Aged 35 to 59)

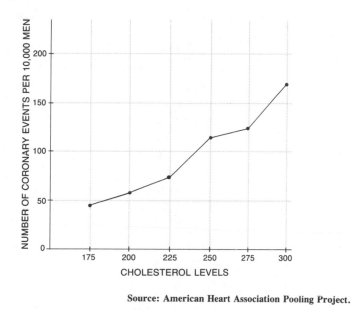

Source: American Heart Association Pooling Project.

Cholesterol levels are easily calculated from blood tests. The results are expressed as the number of milligrams (mg) of cholesterol per deciliter (dl) of blood. For example, the cholesterol level of a person who has 200 milligrams of cholesterol in a deciliter of blood would be 200 mg/dl, simply expressed as 200. A relative scale is used to define the relationship of cholesterol level to cardiac risk. Until recently, the acceptable range was 225 to 275, with a mean of 250. Indeed, many physicians have not considered levels of 260 to be a problem.

For many years, a person with a level of 250 was "normal." Today, health professionals realize that 250 is not "normal." It is "average"—for an American! What has been defined as normal for Americans is considered excessively high in other parts of the world. In Third World nations where plant foods make up most of the diet, the normal cholesterol range is 100 to 140. In the Mediterranean, Latin America and the Orient, "normal" is a range of 150 to 180. "Normal" for Americans may be 250, but only if coronary heart disease is accepted as a normal end point. It's important to understand that "normal" and "healthful" are different terms.

Confusion over cholesterol levels has lulled many people into a false sense of good health. Fitness writer and lecturer Dr. George Sheehan puts this into perspective: "As important as cholesterol is, usually no more than 10 to 15 percent of those who show up at my lectures know what theirs is. Some say they don't know but that their doctors tell them they have nothing to worry about. If they don't know, I say they do have something to worry about." Such changes in thinking by health professionals moved the National Institutes of Health in 1985 to issue new guidelines for cholesterol levels:

Age	Recommended Level	Moderate Risk	High Risk
2 to 19	Under 170	170 to 185	Over 185
20 to 29	Under 200	200 to 220	Over 220
30 to 39	Under 220	220 to 240	Over 240
40 and over	Under 240	240 to 260	Over 260

It should be noted that many health professionals think these standards are still too high but accept them as a first step in a national cholesterol education effort. "We really need to be under 200," one doctor told me, "but so many of us are so high that much of the population would have an anxiety attack if we used 'under 200' as a standard."

This is supported by a study reported in the *Journal of the American Medical Association,* which illustrated that even moderate cholesterol levels dramatically increase the risk of dying from heart attack. The study, conducted on middle-aged men aged 35 to 57, showed that those with cholesterol levels of 182 to 202—certainly low by American standards—had 29% more heart disease deaths than those with levels below 182. According to Dr. Jeremiah Stamler of Northwestern University in Chicago, co-author of the study, "The risk begins much earlier and at lower cholesterol levels than we thought."

"GOOD" AND "BAD" CHOLESTEROL

Blood cholesterol is carried by fat-protein complexes called lipoproteins. This is necessary because all cholesterol is insoluble in water and therefore cannot be transported in a pure state via the bloodstream. It must first be combined with fat and protein molecules in order to become soluble. The two major types of lipoproteins, low-density and high-density, have very different effects on the health of the arteries. A chief distinction is found in their respective chemical packaging.

The *low-density lipoproteins*, or LDLs, carry most of the cholesterol and are considered "bad" because they are primarily responsible for the cholesterol deposited on artery walls. LDL is not a stable chemical package, and it unravels quite easily. Should an LDL escape the bloodstream and penetrate an artery wall, the cholesterol could be released and deposited. When that happens, the clogging process has begun. LDL levels are very sensitive to diets rich in saturated fat.

The *high-density lipoproteins*, or HDLs, are considered "good" cholesterol for two reasons. First, they do not collect on artery walls to block blood flow. This is because HDLs are very stable chemical packages that do not come apart easily. Should an HDL escape the bloodstream and penetrate an artery wall, the package will remain intact— and the cholesterol will have little chance to come in direct contact with the artery. In such an instance, the HDL will return to the bloodstream without causing damage. Second, HDL works to minimize the harmful effects of LDL by causing it to be removed from the bloodstream and excreted. By doing this, HDL actually helps to minimize the arterial buildup caused by LDL. According to Dr. Ken Cooper, HDL cholesterol should constitute no less than 20% of total cholesterol in males (a ratio of 5:1) and no less than 22.5% in females (a ratio of 4.5:1). The greater the percentage of HDL, the more protection from coronary disease.

For both men and women, HDL levels can be increased dramatically by a regular program of aerobic exercise. Researchers have found that joggers who averaged only 11 miles a week had significantly higher HDL levels than did their inactive counterparts, and that HDL in the blood of the runners was raised to a level that could be expected to make a difference in lowering coronary risk.

Studies of families in which one generation after another has lived to age 80 to 90 free of cardiovascular disease have revealed that family members had either very high levels of HDL or very low levels of LDL.

EFFECT OF HDL RATIOS ON RISK
OF CORONARY HEART DISEASE

	Males	Females
Average risk of coronary heart disease in Americans	5:1	4.5:1
Average victim of coronary heart disease	5.5:1	4.6:1
	to	to
	6.1:1	6.4:1
Twice the average risk	9.6:1	7.1:1
Triple the average risk	23.4:1	11:1

Source: American Heart Association.

FOOD AND HIGH CHOLESTEROL

The evidence in heart disease studies illustrates a correlation between dietary habits and the disease. The cause-and-effect relationship involves three steps:

1. A diet rich in saturated fat and cholesterol causes blood cholesterol levels to increase;

2. The higher the blood cholesterol, the greater the number and the size of artery blockages;

3. The more severe the artery blockages, the greater the risk of heart disease and stroke.

At first glance, it might appear that foods high in cholesterol are the chief problem in the development of LDL. Indeed, it doesn't take much of a cholesterol-rich food, such as liver and other organ meats, to exceed the American Heart Association guidelines: no more than 300 milligrams of cholesterol a day. However, foods extremely rich in cholesterol are fairly rare on the American diet, with the notable exception of whole eggs. How many times a year, for example, do you eat liver? Probably not enough to have a significant effect on LDL cholesterol levels. In addition, while foods containing cholesterol can raise blood cholesterol levels, they have less effect on the rate of elevation than does saturated fat.

For many people, then, the primary problem is not foods that are high in cholesterol but those that are high in saturated fat. The prime dietary influence is saturated animal fat, which causes the body to produce excessive LDL and thus raises the total cholesterol level. With 16% of all calories consumed in the American diet as saturated fat (all fat constitutes 42%), it's no wonder that cholesterol levels are so high and that LDL is such a problem.

One of the many studies that proved the relationship between dietary fat and cholesterol levels was conducted by Dr. Ancel Keys, who compared three groups of Japanese each living in a different environment. The first group, who lived in Japan and ate the traditional low-fat Asian diet, showed a low level of cholesterol and a low incidence of heart attack. The second group, who lived in Hawaii and whose diet was a mixture of low-fat Asian and high-fat American foods, had a higher level of cholesterol and a greater incidence of heart attack than the first group. The third group, who lived in Los Angeles and consumed the fatty American diet exclusively, showed the highest cholesterol level and incidence of heart attack of all three groups.

Another relevant study divided Europe into two distinct geographic areas based upon dietary patterns. High-fat Europe, with a diet similar to that of the United States, consisted of the British Isles, Germany, Holland, Scandinavia, Belgium, northern France and northern Switzerland; this group was characterized as a "beer and butter" culture, and their diet pattern, while differing in national foods, was uniformly rich in fat. Low-fat Europe, on the other hand, exhibited a diet pattern that was lower in fats, particularly animal fats; categorized as a "wine and oil" culture, this group consisted of Spain, Italy, southern France, southern Switzerland and Greece. The study illustrated that a high level of cholesterol and a frequency of heart attack existed in high-fat Europe, while the opposite was true of low-fat Europe. It concluded that cholesterol levels and heart attack rates cut across geographic and ethnic boundaries where similarities in fat content of the diet did the same.

While it's an oversimplification to state that HDL cholesterol is "good" and LDL cholesterol is "bad," this relationship is essentially correct. The facts speak for themselves: the amount and type of cholesterol in the blood are critical to coronary health. Lifestyle choices are the greatest controlling factor for cholesterol risk. A diet high in fat, particularly saturated fat, raises LDL and lack of exercise decreases HDL. A diet low in fat, particularly saturated fat, lowers LDL and a regular program of aerobic exercise increases HDL. In either case, it's a choice.

HIGH BLOOD PRESSURE

Many people have the mistaken notion that high blood pressure, or hypertension, has something to do with "hyper" activity or tense, nervous behavior. While there is a correlation between emotional stress and high blood pressure, the word "hypertension" means that the pressure at which the blood is pumped through the arteries is higher than normal.

Blood pressure is measured when the heart beats (systolic) and rests between beats (diastolic) and is expressed as two numbers representing millimeters of mercury (mm Hg). The first number, systolic pressure, is normally between 110 and 130 mm Hg. The second number, diastolic pressure, is normally between 70 and 80 mm Hg. A normal blood pressure might be expressed as 110/70, or "110 over 70." While there is no clear definition of when hypertension begins, most experts agree that a blood pressure reading of 140/90 is the upper limit for the normal range. Anything higher would constitute hypertension.

About 37 million Americans have high blood pressure, which is one of the principal reasons for the high incidence of heart attacks in the United States. This relationship has been thoroughly documented. According to the Framingham Study, for example, a man in his thirties with a diastolic blood pressure between 85 and 94 has five times the risk of a heart attack as a man with a diastolic pressure below 70. Metropolitan Life Insurance Company actuarial studies indicate that the life expectancy of a 35-year-old man with a blood pressure greater than 150/100 is reduced by 16 years.

How does high blood pressure come to be? Cardiovascular researchers believe that many people are born with a genetic susceptibility to hypertension. The potential for the condition is activated by diet, chiefly one high in salt as well as fat. Studies have shown a direct link between a high-salt diet and high blood pressure. In cultures that are salt-rich, such as Japan and the United States, high blood pressure afflicts a significant portion of the population. In contrast, studies by Dr. Lot Page of Harvard have shown that cultures that consume little salt—such as those found in the South Pacific, the Middle East and parts of Brazil— have virtually no high blood pressure.

Excess weight, the product of a high-fat diet, is another significant factor. The risk of high blood pressure is three times as great for overweight people as for those of normal weight. Some tests have demonstrated that blood pressure could be reduced by 41% as the result of a weight control program.

Although high blood pressure constitutes a great risk for heart disease, it is not a natural condition. For most people, it comes about because of lifestyle decisions—principally in the area of diet. By choosing to eat foods rich in salt and fat, by choosing a lifestyle that promotes overweight, many people make a choice for high blood pressure and increased cardiac risk.

OVERWEIGHT

The control of body weight may be the key factor in producing a lifestyle that promotes cardiac health. Of and by itself, excess weight is a risk for coronary disease. Moreover, a lifestyle that promotes overweight is the very same lifestyle that promotes elevated cholesterol and high blood pressure.

It is an established fact that Americans weigh too much. By conservative estimate there are 34 million Americans between the ages of 20 and 75 who are overweight, according to the 1985 consensus report from the National Institutes of Health. Indeed, the U.S. population currently ranks as one of the world's fattest. The typical adult American male weighs 20 to 30 pounds too much, and the typical female is overweight by 15 to 30 pounds.

GENETIC INFLUENCES

Much current scientific thinking involves the impact of heredity on weight, or, as put by one social commentator, "The shape of your genes helps determine the shape of your jeans."

Research shows that fat parents tend to produce fat children. If both parents are overweight, there is an 80% chance that the child too will be overweight. If only one parent is overweight, the chance drops to 50%. And if both parents are average weight, there is only a 1 in 20 chance that the child will be overweight. In a study published in the *New England Journal of Medicine,* Dr. Albert Stunkard and his colleagues concluded that "genetic influences have an important role in determining human fatness in adults." Dr. Stunkard studied 540 middle-aged adults who bore little relation to their adoptive parents with respect to weight. The daughters tended strongly to follow the shape of their biological parents, particularly their mothers, although the sons showed no such relationship to either set of parents. This again emphasizes the complex relationship of genetics to body weight.

Dr. Clifton Bogardus of the National Institutes of Health in Phoenix came to a similar conclusion. Dr. Bogardus found that the amount of calories people burned at rest was a factor of inheritance. Some people naturally burned more calories than others. Those with low calorie-burning capacities tended toward overweight. This study showed that a predisposition to be overweight can be passed down through families.

Setpoints. One of the genetic factors that seem to have a direct influence on weight is the "setpoint," or "settling point," which, according to Dr. Gilbert Leveille and other experts, is a predetermined weight that the body works to keep. Proponents theorize that the brain contains a weight-regulating mechanism that chooses the amount of body fat it considers ideal for a person's needs. It then works tirelessly to defend that weight by controlling how much the person eats and how much body fat will be carried.

In other words, one may be programmed to have weight stay at a certain level. Start a diet, and the body may resist by lowering the rate at which calories are burned to maintain breathing, circulation and other vital processes. By turning down its idling speed by 15% to 25%, the body becomes more energy-efficient and weight loss is harder to achieve.

Even if one is successful in losing weight on a diet, his or her body will strive to get back to its setpoint weight.

According to Dr. Theodore Van Italie of the Obesity Research Center at St. Luke's Hospital in New York, "It's clear that if you lose weight, adaptations come into play that make it possible to regain that weight more efficiently." In support of this theory, studies in which normal-weight people either fasted to lose weight or overate to gain substantial amounts of weight showed that the subjects returned to their original weight after they were told to eat as they pleased. Further support comes from evidence that less than 5% of overweight dieters lose more than 40 pounds and that fewer still can maintain such a weight loss.

Setpoint is a valid factor, but is it set forever? The answer is no. Dieting by itself will not lower the setpoint. In fact, repeated crash dieting can actually raise it, making it more difficult to reach and maintain a weight goal. But when a prudent diet is combined with a regular program of aerobic exercise, the setpoint can be favorably changed. The good news is that hereditary setpoints can be positively altered by lifestyle.

Fat cells. A second genetic factor involves the number of fat cells in the body. Adults have from 30 to 40 billion fat (adipose) cells, which swell and shrink like sponges with the amount of fat inside them. The more fat cells there are, the "heavier" the body wants to be and the harder it becomes to keep weight down.

The number of fat cells a person has is, in part, genetically determined. Contrary to popular thought, crash diets do not melt fat cells. In fact, when the body is starved, says Dr. Irving Faust of Rockefeller University, "fat cells appear to be as fully protected as brain cells." They can become smaller but can never totally disappear. Dr. Faust found that while rats on a starvation diet lost weight— mostly water, muscle, organ and connective tissue—their brain cells and fat cells remained intact even at the point of death. Their fat cells had decreased in size but not in number.

While genetics may provide a base number of fat cells,

overeating can stimulate the production of new cells. For a long time it was thought that fat cells could be produced only during infancy or puberty. New evidence indicates that overeating in adulthood can stimulate new cell production as well.

The number of fat cells is less important to weight control than is their size and content, each of which is influenced by diet and exercise. The amount of fat the cell contains is a product of choice.

Summary. Genetic factors may potentially predispose a person to be overweight, but they do not in the final analysis cause most people to be fat. A study conducted by the Medical College of Wisconsin in Milwaukee on overweight women found that genetics accounted for 12% of the problem, while cultural and environmental influences accounted for 32%. Genetic "baggage" such as high setpoints or multitudinous numbers of fat cells does *not* guarantee overweight. When pro-fat genetics combine with pro-fat cultural influences, however, excess weight is invariably the result.

People should not feel hopeless as a result of genetic research. As Dr. Stunkard says, "What it means is that some people find it easier to gain weight and harder to lose weight than others. We've known that all along. Now we just know more about how it works."

CULTURAL INFLUENCES

It may be consoling to blame genetics for excess body fat ("It's not my fault—I couldn't pick my parents!"), but for many people heredity is not the chief problem. Rather, it's environment. Overweight often runs in families because poor lifestyle habits are passed from one generation to another.

Diet. One of the results of World War II was that the United States became an affluent nation. The middle class greatly expanded and developed an economic capacity that allowed its members to eat as much as they wanted. Access to food became virtually unlimited, a situation that continues today. Now food is abundantly available at all hours, in around-the-clock restaurants and grocery stores or fast-food restaurants that offer takeout and home delivery. The American refrigerator is bulging, and it is our habit to eat from it at all times of the day. As a result, we have developed a pattern of eating when we want to, not when we need to.

Stress. Many medical experts believe that overeating is a result of stress found in the modern American lifestyle. As life became more complex after World War II, anxiety and chronic worry came to the fore. Some people have reacted to modern stress by seeking food as a source of consolation. Says Richard B. Stuart, psychological consultant to Weight Watchers International, "Everyone who goes into the pantry unnecessarily is looking for a solution to one of life's dilemmas—either boredom, frustration, anger, or fatigue." Psychiatrist Dr. Hilde Bruch, author of *The Golden Cage,* puts it this way: "Food may symbolically stand for an insatiable desire for unobtainable love or as an expression of rage and hatred; it may substitute for sexual gratification or indicate ascetic denial . . . it may serve as a defense against adulthood and responsibility. Preoccupation with food may appear as a helpless, dependent clinging to parents, or as a hostile rejection of them."

Tension, aggravation, disappointment, frustration, anger, depression—all lead to the refrigerator. This has become a particularly significant problem for a growing number of overweight Americans caught in a Catch-22 situation. They keep eating because they're tense—but they're tense because they're fat. Many have the feeling that they're not in control of their lives or their bodies, and this feeling—often accompanied by guilt and low self-esteem—drives them to overeat.

Sedentary leisure activities. A good part of why America weighs too much involves choices of leisure-time activities. Instead of burning calories in physical exercise, for example, many Americans spend their free time in front of a TV set, enjoying situation comedies while consuming high-calorie snacks and drinks. Coupled with the increased use of the automobile and the evolvement of more white-collar jobs, the population has become progressively more sedentary.

Television does more than replace exercise; it also promotes overweight by telling us what to eat. Athletes, movie stars and cartoon characters huckster sugary cereals, fatty fast foods and non-nutritive soft drinks. These are the most profitable foods for manufacturers (the rule is, "The more processing involved, the more that can be charged"), so naturally they are the products to be pushed. Less profitable whole foods, such as apples or carrots, are not promoted. Consequently, a contemporary dietary pattern has been developed based not on nutrition but on social and entertainment values.

Summary. In the final analysis, what a person weighs is the consequence of a balance—or an imbalance—between calories consumed and calories burned. If too many calories are consumed and not enough burned, excess fat is created. The post-World War II American lifestyle, which encourages overeating and discourages physical activity, has thrown caloric balances out of whack for many people. The prevalence of excess weight in the American population today is a direct legacy of our modern lifestyle—the same lifestyle that promotes coronary disease.

HEALTH CONSEQUENCES

Even without a complete understanding of the specific role of excess weight in heart disease, enough information has been accumulated to allow the American Heart Association to classify overweight as one of the 11 major coronary risk factors. Dr. Ken Cooper, the father of aerobic exercise, has stated that he now regards overweight to any degree as a significant risk factor for heart disease. "Obesity is one of the top three or four factors in causing coronary problems," he says. "It may even be detrimental alone, that is, it may be unrelated to other coronary risk factors such as high blood pressure, elevated cholesterol, triglycerides and blood sugar. In other words, obesity seems to be an independent coronary risk factor."

Clearly, then, overweight is a serious problem that requires a serious solution. Put simply, choosing a lifestyle that promotes overweight means choosing a lifestyle that also promotes cardiac risk.

It is estimated that approximately 25% of cardiovascular disease is attributed to overweight. According to the National Institutes of Health, a 40-year-old-man who is five feet nine and weighs 178 pounds has a 25% greater risk of coronary heart disease than if he weighed 148 pounds. A 40-year-old woman who is five feet four and weighs 148 pounds has a 25% greater risk than if she weighed 124 pounds. Although the mechanism by which overweight increases the risk of heart disease is not known, many experts believe it is due to the strain placed by excess weight on the heart and lungs, forcing them to work harder.

While overweight is increasingly recognized as a factor in coronary heart disease, a problem exists in determining what constitutes "overweight." The recognized standard has been the height and weight tables issued by the Metropolitan Life Insurance Company. While the company says that the tables reflect desirable weights, those at which people live the longest, these weights have long been interpreted as "ideal." A revised table was issued in 1983 that allowed an increase of 2 to 15 pounds for men and 2 to 12 pounds for women above the levels of the 1959 table. This revision flies right in the face of evidence linking excess weight to cardiovascular disease and has caused concern among many physicians. "In a population in which obesity and cardiovascular disease are major problems," says Dr. W. Virgil Brown of the American Heart Association, "it does not seem prudent to raise the limits for recommended weight."

Dr. William Castelli, director of the Framingham Study,

COMPARING BODY WEIGHT GUIDELINES

1959 Tables

Men

Height	Small Frame	Medium Frame	Large Frame
5'2"	112–120	118–129	126–141
5'3"	115–123	121–133	129–144
5'4"	118–126	124–136	132–148
5'5"	121–129	127–139	135–152
5'6"	124–133	130–143	138–156
5'7"	128–137	134–147	142–161
5'8"	132–141	138–152	147–166
5'9"	136–145	142–156	151–170
5'10"	140–150	146–160	155–174
5'11"	144–154	150–165	159–179
6'0"	148–158	154–170	164–184
6'1"	152–162	158–175	168–189
6'2"	156–167	162–180	173–194
6'3"	160–171	167–185	178–199
6'4"	164–175	172–190	182–204

1983 Tables

Men

Height	Small Frame	Medium Frame	Large Frame
5'2"	128–134	131–141	138–150
5'3"	130–136	133–143	140–153
5'4"	132–138	135–145	142–156
5'5"	134–140	137–148	144–160
5'6"	136–142	139–151	146–164
5'7"	138–145	142–154	149–168
5'8"	140–148	145–157	152–172
5'9"	142–151	148–160	155–176
5'10"	144–154	151–163	158–180
5'11"	146–157	154–166	161–184
6'0"	149–160	157–170	164–188
6'1"	152–164	160–174	168–192
6'2"	155–168	164–178	172–197
6'3"	158–172	167–182	176–202
6'4"	162–176	171–187	181–207

Source: Metropolitan Life.

COMPARING BODY WEIGHT GUIDELINES

1959 Tables

Women

Height	Small Frame	Medium Frame	Large Frame
4'10"	92–98	96–107	104–119
4'11"	94–101	98–110	106–122
5'0"	96–104	101–113	109–125
5'1"	99–107	104–116	112–128
5'2"	102–110	107–119	115–131
5'3"	105–113	110–122	118–134
5'4"	108–116	113–126	121–138
5'5"	111–119	116–130	125–142
5'6"	114–123	120–135	129–146
5'7"	118–127	124–139	133–150
5'8"	122–131	128–143	137–154
5'9"	126–135	132–147	141–158
5'10"	130–140	136–151	145–163
5'11"	134–144	140–155	149–168
6'0"	138–148	144–159	153–173

1983 Tables

Women

Height	Small Frame	Medium Frame	Large Frame
4'10"	102–111	109–121	118–131
4'11"	103–113	111–123	120–134
5'0"	104–115	113–126	122–137
5'1"	106–118	115–129	125–140
5'2"	108–121	118–132	128–143
5'3"	111–124	121–135	131–147
5'4"	114–127	124–138	134–151
5'5"	117–130	127–141	137–155
5'6"	120–133	130–144	140–159
5'7"	123–136	133–147	143–163
5'8"	126–139	136–150	146–167
5'9"	129–142	139–153	149–170
5'10"	132–145	142–156	152–173
5'11"	135–148	145–159	155–176
6'0"	138–151	148–162	158–179

Source: Metropolitan Life.

is even more direct: "The 1983 tables are dangerous because they let people weigh about 10 pounds more. That's a 20% increase in their death rates. The Framingham Study shows that for each pound a person gains over the 1959 tables, he increases his death rate by 2% over the next 26 years. People who are 10% overweight have four times the death rate of someone the same age who remains at the 1959 ideal weights. If you're 25% over the 1959 weights, your death rate is five times higher."

Cardiovascular disease is not a large problem in many other countries. One of the reasons for its epidemic proportions in the United States is because of national overweight.

High blood pressure. One of the most common conditions associated with overweight is high blood pressure, which contributes to stroke and cerebral hemorrhage. High blood pressure occurs 5.6 times more often in overweight people aged 20 to 44 and twice as often in those 45 to 74 than in people the same age or normal weight. Many studies have illustrated that elevated blood pressure can return to normal levels without drugs as a result of weight loss. To make matters worse, excessive body weight often makes blood pressure more difficult to control.

Excess weight may not be the cause of high blood pressure, but it certainly can retard correction of the problem. With so many Americans overweight today, it should be no surprise that almost 40 million people have high blood pressure.

Higher levels of blood fats. Cardiac risk is also increased because of a relationship between excess weight and increased levels of blood fats that could lead to artery blockages. Overweight produces higher levels of LDL cholesterol and triglycerides and lower levels of HDL cholesterol. It is axiomatic that when LDL cholesterol and triglycerides are high and HDL cholesterol is low, the risk for heart attack and stroke is increased dramatically.

A secondary aspect of this relationship is that a lifestyle that produces excess weight—high-fat diet, lack of exercise—is the same lifestyle that fosters unhealthy blood chemistry. A study by Dr. Michael Follick and his associates at Brown University recently illustrated that weight loss could significantly decrease the amount of cholesterol circulating in the bloodstream, thereby greatly reducing the risk of heart disease.

Location of fat deposits. Another facet to the link between overweight and cardiovascular disease involves the location of excessive body fat. According to a Swedish study conducted by Dr. Ulf Smith of the University of Göteburg, people with potbellies are three to five times as likely to suffer heart attacks as those with fatty thighs and hips. This study measured the ratio of waist size to hip size in order to draw its conclusions. Calculating the ratio by dividing hip dimensions by waist size, it found that if a man's waist-to-hip ratio exceeds 1.0 (a 40-inch waist and 36-inch hips, for example, would result in a ratio of about 1.1), his risk of heart attack goes up. The same is true for a woman with a ratio exceeding 0.8 (a 33-inch waist and 36-inch hips would be a ratio of about 0.9).

This effect may result from the fact that fat cells stored in the abdomen are much more metabolically active than those stored in the thighs and buttocks. It may explain why men, who tend to accumulate fat in potbellies, have more heart disease than women, who tend to accumulate fat in thighs and hips.

CHILDHOOD OVERWEIGHT

The link between overweight and risk of heart disease is not limited to adults. Dr. Gerald Berenson of the Louisiana State University Medical Center in New Orleans found that children who became overweight between the ages of 5 and 12 significantly increased their risk of heart disease later in life. Excessive weight gains in childhood were related to changes in blood fat levels that led to the buildup of fatty artery deposits in adulthood.

Childhood overweight, like adult overweight, is influenced by environment. A national sampling of 7,119 children aged 6 to 11 conducted by Drs. William Dietz and Steven Gortmaker found that a 9-state northeastern area had almost twice the rate of overweight children as a 17-state westward stretch starting at Kansas.

Section of Country	% of Children Who Are Overweight
Northeast (Pennsylvania, New York, New Jersey, New England)	22.8%
Midwest (Illinois, Indiana, Iowa, Michigan, Minnesota, Missouri, Ohio, Wisconsin)	18.6
South (ending at the borders of Texas and Oklahoma)	15.3
West	13.9

The study concluded that environmental and cultural influences to a great extent determine the overweight rate in children.

The impact of environment was also covered in a recent report in *Pediatrics*. Researchers found that watching a lot of television—a sedentary activity—is also a significant causal factor. According to the report, the prevalence of overweight among adolescents increases 2% for each hour of television viewed daily.

THE NEED FOR A NEW PERSPECTIVE

Clearly, we need to establish a new, more healthful way of eating—one that will result in weight loss and, more important, offset the aspects of the American diet responsible for high cholesterol levels and high blood pressure. While this is easy to accomplish in theory, it is extremely difficult to achieve in practice.

One of the problems concerns motivation to change. Those who already have a heart disease are generally highly motivated to make lifestyle changes as part of their rehabilitation efforts, but what about those people who are "not sick"? If they have no signs or symptoms, how is it possible to get them to change now—when cholesterol or blood pressure problems do not exist? History illustrates that prevention efforts to reduce risk factors through diet have not been consistent. This, perhaps even more than genetics, may explain why heart disease runs in certain families.

A second problem is the tendency to treat each of the risks that stem from diet—elevated cholesterol, high blood pressure, overweight—independently as if the diet pattern produced just one risk. Even highly motivated cardiac patients make this mistake. They may shift from butter to safflower oil margarine, thus helping to improve their blood cholesterol, and then wonder why their weight hasn't been reduced. They've zeroed in so tightly on the impact of safflower oil margarine on cholesterol that they fail to understand that it has the same number of calories as butter. The same is true for those looking to reduce weight on "high-protein" diets that call for large quantities of red meat. They may lose a few pounds temporarily on such a diet, but they don't understand that their cholesterol may rise as the result of the saturated fat in the meat. The effect of diet on cardiovascular health is multifaceted. When viewed only in terms of its relationship to individual risk factors, dietary change becomes confusing, ineffective and generally short-lived.

Because of these two problems, weight control will be emphasized throughout this book. Excessive weight is a cardiac risk factor in itself—but it is much more. The lifestyle choices, particularly diet pattern, responsible for overweight are the same choices that ultimately dictate elevated cholesterol and high blood pressure. The opposite is just as true. A lifestyle that promotes weight loss and weight control is one that promotes a reduction of cholesterol and blood pressure.

In addition, the fact must be faced: even in light of the staggering statistics regarding heart disease, most Americans are still more concerned about weight and appearance than about cholesterol and blood pressure. Being trim—

which in our society equates to being attractive and successful—is a national fantasy. On the other hand, the reality is that Americans are one of the most overweight populations in the world. There is a fundamental incongruity between how the population lives (pro-fat) and how it would like to look (thin).

THE MYTH ABOUT WEIGHT LOSS

The collective desire to be magically thin has spawned an $18 billion industry that is currently growing at the rate of $1 billion a year. Every year for the last three decades, Americans have been treated to new quick-weight-loss schemes, ranging from fat-burning diets to jaw wiring. These "miracle cures" fluctuate in popularity like a crash-dieter's waistline. People patronize diet doctors, buy the latest diet books, bind their thighs in plastic wrap, let acupuncturists staple their ears, stockpile cases of liquid food and swallow amphetamines that make them crazy but that, they hope, will suppress the desire for a double-scoop cone.

For an example of this craziness, one need only look at the recent action taken by the Food and Drug Administration to prohibit a weight-loss company from selling "vacuum cleaner shorts." The product, knee-length shorts made of an aluminum-foil material, was tied tightly at the waist and the knee; a plastic hose projected from one hip, designed to be connected to a vacuum cleaner. When the vacuum was turned on, body fat was to be sucked away!

Crazy? Yes. But before being closed, the firm reputedly had sold 185,000 pairs of shorts.

Quick-weight-loss gimmicks are expensive and self-defeating—*and they don't work.* Few of the "diet-depressing" pills, for example, are effective in controlling weight; moreover, according to the FDA, many are not safe. So-called starch blockers, whose unproven claim is to allow people to eat bread, potatoes and pasta without absorbing calories, are considered an illegal drug by the FDA. Bulk fillers, promising to swell in the stomach and produce a feeling of fullness, have become popular; these products are safe, says the FDA, but their value in reducing weight has not been proven.

Losing weight through water loss has been touted by producers of diuretics and body wraps, but the loss of water—and the loss of weight—lasts only until the person eats or drinks. Electronic muscle stimulators have also been advertised as a means of losing weight; the FDA states that there is no proof that they work and considers the machines "misbranded and fraudulent when promoted for weight loss purposes."

Special products for cellulite, the dimpled fat that appears most often on women's hips and thighs, are questionable. The advertising treats cellulite as something unique. In actuality, it is not. Cellulite is simply fat, no different from the fat found in other places on the body. Because fat on hips and thighs tends to hang as the result of gravity, it appears pocked, or "cellular." In contrast, fat on the stomach is pushed out, not down. There is no magical way to remove cellulite. It's lost the way all fat is lost—by expending more calories than are taken in. To suggest that cellulite can be removed by external buffing or by the consumption of special herbal tablets is irresponsible and potentially harmful.

CRASH DIETS: LOSERS FOR HEALTH

Nowhere is hucksterism more evident than in the promotion of crash diets. Going on and off diets, losing weight, gaining it back, giving up and feeling desperate is as American as apple pie. Many people live in a polarized state of feast or famine. There are a number of problems associated with on-again/off-again dieting, but the most important is that, as stated by Dr. Henry Jordon, a University of Pennsylvania psychiatrist who specializes in obesity, "Crash dieting just doesn't work."

The truth is that crash diets will not keep anyone thin. According to the National Center for Health Statistics, only

3% of the people who diet will lose weight and keep it off for more than one year; the other 97% not only will regain the lost weight but will put on additional weight as well. This makes the cure rate for overweight worse than for cancer. Bob Schwartz, author of *Diets Don't Work,* has found that crash diets actually encourage weight gain. He uses them in his spas to help beef up underweight members. After putting clients on a crash diet for three days, he has them eat normally for another three. Soon the weight lost on the crash diet is back—along with a few extra pounds. Done often enough, the weight gain can become permanent.

The underlying fallacy in quick-weight-loss methods is that they are short-term solutions to long-term problems. Crash dieting and quick-fix schemes inherently contain the seeds of failure. No one can argue that a drastic reduction in calories will not lead to weight loss. Obviously, if a man regularly consumes 3,000 calories a day, a week on an 800-calorie diet will produce weight loss. But the real questions are:

- Has he really lost fat?
- Can he continue to lose?
- More important, can he keep the lost weight off?

The answer to each is ''no.''

There are five good reasons for the ineffectiveness of crash dieting.

1. Crash diets aren't permanent. Crash diets are unrealistic as a permanent way of eating. They are constructed for short-term use only, the rationale being that weight loss will be rapid if only certain foods are eaten. By dictating exactly what and how often a person eats, they remove the element of choice and are unsuccessful as permanent food management plans because they do not change eating habits.

A number of crash diets that are high in fat and low in carbohydrates do indeed produce an immediate weight loss, but the body is not designed to process only certain types of foods for an extended period of time. If one goes ''off'' the diet, the lost weight reappears; but if one stays "on" the diet too long, serious health consequences can result. According to the Medical Society of New York, prolonged high-fat/low-carbohydrate diets can contribute to kidney disease, ketosis, excess uric acid in the blood, disturbances of heart rhythm, loss of calcium, chronic fatigue and increased serum cholesterol.

Most nutritionists and physicians recommend a diet for adult men and women consisting of 55% to 60% carbohydrates, 25% to 30% fat and 15% to 20% protein. Yet many crash diets combine an unhealthful imbalance of nutrients: a low amount of carbohydrates with a high intake of fat and protein. No matter what they promise, low-carbohydrate diets (including the Atkins, Stillman and Scarsdale plans) are short on nutrition, lack fiber and are high in fat. No wonder such diets may cause liver, blood and kidney problems.

A study at Rutgers University involving 11 well-known diet plans found many to be short on important vitamins and minerals in addition to being too high in fat, cholesterol and sodium. The research showed that the Beverly Hills, Richard Simmons and Stillman diets, each providing less than 70% of the United States Recommended Allowances (USRDA) for more than half the vitamins and minerals studied, were the shortest all around on nutrients. The Stillman, Scarsdale and Atkins plans—each over 50% fat— were seen as unwise for people at risk for heart disease.

2. *Crash diets do not produce fat loss.* Many fad diets are based on the theory that fat can be converted to carbohydrates and "melted away." This is illusory. According to the American Medical Association, which has labeled the theory biologically incorrect, "There is no evidence that permanent weight loss can be achieved by sedentary subjects who consume a carbo-poor diet."

What is really lost on a fad diet is water. Here's how it works: a property of carbohydrate is that it can retain three times its weight in fluid; if less than two ounces of carbohydrates are eaten per day, the body is denied the ability to retain fluid and therefore loses weight—perhaps four to six pounds in a week. But what happens when the person has to return to a normal diet? The water weight comes back twice as fast as it was lost, generally accompanied by a few extra pounds. The crash diet really didn't accomplish anything with regard to loss of body fat.

3. Crash diets lower metabolism. Crash diets produce a condition known as "dieter's dilemma": as caloric intake is lowered, so is the body's need for calories. The ability to burn calories at a certain rate is a function of metabolism. The basal metabolic rate—the rate at which calories are burned while the body is at rest—is the base number of calories needed to keep the body functioning. It operates 24 hours a day. When caloric intake is drastically reduced, metabolism is altered. The body, which doesn't know the difference between the first day of a crash diet and the first day of a famine, thinks it's starving. In defense, it slows down, burning calories at a slower rate and making weight loss more difficult. According to nutritionist Dr. Audrey Cross, "Your body has a sense of survival. Restricting caloric intake makes your body's metabolism more thrifty—adjusting to the calories you take in."

Let's suppose that a woman with a basal metabolic rate of 1,800 calories a day goes on an 800-calorie diet. Her body is shocked by the lack of calories. (Men generally experience this shock when eating fewer than 1,500 calories a day; women, when consuming less than 1,200 calories). Her body dictates a slowing of the metabolic rate in an attempt to conserve energy, and as a result she feels tired and sluggish the first few days of the diet. After losing eight pounds, she goes "off" the diet and returns to her normal eating pattern. Her basal metabolic rate, however, does *not* go back up to normal; it stays low. In other words, the level of calories needed to maintain her body does not automatically readjust upward. This woman suffers the hidden consequence of crash diets: normal eating now produces loads of extra calories—calories that get stored as *fat.* By crash dieting, the woman has primed her body to increase fat storage. She has, in effect, demonstrated that crash dieting is a very efficient way to *gain* weight.

4. Crash diets cause muscle to be lost. Studies show that muscle tissue will be lost if too few calories a day are consumed. The lower the caloric intake, the more muscle is consumed. The lost tissue comes from every organ in the body, including the heart, brain, liver, lungs, kidneys and intestinal tract. According to Dr. George Blackburn of the Harvard Medical School, muscle tissue loss from vital organs is a significant health risk.

The real catch in this situation is that the very muscle tissue lost is what is needed to burn up excess fat. Muscle burns fat. The more muscle in the body, the easier it is for body fat to be utilized as energy. A lot of muscle is akin to a large engine in a car. It has power and it guzzles fuel. Little muscle is like a car with a small engine—not very powerful but very fuel-efficient. This is why people who are fit can eat greater amounts of food. They have more muscle tissue constantly demanding fuel, and therefore they have the capacity to burn fat more easily. The crash dieters are at the opposite extreme: they have lost muscle tissue on the diet, and with it the ability to burn fat. When they go off the diet, body fat piles up.

5. Crash diets produce a dieting mentality. The most common cause of failure is, ironically, dieting itself. Diets cause people to become preoccupied with food and to get into a cycle of starving-bingeing. To paraphrase Mark Twain, "Tell a man what he's not supposed to have, and it becomes the very thing that he can't live without." The result is that people on diets often eat more rather than less.

A man who begins dieting on a Monday, the day when most people start their diets, will spend the entire weekend eating everything in sight. Suddenly he is twice as hungry. Once on the diet, his waking hours are filled with thoughts of food. If he eats one cookie that is not allowed, he considers that he has "blown it," so he eats the whole box. His relationship to food has become unrealistic.

Crash dieting and quick-weight-loss schemes produce

frustration for many people. The only winners from the endless succession of diet gimmicks are those who become rich promoting these fads to a nutritionally naïve and diet-obsessed public. Crash diets and dieting schemes are worthless. Worse than that, they are harmful. As Jane Brody says in her *Nutrition Book,* "Every fad diet is nutritionally unbalanced in one way or another, and some are downright dangerous, even if followed by healthy people for a relatively short time." The sooner the foolishness and hopelessness of crash dieting is understood, the sooner real progress can be made toward weight reduction, permanent weight control and better cardiovascular health.

"DIET" CONFUSION

In our society the word "diet" has come to mean a special way of eating (or not eating), usually for short, predictable periods during the year. In late spring, many people try to shape up for high school reunions, weddings and summer vacations. In late fall, historically the season when most diets begin, they look to lose weight for the holidays. Each New Year's Day millions of Americans share a common resolution to lose weight, but by March the resolve has waned and by late spring they start dieting—again—to greet the summer. Some people leap from diet to diet. For many, it's the only exercise they get! No wonder this cycle allows the average dieter to go on—and off—2.3 diets a year.

The fact is that dieting, by nature a change of short duration, will not produce sustained weight loss. It does nothing to change our basic eating habits. The "grapefruit and hard-boiled egg" diet might produce short-term results, but none of us could expect to eat that way for the rest of our lives.

"Diets" don't work, but a new "diet pattern" does. A diet pattern is a plan for eating that can be used for a lifetime. In the final analysis, enhanced cardiac health and permanent weight control are products not of dieting—but of choosing a new lifestyle.

CHAPTER 3

THE 500-CALORIE SOLUTION TO WEIGHT CONTROL

A Positive Choice

There is no question that the link between lifestyle and cardiovascular health is real and direct. By adopting a lifestyle geared to weight control, we will also be practicing habits designed to reduce the risks of damage to the heart.

The question, then, is how to achieve successful weight loss and permanent weight control. The answer is found in a technique called the 500-Calorie Solution, which recognizes that permanent weight control is the result of a realistic approach based on scientific information. It has nothing to do with crash dieting, rubber exercise suits, grapefruit pills or other quick fixes designed to separate us from our money. Instead, it sets forth a logical, methodical process that determines a proper goal (ideal weight), realistic methods to accomplish that goal, and lifetime habits to keep the goal once it is attained.

FAT VS. WEIGHT

Most people view weight only in terms of pounds. The final arbiter is the bathroom scale. Should it reflect a loss of two pounds, God is in His heaven. Up by that same amount, and it's a major tragedy.

There is a significant flaw in this view: it does not take body composition into consideration. The body is made up of two parts: fat and lean body mass (muscle, bone, teeth and fluids). The bathroom scale measures just one thing: total weight. It does not reveal what makes up that weight— how much is fat and how much is lean body mass. It is not "weight" that affects health and appearance; it is excess body fat. Fat, not weight, is what needs to be lost.

Because weight differs from the body's degree of fatness, scales are unreliable. Not even the most precise set of scales can accurately indicate excess body fat. In addition, body weight can be extremely variable. It fluctuates continuously during the day as a result of a variety of factors, including fluids consumed, amount of salt eaten (salt retains fluids), food in the digestive tract, amount of recent physical activity and sweating, menstrual cycles and some medicines. The scale does not take these factors into consideration, either.

The distinction between "fat" and "weight" is crucial to understanding the problem and the solution. When a person starts to gain body fat, it often is not noticeable. This is because fat first penetrates the muscles, taking the place of lean tissue. The person doesn't look any different or weigh any more. (Ironically, lean body mass weighs more than fat, so that a fit person might actually outweigh a flabby counterpart of the same size. This again shows the fallacy of relying on scales.) Once the muscle is saturated, however, fat begins to accumulate under the skin, where it is noticeable as the unsightly bulges we hate—double chins, potbellies, hamlike thighs. This illustrates a key point: a person gets *overfat* before becoming *overweight*.

Getting slim doesn't come from losing weight; it comes

from reducing body fat. This is precisely why the hundreds of crash diets promoted each year do not work. Indeed, crash dieting actually *increases* the percentage of body fat. Take, for example, a 200-pound man who is 25% fat, which means he is carrying 50 pounds of fat and 150 pounds of lean muscle mass. Bothered by his waist size, he goes on a crash diet and loses 30 pounds in a month. He now loves stepping on the bathroom scale and seeing the needle stop at 170 pounds. But what has he really lost? Crash diets produce water and muscle loss but very little loss of fat—in this case, about 2 pounds. The man may now weigh 170 pounds, but he's carrying 48 pounds of fat. His lean body mass has been reduced to 122 pounds. Before dieting he was 25% fat; after dieting, he's 28% fat.

	Before the Diet	After the Diet
Pounds of lean muscle mass	150	122
Pounds of fat	50	48
Total weight	200	170
Body fat percentage	25%	28%

According to the scale, the man weighs less. In reality, he's *fatter* than when he went on the diet. Eventually he will again eat in his old manner. The water weight will return and, with it, the lost pounds. In addition, because valuable muscle tissue used to burn fat was dieted away, it will be more difficult for him in the future to utilize his body fat as fuel. This man ends up with the worst of all worlds: he again weighs 200 pounds, his body fat percentage is greater than before the diet and his ability to utilize body fat has been diminished.

Fat plays an important and legitimate role in the healthy functioning of the body. It is the fuel the body relies on to run. Without it, you'd have to eat continuously to replenish your fuel supply. Foods rich in fat provide a lot of fuel— nine calories per gram. In addition, dietary fat goes directly to your fat cells. This is very helpful if you're starving, but it's a curse if you're overweight. Protein and carbohydrate, on the other hand, provide less fuel—four calories per gram. Unlike fats, they must be broken down before being stored, and this process burns a lot of calories. The fuel that the food provides is never lost; it's either used up or stored. If you consume more calories than you use up, the extra is stored as body fat.

Body fat accumulates as a fuel reserve primarily under the skin and around the internal organs, where the body can readily draw on it as needed. When the reserve has accumulated approximately 3,500 calories, a pound of body fat has been created. It will take an energy expenditure of 3,500 calories to use up this pound. The ability of the body to store fat as a reserve fuel is virtually limitless. If a person is completely sedentary, which applies to 45% of all Americans, or is not physically active on a regular basis, calories can pile up as body fat. When more calories are taken in than are used—a situation termed "positive energy balance"—the excess is stored as fat throughout the body and often can be seen as unsightly bulges, protruding buttocks and "bay window" bellies.

The utilization of calories has the opposite effect. When more calories are expended in activity than are provided by the foods consumed (a situation called "negative energy balance"), the fat reserves are drained to meet the extra demand. When the energy deficit reaches 3,500 calories, the body has disposed of one pound of fat.

It's not easy to either put on or drop one pound of fat in a single day. In order to increase intake by 3,500 calories, you would have to consume 35 brownies, 3 medium pizzas, a case of beer, or 6 Big Macs and a large cola. On the other hand, since the average person uses between 1,500 and 2,700 calories per day, not even a total fast would result in the loss of a pound of fat. The scale might show a loss of more than a pound, but this would reflect the loss of water, not fat. Even exercise would have to be done in the extreme. You'd have to run 3 or 4 hours or walk 10 hours to burn 3,500 calories.

In other words, gaining or losing body fat is simply not

accomplished in a short time. A few extra calories coming in, a few less calories going out, over time is what causes creeping obesity. As few as 50 extra calories a day—a single chocolate-chip cookie—could add 350 calories a week, or a total of 18,200 in the course of a year. That's equal to over 5 pounds of fat, or 52 in a decade. The basic formula for body fat is simple. If energy intake (calories in food) is greater than energy expenditure (calories used in exercise, basic body functions, physical labor), body fat will be gained. If the intake is less than the expenditure, body fat will be lost.

DETERMINING BODY FAT PERCENTAGE

One of the prerequisites for a successful weight control program is to establish a realistic goal. Some people start a diet to lose weight with no goal in mind; this doesn't make any sense, because if you don't know where you're going, how will you know when you've arrived? Others establish unrealistic goals based on "fantasy weights" that are impossible to achieve. Since fat is ultimately what must be lost, the first step should be to estimate how much body fat you have, calculated as a percentage of body weight. This figure can then be compared with how much body fat you should be carrying.

Health professionals have determined the maximum amount of body fat a healthy adult should have. According to physiologist Dr. David Parker, ideal body fat percentages differ with age:

Age	Ideal Body Fat Percentage	
	Males	Females
16 to 19	15%	19%
20 to 29	16	20
30 to 39	17	21
40 to 49	18	22
50 to 59	19	23
60 and over	20	24

"These are the ideal percentages," says Dr. Parker, "for average people who want to look and feel good, but who are not very active. Athletes—or anyone who exercises aerobically three or four times a week—should be two or three percent less than the ideal in the table."

Unfortunately, there is a disparity between ideal and average body fat percentages in Americans. The ideal range for males is 15% to 20%; American males average about 23%. The ideal range for females is 19% to 24%; American females average about 32%. Ideal percentages are important because they establish the proper balance between fat and lean in the body. If body fat percentage is in line, total weight will be also. Ideal weight is a function of ideal body fat percentage. When the equilibrium deteriorates and body fat escalates, serious appearance and health consequences result. Dr. Ken Cooper puts it well: "Body fat percentage, not weight, is the true indicator of obesity."

A variety of procedures, ranging from the simple to complex, are used to measure body fat. These include the tape measure test, skinfold calipers, bioelectrical impedance and hydrostatic weighing.

TAPE MEASURE TEST

Body fat percentage can be estimated with the use of a simple tape measure. Among the best tape measure techniques is the one shown on pages 70 and 71, by which you can determine your own body fat percentage. Developed by Dr. Jack H. Wilmore, an exercise physiologist at the University of Texas in Austin and the author of *Sensible Fitness,* this technique is considered to have a plus or minus 10% margin of error. Even so, it is still a useful tool for finding out approximate body fat. If, after following the instructions, you calculate that you are 30% fat, for example, applying the margin of error will create a body fat range of 27% to 33%. While not precise, the information is sufficient to indicate that you are carrying too much fat.

MEN

1. Measure your waist exactly at belly-button level.
2. Weigh yourself on an accurate scale.
3. Using a straight edge, line up your waist measurement with your body weight on the chart below to estimate your body fat percentage.

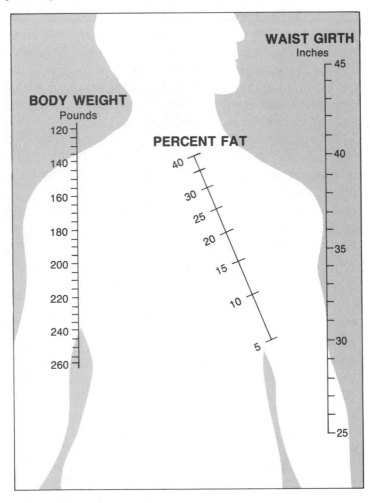

Estimation of relative fat in men from body weight
and abdominal or waist circumference.

WOMEN

1. Measure your hips at their widest point.
2. Measure your height in inches.
3. Using a straight edge, line up these measurements on the chart below to estimate your body fat percentage.

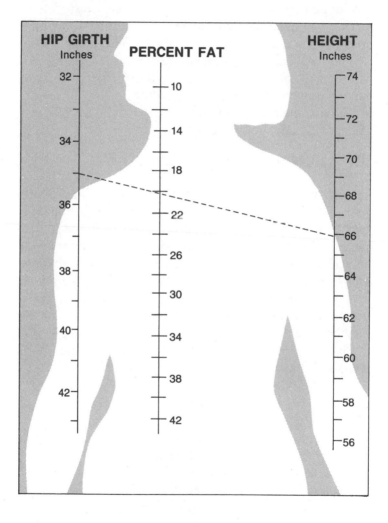

Estimation of relative fat in women from height and hip circumference.

SKINFOLD CALIPERS

This method involves using a set of calipers to measure the thickness of a pinch of skin taken at different points on the body. The points are called universal sites and are generally located on the arms, legs and back. The measurements are used in a formula based on sex, age and sometimes height and weight to estimate body fat percentage. Accuracy in measuring is critical or the test results are flawed. Most technicians are trained in the use of special calipers and in proper site selection. Skinfold testing is readily available at most hospitals, health clubs and YM/YWCAs. The cost is generally about $10.

BIOELECTRICAL IMPEDANCE

In this method, a composition-analyzer machine figures body fat by passing an electric current through the body between two electrodes attached to one hand and two attached to the foot on the same side. (The current is not enough to be harmful or even detectable.) Lean tissue is mostly water and readily conducts electricity, whereas fat resists the charge. The resistance rate is measured and is used to estimate body fat percentage. The accuracy of this method is fairly high. Electronic impedance testing is also available at many health clubs, YM/YWCAs and sports medicine clinics. Costs usually range from $10 to $20.

HYDROSTATIC WEIGHING

Generally considered the most accurate in estimating body fat percentage, this is the standard against which other body fat tests have been gauged. A person is first weighed out of water, then again while totally submerged. Body fat percentage is calculated in part by how much water the person displaces. In effect, the test makes an estimate of the density of body tissue. Lean body mass tends to sink; fat tends to float. Not all health facilities have a dunk tank, which is necessary for this method, but universities and sports medicine clinics often do. The cost for the test ranges from about $20 to $50.

DETERMINING IDEAL BODY WEIGHT

Once body fat has been calculated, the next step is to determine ideal weight. This is a critical calculation. After all, ideal weight is the goal. It tells us where we want to be. Too often weight goals are arbitrarily set as the result of looking in a mirror and have no relationship to ideal weight. They may have no relationship to reality or to good health. Calculated mathematically, ideal body weight represents a realistic goal.

THE STANDARD CALCULATION

To illustrate how ideal weight is calculated, let's use a 35-year-old male who weighs 175 pounds as our subject.

1. Using a scale, he determines that his present weight is 175 pounds.
2. Using one of the available tests, he determines that his body fat percentage is 25%.
3. By multiplying his present weight (175 pounds) by .25, he calculates how many pounds of fat he is carrying.

$$
\begin{array}{r}
175 \text{ pounds present weight} \\
\times \ \underline{.25} \text{ body fat percentage (actual)} \\
44 \text{ pounds of fat}
\end{array}
$$

4. Next, he finds out that the ideal body fat percentage for a 35-year-old male is 17%.
5. He multiplies his present weight by .17 and calculates how many pounds of fat he *should* be carrying.

$$
\begin{array}{r}
175 \text{ pounds present weight} \\
\times \ \underline{.17} \text{ body fat percentage (ideal)} \\
30 \text{ pounds of fat}
\end{array}
$$

6. The difference between actual and ideal pounds of fat is the amount he is "overfat."

$$
\begin{array}{r}
44 \text{ pounds of fat (actual)} \\
- \quad 30 \text{ pounds of fat (ideal)} \\
\hline
14 \text{ pounds overfat}
\end{array}
$$

7. Subtracting the pounds of excess fat (14) from his present weight, he determines his ideal weight.

$$
\begin{array}{r}
175 \text{ pounds present weight} \\
- \quad 14 \text{ pounds overfat} \\
\hline
161 \text{ pounds ideal weight}
\end{array}
$$

Now the man knows what has to be accomplished. He has a goal: to shed 14 pounds of excess fat. When this has been attained, he will have reached his ideal weight of 161 pounds. This goal isn't an arbitrary figure. It represents the best compositional mix for his body—131 pounds of lean muscle mass and 30 pounds of fat.

In order to calculate your own ideal weight, take the following steps:

1. Using a scale, determine your present weight.

1. _____ pounds present weight

2. Using one of the available tests, determine your present body fat percentage.

2. _____ %

3. Calculate how many pounds of body fat you are now carrying by multiplying your present weight by your present body fat percentage.

1. _____ pounds present weight

× 2. _____ body fat percentage (actual)

= 3. _____ pounds of fat

4. Determine your ideal body fat percentage from the chart on page 68.

4. _____ %

5. Determine how many pounds of body fat you should be carrying by multiplying your present weight by your ideal body fat percentage.

1. _____ pounds present weight

× 4. _____ body fat percentage (ideal)

= 5. _____ pounds of fat

6. Subtract the ideal pounds of body fat from the present pounds of body fat to determine how many excess pounds of body fat you are carrying.

3. _____ pounds of fat (actual)

− 5. _____ pounds of fat (ideal)

= 6. _____ pounds overfat

7. Subtract the excess pounds of body fat from your present weight to determine your ideal weight.

1. _____ pounds present weight

− 6. _____ pounds overfat

= 7. _____ pounds ideal weight

THE FREEMAN FORMULA

Health professionals consider the above calculation to be the most accurate method of determining ideal weight. If you don't have access to a body fat test, however, or if it's impractical, you can determine your approximate ideal weight using a formula developed by Dr. Richard Freeman, vice-chairman of medicine at the University of Wisconsin in Madison. The Freeman formula suggests that the ideal female weight is 100 pounds for the first 5 feet of height, plus 5 pounds for each additional inch. Thus the ideal weight for a 5-foot, 5-inch woman is calculated:

First 5 feet of height	100 pounds
5 inches at 5 pounds per inch	+ 25 pounds
Ideal weight	125 pounds

The formula for a male is 106 pounds for the first 5 feet of height, plus 6 pounds for each additional inch. Thus the ideal weight for a 5-foot, 10-inch man is calculated:

First 5 feet of height	106 pounds
10 inches at 6 pounds per inch	+ 60 pounds
Ideal weight	166 pounds

The Freeman formula equates to body fat percentages of 15% to 19% in males and of 18% to 22% in females.

The impact of frame size on the Freeman formula is a legitimate and persistent question. In general, a person with a large frame could add 10% to the ideal weight calculated; a person of small frame could subtract 10%. While this accommodation is valid (not everyone is of "medium" size), it also allows for a fast-and-loose interpretation of ideal weight. In other words, there's room to cheat. One dietitian told me about a patient who epitomized this problem. "She was 5 feet, 2 inches and weighed 109 pounds when I first saw her at age 20," said the dietitian. "She considered her frame to be small. By age 24, she weighed 126 pounds and decided she had a medium frame size. At age 28, now weighing 139 pounds, she determined that all along her size had been large. I last saw her a few years ago when she was 33, her weight at 162 pounds. She had finally run out of frame sizes to justify her ideal weight!"

To find ideal weight by means of the Freeman formula, frame size must be taken into account and arbitrary judgments avoided. There are two ways for frame size to be determined. The simple method involves measuring the wrist just below the wrist bone (toward the hand) with a cloth measuring tape. For women: if the measurement is exactly 6 inches, you have a medium frame; over 6 inches, you have a large frame; under 6 inches, you have a small frame. For men: if the measurement exactly 7 inches, you have a medium frame; over 7 inches, you have a large frame; under 7 inches, you have a small frame.

The more complex method is outlined below.

1. Find your height in inches rounded to the nearest inch (under ½ inch, round down; ½ and over, round up).

1.＿＿＿＿ inches

2. Convert height in inches to height in centimeters by multiplying by 2.545.

1.＿＿＿＿ inches
×   2.545
= 2.＿＿＿＿ centimeters

3. Round to nearest .5 or whole number.

3._____ centimeters

4. Measure wrist circumference using a cloth tape measure and convert to decimals:
$\frac{1}{8} = .1$ $\frac{5}{8} = .6$
$\frac{3}{8} = .4$ $\frac{7}{8} = .9$

4._____ inches

5. Convert measurement in inches to centimeters by multiplying by 2.545.

4._____ inches
$\times$ 2.545
$=$ 5._____ centimeters

6. Round to nearest .5 or whole number.

6._____ centimeters

Frame size is derived by dividing height by wrist measurement.

$$\frac{\text{Height in centimeters}}{\text{Wrist in centimeters}} = \text{Frame size in centimeters}$$

The chart below will give you your frame size.

Female	Male	Frame Size
Greater than 11.0	Greater than 10.4	Small
10.1 to 11.0	9.6 to 10.4	Medium
Less than 10.1	Less than 9.6	Large

Once frame size has been determined by either method, it can be factored into the Freeman formula. If you have a medium frame, the ideal weight in the formula stands as it is. If you have a large frame, add 10%. If you have a small frame, subtract 10%.

DETERMINING CALORIE NEEDS FOR PRESENT AND IDEAL WEIGHTS

Caloric intake has a great deal to do with attaining ideal weight. The proper level of calories for weight loss to occur and weight control to be maintained permanently is based on the needs of the body. The three areas that need to be considered in assessing the total caloric requirements of the body are basal metabolism, physical energy metabolism and digestive metabolism.

BASAL METABOLISM

Basal metabolism, or basal metabolic rate (BMR), reflects the number of calories needed when the body is at rest. Even in this state the lungs are breathing, the heart is pumping, the brain is functioning and other vital organs are at work. Like a car engine at idle, the body is running but not going anywhere.

The basic functions needed just to keep the body alive require energy in the form of calories. According to the Food and Nutrition Board, the average adult male requires between 1,440 and 1,728 calories daily to meet the needs of his basal metabolism. For an average female, the range is 1,296 to 1,584 calories a day.

To estimate the calories needed for basal metabolism, it is first necessary to convert body weight from pounds into kilograms. This is done by dividing pounds by 2.2. For example, a 154-pound person weighs 70 kilograms (154 divided by 2.2 equals 70). To determine your weight in kilograms, use this formula or refer to the following conversion chart.

Pounds =	Kilograms	Pounds =	Kilograms
100	45	155	70
105	48	160	73
110	50	165	75
115	52	170	77
120	54	175	80
125	56	180	82
130	59	185	84
135	61	190	86
140	64	195	89
145	66	200	91
150	68	205	93

Basal metabolic rate, the calories required to turn the body "on," is calculated as a function of kilogram weight. The BMR factors used are 1.0 for men and .9 for women. This is reflected in the following example of a man and a woman, each of whom weighs 70 kilograms.

BASAL METABOLIC RATE FORMULA

Man			Woman
	70	Weight in kilograms	70
×	1.0	× BMR factor	× .9
=	70	= Calories needed per hour	= 63
×	24	× Hours in 1 day	× 24
=	1,680	= Calories needed per day for BMR	= 1,512

To figure your own BMR, use the same formula:

Men			Women
	_____	Your weight in kilograms	_____
×	1.0	× BMR factor	× .9
=	_____	Calories needed per hour	= _____
×	24	× Hours in 1 day	× 24
=	_____	= Calories you need per day for BMR	= _____

PHYSICAL ENERGY METABOLISM

Basal metabolism reflects only a part of the energy needs of the body. We do more than simply stay at rest during waking hours. Therefore, additional calories are needed for physical activities. The more active we are, the more calories we need to consume.

Physical energy needs are estimated as a factor of basal metabolism. Degrees of physical activity are expressed as percentages of the basal metabolic requirement.

Physical Activity Level	Factor
Sedentary most of the time	15%
Sedentary job; regular exercise	20
Physically active job; no regular exercise	20
Physically active job; regular exercise	25

(Regular exercise is defined as at least 20 minutes of aerobic exercise three or four times a week).

Using the same 70-kilogram couple as examples, the formula for physical energy metabolism is easily illustrated. The man has a sedentary job but exercises on a regular basis; his physical activity factor is 20%. The woman has a physically active job and also exercises; her factor is 25%.

PHYSICAL ENERGY METABOLISM FORMULA

Man		Woman
1,680	BMR calories needed	1,512
× .20	× Activity level	× .25
336	= Daily calories needed for physical energy	378

Even though her BMR requires fewer calories than does the man's, the woman has a greater need for additional calories because of her higher rate of physical activity.

To determine the calories you need for physical activity, use the following calculation:

Men		Women
_____	Your BMR calories needed	_____
× _____	Your activity level (from chart)	× _____
= _____	Daily calories needed for your physical energy level	_____

DIGESTIVE METABOLISM

The third area to be measured is the number of calories required for the body to perform digestive functions. This need is a factor of total BMR and physical energy calories. A multiplier of .10 (10%) is used for both men and women. The woman in our example would figure her digestive calories as follows:

DIGESTIVE METABOLISM FORMULA

BMR calories	1,512
Physical activity calories	+ 378
Subtotal	1,890
Digestion factor	× .10
Daily calories needed for digestive functions	189

Thus the woman needs 189 additional calories each day in order to give her body sufficient energy to perform digestive functions.

To figure your digestive metabolism:

Your BMR calories	_____
Your physical activity calories	+ _____
Subtotal	_____
Digestion factor	× .10
Daily calories needed for your digestive functions	_____

TOTAL METABOLIC NEEDS

The caloric requirements of each area—BMR, physical energy and digestion—totaled to a single figure represent the daily calories needed to maintain a certain weight. In the case of the 70-kilogram (154-pound) woman, a total of 2,079 calories are required each day to maintain her weight. This is calculated by the formula on the following page.

TOTAL METABOLIC NEEDS FORMULA

BMR requirements	1,512
Physical activity requirements	+ 378
Digestive requirements	+ 189
Daily caloric requirements to maintain present weight	2,079

To find the calories necessary to meet your total current metabolic need:

Your BMR requirements	————
Your physical activity requirements	+ ————
Your digestive requirements	+ ————
Daily caloric requirements to maintain your present weight	————

Use this same procedure to calculate calories required to maintain your ideal weight.

Most Americans are more familiar with weight loss programs and products that take no thought and that effortlessly produce slimness. Just by plunking down a few dollars for a book or a powdered drink, they expect to shed weight instantaneously. But it doesn't work that way. Permanent weight control, which is the product of fat loss, is not the result of pills, potions or magical incantations. Gimmicks don't produce weight control; *people* do.

The difference between long-term success (attaining ideal weight on a permanent basis) and failure (gain weight, lose it, gain it again) rests with the individual. Success requires a decision to shed excess fat; an understanding that fat loss (like fat gain) has a scientific basis; an awareness that incremental modifications to lifestyle over time can produce tremendous change; and a commitment to shed fat in a logical, methodical manner that leads to a permanent solution. This is why the numeric detail is necessary—to provide an understanding of the problem and the solution.

The following steps must be taken for a weight control effort to be effective:

1. Determine the starting point. Find your present weight and body fat content.

2. Set your goal. Using the recommended body fat content for age and gender, calculate your ideal weight.

3. Determine in concrete terms what has to be accomplished. Subtract ideal weight from present weight to find out the number of pounds of excess fat you need to shed.

4. Determine the dietary parameters. Calculate the number of calories you need daily to maintain your present and ideal weights.

Once this has been accomplished, you're ready to address how the goal may be achieved. The answer is the 500-Calorie Solution.

THE 500-CALORIE SOLUTION

Permanent body fat reduction takes place on a slow, steady basis. Most health professionals counsel a loss of no more than one to two pounds per week. This isn't a great amount when compared with the six or eight pounds that can be lost on a crash diet, but it's realistic in terms of permanency. Remember, crash diets do not reduce fat and the lost pounds come back when the diet is over. A slower rate of loss is the only solution that is permanent. No one gains fat at the rate of six or eight pounds a week, so it's illogical to believe it will come off—and stay off—at that rate.

In order to lose a pound of body fat, you need to be in negative energy balance by 3,500 calories—which means that 3,500 more calories are going out of your reserve tank (fat storage) than are coming in. This can be accomplished by making a 500-calorie adjustment each day. After seven days, 3,500 calories are used and a pound of fat lost. At this rate, in one year 52 pounds of fat will disappear.

Let's use a 175-pound man as an example. Our subject needs about 2,500 calories a day to cover his total metabolic needs. A modest reduction to 2,000 calories daily would produce a 500-calorie deficit and the loss of a pound of fat in one week.

Calculate what it would take for you to lose a pound of fat in one week:

Daily calories needed to maintain
present weight
Minus 500 calories   −   500

Daily calories needed to lose
one pound of fat per week   _____

There must be a 500-calorie-a-day deficit, but it need not come exclusively from dietary reductions. Exercise plays an equally important role in the 500-Calorie Solution. Not only does it burn up calories, but it stokes the BMR so that the body is burning calories at a greater rate even when at rest.

A daily negative energy balance of 500 calories can be achieved by eating less. It can be reached by exercising more. Or it can be attained with a combination of diet and exercise, the most sensible and effective approach. The combination of dietary decrease and exercise increase can produce a negative energy balance of 500 calories with just minor adjustments to daily life. Indeed, these adjustments can easily be made a permanent part of lifestyle without disrupting established living patterns, thus guaranteeing continued success even after the goal is attained.

Let's again use our 175-pound man as an example. He needs to be in negative energy balance by 500 calories, and he intends to achieve this with a combination of exercise and diet. He begins by burning up calories in exercise. This is critical to permanent weight control. As stated above, exercise has many benefits: it burns calories, consumes fat as fuel, builds lean muscle tissue (the fat-burning engine of the body) and increases the metabolic rate, making it possible for more calories to be burned at rest. Gradually working up to the point where he can briskly walk two miles in less than 30 minutes, he burns about 250 calories. This gives him a tremendous start on his goal of 500 calories for the day.

The remaining 250 calories will come easily from small dietary modifications:

- Instead of having a drink before dinner, he sips mineral water and saves 180 calories.

- Instead of spreading mayonnaise thickly on both sides of his sandwich, he puts a thin spread on one side and mustard on the other. The sandwich still tastes great, but it saves 125 calories.

- Instead of eating a doughnut at the morning coffee break, he eats an apple. In addition to the nutrition and fiber, the apple saves 75 calories.

With a little attention, it's fairly easy to trim 250 calories from the typical American diet without sacrificing taste or convenience. These actions allow the man in our example to reach his 500-calorie goal every day:

Daily calories needed to maintain present weight	2,500
Minus calories used in exercise	− 250
Minus calories reduced in diet	− 250
New daily calorie total	2,000

At this rate, the man will lose a pound of fat in one week. More important, the pound will stay off.

Losing fat and keeping it off is simple. Not easy, but simple. It starts with an understanding of the problem, with the selection of a goal and with a method to achieve that goal. The 500-Calorie Solution using diet and exercise is the method, the "what." The "how-to" will be found in the following two chapters.

Says Dr. Victor Katch of the University of Michigan Medical School, "If you talk to anyone who's won the weight loss battle, she'll give you two reasons for her success: she changed her eating habits, and she started and sticks to an exercise program. If she told you anything less, she'd be lying—which is exactly what each fad diet and weight-loss gimmick does."

CHAPTER 4

IMPLEMENTING THE 500-CALORIE SOLUTION WITH DIET

There is no more important lifestyle choice than what to eat. While good nutrition should be of interest to everyone, it's clear that most people are concerned primarily with the impact of food choices on their weight—on how they look. Appearance is an important and legitimate consideration, but it isn't the main reason to eat healthfully. Extra weight, all by itself, is a cardiac risk factor. And the diet that causes overweight also promotes elevated blood cholesterol and high blood pressure—two more significant risks for heart attack.

Controlling weight by following the 500-Calorie Solution involves dietary choices that will help reduce cholesterol and blood pressure. The basic dietary principles of the 500-Calorie Solution are examined in detail on the following pages. These include: reduce fat; reduce sugar; increase complex carbohydrates; reduce salt intake; increase intake of water.

THE FIRST PRINCIPLE: REDUCE FAT

Many people overlook the fact that it isn't necessarily the quantity of food eaten that causes a weight problem, but the caloric concentration—or density—of the food. Calorically dense foods are those that pack a lot of calories in a small volume. They are rich in calories because they contain inordinate amounts of fat and refined sugar. A chocolate peanut butter cup, which crams 143 calories into one ounce, is a good example. Calorically light foods are just the opposite: a quarter of a cantaloupe, for instance, has only 35 calories. A study conducted by Dr. O. W. Wooley, who measured the amount and caloric density of food consumed by a test group, points up the difference between volume and caloric density with respect to weight control. Half the group ate a low-fat diet; half ate a high-fat diet. The results showed that the high-fat group consumed 13% less in volume but took in 56% more calories. This group gained weight on the diet. The low-fat group ate more volume but took in fewer calories—and lost weight.

The average American consumes 130 pounds of fat per year, equal to eating more than a stick of butter each day. Not only is the amount of fat excessive, but half of it is saturated—the type that elevates blood cholesterol. The fat-rich American diet is a prime contributor to the high incidence of overweight and coronary heart disease in the United States.

Reducing dietary fat is essential for good health. Its link to a multitude of diseases and conditions has caused health professionals to recommend that no more than 30% of calories come from fat, with one-third or less as saturated fat. (Actually, many experts view this guideline as too liberal and counsel fat intake of 25% or less.) From a weight control standpoint, the major reason for reducing fat is to cut calories. Indeed, the elimination of fatty foods is the easiest way to meet the dietary goal of the 500-Calorie Solution. This is because a high-fat diet by nature produces a lot of calories. In fact, a gram of fat contains more than twice as many calories as the same amount of protein or carbohydrate.

- One gram of fat contains nine calories.
- One gram of protein or carbohydrate contains four calories.

Compare one ounce of high-fat rib roast with the same amount of low-fat, light-meat chicken, baked without the skin. The rib roast contains 125 calories; the chicken, just 36 calories. *Ounce for ounce, fat really is fatter.*

The relationship between dietary fat and excessive weight isn't always clearly understood. Many who want to lose weight avoid "starch." They think of rice, potatoes, bread and pasta as villains, so they order "diet plates" featuring a hamburger with cottage cheese or a chef's salad with meat and cheese. This thinking is in error. Meat and cheese contain considerable fat and virtually guarantee that the "diet" meals will be rich in calories. Starchy complex carbohydrates are not the caloric problem. Fat is. A medium baked potato has just 90 calories; what causes it to skyrocket to 300 calories is a combination of fatty condiments such as butter, sour cream, bacon bits and cheese. A cup of pasta contains about 200 calories; add a few meatballs, and it can leap to over 500 calories. The effect of added fat on the calories in a meal can be substantial:

Basic Food	Calories	Added Fat	Total Calories
Green salad	20	Oil/vinegar (1 Tbs.)	145
Bread (1 slice)	70	Butter (1 Tbs.)	160
Baked potato	90	Sour cream (2 Tbs.)	150
Peas (⅔ cup)	100	Butter (1 Tbs.)	200
Chicken	150	Gravy (⅓ cup)	210
Total for meal	**430**		**865**

If this difference in calories occurred at one meal every day for a year, it would provide enough additional calories to cause a person to gain 46 pounds!

Fatty condiments can really add on the calories. A three-ounce piece of sole, for example, has about 150 calories; serve it with a tablespoon of tartar sauce, and the calories are raised to 239. Adding a teaspoon of butter to a cup of popcorn or a pancake doubles the calorie count.

Condiment	Calories per Tbs.
Vegetable oil	125
Butter	100
Margarine	100
Mayonnaise	100
Tartar sauce	89
Cream cheese	52
Cream (half-and-half)	32

SOURCES OF DIETARY FAT

Fat is responsible for 42% of all calories in the American diet. Most people like the texture, flavor and satiety that fat brings to food, so it's not surprising to find favorite foods as the chief sources of fat.

Fat appears in the American diet as red meat, including steaks, roasts, ham, hot dogs, hamburger, sausage and luncheon meats; whole-milk dairy products, including milk, cheese, butter, sour cream and ice cream; refined fats and oils used in salads and cooking; commercially baked goods, such as doughnuts, crackers, pies, cakes and cookies; chocolate; processed foods, such as chili, macaroni and cheese, and canned soups; and fast foods, such as fried chicken, hamburgers, deep-fried fish, and shakes.

According to the USDA, the three major sources of fat in the diet are meats, visible fats (cooking oil, shortening) and dairy products.

Sources	% of Total Fat Consumed
Meat (including poultry and fish)	35.2%
Cooking and salad oils/margarine/shortening	28.2
Dairy products/butter	14.5
TOTAL	77.9%

Although fat occurs commonly in the American diet, identifying which foods are high in fat isn't easy for the consumer. This is because fat is not a selling point, so fat content is not highlighted. Would you purchase a steak labeled "75% fat" or a cheese that called itself "90% fat"? Probably not. Savvy food manufacturers realize this and design their advertising to ignore fat in favor of more healthful ingredients—such as protein or calcium.

Red meat and dairy foods are good examples of such efforts. Identifying red meat with protein and dairy products with calcium provides a tremendous health incentive to eat more meat and drink more milk. Advertising stresses the benefits of protein and calcium but avoids addressing how much fat comes along as baggage. According to the USDA, a sirloin steak has about 24% of its calories as protein—and 76% as fat! With over three-quarters of the calories as fat, it's neither accurate nor fair to label sirloin "high-protein" without acknowledging that it is "high-fat" as well. A look at the other so-called "high-protein" red meats illustrates the dominant position of fat.

Food	Calories	% of Calories as Protein	% of Calories as Fat
Bacon (3 slices)	100	20%	78%
Beef fillet (2 oz.)	258	18	80
Bologna (2 oz.)	165	19	76
Frankfurter (2 oz.)	176	16	80
Ham, baked (2 oz.)	160	28	69
Hamburger (2 oz.)	162	33	64
Rib roast (2 oz.)	250	18	81
Lamb, chop (2 oz.)	230	19	79
Liverwurst (2 oz.)	170	19	79
Pork, loin (2 oz.)	205	19	79
Salami (2 oz.)	240	23	83
Sausage, pork (2 oz.)	282	7	93
Veal, chop (2 oz.)	132	46	52

Source: USDA.

Not only does red meat contain substantially more calories from fat than from protein, but much of the fat is saturated—the type associated with increased heart disease risk.

Using the same advertising techniques, dairy foods tout the benefits of calcium without mentioning the drawbacks of fat. Yet the fat content of dairy products is substantial: whole milk is 53% fat, American cheese is 75% fat and ice cream is 91% fat.

Promoting protein and calcium in red meat and dairy products without acknowledging the presence of excessive fat is selective and misleading. Protein in particular has been a major influence on food selection. It is needed for growth and tissue repair; however, the key fact is that *it is not needed in abundance*. The recommended quantity of protein for an adult is no more than 0.8 gram per kilogram (2.2 pounds) of body weight, or about 56 grams for an average man and 46 grams for an average woman. Fifty-six grams of protein are provided by a meal containing four ounces of turkey, two slices of whole-wheat bread, a cup of skim milk and a banana. Most Americans eat twice as much protein as needed for good nutrition. In fact, too much protein can be a health hazard. It can strain the liver and kidneys, which have to process it for excretion, and it can cause calcium loss in the bones. And the type of high-fat animal protein favored by Americans contributes to obesity and heart disease.

Many low-fat sources of protein exist. One cup of low-fat cottage cheese provides 60% of the recommended daily allowance for protein. Beans—kidney, black, lima, navy, garbanzo—and bean curd (tofu) added to soups, rice and salads are a tremendous protein source. Small pieces of poultry or fish added to vegetables, pasta or rice also produce needed protein. The point is that prodigious quantities of red meat or whole-milk dairy products are *not* needed to ensure sufficient protein. This misconception is one reason that Americans currently get 70% of their protein from animal sources and 30% from plant sources. Nutritionists believe the proper ratio to be just the opposite—one-third from animal sources and two-thirds from plant sources.

It's the same story with calcium, which is needed for

strong bones and teeth. The recommended intake for an adult is 800 to 1,200 milligrams a day (more for pregnant or nursing women), although many health professionals are advising women to try to consume 1,500 milligrams a day. The 800-to-1,200 level is provided by three to four glasses of non-fat milk. (In fact, a cup of non-fat milk contains a higher ratio of calcium than does an equal amount of whole milk.) The point is that there is no need to consume tremendous quantities of *high-fat* dairy products to ensure sufficient calcium in the diet. There are many high-calcium, low-fat foods available. Some include:

Food	Calcium Content (mg)
DAIRY	
Non-fat yogurt, plain (1 cup)	452
Low-fat yogurt, plain (1 cup)	415
1% low-fat milk (1 cup)	349
Ricotta cheese, part-skim (½ cup)	337
Non-fat milk (1 cup)	302
Buttermilk (1 cup)	285
Mozzarella cheese, part skim (1.5 oz.)	275
Feta cheese (1.5 oz.)	210
1% low-fat cottage cheese (1 cup)	138
Ice milk (¾ cup)	132
NON-DAIRY	
Turnip greens, cooked (1 cup)	252
Oysters (¾ cup)	170
Broccoli, cooked (1 stalk)	158
Buttermilk pancake (1 6-inch)	157
Tofu (4 oz.)	154
Soybeans, cooked (½ cup)	131
Shrimp, canned (3 oz.)	99
Clams, raw (3 oz.)	59
Orange (1 medium)	54
Okra, cooked (½ cup)	50
Artichoke, cooked (1 medium)	47
Bread, whole wheat (2 slices)	46

Source: USDA.

Red meat is a good source of protein, and whole-milk

dairy products are a good source of calcium. But protein and calcium are secondary components. What these foods primarily contain is fat—a problem for weight control and cardiac health.

HOW TO REDUCE FAT IN THE DIET

A main dietary concept of the 500-Calorie Solution is clear: fat must be reduced. This reduction, however, need not occur overnight. It is quite acceptable to achieve substantial fat reduction *over time*. Gradualism is essential in allowing the diet pattern to be altered slowly and permanently. Going from a meat-heavy diet on a Monday to total vegetarianism on a Tuesday is not realistic. A better way is to institute small actions that over time add up to significant changes.

Reducing dietary fat and calories is possible by following a few fundamental rules.

Learn to Read Labels

A diet designed to promote optimal health and weight control maximizes the use of fresh foods, which generally rank higher nutritionally than their processed counterparts and provide more control over the additives—fat, salt and sugar—favored by food manufacturers. In the fast-paced modern lifestyle, however, it's not realistic to assume that foods from a box, package or can will never be eaten. It is critical, therefore, to know the content of such foods.

Since the basic labeling law was passed in 1938, the government has held that a food processor is obligated to tell the consumer what is in the product by providing information on the food label. Originally intended to reveal nutritional content, particularly in light of deficiency problems, labels were designed to clearly illustrate the USRDA of protein, vitamins and minerals. But concern about nutritional deficiencies is no longer legitimate—when was the last time you purchased a food because of its riboflavin content? What is of concern today is excess—specifically of fat, cholesterol, salt and sugar. Excessive elements, not deficiencies, have made the American diet a health issue.

It should be simple to look at a label and determine how much fat is in the food, but it isn't. This is because fat is commonly listed in grams, which are not a household measurement. Most people do not relate grams of fat to actual fat content. So, instead of educating, the information often serves to confuse. It is technically accurate (the fat *does* weigh X number of grams), but in reality the information is virtually useless. As such, the letter of the labeling law is followed but the spirit is violated.

Unable to determine fat content from the nutritional data presented, many people rely on advertising to tell them what is in the food. For example, a person interested in reducing fat from red meat would be attracted to processed luncheon meats advertised on the label as "95% fat-free—only 5% fat." On the surface, this seems like a good low-fat alternative, but in actuality the luncheon meat is almost 50% fat! The 5% figure advertised relates to *weight*—fat constitutes 5% of the total weight of the package. But consumers aren't interested in what the fat weighs; they want to know how many calories in the meat come from fat. In this example, it is almost 50%.

When expressed as a percentage of a food's weight, the fat content of most foods will sound deceptively low. Even a hot dog can look good with this method. Because about half its weight is water, the fat content of a hot dog is just 30% by weight—but fat supplies over 80% of the calories! Unfortunately, this method has been abused by food processors as a clever way of deceiving consumers about the effective fat content of the food.

The term "low-fat" is another example of advertising that has no basis in reality. Most cream cheese is 90% fat. No one would consider it a low-fat product. But one brand is touted on its label as a "low-fat" alternative, even though it's 79% fat! How can a food that's almost four-fifths fat be "low-fat"? It can't. It may be *lower* in fat than the original product, but it is *not* low-fat. "Low-fat" is therefore a relative term. Consumers should determine how "low in fat" a product is before selecting it.

Another good example of "low-fat" as a misnomer is frozen dinners, including many that are purported to be "light." They are calorically reduced because of smaller portion size, but they are not necessarily low in fat. One such product, a popular spinach-mushroom casserole, is low in calories but is 71% fat. Most frozen dinners, according to the Center for Science in the Public Interest, average 47% fat.

The only way to know for sure how much fat is in the food is to calculate the amount from the nutritional data on the label. All nutrition labels are required by law to state certain things: size of serving; number of servings per container and, for each serving, number of calories; grams of protein, carbohydrates and fat; and percentage of USRDA for protein, vitamins A and C, thiamin, riboflavin, niacin, calcium and iron. Sodium labeling is also required of any product making a nutritional claim such as "low-calorie" or "low-sodium." Other optional information includes grams of saturated and polyunsaturated fat, milligrams of cholesterol, and the percent of USRDA for 12 other vitamins and minerals. Some nutrition labels even include carbohydrate information in a breakdown of starches and sugars per serving.

The following is an example:

NALLEY'S CORNED BEEF HASH

Nutrition Information per Serving

Serving size	1 cup
Servings per container	1¾
Calories	490
Protein, grams	22
Carbohydrate, grams	23
Fat, grams	34
Cholesterol, milligrams	No information
Sodium, milligrams	No information

The two salient pieces of information for fat content are:
- Number of calories
- Grams of fat

In the example on the preceding page, a serving of hash contains 490 calories and 34 grams of fat. What does this tell you? Is the food high-fat or low-fat? The formula for calculating the percentage of calories from fat is simple to use:

1. Multiply the number of grams of fat by 9.
2. Divide the result by number of calories per serving.
3. Multiply the result by 100.

Since fat is 9 calories per gram, the first step is to multiply the grams of fat per serving by 9. In this case it is:

$$34 \text{ grams of fat} \times 9 \text{ calories per gram} = 306 \text{ calories from fat}$$

The second step is to divide the calories from fat by the total calories per serving. In this case it is:

$$\frac{306 \text{ fat calories}}{490 \text{ total calories}} = 0.63$$

The third step is to multiply the result—0.63—by 100 to get the percentage of calories from fat. In this case it is:

$$0.63 \times 100 = 63\% \text{ of calories from fat}$$

This provides a percentage of the calories per serving of hash that come from fat. The hash is 63% fat.

If the label had shown that the food contained 90 calories and 2 grams of fat, the calculation would have been:

$$2 \text{ grams of fat} \times 9 \text{ calories per gram} = 18 \text{ fat calories}$$

$$\frac{18 \text{ fat calories}}{90 \text{ total calories}} = 0.20$$

$$0.20 \times 100 = 20\% \text{ of calories from fat}$$

Fat calculating would not be necessary if labels stated fat content in common terms. Grams of fat have very little meaning for the average person. A more realistic way to determine whether the food is high- or low-fat would be to express fat as a percentage of calories. Until such a change is made, the only way to determine the true fat content of a food is to use the above formula. And remember, for a food to be legitimately low-fat, it should have no more than 25% of its total calories as fat.

Fat information can also be garnered from the ingredients list, which displays all ingredients found in the food in order of prominence by weight. Unfortunately, instead of indicating how much of each ingredient the product contains, the list is simply a relative ranking of ingredients by weight. As a rule of thumb, the higher on the list an ingredient is found, the more there is in the food. Compare the following labels:

Minestrone Soup: Water, red kidney beans, Great Northern beans, green lima beans, green peas, carrots, potatoes, celery, cabbage, green beans, tomato paste, chickpeas, macaroni, salt, *soybean oil,* dehydrated onions, *olive oil,* dehydrated garlic, natural flavorings, spices.

Chunky Creamy Mushroom Soup: Water, mushrooms, *vegetable oil, cream, butter,* bleached enriched wheat flour, sherry wine, potato starch, salt, soy protein isolate, monosodium glutamate, dehydrated onions, natural flavoring, dehydrated garlic.

Although the minestrone soup contains both soybean and olive oils, these ingredients appear fifteenth and seventeenth, respectively. You can assume from this that the soup is not too high in fat. However, the creamy mushroom soup has vegetable oil, cream and butter as the third, fourth and fifth ingredients, respectively. Their position identifies fat as a major component of the product.

Knowing the various names for fat is also important. Fat is listed as lard, animal fat, animal shortening, butterfat, cream, vegetable oil, palm oil and vegetable shortening. Also look for the number of times fat shows up on the ingredients list. While the amount of fat under any one name may be small, taken together the ingredients may supply a significant amount of fat.

Another troubling aspect of label reading involves the term ''no cholesterol.'' The public today understands that dietary cholesterol contributes to coronary heart disease. There is still confusion in the public's mind as to how this happens, but in general people identify cholesterol as negative and many try to avoid it. Some food manufacturers have used this concern as a device to push sales. Crisco, for example, carries a ''no cholesterol'' label. This is accurate but misleading. Vegetables do not contain cholesterol; only animal foods do. Crisco is not an animal product, so by its nature it is free of cholesterol. But that isn't the most salient point. The key fact is that Crisco and other canned shortenings contain saturated vegetable fat, which promotes elevated blood cholesterol levels just as animal fats do. Fat is the real problem for both heart disease and weight control. By focusing exclusively on the product's lack of cholesterol, the consumer may overlook the more serious problem: dietary fat. Another example is a cheese advertised as ''mini-cholesterol.'' It is low in cholesterol—but it is also 85% fat! Other products that use the ''no cholesterol'' device include margarines and peanut butters. ''No cholesterol'' on the label does not guarantee that the food promotes cardiac health or weight control.

Be certain to check ''serving size,'' as there is no standard. Some granola labels indicate that the product contains 150 calories ''per serving,'' but a careful look reveals that a serving is only a quarter of a cup. Most people probably eat twice that amount as a normal serving. A candy bar label notes that it supplies 150 calories per ounce. The catch is that the candy bar weighs two ounces! A ''serving'' of one gourmet ice cream has ''only'' 340 calories. Not only is this a lot of calories, but careful reading of the label reveals a serving to be just one-half cup.

Packaged food is not the only place where ''low-fat'' advertising can be misrepresentative. Fast-food advertising often calls attention to light calories, when in fact the food is rich in fat. Chicken and fish are offered today as healthy alternatives, yet the chicken served is generally from fatty parts of the bird and, like fish, is so heavily fried that the health benefits are lost. McDonald's fillet of fish, touted as high in protein, contains two and a half times as much fat as protein and more calories than a small hamburger. Arby's roast beef sandwich is advertised as "lean," yet it is 40% fat. And the soft-serve ice cream and shakes (they don't contain enough milk to be called "milkshakes") contain so much oil that they might as well be fried. Even the food offered at salad bars in fast-food restaurants is high in fat. Pasta salad, potato salad, macaroni salad and marinated vegetables are doused in mayonnaise and oils.

Under prodding from the public, fast-food chains may be forced to divulge what goes into their food. One can only hope that the fat content of fast foods will be explained in terms common to consumers—percentage of fat calories instead of grams. Based on the practices of food manufacturers, however, this probably won't happen. In the meantime, don't be fooled into thinking fast foods are low in fat.

Reduce Red Meat

The Federal Health and Nutrition Examination Survey (better known as the Hanes study) revealed in 1981 that red meat is the main source of fat in the American diet. It is also a significant source of dietary cholesterol. Typically, red meat constitutes 23% of total fat and 27% of saturated fat consumed by Americans. Despite growing health consciousness, red meat consumption has not dramatically changed since that survey. Consumption of beef, for example, is still about 80 pounds per person per year. No wonder it's hard for so many Americans to keep from gaining extra weight or raising blood cholesterol.

Reduction of calories from meat fat requires planning in advance. Meal planning, which is discussed in more detail on pages 173–177, involves not only the number of meals per week in which red meat will be served but the cut, quantity and cooking methods as well. To control weight and cholesterol, health professionals advise following the guidelines of the American Heart Association: no more than two or three 3-ounce servings of red meat a week. By dividing the week into 21 meals, you can select ahead of time those meals in which red meat will be eaten. The meal plan might look like this:

Day	Menu
Monday	
Tuesday	Grilled Lamb Chops with Rosemary and Garlic (dinner)
Wednesday	
Thursday	Chili con Carne (lunch)
Friday	
Saturday	
Sunday	Spaghetti and meatballs (dinner)

Once the red meat meals have been planned, you can concentrate on the makeup of the other meals. Many Americans have already limited red meat, designing their meals around poultry, fish and vegetables. For them, a formal plan to reduce red meat may not be so essential. However, meal planning is critical for those who eat a lot of red meat: bacon, ham and sausage for breakfast; bologna, salami, hot dogs, hamburgers for lunch; steaks, chops, roasts and casseroles for dinner. It allows for gradual, continual progress until less meat becomes the norm. For some people, this comes quickly; for others, it can take longer. Many people eventually reach a point where red meat only once or twice a month is common.

In addition, when red meat is planned, use cuts lower in fat—such as the loin or rump—and trim all visible fat. The amount of fat on a three-and-a-half-ounce broiled steak can double the calories. The calorie content of low-fat vs. high-fat cuts can be significant:

	Calories		
	Untrimmed	Trimmed	Difference
Rib roast (4 oz.)	499	273	226
Round steak (4 oz.)	296	214	82
Sirloin steak (4 oz.)	463	245	218

	Calories		
	Untrimmed	**Trimmed**	**Difference**
T-bone steak (4 oz.)	536	253	283
Pork roast (4 oz.)	400	277	123
Lamb chop (4 oz.)	460	236	224

Source: USDA.

Obviously, certain meats are too high in fat to be a regular part of a healthy diet. These include sausage, bacon, hot dogs, salami, bologna and other processed meats.

Further reduction can be accomplished by planning meals in which the red meat is stretched. Great slabs of meat as a main course are no longer appropriate in a country fighting obesity and heart disease. Instead, try dishes that allow meat to be stretched, such as spaghetti with meat sauce. Learn from the Orientals, who use meat as a condiment, a garnish and a flavor enhancer. A little meat goes a long way in soups, stir-fries and rice dishes. Stretching meat is the difference between using a pound of hamburger in patties for four people and using it with beans and pasta in chili for eight. It's the difference between serving four steaks, one per person, and using one steak in a stir-fry with vegetables to make a meal for four. Don't overlook delicious and hearty soups that use meat sparingly. Good examples from the recipe section include French Market Soup, Minestrone, and Pasta-and-bean Soup.

Cooking methods also affect the amount of fat from red meat in the meal. Frying sears fat in; broiling, baking, roasting and barbecuing allow fat to drip off. The longer meat cooks, the more fat is lost, so medium and well-done are preferable to rare. Sauté ground beef in a nonstick pan, then drain on paper towels; this will defat the meat as much as possible.

When red meat is served as a main course, reduce its portion size. A key is to increase servings of other foods. (This is done naturally when meat is "stretched" in stir-fries, soups or chili.) If red meat is the entrée, be sure to maximize the use of salads, vegetables, grains and legumes. Instead of a small salad and a huge steak, start dinner with a large salad with plenty of greens and vegetables. A bowl of soup is also a tasty and filling way to start a meal. Serve two cooked vegetables and rice, potato or pasta on the side. By the time you get to the meat entrée, only a small amount will be necessary to satisfy.

Foods served with meat can significantly impact the fat content of the meal. Four ounces of Roast Lamb with Juniper Berries (see our recipe, page 453), for example, contains 229 calories and is 37% fat. The lamb may be lower in fat than many cuts of pork or beef, but it is not low-fat. What you serve with it, however, can make a big difference in the overall fat percentage of the meal:

	Total Calories	Calories from Fat	% of Calories from Fat
Low-fat Choices			
Roast Lamb with Juniper Berries (4 oz.)	229	85	37%
Grilled Tomato (½)	15	1	4
Broccoli with Lemon Mustard Sauce (1 cup)	35	6	18
Roast Potatoes with Rosemary (1 cup)	129	20	16
Total	**408**	**112**	
% of calories from fat for the meal:			**27%**
High-fat Choices			
Roast Lamb with Juniper Berries (4 oz.)	229	85	37%
Green salad with 2 tsp. Thousand Island dressing	90	50	56
Baked potato (1 medium) with:	90	1	1
Sour cream (2 Tbs.)	56	45	80
Bacon bits (1 slice)	43	35	82
Parmesan cheese (1 Tbs.)	31	20	64
Butter (1 Tbs.)	100	100	100
Total	**639**	**336**	
% of calories from fat for the meal:			**53%**

Accompanying the lamb with low-fat foods reduces the total fat content of the meal to 27%. High-fat foods increase the fat content of the meal to 53%. This is a critical point in the 500-Calorie Solution. It illustrates that not just the red meat entrée itself, but those foods served with it, ultimately dictate whether the meal is high or low in fat.

Eat More Poultry

Poultry (except for duck and goose) is generally lower in fat and calories than red meat, and light-meat poultry is lower in cholesterol. Compare the following:

	Calories	% of Calories from Fat
Chicken, white, baked without skin (4 oz.)	144	12%
Turkey, white, roasted, without skin (4 oz.)	150	18
Ground round, broiled (4 oz.)	324	64
Porterhouse steak, broiled (4 oz.)	527	82

Chicken is particularly low in fat when cooked without the skin. Since most of the fat lies just underneath, removing the skin before cooking eliminates a great deal. The difference in calories and fat between skinless chicken and chicken with skin is substantial. The same relationship exists between light and dark meat. Light meat is preferable, as it contains about one-third less fat than dark meat, so opt for breasts over drumsticks. Broilers and fryers are leaner than roasters.

The following illustrates why a skinless breast (light meat) is the best choice for low-fat, low-calorie eating:

Chicken Breast	Calories	% of Calories from Fat
Light meat, skinless (4 oz.)	144	12%
Dark meat, skinless (4 oz.)	160	25
Light meat, with skin (4 oz.)	172	27
Dark meat, with skin (4 oz.)	189	40

One of the major obstacles to changing the American diet pattern is that red meat is so comfortable. Not only is the taste familiar and pleasing, but cooking red meat is simple—you don't need much of a recipe to cook a T-bone steak or a pork roast. In a healthy diet pattern, chicken can be seen in the same light. Chicken breasts pan-fried in a nonstick pan are as easy to cook as minute steaks. Roast or broiled chicken takes no more thought than a pork roast. Chicken stew is an easy replacement for beef stew; skewered chicken for skewered beef; teriyaki chicken for teriyaki steak. Chicken breasts provide tremendous variety and flexibility, as they can be used as a substitute for hamburger in many recipes, including tacos, taco salad, ravioli, and spring rolls. Look for opportunities, and many creative substitutions will become apparent.

There are a lot of ways to get more mileage out of chicken. Pound a breast flat before cooking, and it will double in size—without adding calories. Roll up a flattened breast, and it looks like more food. Fill up a breast by slitting a pocket in it and stuffing it with vegetables or rice. Slice it thin and alternate with sliced vegetables. Use a little bit in stir-fries to enhance flavor without greatly increasing fat or calories.

As with red meat, cooking methods do affect the fat content of chicken dishes. Always cook chicken so that any fat can drip off. Roasting, broiling, barbecuing, baking and steaming are best. When recipes call for sautéing, use wine, vermouth, flavored vinegars or defatted broth. Always use a nonstick pan; never fry in oil and butter.

Another alternative to red meat is turkey. Thirty years ago, 90% of all turkeys were sold in November and December. These months now constitute just 40% of sales. Americans have discovered turkey as a year-round food. It is available fresh and frozen in every supermarket and is less expensive than beef or pork. Turkey parts cook quickly and are good in ethnic and regional recipes such as turkey tacos, curries, stir-fries and pot pies.

The best nutritional buy is a whole turkey. Removing

the skin before cooking allows fat to drip off but can cause the meat to dry out. If the skin is left on during cooking, it should be removed before serving. Never eat the skin. Also, remember that light meat is much lower than dark meat in fat, calories and cholesterol.

Fresh turkey breast can be found in most grocery stores. Roasted or poached, it provides a quick and delicious dinner. Turkey breast also yields leftovers for sandwiches, a great alternative to luncheon meats. Cooked and cured turkey breasts are available but with a drawback: added sodium. Many supermarkets and butcher shops carry ground turkey as a substitute for hamburger. This sounds great, but it may turn out to be a worse choice. Be careful when selecting prepackaged ground turkey; it may contain dark meat, skin and fat. Instead have the butcher grind a turkey breast or grind one at home yourself. A comparison of turkey breast and ground turkey illustrates this point:

	Calories	% of Calories from Fat
Fresh turkey breast, roasted (3 oz.)	133	18%
Ground turkey (3 oz.)	193	52

It's the same for other turkey products such as turkey ham, turkey bologna and turkey franks. Because of added fat, they are usually more than 50% fat.

Eat More Fish

Fish is lower in calories than red meat, so it provides a great alternative. A variety of fish compare very well with four ounces of sirloin steak:

	Calories	Calories Saved
Sirloin steak (4 oz.)	**444**	
Cod (4 oz.)	180	264
Crab (4 oz.)	113	331
Flounder (4 oz.)	90	354

	Calories	Calories Saved
Haddock (4 oz.)	135	309
Halibut (4 oz.)	200	244
Red snapper (4 oz.)	100	344
Salmon (4 oz.)	250	194
Swordfish (4 oz.)	200	244
Tuna, white meat, water-packed (3¼ oz.)	108	336

Source: USDA.

Fewer calories is not the only reason to eat more fish: equally important is the fact that *fish and fish oil are greatly beneficial to cardiac health.* Indeed, researchers have found that fish oil is effective in preventing heart attacks. This was first noticed in Greenland, where between 1950 and 1974 only three heart attacks occurred in an Eskimo population of 1,800. Among a similar American population, over 100 people would have had heart attacks during that time. This finding initially confused the researchers, who were familiar with the link between a high-fat diet and coronary heart disease. Eskimos eat a lot of fat in the form of walrus and seal meat, cold-water fish and whale blubber, yet their incidence of heart attack is low. The reason is that Eskimos eat *marine* rather than animal fat.

One beneficial component of fish oil is an unsaturated fat called Omega-3 fatty acid. According to Dr. William Connor of the Oregon Health Sciences University, there is good evidence that Omega-3's can lower cholesterol and reduce triglycerides; in addition, by keeping the blood thin (technically, making blood platelets slippery), fish oil helps to prevent the blood clots that can cause heart attack or stroke. Other new research also highlights the benefits of fish oil. For example, the *New England Journal of Medicine* has stated that eating "as little as two fish dishes a week may cut the risk of dying from heart attack in half."

Many of the health benefits attributed to fish oil were identified in a Dutch study at the University of Leiden. Researchers monitored the diets of 1,088 middle-aged men from the town of Zutphen for 20 years, starting in 1960.

They found that those who ate no fish had two times the risk of heart attack as those who ate just seven ounces of fish per week. The study showed that moderately fatty fish such as halibut, bluefish, bass, hake, ocean perch, pollock and rainbow trout were as effective as fish with high fat content, such as salmon, mackerel, herring, sardines, sablefish, fresh tuna, whitefish, anchovies and lake trout.

Dr. William Castelli, head of the Framingham Study, advises not to overlook the benefits of shellfish, once accused of being too high in cholesterol. "This was a misconception," says Dr. Castelli. "Sure, shrimp is high in cholesterol, but it is low in saturated fat and loaded with Omega 3's." In particular, he recommends oysters, clams and scallops: "They are the vegetarians of the sea." Each has a fair amount of fish oil yet is relatively low in calories. Four ounces of clams (meat only) have 91 calories; the same amount of scallops have 90; and four ounces of oysters range from 75 calories (Eastern) to 103 (Western).

While the fish oil from two or three servings of fish a week is seen as beneficial, a word of caution is in order. On the basis of the initial research showing fish oil to protect against heart disease, drug manufacturers have rushed to market fish oil capsules and liquid. Their benefit is negligible, according to the American Heart Association, the American Medical Association and many renowned scientists who are studying fish oils. The American Heart Association's recently revised dietary guidelines state that "the limited information available at present does not justify specific quantitative recommendations" for fish oil. In other words, we have no idea what is an optimal—and safe—dose of fish oil. With regard to the general use of fish oil supplements by the public, Dr. Scott Grundy, director of the Center for Human Nutrition at the University of Texas Health Science Center, says, "Most of us feel we're not that far yet." Indeed, there may be a downside to taking great amounts of fish oil supplements:

■ Many are made from fish livers and may contain harmful pesticides or contaminants.

▪ They may thin the blood to a dangerous level, particularly in an accident or during surgery.

▪ Prolonged consumption could result in an excess of Vitamin E.

At this point, most nutritionists and health professionals recommend fish over fish oil supplements, at least until further research is done. In making fish a regular part of the diet pattern, it's important to:

1. Go for the best quality. In the past, this was a problem because much of what was available was frozen and poor in quality. This is no longer the case. Modern handling and delivery methods have cut the time from sea to store, thereby allowing consumers to buy fresh fish of the highest quality in virtually every foodstore and fishmarket.

2. Enjoy a wide variety of fish. It used to be that the availability of fish was restricted to a few kinds—generally, sole, perch, salmon and flounder, plus local varieties. Serving the same type too frequently made for repetitive meals. Poached sole might be healthier than a cheeseburger, but most people found it too boring for steady fare. Today, the list of readily available fish has been expanded to include scallops, halibut, bass, lobster, crab, swordfish, trout, mako shark, mahi mahi, salmon, tuna, black cod, turbot, shad, crab legs, haddock and red snapper. Many new varieties have also been introduced in the last few years, such as squid, orange roughy and monkfish (called the "poor man's lobster"). Eating fish no longer has to be boring.

3. Try new ways to prepare fish. In addition to traditional favorites such as barbecued salmon or poached cod, try new dishes from our recipe section—Seafood Fettuccine, Stir-fried Calamari, Scallops Dijonnaise, Teriyaki Salmon and Blackened Halibut. And don't overlook using fish in hearty and savory soups and stews such as Fisherman's Soup and Seafood Stew.

4. Make food presentation a priority. Serving poached flounder on a white plate invites yawns. Arrange the plate for eye appeal. Add color, for example, by serving two or three vegetables—snow peas, grilled tomatoes and a julienne of carrots and zucchini. The visual sense is important, especially when introducing new and different foods into the diet pattern.

Cooking and preparation methods also make a difference. Fish should be baked, steamed, poached, broiled or barbecued but never fried or deep-fat fried. Frying adds too many calories. Skip the fatty add-ons—a tablespoon of melted butter is 100 calories, and the same amount of tartar sauce is 89 calories. What good does it do to have broiled swordfish rather than prime rib, only to serve the fish swimming in a butter sauce? Instead, use low-fat condiments such as fresh lemons or limes, flavored vinegars, horseradish, tomato salsa, vinaigrettes and oil-free dressings to add flavor without increasing calories. In particular, watch out for marinades. While they keep fish moist and prevent drying out, oil-based marinades can add many unwanted calories. A good alternative is to soak the fish in skim milk before cooking. The fish will stay moist and will not take on a "milky" taste any more than it will take on the "oily" taste of an oil marinade.

Tuna is particularly suitable for sandwiches, salads and casseroles, and just about everyone likes its taste. From the standpoint of cardiac health, tuna—particularly albacore—is rich in protective Omega 3's. The downside is that tuna often provides opportunities for heavy calories. A six-and-a-half-ounce can of tuna in oil has 300 calories more than the same amount packed in water. Also, keep in mind that calories come not just from the fish itself but from added fat—the mayonnaise mixed with it. The key is how much mayonnaise is used:

**Tuna made with 5 tablespoons of mayonnaise =
500 added calories
Tuna made with 3 tablespoons of mayonnaise =
300 added calories**

Cutting the mayonnaise reduces the calories from added fat by 200. This is a step in the right direction, yet the tuna sandwich is still high in calories when compared with a turkey sandwich at 201 calories or a chicken sandwich at 220 calories. The point is not to be misled: tuna is a healthful fish, but in a sandwich or salad loaded with mayonnaise it could be a 500-calorie lunch!

The same rules for healthy eating at home apply to restaurants. Order fish baked, poached, or broiled in lemon, but never fried. Skip the butter and tartar sauce in favor of fresh lemons or a little reduced-sodium soy sauce. One good way to control calories and fat in a restaurant is to order a seafood appetizer and soup or salad, and skip the entrée. For example, a half-dozen oysters followed by a large green salad or a bowl of cioppino offers variety without the calories.

Switch to Low-Fat Dairy Products

Dairy products can range from those extremely low in fat (skim milk at about 2% fat) to those very high in fat (cream cheese at over 90% fat). In addition, much of their fat is saturated. It's important to know which dairy products enhance weight control and heart health.

The best choice for milk is non-fat, also called skim, which contains about 90 calories a cup and is just 2% fat. The same amount of so-called "2% milk" has 120 calories and is 38% fat; a cup of whole milk has 160 calories and is 53% fat. Non-fat milk has the same minerals, vitamins and protein as, and a greater percentage of calcium than an equal amount of whole milk. The difference is in the fat and calories. Think of whole milk as non-fat milk with two pats of butter added. If you drank three glasses of milk a day, the difference in calories between whole and non-fat milk would be 210 calories—enough to produce 22 pounds of excess weight a year.

Some people find non-fat milk hard to like. When we began to change our way of eating after my surgery, the jump from "2%" to non-fat milk was too great for our taste buds. The solution was to make the change gradually, giving our taste buds sufficient time to adapt. We began by mixing three parts "2% milk" with one part non-fat. Each week we added more non-fat and less "2% milk," until finally we were drinking 100% non-fat milk. (Frankly, the kids were never wild about this. The secret to success with them was that we continued to serve the mixture in a "2% milk" carton. By the time the kids found out that they were drinking non-fat, they were used to it. Now they'll go without milk before drinking whole or "2%" milk, which is too creamy for their taste.)

In recipes that call for milk, evaporated milk or cream, two good substitutions are low-fat buttermilk and skim evaporated milk. Low-fat buttermilk is relatively low in calories yet still gives a rich flavor in pancakes, waffles and baked foods. Skim evaporated milk can be substituted in soufflés, puddings and ice cream. A look at the difference in fat and calories should be a real inducement to recipe modification:

	Calories	% of Calories from Fat
Cream (½ cup)	419	96%
Evaporated milk (½ cup)	170	53
Skim evaporated milk (½ cup)	100	2

Cheese, according to the Stanford Heart Disease Prevention Clinic, is the hardest food for Americans to trim from the diet. This is because we love cheese. We eat about 26 pounds per person each year in sandwiches, casseroles, hors d'oeuvre and pizza. Unfortunately, while it's a good source of calcium and protein, cheese is a concentrated form of milk (about eight pounds of milk goes into one pound of cheese), so most cheese is between 65% and 75% fat. This means that a typical 1½-ounce serving, about two slices of American cheese, contains as much fat as three and a half pats of butter—and most of the fat is saturated. As a result, cheese packs a lot of calories into a small space. This isn't always understood. Some people will reduce the meat in a recipe and increase the cheese, thinking that fat is being cut. In truth, the modified recipe may contain more fat and calories than the original. For example, the recipe for a ''Hungry Joe Special'' (a combination of hamburger, spinach, mushroom, egg and cheese) calls for one pound of hamburger and one-fourth pound of cheese. By eliminating the hamburger and doubling the cheese, the calories are raised from 242 to 445 per serving and the fat content from 54% to 58%.

The successful use of cheese on a healthy diet takes perspective. It must be understood that almost all cheese is too fat to be eaten regularly. One ounce of Cheddar is 70% fat and contains 115 calories. The same amount of blue cheese is 72% fat with 100 calories, while Camembert is 81% fat with 115 calories. These and other high-fat cheeses such as Brie, American, cream, Monterey Jack, Roquefort and Swiss must be severely moderated if excessive calories are to be avoided.

Full-fat cheese must be used sparingly as an occasional garnish or treat rather than as a dietary staple. Free reign with cheese cubes served at a cocktail party (each cube is about the same as one slice of American cheese) means no caloric control. If you do plan to eat a small slice of Brie from time to time, by all means enjoy it. Understand what it represents in terms of fat and calories, but don't feel guilty. You'll like yourself better and have more opportunity for keeping the amount eaten under control.

In addition to cutting volume, switch to low-fat cheese. Varieties are available, but they may take some effort to search out. Just because the label states that the cheese is ''part-skim,'' ''low-fat'' or ''semi-soft'' doesn't make it legitimately low in fat. Some part-skim mozzarella contains only one-fourth less fat than its full-fat counterpart; with 55% of its calories from fat, it can hardly be called ''low-fat.'' If you can't find out the fat content from the label, check with the dairyman at your food store. Specialty cheese shops often carry more of a variety of low-fat cheese. You can also refer to a calorie guide that provides caloric content of cheese by brand name.

A second problem is taste. Low-fat cheese is often so bland that it isn't worth the saving in fat or calories. The solution is to find a few tasty, relatively low-fat cheeses that you can depend on, and use them judiciously. In the Northwest, our area of the country, there is a part-skim Cheddar that we can use in recipes calling for yellow cheese. Part-skim mozzarella is used in those calling for white cheese. We have also found that hoop cheese sliced thin is great on sandwiches. Part-skim ricotta and low-fat cottage cheese are additional good choices. The critical point to remember is that even legitimately low-fat cheese is high in calories and fat and therefore must be eaten in moderation. The difference between a plain turkey sandwich and one made with an ounce of part-skim mozzarella cheese is 90 calories; with full-fat American cheese the difference is 115 calories!

Yogurt is available in low-fat and non-fat varieties. Low-fat yogurt is about 25% fat; non-fat yogurt is about 3% fat. Both types are available in most supermarkets. Look for true low-fat brands that also taste good. Dannon, for example, has a peach yogurt that is 13% fat and contains 190 calories in six ounces. Be aware that some brands come in eight-ounce containers. The difference between a six- and an eight-ounce serving can be as much as 50 calories— so choose well. Plain yogurt is a valuable substitute for sour cream or whipped cream.

Ice cream, America's favorite dessert, is too rich in fat calories to be eaten on any but the most special occasions. Better choices are fruit sorbets, frozen yogurt and fruit desserts. The following list illustrates the differences in calories and fat in various desserts.

	Total Calories	% of Calories as Fat
Häagen-Dazs, vanilla (¾ cup)	401	60%
Frusen Glädjé, vanilla (¾ cup)	413	61
Regular vanilla ice cream, 12% (¾ cup)	208	52
Sealtest Light n' Lively Ice Milk (¾ cup)	150	26

	Total Calories	% of Calories as Fat
Yoplait Strawberry Frozen Yogurt (¾ cup)	135	10%
Dole Sorbet, peach (¾ cup)	180	No fat
Yodolo Strawberry Soft-Serve Dessert (¾ cup)	150	No fat

One must be very careful in choosing alternative frozen desserts. For example, Tofutti, a popular non-dairy dessert, contains no cholesterol and no butterfat but is rich in sugar, calories and oil. According to the Center for Science in the Public Interest, it has *very* little tofu. Three-quarters of a cup of Tofutti vanilla almond bark has 345 calories and is 58% fat, making it relatively calorically dense. Indeed, all non-dairy desserts must be examined closely. They contain less saturated fat than ice cream, but many are too rich in calories to be included frequently in a weight control diet pattern.

This is a good place to call attention to eggs, although they're not technically a dairy item. Eggs are responsible for about 35% of the cholesterol intake on the American diet. If you're eating eggs for nutritional reasons, the following table will show you that, calorie for calorie, one cup of skim milk contains more protein and calcium—and less cholesterol and fat—than a whole egg.

	One Egg (Large)	Non-fat Milk (1 cup)
Calories	94	90
Protein (g)	7.4	8.8
Fat (g)	6.6	Trace
Calcium (mg)	31	296
Cholesterol (mg)	251	5

Sixty-three percent of the calories found in a large egg come from fat. In addition, the egg contains 251 milligrams of cholesterol. Two eggs at breakfast contain far more cholesterol than the daily maximum of 300 milligrams recommended by the American Heart Association.

This isn't to say that whole eggs should never be eaten. For most people, two or three a week is no problem. Those concerned with high cholesterol, however, should moderate their consumption of whole eggs. The problem is not the egg—it's the egg yolk, which contains 90% of the cholesterol, 79% of the fat and the vast majority of the calories. The egg white, on the other hand, contains most of the protein. The challenge is how to eat the whites and avoid the yolks. Commercial egg substitute, made primarily from egg whites and found in the frozen foods section of most supermarkets, works for scrambled eggs, French toast, omelets and pancakes. The problem here is that the substitute contains many preservatives. There are two ways to get around this. The first solution is to make your own egg substitute. The second is to cut the number of egg yolks called for in a recipe and increase the egg whites. For example, an eight-egg omelet for a family of four can be made with four whole eggs and four additional egg whites. This preserves the taste of the food while reducing fat, calories and cholesterol.

Reduce Fats and Oils

From the standpoint of coronary health, all fats and oils are not equal. Some are more heart-healthy than others. Depending on their fatty acid composition, fats and oils can be categorized as saturated, polyunsaturated or monounsaturated.

Saturated fat. This is the most harmful type of fat. It elevates blood cholesterol levels and is a significant risk for heart attack. Most saturated fat comes from animal foods. Examples include butter, lard, chicken fat and the visible fat on meat. A characteristic of saturated fat is that it will stay hard at refrigerator temperatures.

Polyunsaturated fat. On the other extreme, polyunsaturated fat provides coronary protection by lowering cholesterol in the blood. It is a healthy alternative to saturated fat. All polyunsaturated fat comes from vegetables in the form of oil. Characteristically, polyunsaturated oils remain liquid at refrigerator temperatures. The polyunsaturated oils in order of preference are:

Safflower oil
Soybean oil
Sunflower oil
Corn oil
Cottonseed oil
Sesame oil

Because they are healthier, products made with polyunsaturated oils are recommended over those rich in saturated fats. Safflower oil, for example, is preferable to butter. There are, however, two exceptions to this rule. The first involves *palm oil* (or *palm kernel oil*) and *coconut oil,* two vegetable oils that are heavily saturated and should be avoided. Palm oil is 51% saturated (palm kernel oil, 86% saturated, is even worse); coconut oil is 92% saturated. By comparison, lard is 41% saturated. Tests show that diets rich in palm and coconut oils elevate blood cholesterol and increase the risk of heart attack. Unfortunately, these oils are used freely in processed foods because they cost less than unsaturated oils. They are listed among the ingredients of scores of products, including bread, imitation whipped-cream topping, non-dairy creamers, frosting, soups, cheese-flavored snacks, peanuts, prepared breading for chicken, potato chips, cookies, frozen dinners, salad dressings, cake mixes, pie crusts, rolls, tortilla chips and crackers. Palm oil and coconut oil are found in so many processed foods today that on average each American consumes over seven pounds of these oils annually. Even so-called health foods contain them. A carob candy bar made with palm oil is far more harmful to cardiac health than is a chocolate bar.

A key to avoiding these oils is to read labels. If palm oil or coconut oil is on the list of ingredients, avoid the food. Beware of terms like ''all-vegetable oil'' and ''made with 100% vegetable oil,'' as they do not identify the oil used; many canned shortenings, for example, brag about being ''all-vegetable'' on the label but do not acknowledge the presence of highly saturated palm oil. Another favorite

advertising term is "made with one or more of the following oils—soybean, cottonseed, palm, and/or coconut oil."
You can't tell from this description which oil is used. The
label on Nabisco Nutter Butter Cookies, for example, states
that the product contains "peanut butter (roasted peanuts,
hydrogenated palm and/or peanut oil, salt)." There's a big
difference between using peanut butter made with palm oil
and that made with peanut oil. If the label isn't specific,
assume the worst.

The second exception involves *hydrogenation,* the chemical process used to harden liquid oil. Hydrogenation is
critical to the production of shortenings and stick margarine. Unfortunately, the process can produce a chemical
change that increases the saturated fat in the product. In
general, the softer the margarine, the less saturated fat it
contains. Soft-tub margarines are better than soft sticks,
which in turn are better than hard sticks. Again, a key is
label reading. Acceptable margarines must list "liquid"
vegetable oil, such as corn or safflower, as the first ingredient. (Diet margarines list "water" as the first ingredient.
Liquid corn or safflower oil should be the second.) If the
first ingredient is "partially hydrogenated" or "hard-
ened," don't buy the product.

Monounsaturated fat. In the past, healthy heart diets
were concerned with avoiding saturated fat (bad) and including polyunsaturated oils (good). A third type of fat,
called monounsaturated, was seen as neutral—not harmful
like the cholesterol-elevating saturated fats, but not as
healthful as the cholesterol-lowering unsaturated oils.
Monounsaturated oils include olive oil and peanut oil.

New information has changed the perception of monounsaturated fats and of olive oil in particular. Recent studies conducted by Dr. Scott Grundy indicate that, like fish
oil, *olive oil may be instrumental in reducing the risk of
coronary heart disease.* In his study, Dr. Grundy devised
three different liquid diets, each containing either saturated,
polyunsaturated or monounsaturated fat but all providing
40% of total calories. The diet was given to a test group

of 20 people, who stayed on it for four weeks. The results showed that the monounsaturated diet was just as effective as the polyunsaturated diet in lowering cholesterol. This may explain why populations using olive oil—Italians, Greeks, Cretans—have fewer heart attacks than other populations do. "We knew that the rate of cardiovascular disease was very low in the Mediterranean region, where people cook primarily with olive oil," says Dr. Grundy. "Unfortunately, a thorough clinical comparison of monounsaturates and polyunsaturates had not been made, so no one knew whether monounsaturates lowered cholesterol levels as effectively. We now know they do."

A critical aspect of Dr. Grundy's work examined the cholesterol-lowering properties of olive oil. One of the reasons that polyunsaturated fats have been seen as healthful is their ability to lower cholesterol. Unfortunately, they lower *all* cholesterol: HDL (high-density lipoprotein), the "good" cholesterol, is reduced as well as LDL (low-density lipoprotein), the "bad" cholesterol. Olive oil, however, seems to reduce only LDL cholesterol, that most responsible for artery blockages; it doesn't reduce HDL cholesterol, that associated with reduced heart attack risk. The results of this study are preliminary, and more work needs to be completed. As of this writing, however, olive oil can be said to rank in healthful properties with fish oil and with the unsaturated oils. Indeed, many health professionals already consider it the oil of choice.

In considering the significant cardiac-health differences between individual fats and oils, it's important not to lose sight of permanent weight control. From the perspective of the 500-Calorie Solution, all fats and oils are the same, uniformly rich in calories. A single tablespoon of oil, any oil, is 125 calories. One tablespoon of butter is 100 calories, as is the same amount of regular margarine. (Diet margarine is about 50 calories). A tablespoon of mayonnaise is 100 calories.

In addition, not all calories are the same. A hundred calories' worth of fruit and vegetables is not the same as

100 calories' worth of French fries. This is because not just the total calories count in weight control, but also the type of calories. According to Dr. Wayne C. Miller at the University of Illinois, if the bulk of your calories comes from fat, you're apt to gain weight even if you're counting calories and not overeating. The reason is found in the way food is metabolized. All food is either carbohydrate, protein or fat. Carbohydrates are quickly converted to glucose, the body's main fuel. Protein breaks down into amino acids. These conversions take energy. The body burns calories when digesting carbohydrate and protein. Fat, however, is not converted but is stored directly as fat. This is easily done by the body without an expenditure of calories. Animal tests conducted by Dr. Miller bear this out. Two groups of animals were fed the same number of calories per day and had the same rate of activity. One group was fed a high-fat diet, the other a low-fat diet. The high-fat group gained 32% in weight and 20% in body fat over the low-fat group. Even though the calories were the same, fat-rich diets produced extra body fat.

It's impossible to significantly reduce calories eaten and body fat stored when the diet is rich in fat—even if the fat eaten is a "good fat." A diet pattern designed to promote permanent weight control and cardiac health, therefore, incorporates a plan for two actions: 1) a switch from saturated to polyunsaturated and monounsaturated fats, and 2) a reduction of all fats and oils. Tips for reducing fats and oils include:

■ Use safflower oil or olive oil in a recipe that calls for vegetable oil. Also, these oils are interchangeable. If the recipe calls for olive oil, safflower will do, and vice versa.

■ A feature of olive oil is its strong flavor, so a little goes a long way. Sample French, Greek, Spanish and Italian oils. Olive oil ranges in color from pale yellow to dark green, and in taste from mild and delicate to rich and fruity. The finest quality is extra virgin or virgin. With a good oil, you can use a little and still produce the desired taste—with fewer calories.

■ Every time oil is listed as an ingredient, question it. Not all recipes that call for oil really need it. For example, we were concerned about calories in our oil-based salad dressings, so we changed to commercial diet dressings. This saved calories but provided another problem: unwanted additives. By experimenting with the list of ingredients on the diet dressing labels, we were able to make an oil-free dressing without additives. It has no oil and very few calories.

■ When making a sandwich, put margarine or mayonnaise on one slice of bread and mustard on the other slice. This will cut the added fat calories in half. Using diet margarine and "light" mayonnaise will reduce the calories and fat even more. The goal is to wean taste buds gradually away from greasy spreads, until you enjoy a sandwich with mustard—and no mayonnaise or butter.

■ Substitute plain non-fat yogurt for sour cream. This can save almost 175 calories per half-cup.

■ Use mayonnaise judiciously in tuna salad, coleslaw, macaroni salad and potato salad. The difference in calories depends on the amount of mayonnaise used.

■ Learn to appreciate the natural flavors and textures of foods. Avoid using butter, margarine and mayonnaise as add-ons. For enhanced flavor, look for low-fat alternatives like lemon juice, flavored vinegars, Tabasco or reduced-sodium soy sauce.

■ Defat all soups and stocks by refrigerating them for 24 hours before using them. Even canned soup will yield fat to be skimmed after refrigeration.

■ Use nonstick pans for "sautéing." Don't fry in lard, bacon fat, butter or margarine. Instead, use wine, vermouth, lemon juice, flavored vinegar or water to provide flavor but few calories. If two tablespoons of oil are saved, the calories are reduced by 250.

■ Cook vegetables without added fat by steaming or microwaving. Try sautéing them in broth or flavored vinegar. For example, one pound of mushrooms sautéed in butter has 324 calories; the same amount sautéed in broth has just

129 calories. For convenience, freeze defatted chicken broth in ice trays and store in freezer bags. One or two cubes yield just the right amount of liquid needed for most sauté and stir-fry recipes.

- Use flavored vinegars such as raspberry, strawberry and blueberry to put zing, but few calories, into sautéed foods. For example, sauté a boned, skinless chicken breast with nothing added to a nonstick pan; just before it's finished, deglaze the pan with raspberry-flavored vinegar to give the chicken a distinct flavor and aroma.

- Reduce fat and calories by using commercial diet salad dressings. One teaspoon of regular Italian dressing is 75 calories; the same amount of diet dressing is 7. A teaspoon of Thousand Island dressing is 70; in diet form, it's 28. Serve the dressing on the side. This will provide control over how much is used. I've also come to like salad with vinegar, flavored vinegar, salsa or lemon and pepper dressings. They contain virtually no calories. The oil-free dressings found in the recipe section are a real bonus; they add flavor but few calories to salads.

- Watch out for nuts and seeds. They don't contain cholesterol or a high proportion of saturated fats, but they're rich in calories. A half-cup of peanuts, about two handfuls, contains 760 calories. A half-cup of trail mix has over 600 calories.

- Peanut butter is a great food, but it should be eaten in moderation, as one tablespoon contains 95 calories—about the same as butter or mayonnaise. It's relatively easy to make a peanut butter-and-jelly sandwich worth over 400 calories!

- Watch out for avocados, which are rich in fat and high in calories. One-half an avocado is about 190 calories and 85% fat. Olives have the same problem: they are 96% fat.

Eat Smart in a Restaurant

Fast food, deli, gourmet, ethnic—Americans love restaurant food. Unfortunately, much of it is high in fat and calories and poses an issue for coronary health and weight control. Many foods contain oil, butter, cream, lard, meat drippings, fatty meat, mayonnaise, cheese, and cheese sauce. In addition, these foods are fried, sautéed, pan-fried and deep-fat-fried, thereby increasing the fat and the calories. Perhaps the best example is fast-food restaurants. In a single day, almost 46 million people—a fifth of the entire population—eat at one of the 60,000 fast-food restaurants in the United States. Annual sales of the 340 fast-food chains now top the $50 billion level. "Fast foods" are really "fat foods." A Burger King chicken sandwich contains as much fat as one and a half pints of Scaltest ice cream. A Wendy's cheese-stuffed potato contains fat equal to nine pats of butter. An examination of some of our most popular fast foods reveals much about total calories and fat content:

Chain	Calories	% of Calories from Fat
ARBY'S		
Super Roast Beef Sandwich	501	40%
Potato Cakes	201	63
Sausage and Egg Croissant	499	59
BURGER KING		
Whopper	626	55
Hamburger	275	39
Bacon Double Cheeseburger	510	55
Specialty Chicken Sandwich	688	52
French Fries, regular	227	52
Vanilla Shake	321	28
Onion Rings	274	53
McDONALD'S		
Big Mac	570	55
McD.L.T.	680	58
McNuggets (6)	323	56
Egg McMuffin	340	42

Chain	Calories	% of Calories from Fat
McDONALD'S (cont'd)		
French Fries, regular	220	47%
Chocolate Shake	383	21
Apple Pie	253	51
KENTUCKY FRIED CHICKEN		
Extra Crispy or Spicy Thigh	371	64
Original Recipe Side Breast	276	56
Nuggets (6)	276	57
WENDY'S		
Double Cheese Burger	630	57
Cole Slaw	90	80
Chicken Filet Sandwich	320	28
Home Fries	360	55
Frosty Dairy Dessert	400	32
Breakfast Sandwich	370	46
Chili	260	28
SKIPPER'S		
Clam Chowder	102	35
Fish Filet	227	65

Source: Center for Science in the Public Interest.

A principal problem with fast foods is excessive calories. A Kentucky Fried Chicken Extra Crispy dinner (three pieces of chicken) contains 1,100 calories. A Burger King Whopper is over 600 calories, and a Dairy Queen banana split approaches 550. A typical fast-food meal of a quarter-pound cheeseburger, fries and a shake has more than 1,000 calories. That's about 40% of a 165-pound man's needs for the day and about 60% of a 128-pound woman's. (The meal also provides a teaspoon of salt.) A great many fast foods are also high in saturated fat. You'd expect this to be the case with hamburgers, hot dogs and roast beef sandwiches, but a lot of saturated fat is also found in non-beef items that are deep-fat fried, such as chicken, fish and potatoes. A study conducted by Dr. Frank Sacks at Harvard

University revealed that many of the nation's largest fast-food chains fry their foods in saturated fat, thus promoting high blood cholesterol. McDonald's, Burger King, Wendy's, Arby's, Hardees, Big Boy and Popeye's fry in beef tallow; Howard Johnson's uses saturated palm oil. Both beef tallow and palm oil are more saturated than lard.

Health professionals are particularly concerned about the effect of saturated fat on children, the chief consumers of fast food. Children are susceptible to coronary artery disease from about age two, but it generally doesn't manifest itself until after age 11. Recent research now indicates that the disease is occurring more frequently in children, and much of the reason is saturated fat in the diet. "We're clogging up their arteries," says Dr. Tazwell Bank, director of the Heart Station at Washington, D.C.'s General Hospital. This point is reinforced by the fact that, by age 22, 46% of American men already have coronary heart disease, a product of childhood lifestyle. In a study at Louisiana State University of 35 youths aged 7 to 24, only 6 did not demonstrate manifestations of the disease. Children and adolescents are most susceptible to fast-food advertising—a fact not lost on McDonald's, Wendy's and Burger King, who together spent over $457 million in advertising in 1984.

To be fair, not all fast-food choices are lethal. Some chains offer grilled plain hamburgers that compare very well with fried cheeseburgers in fatty "special sauce." Most chili contains much less fat than a triple cheeseburger. Surprisingly, pizza can be a good choice. A typical slice runs less than 30% fat and is almost 60% carbohydrate. Good fast-food choices eaten in moderation will not upset a healthy diet pattern. However, a steady diet of hamburgers, fried chicken and fish, shakes and fries, is inconsistent with the principles of a positive eating program.

Sit-down restaurants generally pose less of a problem because they offer a wider range of possibilities, such as salads, vegetables, fruit, whole-grain breads, fewer heavy sauces, and more chicken and fish. Also, their personnel are more apt to make requested changes. A number of restaurants offer "heart-healthy" menus based on American Heart Association guidelines. These meals are lower in fat and calories than their regular items.

What it takes to eat well in a restaurant is the ability to make sensible food selections. This is often the product of practicing a positive diet pattern at home. Sensible selections are the result of perspective and planning: dwell on what you *can* have rather than on what you *can't* have, and know ahead of time where the restaurant meal falls into your dietary plan. If you don't want to overeat, for example, plan to order a salad and an appetizer rather than an entrée. Plan to drink mineral water or a nonalcoholic beverage. Restaurant food doesn't have to happen *to* you. Planning provides control. It even works with heavy restaurant meals. Plan for the increased calories by cutting back on your other meals and increasing your exercise. Then your calories for the day won't be too far off.

If you arrive at the restaurant hungry, planning can be even more important. If you know dinner will be late, make provisions to eat some fruit or drink a glass of skim milk earlier in the evening to take the edge off your hunger. Smart planning can prevent overeating. For people who eat in restaurants a lot, as many traveling business people do, a good plan when famished is to ignore the menu. Find out from the waiter what fish is fresh, then order it broiled and served with plenty of lemons, a tossed green salad with oil and vinegar on the side, steamed vegetables, and rice or baked potato. Another good choice is broiled veal. This technique can save agonizing over temptingly rich offerings and prevent the ordering of fat- and calorie-rich foods.

Breakfast is often the most difficult meal to eat in a restaurant, as so many choices include excessive fat. Bacon, ham and sausage, eggs fried in butter, fried potatoes, butter on toast, cream in coffee—all pose a serious dietary problem. The best choice is hot cereal with fruit and non-fat or 1% milk. Oatmeal, oat bran and cream of wheat are satisfying and low in calories. Dry cereals such as Shredded

Wheat and All-Bran are low in sugar and high in fiber, and are good with fresh fruit. Some restaurants—Denny's, for example—offer scrambled eggs made with egg whites. If you can stand the cholesterol, a poached egg on an English muffin or eggs Benedict without the Hollandaise sauce can be ordered occasionally. Many restaurants will use non-stick pans for eggs, pancakes and waffles, if requested. If you order pancakes or waffles, go easy on the margarine and the syrup.

A restaurant or hotel buffet provides a greater choice for a healthy breakfast. It generally offers a variety of fresh fruit, light salads, and baked goods such as whole-wheat rolls and bran muffins. Many feature seafood, such as poached salmon, clams, oysters and mussels. The best approach is to maximize the healthy foods—fruit, seafood, vegetables—and *sample* the foods you normally avoid. A buffet is a good chance to have a taste of ham or Canadian bacon, for example. If you do eat at a buffet, be aware that you'll probably take in a fair amount of calories. Plan for a lighter evening meal like soup or salad. For hearty soups that satisfy with few calories, see our recipes for Swiss Barley Soup (only 51 calories per cup) and French Market Soup (68 calories per cup).

Lunches can be a problem, especially for those in a hurry. Again, planning is the key. Keep a mental list of restaurants where you can get a healthy meal. This will minimize the risk of getting stuck at a high-fat restaurant. Also, keep a mental list of healthy lunches that you like: sliced fresh turkey or roast chicken on a crusty French roll with Dijon mustard . . . pasta salad . . . minestrone soup with a French baguette . . . tuna salad on dill rye . . . fresh fruit. If you have five or six core luncheon items in mind, making healthy selections becomes easier.

Many restaurants offer an interesting variety of salads. Hold the fatty add-ons such as cheese, egg, ham, bacon, sunflower seeds, avocados, olives and croutons. The most critical aspect is the dressing. Some are very high in fat calories—Thousand Island, Russian, blue cheese, for example—and can easily add 250 calories to the meal. If you decide on an oil dressing, always have it served on the side. The best approach to saving calories is to use dressings made without oil, such as flavored vinegars, tomato salsa or lemon juice. Many restaurants serve oil-free diet dressings. Don't overlook fresh fruit salads, as they can be sumptuous. Check the dessert menu for fruit—fresh strawberries, for example—and have it served as a salad.

Salad bars are a mixed bag. On the one hand, they offer variety; on the other, the add-on's, toppings and dressings can sabotage your meal and send calories sky-high. The following gives you an idea of how many calories are packed into some salads:

Salad	Calories per ½ Cup
Chicken and celery	200
Coleslaw	212
Fruit salad	115
Gelatin, fruit and cottage cheese	140
Kidney bean	174
Macaroni	217
Potato	124
Three-bean	147

It's relatively easy to pack 800 to 1,000 calories onto a salad-bar plate. Part of the problem is the high-fat items: one-eighth of a cup of sunflower seeds is 100 calories; three ripe olives are 57 calories; a quarter-cup of Cheddar cheese is 230 calories. But part also stems from oversize utensils that make for too generous a serving. A typical ladle holds two teaspoons of dressing, or about 150 calories—double the recommended amount. A serving spoon holds one-third cup. Using common sense in selection and portion size is the key.

Ask for bread or rolls with whole grains—whole wheat, rye and sour-dough are preferable to croissants, butter rolls and white bread. Be careful with butter. A single pat of butter adds 35 to 50 calories to any kind of bread. The secret is to do without butter, or to use it very sparingly.

Desserts can kill attempts to control weight. Pastry, pie, cake, ice cream and candy have calories so concentrated that even a small portion can undo an otherwise prudent meal. Make your decision ahead of time—a bad on-the-spot choice can negatively affect the whole meal. If you plan for dessert, the best choice is fresh fruit. Fresh strawberries or raspberries are sweet and satisfying yet light in calories. If you just can't turn down a gooey dessert, plan the rest of the meal around it. Eat a light appetizer and a salad, and allow for the calories at dessert. Or order one dessert for four people. Often just one bite is all that's needed to satisfy.

Planning also extends to the type of restaurant. Seafood restaurants generally have many good choices. Start off your meal with oysters, clams or mussels (raw, baked, steamed), crab or shrimp cocktail, or seviche. Select the best of the local shellfish—cherrystones in New England, Gulf shrimp in the South, Olympia oysters in the Pacific Northwest. Many seafood places offer a wide variety of fresh fish items—lobster tails, broiled swordfish, poached salmon, baked trout, crab legs, baked oysters and blackened redfish. Don't overlook nontraditional fish on the menu, such as shark, orange roughy or mahi mahi. The key to ordering fish is to have it cooked and served without butter. Fresh lemons are a low-calorie alternative. If you're planning to have a low-calorie meal, order two seafood appetizers and have one served as the main course.

American restaurants usually center on red meat, but often roasted or broiled chicken, turkey and veal are available. Ethnic restaurants provide a number of tasty and nutritious possibilities. Italian restaurants almost always feature veal and chicken over beef, and offer healthy and hearty pasta-based soups. If you like pasta, there are many sauces that will not add heavy calories—a meatless marinara and red clam sauce are two examples. Skip pasta with meatballs, sausage or cream. Oriental restaurants specialize in stir-fry cooking, which maximizes vegetables and minimizes red meat. Plan to avoid tempura, pork-fried rice and other fried foods. Many soups, such as won ton and hot and sour, are made with chicken broth. Steamed rice is always available. Even appetizers such as pot stickers and spring rolls can be steamed rather than fried. You can also plan to eat light in a Mexican restaurant: order taco salad with half the meat and double the lettuce, tomato salsa for topping, and steamed tortillas instead of chips.

Moderate Processed Foods

Processed foods appeal to Americans. Tasty, quick and convenient, they fit well into our fast-paced lifestyle. It's estimated that processed food makes up about half of what we eat today. The industry has grown so rapidly that 10 years ago most of these foods didn't even exist. Unfortunately, many of them are nutritional travesties predominantly consisting of fat, salt, sugar and empty calories. Some are so fiber-poor that they can't satisfy hunger for any length of time and thereby encourage overeating.

Perhaps the greatest drawback to many processed foods is that they're calorically dense, packing a lot of calories into a small serving:

Food	Calories
Swanson Hungry Man Turkey Dinner, frozen (19 oz.)	740
Banquet Bean and Frankfurter Dinner (10¾ oz.)	591
Libby's Corned Beef Hash, canned (1 cup)	454
Van de Kamp's Chicken Pie, frozen (8 oz.)	427
Nalley's Big Chunk Chili, canned (1 cup)	404
Carnation Instant Breakfast (8 fluid oz.)	280
Frito-Lay's Potato Chips (1 oz.)	157
Jeno's Pizza Roll (1)	45

Even some of the so-called "light" meals have a lot of calories. They're light because the portion size has been reduced, so often they fail to satisfy. Still, it's not reasonable to outlaw processed foods altogether. Again, the key is moderation, both in the amount of times these foods are eaten and in the fat/caloric content of the foods selected.

Quick-to-fix, healthy meals can be planned for at

home. We keep a list of quick recipes posted inside a cupboard door for easy reference. Pan-fried chicken breasts take less than 20 minutes; while they're cooking, rice can be prepared. Poached or pan-fried scallops cook in under five minutes. Other fast meals include pasta with marinara sauce, macaroni and cheese, and vegetable stir-fries. The key to quick-to-fix meals is planning. The next time you cook spaghetti, for example, make extra sauce and freeze it. For a quick pasta dinner, heat the sauce while the pasta is cooking; serve with a salad and a French bread. Chicken stock can also be prepared and frozen ahead of time; when you're ready to use it as a quick soup base, just thaw the stock and heat it with leftovers.

Our family often enjoys pizza as a quick-to-fix meal. When we're making our own pizza, we double the recipe and freeze the second pizza. A quick pop in the oven, and we have pizza faster than if it were delivered—and much lower in fat and calories.

THE SECOND PRINCIPLE: REDUCE SUGAR

Americans love sugar. The average American adult consumes one-third of a pound a day—128 pounds per year. The figure is even higher for adolescents—274 pounds per year. Thus sugar accounts for 24% of total calories in the contemporary American diet, or 600 calories per day for adults.

SOURCES OF DIETARY SUGAR

Table sugar, or sucrose, is responsible for about 30% of total sugar intake. Mostly, it's added to drinks such as coffee, tea, lemonade and Kool-Aid, used in cooking and baking, and liberally sprinkled on cereal and fruit. A much greater problem is sugar added to processed foods—soups, cured meats, gravies, canned fruit, salad dressing, ketchup, bread, crackers, spaghetti sauce, pies, cakes, jams, ice cream and candy. Processed foods are responsible for fully 70% of American sugar consumption. Sugar has become by far the nation's most popular food additive. According to the Hanes study, there are five principal sources of sugar in the American diet:

- Soft drinks contribute 21% of sugar calories. For those aged 15 to 34, it's even higher—32% to 40%.

- Sweets such as syrups, jellies, jams, ices and gelatin desserts contribute 18.4%. Consisting of empty calories, these sweets promote obesity and yet are the largest source of sugar for people over the age of 35.

- Sugar-rich bakery goods such as cakes, cookies, pies, pastries and crackers contribute 13.3% of sugar calories.

- Milk products contribute 9.6%. These include ice cream, milkshakes, flavored yogurt and chocolate milk.

- Bread and grain foods contribute 6.2%. These include pasta, rice, baby cereals, cooked cereals, crackers and many salty snacks. (Actually, these foods are not high in sugar; the amount adds up because they're eaten so often.) Cold cereals rank sixth, producing 4.6% of calories from sugar. This in itself is staggering; however, for children aged one to 10, cold cereal supplies 9%.

There are two principal problems with sugar from a cardiovascular health standpoint. The first is that refined sugar elevates triglycerides, a blood fat that can work like cholesterol to clog coronary arteries. (About 20 million Americans have a genetic predisposition to high triglycerides, which can be triggered by excessive sugar in the diet.) A greater problem is the impact of sugar on overweight. Sugar is fat's twin when it comes to increasing weight. Actually, a teaspoon of sugar is just 16 calories, which makes it no more fattening than protein or starch and less than half as fattening as fats and oils. The problem is that we do not consume quantities of sugar by itself, teaspoon by teaspoon. The greatest amount comes from processed foods. The manufacturing process allows for tremendous amounts of sugar to be packed into small quantities of food, making the product high in calories. A one-and-a-half-ounce milk chocolate bar, for example, contains seven teaspoons of sugar—48% of the 233 calories in the bar. Eight ounces of eggnog has eight teaspoons of sugar—42% of its 342 calories. A 12-ounce Coke contains over nine teaspoons of sugar—100% of its 144 calories.

Sugar-rich food, such as brownies, is extremely high in calories but has very little bulk so it takes a lot to feel "full" and there is a tendency to overeat. It's just the opposite for foods with low caloric density, such as cantaloupe or strawberries, which are low in calories but high in fiber and therefore produce a feeling of satisfaction. Compare two sweet-tooth reactions: a person who satisfies a craving with plump, juicy strawberries, at 55 calories a cup, consumes very few calories before feeling too full to eat another berry; a person who satisfies a craving with a couple of Baby Ruth candy bars, at 260 calories per bar, can consume a tremendous number of calories before feeling full. It's the same for M&M's and apples: eat a pound of apples and you'll take in 242 calories; eat a pound of M&M's and you'll take in 2,240 calories.

For a better understanding of the impact of sugar on caloric intake, let's examine the sugar content of some common foods according to the American Society of Dentistry for Children:

Food	Total Calories	Tsps. of Sugar	% of Calories from Sugar
SOFT DRINKS (12 oz.)			
Shasta Orange Soda	172	11.8	100 %
Mountain Dew	178	11	100
On Tap Root Beer	162	10.3	100
Pepsi-Cola	158	10	100
Coca-Cola	144	9.3	100
Sprite	142	9	100
Canada Dry Tonic Water	140	8.4	97.7
Canada Dry Ginger Ale	130	8	94.8
Shasta Ginger Ale	118	8	100

Food	Total Calories	Tsps. of Sugar	% of Calories from Sugar
OTHER BEVERAGES			
Hawaiian Punch (8 oz.)	100	6.5	100%
Kool-Aid, unsweetened (8 oz.)	100	6.3	100
Country Time Lemonade Flavor, frozen concentrate (8 oz.)	91	6	100
Nestlé Hot Cocoa Mix (1 oz.)	110	5.8	84
Kool-Aid, sweetened (8 oz.)	93	5.5	100
Hi-C, Grape (6 oz.)	89	5.5	88
Tang (4 oz.)	64	3.8	100
CANDY			
Milky Way (2.1 oz.)	270	9.0	21
Snickers (2 oz.)	258	7.3	42
M&M's, plain (1.7 oz.)	238	6.8	46
Jelly beans (10 pieces)	104	6.6	100
Marshmallows (1 oz.)	111	4.8	100
Nestlé's Milk Chocolate (1 oz.)	150	4.0	43
Mr. Goodbar (1 oz.)	155	3.0	31
DAIRY PRODUCTS			
Dannon Frozen Yogurt, peach (½ cup)	260	3.3	50
Vanilla ice cream, 12% fat (½ cup)	147	3.2	37
Chocolate milk, 2% fat (1 cup)	180	2.7	24
OTHER DESSERTS AND SWEET SNACKS			
Popsicle (1)	70	4.5	100
Hunt's Snack Pack, vanilla (1 can)	180	4.4	37
Canned pears, heavy syrup (½ cup)	87	3.6	59
Orange sherbet (½ cup)	120	2.8	33

Food	Total Calories	Tsps. of Sugar	% of Calories from Sugar
BREAKFAST CEREALS (1 oz.)			
General Mills			
Boo Berry	110	3.3	47%
Count Chocula	110	3.3	47
Trix	110	3.0	44
Cocoa Puffs	110	2.8	40
Lucky Charms	110	2.8	40
Total	110	0.8	11
Wheaties	110	0.8	11
Kix	110	0.5	7
Cheerios	110	0.3	4
Kellogg's			
Froot Loops	110	3.3	47
Sugar Corn Pops	110	3.0	44
Frosted Flakes, sugar	110	2.8	40
Product 19	110	0.8	11
Rice Krispies	110	0.8	11
Corn Flakes	110	0.5	7
Post			
Super Sugar Crisp	113	3.5	51
Raisin Bran	102	2.3	40
Honeycomb	113	2.8	40
Grape-nut Flakes	108	1.3	20
Ralston Purina			
Sugar Frosted Flakes	110	2.8	40
Raisin Bran	100	2.3	36
Rice Chex	110	0.5	7
Quaker Oats			
Cap'n Crunch	121	3.0	44
King Vitaman	120	3.0	44
Quisp	121	3.0	44
Life	105	1.5	22
Shredded Wheat	75	0.3	3
Puffed Rice	55	0	0

A number of high-sugar foods are also rich in fat, a double whammy for calories. A one-ounce Hershey's Milk Chocolate bar gets almost twice its calories from fat as from sugar; 2% chocolate milk gets 24% of its calories from sugar and 38% from fat. This is especially important in light of research showing that overweight people crave fat more than sugar. In a study conducted at the University of Michigan and at Vassar College, overweight and normal-weight people rated various combinations of sugar and fat given to them in the form of a whipped dairy drink. The overweight people preferred a drink that was 34% fat and 4% sugar, while the normal-weight people liked a drink that was 8% fat and 21% sugar. This illustrates that in many cases it isn't a "sugar fix" that drives overweight people to a chocolate bar—it's a "fat fix"!

HOW TO REDUCE SUGAR IN THE DIET

Humans are born with a sweet tooth, so the craving for sugar is legitimate, but there is no room for large quantities of sugar in a diet designed for heart health and weight control. All refined sugar, particularly table, brown and confectioners', should be moderated. If you have to have a sweetener, you might use a bit of honey, maple syrup or molasses; they're so much sweeter than sucrose that a little will go a long way. The chief problem, however, is not the sugar bowl—it's the sugar found in processed foods.

Learn to Read Labels

With sugar the number one additive in processed foods, label reading is essential in determining whether or not the food is sugar-rich. This is not as easy as it may seem, because the ingredient list doesn't always show sugar as "sugar." Numerous other names are used to describe refined sugar: sucrose, maltose, dextrose, lactose, fructose, malt, corn solids, corn syrup, honey, molasses, invert sugar, raw sugar, maple syrup, corn sweetener, malted barley, date sugar and turbinado, to name a few.

A good example of label confusion involves a popular soft drink touted as containing "no sucrose." Many people purchase the drink because they equate "no sucrose" with "no sugar," but according to the ingredients list the beverage contains "high fructose corn syrup" and is therefore not free of sugar. What the manufacturer is really saying is that the product contains no table sugar—no sucrose. Similarly, foods labeled "sugar-free" or "sugarless" can't contain sucrose, or table sugar, but they can have other sweeteners such as honey, corn syrup and fructose. Sometimes these ingredients make a food just as high in calories.

Bending the labeling rules with regard to sugar content is not new. A few years ago, a large breakfast cereal manufacturer created a product that was almost 60% sugar. It contained white sugar, brown sugar and turbinado, along with wheat, rice, oats and bran. Just as the cereal was about to hit the market, there was a backlash caused by angry parents tired of advertising designed to sell sugar cereals to children. The cereal manufacturer was tempted to hold back the product, but economics dictated that it be put out—with a labeling change. The list of ingredients showed that the four cereal grains had been combined into a new category, "cereal grain," while the three sugars were kept separate. This allowed cereal grain to appear first on the list, followed by white sugar, brown sugar and turbinado. This gave the impression that the food consisted primarily of cereal grain. It did not. It was still 60% sugar.

Reading and understanding labels is the only true way to know whether or not a food contains excessive sugar and calories. Most foods do not give sugar content, so you must make a decision from the list of ingredients. A rule of thumb is that if a label lists sugar, under any name, as one of the first three ingredients, consider the food too sugar-rich and avoid it. Also, look for the number of times sugar appears on the list. A box of cookies might list "sugar" third, "corn syrup" fifth and "honey" eighth. Together they might add up to first.

The labels that do provide information on sugar content generally don't use household measurements. Many breakfast cereal labels give grams of sugar under the category "sucrose and other sugars." Most people aren't comfortable with metric weights. In order to calculate sugar content in real terms, it's necessary to translate grams into teaspoons. Just remember that 4 grams equals one teaspoon. If, for example, a label indicates that a one-ounce serving of the cereal contains 12 grams of sucrose and other sugars, divide the grams by 4 to get teaspoons of sugar:

$$\frac{12 \text{ grams}}{4 \text{ grams}} = 3 \text{ teaspoons}$$

Now you know that a serving contains 3 teaspoons—before any more is added from the sugar bowl!

Avoid Soft Drinks

Soft drinks are the single greatest source of sugar in the American diet and in 1985, according to *Advertising Age,* replaced water as America's most consumed beverage. Soft drinks harm weight-control efforts because they are high in calories. It would be relatively easy for a person who likes Coca-Cola, for example, to consume almost 450 calories in a single day. Many people could drastically reduce their sugar consumption by cutting down on soft drinks.

Soft drinks also increase the desire for sweets. According to research done at the Eating Disorder Clinic of Brigham Young University, sweet-tasting drinks cause a craving for more sugar and more calories. So, the more sweet drinks you have, the greater the demand for more sugar and the greater the increase in eating or drinking high-calorie food and drink. It works the same way with diet soft drinks. Artificial sweeteners used in diet sodas are 100 times sweeter than sugar. The body is tricked into thinking it's eating tremendous amounts of sugar, and it adjusts metabolism accordingly. Soon the person will feel tiredness and hunger, common sugar-blues symptoms, and will search for something sweet to eat to energize his or her system.

Another problem is the health effect of artificial sweeteners used in diet drinks. Saccharin, linked to cancer in laboratory animals, has been replaced in many diet drinks by aspartame or a mixture of saccharin and aspartame. While presently declared "safe," the final word is not yet in on aspartame. Some health professionals consider it little better than saccharin. In addition, artificial sweeteners may cut calories, but they keep up the craving for sweet taste.

One of the keys to reducing sugary drinks in the diet is to drink six to eight glasses of water a day. Not only does water keep you full and help avoid overeating, but it increases fat metabolism. You might try keeping a pitcher of ice water and sliced lemons or limes in the refrigerator. You should also drink three glasses of non-fat milk each day for calcium. If you drink water and milk every day in the proper amounts, your body will have sufficient fluid and your desire for soft drinks will diminish.

There are other alternatives to soft drinks, such as bottled mineral water. Fruit juice diluted with club soda or mineral water is refreshing and cuts the natural sugar and the calories in half. Try an apple spritzer—one-third cup apple juice mixed with two-thirds cup club soda, mineral water or seltzer.

Moderate Alcohol Intake

Alcohol is technically a refined sugar, and as such its intake must be moderated. From the standpoint of cardiovascular health, there is much thought that excessive drinking is a risk. High intake of alcohol can raise blood triglycerides, which can clog arteries. Excessive alcohol has also been linked to the production of high blood pressure. The information concerning moderate intake of alcohol, however, is not so clear: while non-drinkers and heavy drinkers tend to have heart attacks at the same rate, moderate drinkers who consume about one and a half ounces of alcohol a day suffer fewer heart attacks. Some research shows that moderate drinking elevates HDL, or "good" cholesterol, which tends to prevent the accumulation of arterial blockages. Other studies counter that the HDL benefits of alcohol are an illusion. Recent data show that one or two drinks a day raises an HDL component called HDL3 but does nothing to promote HDL2, the component most identified with coronary protection.

The general consensus at this time is that a moderate

amount of alcohol—a glass of wine, a beer or two, a cocktail—may be beneficial to cardiovascular health. No one is quite certain why. It could be the HDL or the fact that a small amount of alcohol reduces stress. Whatever the reason, people who are light drinkers have fewer coronary problems than do heavy drinkers or non-drinkers.

Moderate alcohol intake may even be beneficial to a weight control program *after* ideal weight has been reached. Many people find that a glass of wine with dinner relaxes them and releases stress, so they're not driven by tension to overeat. (Note: exercise accomplishes the same thing with less risk and no calories!) The effect of a glass of wine with food is different from the effect of alcohol on an empty stomach, which can create a false hunger so strong that it can overwhelm good dietary intentions.

Alcohol has no place in a weight loss program. Not many people concerned with weight loss could tolerate the calories produced by even moderate amounts of alcohol. This is because alcohol is basically empty calories—pure fuel waiting to be stored as body fat—and ounce for ounce has almost as many calories as fat. The following illustrates the concentrated caloric punch supplied by alcohol:

Beverage	Calories
Scotch, whiskey, gin, vodka (1½ oz.)	
80-proof	97
86-proof	105
90-proof	110
94-proof	116
100-proof	125
Brandy, cognac (1 oz.)	65
Liqueurs (1 oz.)	75–100
Dry wine (3½ oz.)	87
Sweet wine (3½ oz.)	142
Beer, ale (12 oz.)	140–165
Light beer (12 oz.)	95–105

Restaurants and social gatherings often prove to be the biggest problem in moderating alcohol. If you do choose to drink socially, plan for it ahead of time and decide what you're going to drink. You may determine that a nonalcoholic cocktail such as a Virgin Mary, a screwdriver without vodka, or mineral water with a piece of lime is all you need to be satisfied. These drinks allow you to be part of the group, to have something in your hand, without adding calories.

You might also limit the number of drinks. Have one cocktail and make mineral water the second. Plan the drinks to be calorically light. Stay away from high-calorie mixers and sweet liqueurs. Have a glass of champagne—three ounces is only 60 calories. Or try a wine spritzer, two ounces of dry white wine mixed with club soda or mineral water. Smart planning provides you with control over the impact of alcohol on your diet pattern.

Eat Fresh Fruit for Dessert

Sugary, creamy desserts and candies can undo a meal designed for weight control. A cream puff has over 300 calories; a piece of chocolate cake, 365 calories. The best alternative is fresh fruit, which contains vitamins, minerals and fiber as well as natural sugars. Look to the fruit of the season for best buys and the sweetest taste. Frozen honeydew and bananas are sweet and satisfying, as are baked bananas and applesauce. Fruit purées make elegant and attractive desserts without heavy calories. Our recipes include Fresh Peaches with Strawberry and Banana Purées (just 94 calories) and Poached Pears with Raspberry Purée (just 125 calories).

Avoid canned fruits in syrup, as they are loaded with sugar. Dried fruits—dates, figs, raisins, apples, apricots— are a good alternative to candy bars. They have a high concentration of sugar and calories (two large apricot halves are 25 calories), so eat them in moderation.

If you want to have a richer dessert, plan for it. Don't decide on a slice of apple pie after a heavy dinner. If you want the pie, opt for a lighter dinner—perhaps soup or salad. Commercially baked cake, cookies or pies are very rich in fat, sugar and calories, so get the best quality if you're going to have them. Don't take in high calories with a packaged doughnut. Often, hot homemade bread will satisfy with fewer calories than a commercial dessert. Try our recipes for Blueberry Muffins, Cranberry Bread, Banana Currant Muffins, or Popovers with low-calorie Apple Butter. Instead of high-fat, creamy commercial desserts, try some of our dessert recipes: Spanish Cream (64 calories), Cranberry Custard (88 calories), Banana Cream Pudding (111 calories) or Cold Lemon Soufflé (112 calories).

THE THIRD PRINCIPLE: INCREASE COMPLEX CARBOHYDRATES

An important premise of the 500-Calorie Solution is the fact that a long-term diet pattern cannot be successful if it's based exclusively on negatives—on foods you can no longer eat. To create a new and permanent way of eating healthfully, the diet pattern must be centered on foods you can have. Complex carbohydrates fill this need. They are the secret to a diet pattern that is healthful, promotes weight control and includes food that tastes good.

The third basic principle, then, is to replace foods rich in fat and sugar (calorically dense) with complex carbohydrates (calorically light), including vegetables, fruits, whole grains, pasta, beans and peas, rice, cereal and breads.

Historically, carbohydrates have been the chief source of calories for humans: corn for American Indians, bread for Europeans, rice for Asians, grains and beans for Africans and South Americans. In many parts of the world starchy carbohydrates still make up the bulk of the diet, but in the United States and other industrialized civilizations the proper role of carbohydrates in the diet has been altered. Since the early 1900s, the American diet has systematically substituted fat for carbohydrates. Foods rich in fat were considered the mark of an affluent, civilized culture. This was especially true after World War II, when animal sources of protein—principally red meat and whole-milk dairy products—became very popular. The result is a diet in which carbohydrates make up 45% of calories while fat makes up 42%. By comparison, the U.S. Senate Select Committee on Dietary Goals recommends a diet consisting of about 60% carbohydrates and 30% fat.

Two significant changes have occurred in the eating pattern of Americans with regard to carbohydrates. First, the consumption of all carbohydrates has fallen in favor of fat. The switch from grains, beans and vegetables to animal foods has negatively impacted heart disease and overweight for Americans. In addition, much of the fat eaten is saturated, so this change must bear responsibility for elevated cholesterol in the population. The second change concerns a switch in the type of carbohydrates eaten. In the past Americans ate most of their carbohydrates in the form of complex starches, such as beans and grains, and natural sugars, such as those found in fruits and vegetables. Today, most carbohydrates come from refined and processed foods such as commercially baked goods, packaged grains, canned vegetables, candy and junk food. For example, Americans are eating more fruit now than in the past, but fresh fruit consumption is down by over 30%. Canned fruit in heavy syrup and fruit juice constitute the greatest sources of fruit in the diet. The same problem exists with fresh vs. canned vegetables and whole grains vs. refined flours. Refined and processed carbohydrates make up almost 20% of the calories in the modern American diet, instead of the 10% recommended by health professionals.

The American diet pattern is woefully short of complex carbohydrates. There are three good reasons why this should not be so.

1. Complex carbohydrates are not fattening. Of all the misconceptions surrounding carbohydrates, none is farther from the truth than the notion that carbohydrates cause people to get fat. Indeed, a diet rich in complex carbohydrates actually promotes weight loss and provides a tool for long-term weight control. The caloric difference between complex carbohydrates and high-fat/sugar foods is significant. A five-ounce potato, for example, contains about 90 calories, or 18 calories per ounce; the same amount of steak contains about 500 calories, or 100 calories per ounce.

The misconception that bread, pasta and rice—"starchy" foods—are fattening has moved many dieters toward red meat. They go on meat-heavy, carbohydrate-poor diets, such as the Scarsdale Diet. They order the "dieter's special"—ground sirloin, cottage cheese and sliced tomato—without realizing that the meal is about 700 calories and 70% fat. What many do not understand is that fatty animal products constitute the easiest way to overconsume calories. In other words, it isn't the potato that is a threat to slimness; it's frying it in fat or topping it with butter and sour cream. It isn't the rice that is a problem; it's the butter. It isn't the pasta that adds pounds; it's the meatballs, sausage and cream sauce.

In addition to being higher in calories, fatty foods are low in bulk and can therefore be eaten in greater amounts. (This is especially true of processed foods, which often are so highly refined and fiber-depleted that they cannot satisfy natural hunger.) Complex carbohydrates arc just the opposite. They are low in calories and are filling. Foods that take a lot of chewing, like apples or carrots, take a long time to eat, providing sufficient time—20 minutes—for satiety to be attained.

Complex carbohydrates also absorb water in the digestive system, thereby helping to create a feeling of fullness and satisfaction that offsets the deprivation associated with dieting. Eating complex carbohydrates exercises caloric control because 1) the food contains fewer calories, and 2) a point of satisfaction is reached before excessive calories can be consumed.

2. Complex carbohydrates contain fiber. The American diet is criticized as being fat-rich and fiber-poor, a combination that contributes to a number of serious health problems: cancer of the colon and rectum, diverticulosis, gallstones, varicose veins, hiatus hernia, appendicitis, hemorrhoids . . . and heart disease. According to a recent report of the National Cancer Institute, Americans consume on average 15 grams of dietary fiber each day—an amount that many health professionals believe should be doubled or tripled.

What is fiber? Often called roughage, bulk or bran, fiber is simply the nondigestible part of plant food. It passes through the digestive system intact. This is an important concept for weight control. It means that with certain foods, notably complex carbohydrates rich in fiber, not all the calories consumed stay with the body. Not only are complex carbohydrates lower in calories than high-fat foods, but some of their calories don't count!

The following table shows some of the foods that are rich in dietary fiber:

Food	Fiber Content (g)
All-Bran or 100% bran (1 cup)	23.0
Apple (1 small)	3.1
Applesauce (½ cup)	1.7
Cucumber (½ of 7-inch cucumber)	1.5
Graham crackers (2)	1.5
Grapefruit (½)	2.6
Grape-Nuts (⅓ cup)	5.0
Grits, dry (¼ cup)	4.8
Kidney beans, cooked (1 cup)	3.6
Lentils, cooked (½ cup)	4.0
Lettuce (1 cup)	0.8
Oats, rolled, dry (½ cup)	4.5
Orange (1 small)	1.8
Peach (1 medium)	1.3
Pear (1 medium)	2.8
Peas, cooked (½ cup)	3.8
Plum (2 small)	1.6
Potatoes, cooked (⅔ cup)	3.1
Rice, brown, cooked (1 cup)	1.1
Rice, white, cooked (1 cup)	0.4
Rye bread (1 slice)	2.0
Rye crackers (3)	2.3
Strawberries (½ cup)	2.6

Food	Fiber Content (g)
Wheat, cracked, dry (⅓ cup)	5.6
Wheat, shredded (2 biscuits)	6.1
Whole-wheat bread (1 slice)	2.4

Source: USDA.

3. Complex carbohydrates lower blood cholesterol. It has long been known that certain complex carbohydrates can have a positive impact on blood chemistry. A study at the University of Wisconsin, for example, found that whole-grain barley may block the production of cholesterol in the liver. Other studies show that pectin, a component of certain fruit such as apples, lowers blood cholesterol and that garlic and onions thin the blood.

These findings have been encouraging, but perhaps the most important research concerns the effect of soluble fiber on cholesterol. Soluble fiber, of which oats are one of the best sources in the American diet, forms a gel as it moves through the digestive system and interferes with the absorption of cholesterol. The positive impact of soluble fiber in oats was shown in testing done at the University of Kentucky by Dr. James Anderson, who took two groups of men with high cholesterol and had them eat a diet rich in fat and low in fiber—the typical American diet. A second group supplemented their diet with one bowl of hot oat-bran cereal and five oat-bran muffins each day. The cereal, muffins and other food produced 47 grams of fiber per day, of which 17 were soluble. After 10 days on such a diet, the second group had blood cholesterol levels fall an average of 13%. The experiment was repeated a year later, and this time cholesterol levels fell by 19% in three weeks. Similar results were produced in a test group who consumed soluble fiber from legumes: eating one and a half cups of navy or pinto beans a day, enough to equal the soluble fiber intake of Dr. Anderson's oat-bran study, the group showed a 13% to 19% decrease in cholesterol levels.

These early studies clearly illustrate that soluble fiber lowers blood cholesterol in people who have extremely high levels. A new study now shows that the fiber in oats may

produce the same result for people with moderate cholesterol levels. Researchers at Northwestern University School
of Medicine placed 208 people, aged 30 to 65, on a low-
fat, low-cholesterol diet. After about six weeks, cholesterol
levels dropped from an average of 208 to 198. The diet
was continued for another six weeks, but with one change:
two-thirds of the group ate two ounces of oat products every
day, in the form of hot oat cereal or foods made with oat
bran. Their blood cholesterol level dropped to 190, while
the level of the non-oat group stayed at 198. According to
the National Institutes of Health, a 1% reduction in blood
cholesterol produces a 2% drop in the risk of heart attack.
Therefore, the cholesterol reduction induced by oat fiber is
of tremendous significance.

The best source of such fiber is oat bran, which has
twice the fiber of oatmeal. Oat bran can be eaten as a hot
cereal or in muffins. Hot cereal is the better choice because
many muffin recipes are higher in calories. Other complex carbohydrates containing soluble fiber include grains
(rye bread, whole-wheat bread), dried beans and peas
(black-eyed and split peas, lentils, kidney, navy and pinto
beans), vegetables (peas, corn, sweet potato, zucchini,
cauliflower, broccoli) and fruit (pears, prunes, apples, bananas, oranges).

SOURCES OF COMPLEX CARBOHYDRATES

Complex carbohydrates are central to the 500-Calorie Solution. Some key foods are discussed below.

Vegetables and Legumes

Dried beans and peas are good sources of fiber and other
nutrients. Legumes such as navy beans, lentils, pinto beans,
black-eyed peas and soybeans are particularly rich in protein, which makes them a low-fat alternative to red meat.
A good way to include them in the diet is to mix them with
other foods—rice with lentils or black beans, pasta and

beans, or bean tacos—or to use them in soups with pasta, rice and other grains.

Most vegetables are a nutritional bargain, providing vitamins and minerals but relatively few calories. High in water content, they provide bulk and are filling. One-half cup of the most watery vegetables, such as asparagus, green beans, tomatoes, summer squash and broccoli, contains less than 25 calories. Lettuce, radishes, celery and raw greens are so low in calories that they can be eaten freely on a weight-loss program. Even a half-cup of the starchy vegetables, such as corn, potatoes, lima beans, winter squash, peas and beans, provides under 100 calories—still less than one tablespoon of oil or butter.

Raw vegetables are more nutritious than cooked and are far superior to their processed counterparts. The best way to cook vegetables is to steam lightly, microwave or stir-fry. In general, the crunchier after cooking, the better.

Fruit

Fresh fruit is a basic element of a healthy diet. Fruits are low in calories and sodium, high in carbohydrates and fiber, and practically devoid of fat. Apples and many other fruits contain pectin, a type of fiber that helps to lower blood cholesterol. In addition, fruits can meet the sweet-tooth cravings in a nutritious, nonfattening way. They are not calorie-free but are sufficiently low to provide good caloric mileage. This is illustrated by comparing fruit with one tablespoon of oil, or 125 calories. For this amount of calories, you could eat:

6 apricots	1¾ cups of papaya
1½ cups of blackberries	3 peaches
1½ cups of blueberries	1½ cups of pineapple
1 whole cantaloupe	5 Japanese plums
1 pound of casaba melon	1 cup of prunes
1 cup of pitted sweet cherries	1½ cups of raspberries
8 ounces of currants	2 cups of strawberries
4 figs	3 tangerines or mandarin
1 whole grapefruit	oranges

2 guava   3 slices of watermelon
4 2-inch wedges of honeydew melon   2 apples
6 lemons   1½ bananas
8 limes   3 bunches of grapes
3 nectarines   1½ mangos
2 oranges   1 pear

Breakfast Cereals

Cereals in their natural state are a low-calorie way to get good nutrition. They have vitamins, minerals and fiber. As cold breakfast cereals, however, many have a dual problem: they've been processed to the point where fiber is minimal, and they contain excessive refined sugar—white and brown sugar, honey, molasses and corn syrup.

The recommended cold cereals are those made with whole grains and with no added sugar. Some of the best are listed here.

Cereal (1 oz.)	Main Ingredients	Calories	Fiber Content (g)
Fiber One (General Mills)	Wheat bran, corn bran, NutraSweet	60	11
Bran Buds (Kellogg's)	Wheat bran, corn syrup	70	8
Raisin Bran (Post)	Whole wheat, wheat bran, raisins	90	4
Bran Flakes (Kellogg's)	Wheat bran, wheat parts	90	4
Shredded Wheat (Nabisco)	Whole wheat	110	3
Wheat Germ Flakes (Kretschmer)	Cracked wheat germ, wheat flour	100	3
NutriGrain (Kellogg's)	Whole wheat	110	2
Puffed Wheat (Quaker)	Wheat	100	1

Hot cereals generally are a better choice because they're low in calories and high in fiber and nutrition. Best bets for hot cereals are oatmeal and oat bran. Give them a fiber boost by adding fresh fruit and berries. Watch out for the "instant" cereals, as many are rich in sugar and salt.

Bread

White bread constitutes three out of every four loaves purchased by Americans. A better choice is whole-grain bread made from stone-ground flour, rich both in fiber and in nutrients. The next-best bread is 100% whole-wheat or other whole-grain bread, such as rye or pumpernickel.

Read the labels carefully when buying whole-grain breads. The words "wheat flour" instead of "whole-wheat flour" mean that the wheat bran and germ have been removed. You can't tell how much fiber is in a loaf of bread by its dark color, since raisin juice or other coloring may have been added. Ethnic breads, such as French or Italian, often contain little or no shortening; from a fat standpoint these are a good choice, but their crunchy crusts are no higher in fiber than plain white bread because in all cases the bran has been removed.

A comparison of commercial bread illustrates the wide variations in fiber content:

	Calories per Slice	Fiber Content (g)
Whole wheat	70	3.2
Pumpernickel	70	3.0
Rye	70	2.4
Cracked wheat	70	2.2
White, enriched	80	1.1
French, enriched	75	.1
Bagel (½)	85	.1

Pasta

Made from hard durum wheat that has been ground into semolina flour, pasta comes in a variety of shapes and sizes and lends itself to an assortment of dishes. Spaghetti, linguine, rigatoni, penne, fettuccine and vermicelli offer low-calorie main courses when served with marinara or red clam sauce. Rotelle, rotini and shells make terrific salads with fresh vegetables. Orzo is a delicious side dish. And tortellini, pastina and shells make hearty soups even heartier.

Keep in mind that there can be a great difference in quality among brands. It's important to use the best pasta available, as the quality of the meal is only as good as the quality of the pasta. Many Italian markets and supermarkets offer high-quality imported and domestic brands.

Don't overlook Oriental noodles such as soba (buckwheat) and saifun. Found in Japanese and Chinese markets and in the Oriental section of many supermarkets, these noodles are particularly good in chicken broth with vegetables and make a delicious main course.

Potatoes

A medium potato has just 90 calories and contains important nutrients. Skip the fatty condiments—butter, sour cream, bacon bits and cheese—to keep the low-calorie content. Instead of sour cream, try non-fat yogurt. Other low-fat condiments include salsa, black pepper, garlic powder, chopped dill, parsley and chives.

Don't overlook other ways to use potatoes. We enjoy bite-size red potatoes in a salad with a vinaigrette of warm lemon juice and a touch of olive oil. Steamed red potatoes are also delicious with this vinaigrette. Bite-size red potatoes, split in half and served with a dab of yogurt and crab, also make a great-tasting hors d'oeuvre.

Commercial potato chips and fried potatoes are drenched in fat during the cooking process, resulting in foods that are high in calories. To illustrate the effect of cooking fat on the makeup of the potato, consider that turning a 90-calorie potato into French fries adds about 350 calories. An ounce of potato chips has over 150 calories. A good alternative is to select four large potatoes, thinly sliced, and toss with one tablespoon of olive oil. Then fry in a non-stick pan. By adding the oil to the potatoes, instead of to the pan, less oil is needed. Sliced or French fry-cut potatoes can also be cooked in the oven on a nonstick baking sheet as a low-fat alternative to French fries.

Rice and Other Grains

Rice, a dietary staple for millions of people, is rich in nutrients. White rice is polished, a process that makes it more attractive to the Western palate but one in which protein and nutrients are sacrificed. A better choice is whole-grain brown rice; not subject to processing, it retains all the nutrients of the rice kernel.

An increased interest in complex carbohydrates has improved the availability of many grains. One is wild rice. It is excellent as a stuffing for poultry and as a side dish. Barley, used since Colonial times, is experiencing a resurgence in soups and as a side dish. It swells larger than other grains in cooling, so a little used in chicken broth will feed an entire family. Bulgur, a favorite in the Middle East, is quick-cooking and is a nice alternative to rice. It is the main ingredient in tabbouli, a delicious salad. Other grains to try include millet, buckwheat (kasha) and whole-rye or wheat berries.

Don't overlook corn, a primary source of protein and carbohydrates in many parts of the world. Try cornmeal in bread or as a side dish.

HOW TO USE COMPLEX CARBOHYDRATES FOR WEIGHT CONTROL

Making complex carbohydrates an integral part of the diet pattern is essential to successful, permanent weight control. The human stomach is designed to accommodate bulky foods. Rice, pasta, potatoes, apples and other complex carbohydrates are filling and provide satisfaction without producing excess calories. Conversely, it takes a great amount of high-fat foods—chocolate bars, TV dinners or French fries—to produce a satisfied feeling. The price for that satisfaction is excessive calories and extra weight.

Successful weight control is linked to being satisfied. This is why most diets fail. In limiting the amount of food, the dieter is left hungry, soon feels ''deprived'' and quickly goes "off" the diet. This problem is evident even among people who eat "light" frozen dinners. These products restrict calories primarily by controlling portions. Small amounts of food may not satisfy and can lead to snacking or a second dinner later in the evening. In the final analysis, restricting calories by cutting food volume sharply doesn't work for permanent weight control.

On the other hand, reaching a point of satisfaction on the high-fat American diet necessitates a high caloric intake. Consider a typical American dinner: cocktails and peanuts, a small salad with lots of Thousand Island dressing, steak, French fries, rolls and butter, all topped off with a piece of apple pie. For many people, consuming such a dinner is not considered overeating. They are not "stuffed" to the point of unpleasantness—yet look at the calories consumed. This meal might easily contain 2,500 to 3,500 calories. The problem here is not food volume but caloric density. This example illustrates a critical point: *incorrect food choices, not food volume, cause overweight.*

A diet pattern rich in complex carbohydrates is the solution. Carbohydrates produce satisfaction without excess calories and offer a reasonable alternative to "porking out" on high-fat meals or to starving because of inadequate food volume. A good example is pasta. A one-cup serving, about five ounces of cooked pasta, is 200 calories. (The average adult, in order to consume 3,000 calories in a day, or the amount most need to maintain body weight, would have to eat over 15 cups of pasta!) For pasta-based dishes that are delicious and satisfying yet low in fat and calories, see our recipes for Pasta with Marinara Sauce, Scallop-and-pesto Fettuccine, Pasta Salad, Linguine with Clams and Artichoke Hearts, Pastina in Brodo, and Fettuccine Primavera. It's rarely necessary to limit grains, fruits, vegetables or legumes in order to lose weight and exert permanent weight control. A person generally will fill up before overconsuming calories. You could even preserve the predinner cocktail-hour format if that is important, but without the alcohol and peanuts. Instead, have mineral water with a slice of lime, a Virgin Mary or a white wine spritzer. For munchies, eat your fill of crudités—these will take the edge off your hunger without providing excessive calories.

THE FOURTH PRINCIPLE: REDUCE SALT

For many Americans, salt is a basic dietary component. It is used in cooking and as a condiment, and next to sugar is the most widely used additive in processed foods. Within the last few years, however, many people have begun to question the amount of salt found in the American diet. The reason is that excessive salt has been linked to high blood pressure, stroke, and kidney and thyroid disease. It also causes fluid retention, which impacts weight and appearance. The U.S. Senate's Select Committee on Nutritional Goals, the American Heart Association and the Surgeon General have called for a reduction in salt intake. As noted food expert Craig Claiborne, himself a victim of high blood pressure, says: "They should label salt, just as they do cigarettes, saying it is injurious to your health."

A certain amount of sodium is needed in the diet for good health. The National Research Council recommends an "adequate and safe" level of 1,100 to 3,300 milligrams of sodium daily, or about one-half to one and a half teaspoons of salt. The actual physiological requirement is only 220 milligrams a day, or about one-tenth teaspoon of salt. The average American consumes two to four teaspoons of salt each day, which translates into 4,000 to 8,000 milligrams daily—and 15 pounds of salt per year.

WHAT SODIUM DOES

The principal problem resulting from excessive dietary salt is high blood pressure, or hypertension, which affects almost 40 million Americans. While we are quick to cite "salt" as the problem, this is a misnomer. Salt is the combination of two minerals: sodium and chloride. Sodium, which makes up about 40% of salt, is the health issue.

Sodium is not inherently negative. Indeed, in the proper amount it is essential for good health. This is because each cell of the body must be bathed continually in a saline solution. If the solution carries a balanced sodium-to-fluid ratio, proper metabolic functioning will take place; however, if the ratio is off because of too much sodium, proper functioning is harmed. A person who eats salty foods will take in excess sodium. If a person exercises and loses fluid as sweat, sodium concentration will increase. In each instance, the sodium-to-fluid balance will be disrupted. The proper ratio is restored by a regulating mechanism in the body that reacts to excessive sodium by triggering a thirst sensation, causing anyone who exercises or eats salty foods to be thirsty. In drinking to satisfy thirst, however, proper fluid balance is restored.

A characteristic of sodium is that it retains fluid. Consequently, when the body contains too much sodium, it also contains too much fluid. Excessive sodium and fluid are eliminated through the kidneys. If this is a constant condition, the kidneys may be overworked, become strained and ultimately fail to work properly. They simply become unable to perform the required level of elimination, and kidney damage or failure takes place. Since sodium holds more fluid, excessive sodium in the body means that the volume of blood is increased. In order to circulate a greater amount of blood, the heart has to pump harder. In doing so, blood pressure is increased. At the same time, sodium causes small blood vessels to constrict, thereby increasing resistance to blood flow. The heart is again forced to increase blood pressure and is put under serious strain.

Hypertension, or high blood pressure, may be the permanent result of excessive sodium in the diet. The condition affects one out of every six adults and directly causes

100,000 deaths annually. In addition, it is a major threat for heart attack. Like coronary heart disease, high blood pressure progresses silently over many years without any outward manifestation. Then one day it appears. But by the time it is detected, it is usually too late to repair heart, blood vessel or kidney damage. Chronic illness and death can result. According to the National Heart, Lung and Blood Institute, about half of all Americans with high blood pressure are unaware that they have it.

The causes of high blood pressure are not fully understood, but considerable research links its development to excess salt in the diet. Studies have shown that in low-salt cultures, such as New Guinea, the Kalahari Desert and parts of Brazil, high blood pressure is virtually non-existent. In high-salt cultures, such as Japan and the United States, high blood pressure is rampant. Forty percent of adults in northern Japan, where salt consumption is almost six times that of the West, suffer from high blood pressure.

Not everyone who eats too much salt is susceptible to hypertension. According to a Harvard Medical School study, some two-thirds of all Americans could eat at a salt lick without harming their health. One-third, however, are genetically predisposed to high blood pressure. For these people, a diet high in salt can bring on the condition. The problem is that there is no procedure by which to identify those who have the genetic weak-link, so a sodium-rich diet means rolling the dice with your health.

SOURCES OF DIETARY SALT

Dietary salt comes from a variety of sources. About 15% comes from foods that contain sodium naturally—meat, milk, fish and water. Some 35% comes from the salt shaker, used in cooking and at the table. But over 50% comes from processed convenience foods found on the American diet. Using the recommended guideline as a standard, it's easy to see how much excess sodium is contained in common foods:

	Sodium Content (mg)
Dill pickle (1 large)	1,940
Sauerkraut (1 cup)	1,755
Salted popcorn (2 oz.)	1,100
Soy sauce (1 oz.)	2,077
Ham (3 oz.)	1,114

It's no surprise that these items contain salt—they taste salty. What *is* a surprise is the number of low-sodium foods made into high-sodium products by added salt. A 5.5-ounce potato, for example, has just 5 milligrams of sodium; processed as potato chips, it contains 1,562 milligrams. A tomato has 14 milligrams of sodium; processed as tomato sauce, one cup contains 1,498 milligrams. According to a sodium study in *Consumer Reports,* one ounce of corn flakes has nearly twice the sodium as an ounce of salted peanuts, two slices of white bread have more sodium than 14 potato chips and one-half cup of prepared chocolate pudding has more sodium than three slices of bacon. The sodium content of canned, frozen and packaged foods is staggering, as shown in a USDA listing of common foods.

Food	Sodium Content (mg)
Jell-O Instant Lemon Pudding (½ cup)	406
Underwood Deviled Ham (4½ oz.)	1,156
Oscar Mayer Ham and Cheese Loaf (1 slice)	287
French's Au Jus Gravy Mix (¾ oz.)	2,400
Vita-Crunch Granola (½ cup)	328
Duncan Hines Fudge Cake Mix (¹⁄₁₂ of cake)	439
Aunt Jemima French Toast, frozen (1 slice)	220
Oscar Mayer Frankfurter (1⅔ oz.)	364
Swanson's Fish Dinner, frozen (9¾ oz.)	1,368
Old London Corn Chips (1¾ oz.)	921

Food	Sodium Content (mg)
Hormel Corned Beef Hash (7½ oz.)	1,480
Campbell's Chunky Manhattan Clam Chowder (1 cup)	1,055
Hunt's Chili Sauce (½ cup)	1,549
Heinz Chili Beef Soup (1 cup)	1,130
Lipton Chicken Cup-a-Soup (⅓ oz.)	931
Chef Boyardee Beefaroni (7½ oz.)	1,186
Heinz Baked Beans (8 oz.)	1,307
Prince Spaghetti Sauce (4 oz.)	1,030
Shake 'n Bake Chicken Coating (2⅜ oz.)	2,557
Chicken of the Sea Tuna, oil-packed (6 oz.)	1,196
Oscar Mayer Bologna (1 slice)	342
Green Giant Broccoli Spears (3½ oz.)	444
Pepperidge Farm Herb Stuffing (8 oz.)	3,931
Betty Crocker Bisquick (8 oz.)	1,475

Sodium is added in tremendous amounts to processed foods for a number of reasons. First, it's a cheap filler that adds weight and substance to the food. Second, it adds a semblance of recognizable flavor to the bland-tasting product that often results from food processing. And third, Americans like the taste of salt. Many people are virtually addicted to salt, a fact not lost on food processors. As Senator Albert Gore points out, "There is a tremendous competitive advantage to loading food with salt and not telling people about it."

HOW TO REDUCE SALT INTAKE

Humans are not born with a craving for salt. It is an acquired taste. Many people learned to like the taste of salt as babies when their mothers salted their food or served them commercial baby food laced with salt. Dr. Lot Page, a Harvard hypertension specialist, states that "salt appetite is determined by early dietary habits and has no relationship to salt need.'' This means that a taste for salt can be *un*learned. By being weaned from salt, taste buds can be freed to savor the natural flavors of food. When that happens, the craving for salt and salty foods diminishes. Some suggestions for cutting salt in the diet are listed below.

Learn to Read Labels

It is imperative to identify the high-salt foods in your diet. This may be easily done for pickles or pretzels, but it is more difficult for processed convenience foods. The key is learning how to read the label.

Sodium is not listed on the label of processed foods merely as ''salt.'' Be aware of its other names: sodium benzoate, sodium nitrate, MSG, sodium caseinate and sodium citrate, to name a few. A good example is Kraft Chunky Blue Cheese Salad Dressing. The label shows that it contains: ''water, blue cheese (milk, cheese culture, *salt,* enzymes, artificial color), vinegar, sugar, soybean oil, *salt,* kanthan gum, propylene glycol alginate, polysorbate 60, with *sodium benzoate* and *calcium disodium* ETA to protect flavor.'' This dressing contains 240 milligrams of sodium per tablespoon.

Some labels do reveal the sodium content of the food, but most do not. The label on a can of Campbell's Cream of Mushroom Soup, for example, shows that it contains 941 milligrams of sodium in one cup. That's a lot of sodium, but hats off to Campbell's! At least they're telling what's in their soup. Then the consumer is in a position to make an intelligent decision. The sodium content of specific foods by brand name is listed in a good sodium guide, available at most bookstores.

Since most labels do not reveal the exact sodium content of the food, a rule of thumb is that if salt or any sodium product is one of the first three items on the list of ingredients, consider the product to be too high in salt and avoid it. Also, since July 1, 1986, certain claims on labels have been defined by the FDA.

Claim on Label	FDA Requirement
Low sodium	Less than 140 mg per serving
Very low sodium	Less than 35 mg per serving
Sodium-free	Less than 5 mg per serving
Reduced sodium	75% or greater reduction
Unsalted	No salt added

These are helpful in determining the sodium content of processed foods. But be careful—"unsalted" does not mean sodium-free.

Get Rid of the Salt Shaker

The use of salt as a condiment is common in the American diet. With a single teaspoon containing 2,300 milligrams of sodium, added salt can increase the sodium content of meals tremendously. It is critical, then, to reduce the use of the salt shaker—or better yet, eliminate it altogether. This is often difficult if you've been conditioned to shake salt on food out of habit or for enhanced flavor. A better choice is to use a combination of dried herbs and seasonings. Many are available commercially (Mrs. Dash, Spike), or you can blend your own. Non-sodium seasoning will add zip to food and satisfy the need to move your wrist without threatening your health.

If nothing but salt will do, consider using a one-hole shaker. Your wrist will give out before you get too much salt on your food. You can also switch the salt and pepper shakers. Since pepper shakers have fewer holes, you'll get less salt with the switch. You might also decide to put the salt shaker out only on certain days, leaving others to be salt-free.

Salt substitutes, technically potassium chloride, are not a good alternative. They trick the taste buds into thinking you're still a salt eater, so the craving for salt and salty foods doesn't go away. The only way to successfully restrict sodium in your diet is to wean your taste buds away from salt. Only then will you be satisfied with less salt in and on your food.

Limit Salt in Cooking

Many recipes, especially those using processed foods, call for too much salt. Your first step should be to question whether salt is really needed. A good example is a common recipe for French toast, which calls for one-fourth teaspoon of salt. What is salt doing in French toast? If it isn't needed, don't use it and save the sodium.

If the recipe truly needs salt, cut the amount called for by at least 25%. You will not experience any change in taste. After a time, you can cut it by that same amount again. Eventually, you'll find that your taste for salt has diminished.

Avoid salty condiments such as sea salt, garlic salt and soy sauce. (Reduced-sodium soy sauce at about 160 milligrams per teaspoon can be used in moderation.) Instead, use low-sodium herbs and spices to enhance flavor. The following herbs contain less than two milligrams of sodium per teaspoon:

Allspice	Curry powder	Oregano
Basil leaves	Dill seed	Paprika
Bay leaves	Fennel seed	Pepper (black, red, chili)
Caraway seed	Garlic powder	Poppy seed
Cardamon seed	Ginger	Rosemary leaves
Celery seed	Mace	Sage
Cinnamon	Marjoram	Savory
Cloves	Mustard powder	Sesame seed
Coriander seed	Nutmeg	Tarragon
Cumin seed	Onion powder	Thyme

Lemon juice, which cuts down the desire for salt, is a particularly good substitute.

Moderate Fast Foods

The chart on the facing page shows that fast foods, like processed foods, contain a large amount of added sodium. Since they're also high in fat, this causes a double problem in terms of heart health.

Food	Sodium Content (mg)
BURGER KING	
Double Beef Whopper with Cheese	1,206
Apple Pie	412
Whopper	842
Specialty Chicken Sandwich	1,423
McDONALD'S	
Big Mac	979
Quarter Pounder with Cheese	1,226
Fillet O' Fish	799
Egg McMuffin	885
Chocolate Shake	512
KENTUCKY FRIED CHICKEN	
Kentucky Nuggets (6)	840
Extra Crispy or Spicy Side Breast	797
ARBY'S	
Beef 'n Cheddar	1,520
Super Roast Beef	800
DAIRY QUEEN	
Chocolate Malt (large)	840
Double Hamburger with Cheese	980
Super Hot Dog with Chili	1,595

Source: Center for Science in the Public Interest.

Eat More Fresh Foods

Avoid obviously salty foods such as potato chips, salted nuts, French fries and sauerkraut. The fewer processed and fast foods in your diet pattern, the more control you have over salt intake. The key is more fresh foods—they taste better, they're fresher and they have no added sodium.

THE FIFTH PRINCIPLE: INCREASE WATER INTAKE

There are a number of reasons for increasing the intake of water. First, water is filling, so it helps with weight control. In analyzing why most short-term diets are not successful, many health professionals have concluded that the calories on these diets are so low that dieters feel deprived and dissatisfied immediately after eating. They simply aren't getting enough food to feel full, so they become discouraged and revert to the old way of eating. Water, along with complex carbohydrates, helps to maintain satisfaction without adding calories. Six to eight glasses, or two quarts, of water a day not only keeps the stomach feeling full but actually decreases hunger pangs and prevents snacking and overeating. Research shows that snacking in particular is often the result of mistaking thirst for hunger.

Water also helps the body to use stored fat more efficiently as fuel. Studies show that the kidneys need a sufficient supply of water to function properly. When the water supply is insufficient, the liver is forced to pick up some of the kidney's functions. One of the principal jobs of the liver is to metabolize body fat into usable energy. However, if the liver is busy doing the kidney's work, its own ability to metabolize fat is impaired. As a result, the body burns less fat as fuel and more is stored for future use.

Sufficient water in the diet also relieves fluid retention, the cause of unattractive "puffiness." The body sees insufficient water as a threat to survival. As a result, it holds on to every drop (much as it conserves fat cells during a crash diet). Emergency rations of water are stored outside the cells, ready for immediate use. The storage of this water shows up chiefly as swollen feet, ankles, wrists, hands and legs. Diuretics, which force the body to eliminate some of the stored water, can provide relief but are not a good solution. They force nutrients to be expelled along with the water, and their effect is not permanent. In the view of the body, the forced loss of water only heightens the threat of insufficient water. Virtually as soon as the diuretic works, the body will replace the expelled water and fluid retention will once again result.

Two quarts of water a day satisfies the body's needs and dissipates the perceived threat to health. Water is processed and excreted on a regular basis. No "emergency" supply is retained.

When considering the need for water, many people make the mistake of equating "fluids" with "water." Water, or H_2O, is specifically what the body craves. It is especially important in a weight control program, as other beverages can contain a great amount of calories and can sabotage a diet. (Consider this: a glass of whole milk, generally not considered "diet-busting," is 159 calories; a brownie, which everyone knows is high in calories, contains just 97!) For some people, beverages may account for half the total caloric intake. Beverages, rather than solid food, may be their biggest calorie problem.

Finally, water contains no calories. A comparison to other beverages illustrates why water should be the beverage of choice.

Beverage	Calories	Calories per Oz.
BEER (12 oz.)		
Beck's Dark	156	13
Budweiser	150	13
Coors	142	12
Coors Light	102	9
Guinness Extra Stout	192	16
Heineken	152	13
Michelob	163	14
Miller High Life	150	13
Miller Lite	96	8
WINE (3½ oz.)		
Champagne	71	20
Dessert, sweet	142	44
Red table	76	22
Sherry	147	42
Vermouth, dry	105	30
White table	80	23
LIQUOR		
Bailey's Irish Cream (1 oz.)	85	85
Brandy (1 oz.)	69	69
Cordials, liqueurs (1 oz.)	97	97
Daiquiri (3½ oz.)	122	35

Beverage	Calories	Calories per Oz.
LIQUOR (cont'd.)		
Gin, rum, vodka, whiskey, 86-proof (1½ oz.)	105	65
Gin, rum, vodka, whiskey, 100-proof (1½ oz.)	125	83
Manhattan (3¼ oz.)	233	72
Martini (2¼ oz.)	152	61
Piña Colada (3 oz.)	450	150
SOFT DRINKS (12 oz.)		
Quinine soda	113	9
Club soda	0	0
Dad's Root Beer	158	13
Shasta Orange Soda	172	11
Bitter lemon	192	16
Pepsi	158	13
Diet Pepsi	0	0
Coca-Cola	144	12
Diet Coke	0	0
Dr Pepper	144	12
7-Up	146	12
Diet 7-Up	0	0
Mountain Dew	178	15
MILK DRINKS		
Whole milk (8 oz.)	159	20
2% milk (8 oz.)	120	15
1% milk (8 oz.)	102	13
Skim milk (8 oz.)	90	11
Buttermilk (8 oz.)	99	12
Eggnog, no alcohol (4 oz.)	171	43
Malted milk, chocolate (8 oz.)	233	29
Chocolate milk, whole (8 oz.)	208	26
Hot cocoa (8 oz.)	218	27
Nestlé Quik chocolate milk mix (8 oz.)	245	31
Nestlé Quik chocolate milk mix, sugar-free (8 oz.)	140	18
Burger King vanilla shake (16 oz.)	340	21

Beverage	Calories	Calories per Oz.
MILK DRINKS (cont'd.)		
McDonald's chocolate shake (16 oz.)	383	24
Dairy Queen chocolate shake, regular (16 oz.)	710	44
FRUIT JUICES (8 oz.)		
Apple juice	118	15
Coconut milk	605	76
Cranapple juice, regular	173	22
Grape juice	170	21
Grapefruit juice, canned	101	13
Grapefruit juice, fresh	96	12
Orange juice, fresh	112	14
Orange juice, canned, unsweetened	120	15
Orange juice, frozen, reconstituted	122	15
Orange juice, imitation	120	15
Pear-apple juice	110	14
Pineapple juice, canned, unsweetened	138	17
FRUIT DRINKS (8 oz.)		
Country Time drink mixes, all flavors	88	11
Crystal Light drink mix, orange, sugar-free	4	0.5
Del Monte pineapple-orange juice drink	120	15
Gatorade bottled drinks, all flavors	56	7
Hawaiian Punch canned drinks, all flavors	120	15
Hawaiian Punch drink mix	104	13
Hi-C canned drinks, all flavors	120	15
Hi-C drink mixes, all flavors	104	13
Kool-Aid drink mixes, all flavors except lemonade	104	13
Kool-Aid drink mixes, all flavors, sugar-free	4	0.5
Kool-Aid lemonade drink mix	104	13

Beverage	Calories	Calories per Oz.
FRUIT DRINKS (8 oz.) (cont'd.)		
Lemonade from frozen concentrate	107	14
Tang drink mixes, all flavors	120	15
VEGETABLE DRINKS (8 oz.)		
Carrot juice	93	12
Mott's Clamato	114	14
Tomato juice	46	6
V-8 vegetable juice cocktail	52	7
COFFEE AND TEA (6 oz.)		
Tea, clear	2	0.3
Tea, instant, sweetened	86	11
Tea, instant, unsweetened	0	0
Magic Mountain instant herb tea	4	0.5
Postum cereal beverage	36	5
Coffee, black	2.7	0.3
Coffee, instant, black	1.3	0.2
General Foods "International Coffee," Irish Mocha Mint	67	8

Source: USDA.

Drinking six to eight glasses of water each day is essential for good health. Without sufficient water, the body can't metabolize stored fat efficiently or function properly. In addition, drinking enough water each day will help wean you from soft drinks and other beverages. Cold water is absorbed into the system more quickly than warm water. Moreover, some evidence suggests that drinking cold water may help you to burn extra fat. Plan your water intake and try to make it a habit. For example, automatically drink a glass of water before each meal. At first such scheduling is a hassle, but soon it can become routine.

A WORD ABOUT CAFFEINE

Americans consume 33 million gallons of coffee a day, equal to 30 seconds of full flow at Niagara Falls. The average person drinks about 450 cups of coffee a year. One of the chief by-products of such a high level of coffee consumption is an inordinate intake of caffeine.

Caffeine negatively impacts cardiovascular health and weight control efforts. It is a drug that stimulates the heart, forcing it to work harder and in some instances producing extra heartbeats. Caffeine can also increase blood pressure and, according to some studies, increases the amount of fatty acids in the bloodstream. A Johns Hopkins University study of over 1,000 men found that those who drank five cups of coffee a day had nearly three times the risk of heart disease as those who drank no coffee. Research to date has not conclusively linked heart disease to moderate consumption of coffee, but it seems reasonable that those concerned with cardiac health should avoid overstimulation of the heart by caffeine.

From a weight control standpoint, caffeine is also negative. First, it causes blood sugar to drop, causing feelings of hunger. In addition, caffeine is a diuretic, causing the body to expel fluid. So, if you're counting on coffee or tea to increase body fluids, this won't happen. The same holds true for cocoa, chocolate and soft drinks.

	Caffeine Content (mg)
COFFEE (1 cup)	
Drip	146
Percolated	110
Instant, regular	53
Decaffeinated	2
TEA (1 cup)	
Brewed, U.S. brands	40
Brewed, imported	60
Instant	30
COCOA AND CHOCOLATE	
Cocoa Beverage (6 oz., water mix)	10
Milk Chocolate Candy (1 oz.)	6
SOFT DRINKS (12-oz. can)	
Diet Mr. Pibb	52
Mountain Dew	52

	Caffeine Content (mg)
SOFT DRINKS (12-oz. can) (cont'd.)	
Mellow Yellow	51
Tab	44
Dr Pepper	38
Pepsi-Cola	37
Diet Pepsi	34
Coca-Cola	33

Many health professionals feel that a cup or two of coffee a day may be fine. However, a diet pattern that contains too much coffee, tea, soft drinks or candy bars will not provide for good health.

STARTING THE 500-CALORIE SOLUTION

Freestyle eating, or consumption without thought, and crash dieting represent negative dietary choices that are neither beneficial to health nor effective for permanent weight control. Choosing to eat for permanent weight control (and thus for cholesterol and blood pressure control) is one thing; making it work is quite another. A healthy diet pattern must be based on accepted nutritional principles, but that alone will not ensure success. It must also:

■ Be realistic, attainable, and compatible with the modern American lifestyle. Spending eight hours in the kitchen preparing healthy food is not feasible. Few people have the time; still fewer have the interest. Food preparation must be practical. It is the same with eating out. If going to a restaurant means bringing along homemade salad dressing, the diet pattern won't work. It must offer realistic choices at home and in a restaurant.

■ Include food that tastes good. There is no argument that a diet pattern based on sound principles is better—but no one eats principles! No matter how healthy it is or how much weight is lost, few people will accept the new way of eating if the food isn't appetizing.

■ Focus on familiar foods. For example, fatty red meat,

such as sirloin steak, is central to the American diet. However, it is very high in fat—contributing to both excess
calories and cholesterol—so its consumption should be reduced. Tofu is a healthy alternative: high in protein, low
in fat. Despite understanding that it is a healthier choice,
most Americans would not trade beef for tofu on a regular
basis. Permanent change is established by making familiar
foods healthier—in this instance, by choosing fish, fowl or
leaner cuts of red meat to reduce fat.

▪ Avoid emphasizing the negative. Most dietary
changes are thought of exclusively as foods to be avoided.
Obviously, this must be a consideration. It's tough to control weight or cholesterol if the consumption of French fries
is open-ended. But to view diet pattern in a totally negative
light causes feelings of deprivation that invariably lead back
to the old diet. Positive change is not so much the loss of
old foods as the gaining of new ones. If you're enjoying
healthy, low-calorie food that tastes great, there's less reason to miss unhealthy, high-calorie foods.

▪ Be moderate. It's unrealistic to ban certain foods forever. For example, fresh fruit is better than pie or cake as
a dessert choice, but a peach with a candle in it may not
do much for a birthday celebration. For some, a birthday
is not a birthday without chocolate cake, so the positive
choice is to eat *some* cake. By enjoying a piece without
guilt, taste buds and emotions are satisfied. Afterwards, it's
easy to resume the healthy diet pattern. This establishes a
realistic perspective . . . just be sure not to celebrate a
birthday once a week!

A word of caution: while it's very important in the initial
period of diet pattern change to write down meal plans and
actual behavior daily, it's also important to *avoid* one daily
activity—weighing yourself! The body doesn't drop weight
in a predictable, orderly way. When you climb on the bathroom scale every day, you set yourself up for failure. As
nutritionist Dr. Sandra Haber says, "The scale becomes a
judge of how well you've done that day. You may know
that you haven't overeaten, but if the scale needle hasn't

moved, or worse, it's inched upward, you believe the scale, not your own actions." Discouragement can cause over-eating. Remember, the scale measures weight, not fat. Weigh yourself no more than twice a week—first thing in the morning, naked, and on an empty stomach.

KEEP A DIARY

Most people assume that they eat—and overeat—because of physical hunger. They do not. A great many are moved to eat and to select certain foods by external or internal cues that associate eating and/or food with activities, people and mood. For example, a person might eat because of the clock, an external cue. When it strikes noon, it's lunch-time—time to eat, whether hungry or not. Coffee breaks automatically call for certain foods, usually calorically dense doughnuts or Danish pastry. Another external cue is the smell of food. The aroma of frying hamburgers or freshly baked cookies can signal false hunger. Some activities—driving, reading, watching a movie and especially watching television—can cause mechanical eating. People tend to become so involved in what they're doing that they lose track of what's going into their mouths. Other people can be a cue to eat. Associating a favorite aunt with pies and cookies from childhood might cause a person to over-eat when visiting her. Many people continue to "earn" parental love by leaving a clean plate.

Internal cues to eat are just as motivating. These include anger, happiness, anxiety, boredom, depression and lone-liness. Food is often a reward, a consolation prize, a pac-ifier, a stimulant or a security blanket. It can be an easy fix for whatever ails. Emotions do not provide good rea-sons to eat, yet many health professionals believe them to be the single greatest reason for overeating by Americans.

A good way to begin to monitor your eating is to record daily habits for a week or two. This is a hassle initially but is critical to revealing dietary habits that need to be changed. The real bottom line is that recording behavior provides us with a better awareness of what, when and why we eat. Overeating and poor food selection are not isolated events; they're linked to lifestyle influences. If eating cues are understood, changing behavior and diet pattern becomes easier. On the next page is a sample food diary that shows how to record your eating habits.

It's also important to track calories when recording present food habits. This provides awareness of how many calories you're taking in. For this reason, the recipes in this book provide caloric information. In addition, you may want to consult a calorie dictionary, available at most bookstores, which provides caloric content of all foods, including brand names. This process allows you to relate present caloric intake to the calories necessary to sustain ideal weight. If you don't know the number of calories taken in, you won't be able to utilize the 500-Calorie Solution effectively.

Recording calories is a must for the first month or two, but it need not go on forever. It is *not* a way of life on the 500-Calorie Solution. In establishing a new, permanent way of eating, more emphasis is placed on healthy dietary principles than on counting calories. Understanding dietary principles and how to apply them to everyday life is the secret to long-term healthy eating. However, recording eating behavior and calorie consumption is the first step in the process of change.

For those primarily interested in weight control, the food diary is even more important. It allows for a comparison at the end of the day between your meal plan and what has actually been eaten. If you find that the plan called for 2,000 calories but 2,800 calories were consumed, a problem is evident. Whatever contributed to the extra calories— second helpings, bedtime snack, afternoon binge—is clearly identified in writing. Then you can take action to be more careful. On the other hand, if you planned to skip the cheeseburger and fries in favor of broiled chicken—and you did!—celebration is in order. In either case, the diary provides the information necessary to make adjustments

FOOD DIARY

Day of the Week: *Wednesday*

When	Where	With Whom	Why	Level of Hunger	Activity	What Food/ How Much	Calories
8 to 9 A.M.	Den	Alone	Bored	Moderate	Watch TV	4 doughnuts	800
12 noon	McDonald's	Kids	Lunch	Hungry	Supervise Lunch	Big Mac	570
						French fries	220
						Coke	72
3:30 P.M.	Kitchen	Mom	Happy	Low	Talking	Coffeecake	150
						Coffee	
6:00 P.M.	Kitchen	Family	Dinner	Moderate	Supervise Dinner	Fried chicken	
						Drumstick	87
						Breast	160
						1/4 cup mashed potatoes	92
						Gravy	50
						1/4 cup beans, buttered	40
						Milk	157
10:30 P.M.	Den	Bob	Tired	Moderate	Watch TV	12 Oreos	600
						Milk	157

TOTAL CALORIES: 3,155

and keep moving in the right direction. As Will Rogers once said, ''You can be on the right track, but if you don't keep moving, you're going to be hit.''

MEAL PLANNING: ESSENTIAL FOR CHANGE

Planning is essential to the success of most endeavors, whether it's to break old habits or to attain financial security. This is particularly true with regard to permanent dietary change. For it to succeed, the technique of meal planning is critical. If it's five o'clock and you haven't planned for a healthy dinner, it's too easy to gravitate to the old, familiar food pattern. If you haven't planned for lunch and you're pressed for time, anything that is quick might do—a Big Mac, a hot dog on the street or a candy bar. If you don't plan ahead to trade your breakfast croissant for a bagel or bran muffin, it won't happen.

Eat Calories Earlier in the Day

In the modern American lifestyle, the main meal of the day is dinner. The pace of life today is such that many people skip breakfast or lunch. Of those who do eat these meals, a number get insufficient nutrition—coffee and a roll for breakfast, fast food for lunch. When they get home in the evening and relax, many times with the use of alcohol, they often become ravenous and eat much more than they need. This eating pattern does not promote weight loss, weight control or good health.

A better way is to eat the majority of calories at breakfast and lunch so that they can be burned during the course of the day. New York *Times* columnist Jane Brody offers the following example to put this concept into perspective. ''If you're driving from New York to Los Angeles, does it make more sense to fill the gas tank after you've arrived in Los Angeles? . . . or before you leave New York?''

A recent study illustrated how timing affects caloric utilization. Two groups of women were fed 2,000 calories a day. The only difference was that the first group received all 2,000 at breakfast; the second group ate all 2,000 at dinner. The results were direct: every person in the first group lost weight, and every person in the second group gained weight. A test by the USDA of the feeding habits of yearling steers produced similar results. Two groups of steers were fed two pounds of cracked corn a day. One group was fed at 8:00 A.M., the other at 1:30 P.M. After 72 days, the afternoon steers had gained 30% more weight than the morning group.

Shifting calories from late in the day to earlier is a product of planning. Breaking a pattern of nothing or a sweet roll for breakfast—and a double helping of roast beef for dinner—will not happen without planning. It takes some effort, but it is a weight control technique that brings long-term results.

Use a Meal Planner

Meal planning is simply deciding beforehand what you'll eat for a particular period of time. By making these decisions in advance, much of the "on-the-spot" stress is alleviated. With a meal plan designed for health, you can have confidence that you'll be eating for health and weight control.

Start by making a meal plan for a week in advance. The Meal Planner on the facing page shows breakfast, lunch and dinner, plus a snack, for two days. Writing the plan will serve as a reminder and will foster commitment and incentive to succeed. Remember, planning means control.

Substitution

A key to successful meal planning is an understanding of creative substitution—the replacing of unhealthy foods or ingredients in the meal with healthier ones. The easiest substitution is a one-for-one exchange: roast chicken for roast beef; salmon or halibut for sirloin steak; fresh apples for apple pie; unsalted chips for salted chips; skim milk for whole milk; fruit juice for soft drinks. These changes

MEAL PLANNER

Day: *Monday*

Meal	Menu	Calories
BREAKFAST	Scrambled egg with tomato salsa; English Muffin Bread with Strawberry Preserves; ¼ cantaloupe; skim milk	364
LUNCH	Cup of chicken broth (defatted); sliced breast of turkey on rye bread with hot Chinese mustard, tomato, onion and lettuce; Granny Smith apple; iced tea	307
DINNER	Poached Salmon with Lemon; Vermicelli-Stuffed Tomatoes; Steamed Snow Peas; Fresh Raspberries with Strawberry Purée	540
SNACK	Popcorn	23
	TOTAL CALORIES:	1,234

Day: *Tuesday*

Meal	Menu	Calories
BREAKFAST	Oat-bran Muffin with Apple Butter; fresh blueberries; skim milk	337
LUNCH	French Market Soup; French baguette; mandarin oranges; skim milk	298
DINNER	Pan-fried Chicken; Roast Potatoes with Rosemary; Pan-steamed Asparagus; fresh pineapple and papaya	402
SNACK	¼ cantaloupe	35
	TOTAL CALORIES:	1,072

are simple but effective. The calories saved in a year by switching from a glazed doughnut daily to a bran muffin, for example, represent a weight loss of 11 pounds.

A more sophisticated form of substitution involves modifying recipe ingredients and cooking methods. This is a key concept in the 500-Calorie Solution. It calls for the substitution of low-calorie, healthful ingredients for high-calorie, not-so-healthful items in a recipe—while preserving the food's familiar flavor.

A good way to start creative substitution is simply to change the red meat in a recipe, leaving all other ingredients the same. For example, most taco recipes call for hamburger, which is high in fat and calories. By substituting shredded chicken or ground turkey for hamburger, the best of both worlds is gained. The taco is lower in fat and calories—good for weight control and lower cholesterol—and one can still eat a favorite food.

Next, learn to change other ingredients to reduce fat, salt and sugar, and calories. Instead of sour cream in a recipe, use non-fat yogurt. If it calls for two eggs, use one egg yolk and two egg whites. If the recipe is made with evaporated milk, use skim evaporated milk. Instead of butter or shortening, use safflower oil margarine.

Also, begin to question ingredients. Is salt necessary in the recipe? Can it be made with less oil? As you progress with a healthy eating pattern, many opportunities to improve recipes by lowering fat and calories—without sacrificing flavor—become apparent.

Cooking methods also should be questioned. Rather than sautéing mushrooms in a butter-drenched skillet, cook them in a nonstick pan using chicken broth, flavored vinegar or wine. Instead of deep-fat-frying potatoes for French fries, oven-bake them. Such changes preserve taste but reduce unhealthy ingredients—and calories.

The 500-Calorie Solution, through meal planning and creative substitution, recognizes that there must be a balance between health and quality-of-life concerns. In doing so, it creates a diet pattern that can be enjoyed as a way of life. Formal meal planning doesn't need to go on forever. At the start, it is a necessity. After a while the process will become so second nature that you'll automatically gravitate to healthier foods, ingredients and cooking methods. Be sure to include all meals in your plan. The typical American pattern of no breakfast, skipping lunch, eating an enormous dinner and snacking from dessert to bedtime produces excess weight. Skipping meals as a means of cutting calories often backfires. Research shows one result is the Restrained Eaters Syndrome. When a chronic meal skipper sits down to eat, the body—used to being starved—encourages overeating to store food by ignoring satiety signals and stimulating the appetite.

The result is that meal skippers often eat more calories at one meal than they would have at three meals. According to Dr. Wayne Calloway, director of the Center for Clinical Nutrition at George Washington University, "Animals do the same, so it may be an innate biological response." Others believe this to be a psychological reaction to deprivation. Because you haven't had a cookie for a while, it tastes extra good—so you eat the whole package! In addition, meal skipping works like crash dieting—it tends to lower metabolism by 10% to 30%. This means that you burn calories more slowly and need fewer calories to survive, making it easier to gain weight.

Snacks are not necessarily diet villains, so you don't have to cut them out. Instead, plan for them. Studies show that snackers can get essential nutrients from between-meal eating. Obviously, this is not a license for open-ended consumption of candy and junk food—Twinkies or Snickers will provide little more than empty calories. But apples, carrots and popcorn as snacks can fill and keep an appetite under control. If you're used to a snack, it's more realistic to plan for a healthy one than to deny. Schedule a bowl of strawberries, for example, instead of a bowl of strawberry ice cream. Studies show that incorporating healthy snacks into the plan can result in more frequent but smaller meals and actually help to reduce weight.

CHOOSING TO EAT HEALTHFULLY

It is possible to create a diet pattern that promotes cardiac health and permanent weight control. A new "diet" isn't needed—a new style of eating is, and this new style is reflected in the 500-Calorie Solution. "Diet" should be thought of as the foods eaten daily, not as a torturous starvation regimen or a set of do's and don'ts. In short, it is essential to learn how to eat well naturally. Permanent dietary change is the only way that long-term success can be achieved. It is the key to making healthy eating the rule rather than the exception.

In constructing your diet pattern, it's important to keep the following two concepts in mind:

- First, understand clearly that what you eat is a choice. Every day you make decisions about what, when and how much to eat. Even a poor eating pattern that leads to overweight or coronary heart disease is a choice. Therefore, if negative choices can be made, so can positive ones. The 500-Calorie Solution gives you the tools necessary to choose a healthful diet pattern and to put that choice into action. But it all starts with you. A healthy diet pattern is within your power.

- Second, think in terms of permanent changes in the way you eat. Eating in a healthy manner for a week or two, then reverting to your old dietary lifestyle, doesn't accomplish anything. The 500-Calorie Solution is designed to fundamentally change eating habits so that healthful eating becomes a lifetime affair.

Sound dietary principles and low-calorie, heart-healthy recipes are the foundation, but by themselves they will not produce results. The key component is *you*. If you truly desire to eat in a healthy manner to foster cardiac health and weight control, if you've made healthy eating a lifestyle choice, then you'll be able to use the tools provided to succeed.

A healthy diet, like good health itself, is a choice.

CHAPTER 5

IMPLEMENTING THE 500-CALORIE SOLUTION WITH EXERCISE

Neither cardiovascular health nor permanent weight control comes about through diet exclusively. A sound diet pattern needs to be balanced by a program of regular exercise. This is why the 500-Calorie Solution has two components: diet *and* exercise.

Many people have the impression that exercise is not a problem in the American lifestyle—that today we're in the midst of a fitness boom. Almost everyone seems to be involved in jogging, walking or biking. Aerobics classes are full. Sales of exercise books, tapes and equipment have skyrocketed. Shorts, shirts, sweats and other exercise gear have become *de rigueur* for men and women of all ages. Indeed, 25% of all shoes sold today in the United States are athletic shoes. It seems as if everyone is exercising. Unfortunately, this is a myth. In reality, 45% of the population admits to being completely sedentary. And of the 55% that claim to exercise, it's estimated that fewer than one in three do it often or hard enough to benefit weight control or cardiovascular health.

There's a further problem—one that may explode like a time bomb. The few people who do exercise regularly are adults. Recent studies illustrate that children and adolescents are barely active at all. There are numerous indications that many of today's children and adolescents have never been in shape and, given a continuation of their present lifestyle, may never get in shape. The implications for future overweight and coronary heart disease problems are frightening.

Fitness experts agree that physical activity is fundamental to fat loss and sustained weight control. That there is a direct link between exercise and weight control is hardly news today, but it wasn't always that way. The concept of weight "control" as opposed to weight "loss" is relatively new. In the days when most people slimmed down by dieting alone (and then regained the weight and dieted again), there was no goal but to lose weight. People went on crash diets, often successfully, but then they faced the problem of what to do next. They couldn't stay on the crash diet forever, as that would impair health. If they came off the diet, however, and returned to the old way of eating, the lost weight would reappear.

Recent studies have shown that many overweight people do not on average consume more calories than people of normal weight. Obviously, they consume sufficient calories to stay overweight, but they do not necessarily eat more than other people do. A study of San Francisco area runners, for example, showed that the men consumed an average of 2,960 calories a day but weighed 20% less than inactive men their age who consumed only 2,360 calories a day; the women averaged 570 calories more per day, but they weighed 30% less than their inactive counterparts. Other studies have yielded the same results. One involving 350 overweight subjects showed that in 70% of the group the excess weight was related to inactivity; in only 3.2% was it linked to increased food intake.

The difference between overweight and normal weight, these studies suggest, is not solely a product of caloric intake. It is also the result of physical activity levels. A man who has an office job and sits most of the day burns up only 2,500 calories a day. A man doing heavy physical labor, however, will burn up as much as 4,500 calories a day, while one involved in sports and very heavy physical work may burn up to 6,000 calories daily. The vast majority of the overweight people involved in these studies were not as physically active as the people of normal weight. They were much more efficient in the use of their bodies in daily tasks, thereby burning fewer calories in the course of a day. In a study using pedometers to measure distances walked by overweight and normal-weight women in the same occupation, it was found that the former walked about 2.1 miles every day while the latter averaged 4.9 miles.

Even during formal exercising, overweight people often move less than persons of normal weight. In a Harvard University study conducted by Dr. Jean Mayer, a comparison of the amount of physical activity between overweight and normal weight high school girls was made by taking 30-second motion pictures every three minutes of the girls playing volleyball and tennis. The overweight girls were inactive (standing still) 80% to 90% of the time, hitting the volleyball when it came directly to them but seldom moving to go after it.

A number of experts have concluded that a sedentary lifestyle is a prime cause of chronic overweight. According to physiologist Dr. William Haskell of the Stanford Medical School, lack of exercise is "the major culprit in the weight gain most Americans are faced with." He speaks for many health professionals when he says that there has been an overemphasis on caloric intake, with "too little emphasis placed on the role of energy expenditures."

While it's crucial to emphasize the benefits of regular exercise for fat loss and weight control, the 500-Calorie Solution doesn't lose sight of an important perspective: exercise by itself is not a good method of losing weight in a timely fashion. Physical activity does burn up calories, but at a very slow rate. The following chart illustrates the number of calories burned for each minute of continuing activity in various forms of exercise.

CALORIES BURNED PER MINUTE

	Weight in Pounds				
Activity	Up to 130	131 to 152	152 to 170	171 to 187	188+
Badminton/volleyball	4.4	5.4	6.1	6.8	7.4
Baseball	3.6	4.5	5.0	5.6	6.1
Basketball	5.5	6.7	7.5	8.4	9.2
Bowling (nonstop)	5.2	6.3	7.1	7.9	8.7
Calisthenics	3.9	4.8	5.4	5.9	6.5
Cycling:					
5½ mph	3.9	4.8	5.4	5.9	6.5
13 mph	8.3	10.2	11.5	12.7	14.0
Dancing:					
Moderate	3.3	4.0	4.4	5.0	5.5
Vigorous	4.4	5.4	6.1	6.7	7.4
Golf:					
Twosome	4.2	5.2	5.8	6.4	7.1
Foursome	3.2	3.9	4.4	4.8	5.3
Handball/squash/ racquetball	7.6	9.3	10.4	11.6	12.7
Housework	3.2	3.9	4.4	4.8	5.3
Rope skipping:					
70 counts/minute	6.0	7.4	8.3	9.2	10.0
100 counts/minute	9.9	12.0	13.6	15.0	16.5
Rowing:					
Leisurely	3.9	4.8	5.4	5.9	6.5
Vigorous	10.6	13.0	14.6	16.2	17.8
Running:					
5½ mph	8.3	10.2	11.5	12.7	14.0
7 mph	10.8	13.3	14.9	16.6	18.0
9 mph	12.9	14.8	16.6	19.9	20.2
Skating	4.4	5.4	6.1	6.6	7.4
Soccer	6.9	8.5	9.6	10.6	11.7
Swimming:					
Crawl (moderate)	3.8	4.6	5.1	5.7	6.3
Crawl (vigorous)	8.3	10.1	11.4	12.6	13.9
Sidestroke	6.5	7.9	8.9	9.9	10.9

Activity	Weight in Pounds				
	Up to 130	131 to 152	152 to 170	171 to 187	188+
Tennis:					
Moderate	5.4	6.6	7.4	8.2	9.0
Vigorous	7.6	9.3	10.4	11.6	12.7
Walking:					
2 mph	2.7	3.3	3.8	4.2	4.6
4½ mph	5.0	6.3	7.1	7.9	8.6
Up/down stairs	9.3	11.4	12.8	14.2	15.6
Weight lifting	6.0	7.2	8.2	8.9	9.4

Source: American College of Sports Medicine.

Because fat is such a highly concentrated form of energy, it takes a long time to burn. Losing a pound of fat— 3,500 calories—requires hours of strenuous physical activity. A 150-pound woman, for example, would have to walk for more than 9 hours at an aerobic pace (4 miles per hour) to burn 3,500 calories. A fit runner burns fewer than 1,000 calories on a 10-mile run (the winner of the New York Marathon loses about three-quarters of a pound of fat!), which barely covers a hot fudge sundae with whipped cream and nuts. It doesn't take a trained mathematician to conclude that losing weight exclusively through calories burned is painfully slow.

Exercise by itself will produce weight loss of about one-third of a pound a week in fat people and about one-tenth of a pound a week in people of essentially normal weight. Because this rate seems too slow for many individuals, fad diets geared for rapid weight loss have continued to be more popular than exercise programs even though such diets do not produce permanent results.

For years, exercise was viewed in one way: its only benefit in relation to weight loss came from the calories burned in the exercise itself. That's the reason some medical professionals have historically denigrated the importance of exercise. Indeed, certain doctors in the past told their overweight patients to cut calories and forget exercise, advising that "the best exercise you can get is pushing yourself away from the table.'' This view has changed, but it's important to keep in mind that exercise alone is not effective. The 500-Calorie Solution, by combining diet and exercise, results in fat loss and permanent weight control. A little exercise and a little calorie cutting can add up pretty quickly to 500 calories a day and weight loss of about a pound a week.

The need for a diet/exercise balance is not always understood. Problems can occur when people justify huge amounts of extra calories because they're on an exercise program. They figure that because they run, for example, an extra one or two jelly doughnuts won't hurt. It's great to run, but fueling that running with cheeseburgers and shakes won't result in cardiovascular health or weight control. This is confirmed by research into the amount of exercise time needed to offset high-calorie foods:

		Minutes to Work Off Food			
Food	Calories	Walking 4 mph	Cycling 10 mph	Swimming Crawl	Jogging 11 Minute/Mile
Bagel (1)	165	28	20	19	18
Bourbon/Scotch (1 glass)	110	19	13.5	12.5	12
Beer (12 oz.)	150	26	18.5	17	16.5
Big Mac (1)	570	98	70	66	63
Brownie (1)	97	17	12	11	10.5
Butter/margarine (1 Tbs.)	100	17	12	11	10.5
Cinnamon roll (1)	174	30	21	20	19
Chocolate (1 oz.)	152	26	19	17.5	16.5
Cookie (1 small)	50	8.5	6	5.5	5
Corn chips (1 oz.)	160	28	20	18	17.5
Crackers (5)	105	18	13	12	11.5
Cream puff (1)	296	51	37	34	32.5
Danish (1 small)	148	26	18	17	16
Jelly doughnut (1)	226	39	28	26	24.5
French fries (1 serving)	220	37.5	27	25	24
Ice cream (1 scoop)	186	32	23	21	20
Ice cream bar	144	25	18	16.5	15.5

		Minutes to Work Off Food		
Food	Calories	Walking 4 mph	Cycling 10 mph	Swimming Crawl	Jogging 11 Minutc/Mile
Mayonnaise (1 Tbs.)	100	17	12	11	10.5
Milkshake	324	56	40	37	35.5
Peanuts (10)	50	8.5	6	5.5	5
Pie:					
Apple	410	71	51	47	45
Pecan	668	115	82	77	73
Pizza (½ of 10″ pie)	500	86	62	57	55
Potato chips (10)	110	19	13.5	12.5	12
Salad dressing					
(1 Tbs.)	80	14	10	9	8.5
Soft drink,					
sugared (8 oz.)	100	17	12	11	10.5
Sunflower seeds					
(¼ cup)	203	35	25	23	22
Tartar sauce (1 Tbs.)	89	15	11	10	9
Trail mix (½ cup)	600	103	74	69	66
Vegetable oil					
(1 Tbs.)	125	22	15.5	14.5	13.5
Wine (1 glass)	140	24	17	16	15

Source: The Bob Hope International Heart Research Institute.

While it must be acknowledged that exercise of and by itself is not a very effective weight loss technique, neither is diet. Crash diets have done more for weight gain than for weight loss in the United States; indeed, if dieting by itself resulted in permanent weight control, we would be a nation of thin people. Taken together, diet and exercise can produce the 500-Calorie Solution, the most effective way to lose weight and keep it off permanently.

EXERCISE FOR WEIGHT CONTROL

Physical activity is essential for weight loss and weight control. Unfortunately, many misconceptions exist concerning an effective exercise program. One is the belief that housework or "running around the office" constitutes exercise. People often are tired at the end of a day from these activities and think their fatigue is evidence of a physically active life; for most people, however, that tired feeling comes from mental not physical exertion. Meetings, car pools and cooking may cause stress in our lives, but they offer too little opportunity to burn calories. Neither office-work nor housework effectively promotes weight control.

A second misconception is the belief that certain exercises can burn fat from specific parts of the body. Many people who subscribe to this theory recognize the need for physical activity but concentrate their efforts on shaping certain areas of the body. They use spot reduction exercises, such as situps and leg lifts, which are essentially weight-lifting activities and are great for muscle tone but have little effect on body fat. Much of the popularity of spot reduction exercise stems from a lack of understanding about the relationship between muscle and fat. A man with a potbelly, for example, might start a situp program because he thinks there's a connection between the stomach muscles and the fat that makes up his potbelly. In reality, however, no connection exists between the two. The layer of fat on top of the muscle doesn't belong to that muscle; it belongs to the whole body. It will ''melt away'' only if the demand for calories from the entire body is so great that the fat is burned for energy. Situps can result in larger, stronger and firmer stomach muscles, but will have little effect on the fat deposit sitting on top of those muscles.

The best fat reduction exercises are those that involve the most muscle tissue. The more muscle involved in the activity, the greater the demand for fat as fuel. Spot reduction exercises do not demand a great deal of energy and are therefore ineffective in burning fat; however, when large sets of muscles, such as those of the legs, are exercised continuously, fat will be drawn from all parts of the body to fulfill energy requirements—and body fat will be lost.

The same rationale applies to a woman with excess fat. Generally when a woman gains weight, subcutaneous fat (which lies just under the skin) is deposited from bottom to top—first at the back of the thighs, then on the outside of the thighs, the hips, around the waist and finally on the upper body, especially on the upper arms. Fat deposits typically melt away in reverse order from how they were put on, that is, from top to bottom. The puckering in a woman's legs, popularly called cellulite, is simply lots of fat under a different skin texture. The skin texture, rather than the type of fat, causes the ''dimples''; the fat itself is the same as that found in other parts of the body. There is nothing special about cellulite or its removal. The term exists in order to sell gimmicks and notions that promise effortless fat reduction but simply do not work.

What does work to reduce body fat is exercise, specifically what is known as aerobic exercise. This type of physical activity makes it relatively easy for exercise to contribute 250 calories to the 500-Calorie Solution.

The following example illustrates the time needed in a variety of aerobic activities for a 150-pound person to burn 250 calories. A person weighing more than 150 pounds would burn more calories; one weighing less would burn fewer calories.

Activity	Calories per Hour	Minutes to Burn 250 Calories
Walking (4 mph)	355	42
Tennis (moderate)	425	35
Swimming (crawl 45 yards/ minute)	530	30
Downhill skiing	585	27
Handball/squash	600	25
Tennis (vigorous)	600	25
Jogging (5.5 mph)	650	22
Biking (13 mph)	850	18

Often it's discouraging to review the exercise/calorie charts and realize how much time and effort go into the loss of a single pound of fat, but from the perspective of permanent weight control rather than fast weight loss one can see that less than 45 minutes of effort daily can consume 250 calories—halfway toward the 500-calorie goal.

EXERCISE BURNS BODY FAT

Being "overweight" is really being "overfat." Since excess body fat is what produces a blimp-like appearance, the fundamental intent of permanent weight control is to lose body fat and keep it off; body fat cannot be dieted away, but it can be burned as fuel for exercise. This has been demonstrated in many studies, including one that examined overweight women in three separate groups. The first group reduced their caloric intake by 500 calories a day but did not increase physical activity; the second reduced calories by 250 a day but increased exercise by that same amount, producing a 500-calorie deficit; the third did not change their eating pattern but increased physical activity, burning up 500 calories a day. The results showed that the two groups involved in exercise lost significantly more body fat than the first group.

Mild to moderate physical activity uses fat as an important source of energy. When a person exercises regularly, then—and *only* then—will the body utilize its stored fat as fuel. Moderate daily exercise can produce an energy deficit that requires the burning of stored body fat. This deficit over time can result in a substantial amount of fat being used. The calories burned directly from exercise are critical to a successful long-term weight control program.

Most health professionals feel that weight loss of one to two pounds per week is optimal if the weight is to stay off. A person can lose a greater amount with a crash diet or other gimmick, but the weight loss isn't fat and it won't be permanent. Prudent weight loss and permanent weight control can be accomplished by burning 200 to 250 calories daily through physical activity and by reducing caloric intake by the same amount. In this way, exercise functions as an integral part of the 500-Calorie Solution.

EXERCISE RAISES METABOLISM

In addition to burning up calories, exercise causes an increase in the basal metabolic rate, or BMR. This means that even after exercise stops, the body needs more calories just to exist and function. In effect, exercise revs up the engine and keeps it running—burning calories—at a higher level for hours after the exercise is completed.

Exactly why and how much the BMR is changed by exercise is unclear, in part because basal metabolism is hard to measure and can vary by as much as 30% among persons of the same weight, age and sex. What *is* clear, however, is the positive effect of exercise on the BMR. This phenomenon was first noted by scientists in a 1935 study of Harvard football players, which found that "even 15 hours after a game or strenuous practice . . . the metabolic rate is in general distinctly elevated . . . by as much as 25% above normal."

In a 1960 study, subjects walked 10 miles at a rate of 4 miles per hour—an aerobic level—and showed BMR 14% to 18% above normal for 7 hours. A more recent study at the University of Southern California showed that people who exercised had a metabolic rate 7.5% to 28% higher than if they had not exercised and that the higher rate continued for 4 hours after they stopped.

Exercise causes the metabolic furnace to burn at a higher level and, in doing so, makes it harder for the body to conserve energy (calories) and easier for it to lose weight. This is why, in many medically supervised weight loss programs, patients will exercise moderately two times a day—once in the morning and once in the evening. Such a schedule keeps their BMR raised virtually all day and all night, and helps them to burn calories and lose weight more efficiently.

So it's not just the calories burned by the exercise that are important to weight control, but the increase in the BMR as well. The benefit of an enhanced BMR—running the engine consistently at a higher level—can have a dramatic impact on weight loss all by itself. "If exercising regularly changes your metabolism even slightly, so that you burn an extra 100 calories a day," says exercise physiologist Dr. Jack H. Wilmore, "that small change can add up to 10 pounds of weight loss a year."

EXERCISE LOWERS THE "SETPOINT"

Current thinking holds that body fat is regulated to a great degree by a control center in the brain which "chooses" the amount of weight it considers ideal. The level chosen is called the "setpoint" weight, which the control center works continuously to maintain. It does this by influencing the amount of calories eaten and the efficiency of calories burned. It's ironic that crash dieting may actually cause the setpoint to be elevated, thus explaining why dieters often have difficulty passing below a certain weight. When threatened by weight loss, the control center defends the setpoint weight by increasing appetite and caloric intake while simultaneously diminishing the ability of the body to burn calories. From a fat control standpoint, this is the worst of both worlds: more calories coming in, fewer calories being burned. With the body itself working against sustained weight loss, it's no wonder that so many dieters reach a plateau and become frustrated.

While crash dieting alone can raise the setpoint, studies show that exercise will lower it. The two effects seem to cancel each other out in dieters who have added exercise to their program, leaving the subjects with normal metabolic rates and the ability to produce sustained weight loss. "The body seems to sense that an active person needs to be thin," says obesity expert Dr. Dennis Remington of Brigham Young University, "and it reacts by adjusting its concept of what constitutes the proper amount of body fat. By lowering the setpoint, it allows the body to process calories more efficiently."

A lower setpoint can also mean better control over the appetite. For many years, it was thought that exercise decreases appetite; while this may be true for extremely strenuous activities such as running in a marathon, moderate exercise often has the opposite effect. A walk before dinner, for example, may enhance appetite. The key word today is "control." Once an exercise program is started, the body senses that it must find a new weight level, and a new balance of fat to muscle, in order to sustain activity. The lowering of the setpoint can produce a decrease in the desire for food, thus allowing better control over caloric intake. This point was illustrated by researchers at St. Luke's-Roosevelt Hospital in New York, who conducted a test on obese women. The group was monitored during three 19-day phases: first a period of no exercise at all, then mild exercise, then moderate daily workouts on a treadmill. Interestingly, the women continued to consume the same amount of calories as during the resting phase, no matter how much more active they became. Exercise did not cause them to become ravenous so that they overate; instead, it helped them to control their diet while drawing on their stored energy reserves of fat.

EXERCISE CREATES MUSCLE

Regular exercise creates new muscle tissue, a critical factor because muscle is what burns fat. "Diet alone can't build lean body mass (muscle tissue)," says Georgia Kostas, R.D., director of the nutrition program at the Cooper Clinic. "But exercise will. In fact, the more muscle you have, the easier it is to burn fat—even while sitting down." Fat is the fuel, but muscle is the engine. The bigger the engine, the more fuel can be burned.

The relationship of fat to muscle in the body is also critical because body fat needs fewer calories to maintain itself than does lean muscle tissue. Studies show that overweight people need a third to a half fewer calories to maintain their weight than do people of normal weight. This is why, of two people who eat the same amount of food, the fat person gets fatter and the lean person stays thin. Building up lean muscle tissue through regular exercise dramatically increases the body's ability to burn calories. Not all types of exercise are equally effective. Aerobic exercise has little impact on muscle growth. Its main benefit is the reduction of body fat. Weight training is more effective. Many health professionals suggest a balance of aerobic and weight-training activities to produce the best of both worlds: fat reduction and muscle increase. A study conducted at Stanford University of middle-aged, previously sedentary men showed that after two years of running an average of 12 miles per week, their body fat fell from an average of 22% to 18%—while eating an average of 15% more calories!

EXERCISE REDUCES STRESS AND PROVIDES LIFESTYLE CONTROL

Exercise offers psychological benefits that are important for weight control. It helps us view the body more realistically and improves a psychological measurement known as "locus of control." In effect, it demonstrates how much control we think we have over our lives and how much we feel external events are in charge.

Overeating is often dictated by stress, anxiety and lack of self-esteem. Food becomes a consolation to people who feel their lives are out of control—that life is happening to them. Exercise can change that viewpoint. People who commit to an exercise program and keep that commitment see themselves as being in charge of that part of their lives. A reduction in tension and anxiety, and an increased feeling of self-worth, often result and help prevent overeating.

In addition, there is often a carryover into other lifestyle habits. A person who exercises often will decide to stop smoking, for example, and to eat in a healthier fashion. "Success breeds success" is an old axiom, but it's true. Success with exercise often provides the incentive and the motivation to make healthy changes in other areas of life. Finding ways to be more active places the emphasis on the positive—what one *can do* rather than *can't have* in order to lose weight. It's a joyful approach as opposed to a negative, deprived feeling. Doing something positive and succeeding can provide a real boost to a person's self-image. Moreover, exercise can serve as an important distraction, according to experts such as Dr. Scott Weigle of the University of Washington Medical School, by giving people "something to focus on besides food."

The importance of regular physical activity as part of a weight control program cannot be overemphasized. The burning of fat, the raising of metabolism, the creation of new muscle tissue, the lowering of the setpoint, the dissipation of stress—these benefits are critical to losing and controlling weight. And when this activity is combined with diet in the 500-Calorie Solution, each element increases the effectiveness of the other. The result is weight lost more easily and kept off permanently.

EXERCISE AND CARDIOVASCULAR HEALTH

Physical inactivity has been linked to a number of illnesses and degenerative conditions—overweight, depression, osteoporosis, chronic stress—but its relationship to coronary heart disease is the most critical. While physical inactivity all by itself may not bring on a heart attack, numerous studies strongly suggest that a prime connection exists. Conversely, these same studies illustrate an association between regular exercise and protection from heart attack.

One such study, conducted by Dr. J. N. Morris, compared drivers with conductors on London's double-decker buses. While the drivers remained sedentary all day, the conductors went up and down stairs continuously as they collected tickets. The study illustrated that the sedentary drivers had 30% more heart attacks than the more active conductors. This finding was supported by a similar study at the University of Minnesota involving thousands of railroad engineers and switchmen.

A very significant study was conducted by Dr. Frederick Stare at Harvard University. He selected 500 pairs of Irish brothers, of whom one emigrated to the United States while the other stayed in Ireland. Because of the filial relationship, environmental rather than genetic factors were the focal point. Dr. Stare found a key difference to be the activity levels of the two groups. The brothers who stayed in Ireland continued to farm, doing physically demanding work. The brothers who came to the United States, however, settled in urban areas and led a more "citified" existence involving much lower levels of physical activity. After 10 years, reported Dr. Stare, the brothers in the United States had suffered 50% more heart attacks than the brothers who remained in Ireland.

A landmark study of the lifestyles of Harvard alumni, conducted by Dr. Ralph Paffenbarger, Jr., of the Stanford University School of Medicine, revealed that active men reduced their risk of heart attack by 35% and lived longer—about 30 months—than their sedentary classmates. This study produced a gauge of physical activities tied to calories burned. Dr. Paffenbarger found that benefits began to appear as soon as the men expended 500 calories a week in exercise (less than two hours of brisk walking), with peak benefits coming between 2,000 and 3,500 calories a week (a daily 20-minute run). Interestingly, he also discovered that benefits tapered off after 3,500 calories. His work brought forth an additional important point: the incidence of sudden death (at the time of the attack) was much lower in the physically active groups, prompting the conclusion that people who work out regularly have fewer and milder heart attacks than those who do not.

These and other studies illustrate that a link between physical inactivity and heart attack does exist. More important, they suggest a strong correlation between physical activity—even if moderate—and protection from coronary heart disease.

EXERCISE STRENGTHENS THE HEART

All muscle tissue responds to exercise by increasing in size and strength. A person who lifts weights soon finds biceps growing and arm strength increasing. It's the same with the cardiac muscle: when exercised, it gets stronger and becomes a more efficient pump.

Increased efficiency, the ability to perform with less effort, can greatly reduce strain on the heart. For example, a "normal" heart rate requires the heart to contract about 72 times every minute to pump sufficient blood throughout the body. Regular physical activity strengthens the heart and allows it to pump the same volume of blood in fewer strokes. Additional strength means additional efficiency. This is how it works. With an average resting pulse of 72 beats per minute, the heart is required to beat 103,680 times a day. But if exercise is used to strengthen the muscle and gain cardiac efficiency, the resting pulse can be reduced tremendously. If it were to come down to 58 beats per minute, the heart would beat 80,040 times during 23 hours at rest. Add in 8,640 heartbeats for one hour of exercise (at the rate of 144 beats per minute) and the net savings is tremendous:

> 103,680 heartbeats at 72 per minute (24 hours)
> − 80,040 heartbeats at 58 per minute (23 hours)
> − 8,640 heartbeats at 144 per minute (1 hour)
> 15,000 heartbeats saved each day

Exercise has allowed the heart to pump an equal amount of blood using 15,000 fewer beats a day!

A reduction in resting pulse is possible for virtually anyone involved in regular aerobic exercise. Some highly trained world-class athletes have resting pulses under 40 beats per minute. While the vast majority of us will never reach that level, any reduction will ease the workload and reduce cardiovascular strain.

A conditioned cardiac muscle may also prevent extremely rapid heart rates resulting from physical or emotional stress. Everyone has a maximum heart rate, the most heartbeats per minute that can safely take place. This is generally estimated by subtracting age from 220. Thus, the maximum heartbeat of a 30-year-old would be 190 (220 − 30 = 190), while that of a 40-year-old would be 180 (220 − 40 = 180). Maximum heart rate changes with age; it gets lower as you get older.

Maximum heart rate is regulated by a mechanism within the heart that limits it from overbeating and straining itself. A conditioned heart generally responds well to this mechanism, but in a deconditioned heart the regulator may not work. Then, when the heart is called upon to beat faster because of a strenuous activity like shoveling snow, for example, it may speed up to 250 beats a minute or more in an effort to supply blood to the muscles. This can strain the heart to the breaking point and cause a heart attack.

It's the same for emotional stress. In this situation, certain chemicals are secreted that cause the heart to speed up. We've all experienced near-misses with a car and the "heart in your throat" feeling. In a conditioned heart, the slowdown mechanism will keep the racing heartbeat in check; a deconditioned heart, however, may refuse to slow down and instead speed up and beat itself to death.

A conditioned heart, then, provides pumping efficiency, less strain on the cardiac muscle and more protection from extremely rapid heart rates. And regular exercise is the single best way to condition the cardiac muscle.

EXERCISE IMPROVES BLOOD FLOW

The positive effect of exercise has long been acclaimed by cardiac researchers. A number of studies suggest that sustained aerobic exercise can dramatically improve blood flow. One such study, conducted at Boston University, has shown that regular exercise increases the diameter of blood vessels, including the coronary arteries. Such expansion doesn't alter the absolute size of any coronary artery blockage, but it does change the amount of artery channel occluded. By "opening" the artery, exercise allows more blood to reach the heart. This may also be the mechanism by which it lowers blood pressure. Numerous studies have illustrated a relationship between regular exercise and the control of blood pressure in borderline hypertensives.

Other studies, principally by Dr. Gabe Mirkin at UCLA, suggest that exercise may result in the formation of new blood vessels and capillaries to the heart, allowing the cardiac muscle to receive more blood. In effect, by promoting the growth of new blood vessels, exercise may produce a natural bypass operation for those with artery blockages.

The health of the body depends upon the health of the heart, and the key to cardiac health is a sufficient blood supply. By enlarging arteries and promoting new growth of blood vessels, exercise promotes good health.

EXERCISE IMPROVES BLOOD CHEMISTRY

When the blood contains elevated levels of cholesterol and triglycerides, cardiac risk is increased. It is an accepted fact that the higher the blood cholesterol, the greater the risk of heart attack. The M.R.F.I.T. study showed a death rate of 2.3 out of 1,000 people in those with cholesterol levels lower than 203; the death rate for those with cholesterol levels greater than 263 was 8.6.

But total cholesterol level is not the whole story. The makeup of that cholesterol may be of greater importance. As explained previously, there are two types of cholesterol: LDL (low-density lipoprotein), the "bad" cholesterol, and HDL (high-density lipoprotein), the "good" cholesterol. LDL sticks to the walls of the coronary arteries and produces blockages; HDL does not. HDL acts as a scavenger, scoops up the LDL and delivers it to the liver for breakdown and excretion into the bile. A high level of HDL is associated with lower heart attack risk and is desirable.

Recent research conducted by Dr. William Haskell and his associates at Stanford University shows that aerobic exercise causes a decrease in LDL cholesterol and in triglycerides. (Some researchers believe this reduction to be the result of weight loss, one of the products of regular exercise; others believe that exercise itself produces the change in blood chemistry. No one knows for certain, but either way the reduction of LDL cholesterol and triglycerides is welcome.) What made Dr. Haskell's study a landmark was that it demonstrated that *exercise increases HDL cholesterol.* This is most important because protective HDL responds to only a few lifestyle areas, notably weight reduction, smoking cessation and certain foods. Indeed, exercise may be the most effective way to raise HDLs substantially. This is particularly good news for men, who do not have naturally high levels of HDL.

According to many health professionals, the ratio of HDL to total cholesterol is much more important than just total cholesterol. In a man, HDL should constitute no less than 20% of total cholesterol, or a ratio of 5:1 (1 part HDL in 5 parts total cholesterol). In a woman, it should constitute no less than 22.5% of total cholesterol, or a ratio of 4.5:1. The lower the HDL percentage, the higher the ratio and the greater the risk of heart attack. Conversely, the greater the HDL percentage, the lower the ratio and the lower the risk of heart attack.

To understand the critical importance of this information, compare the HDL ratios of three men shown in the table below. Each has a total cholesterol level of 225 but a different level of HDL, resulting in different HDL ratios.

	Total Cholesterol	HDL Cholesterol	HDL Ratio	HDL Percentage
#1	225	45	5:1	20%
#2	225	25	9:1	11
#3	225	75	3:1	33

Man #1 exercises moderately and has an average HDL level of 45, which provides him with a ratio of 5:1, an "average risk" for coronary heart disease. He has achieved the recommended minimum: 20% of his total cholesterol is HDL. Man #2 is sedentary. He doesn't exercise and is involved in little or no physical activity. Thus his HDL level is only 25. His ratio is 9:1—only 11% of his cholesterol is HDL, far below the desired level—and constitutes a "high risk" for coronary heart disease. Man #3 is an endurance exerciser (marathon runners average HDLs of 75). He has a high level of HDL and a 3:1 ratio, which is extremely good. With 33% of his cholesterol as HDL, he has a "low risk" for coronary heart disease.

In each case, the man has a total cholesterol level of 225. If judged solely on this information, all three would have been seen as having an average risk for heart disease. But taking HDL ratios into consideration produces an entirely different finding: one person with average risk, one with high risk and one with virtually no risk.

HDL cholesterol provides significant cardiovascular protection. Must one be a marathoner to acquire this protection? The answer is no. Studies have shown that joggers who averaged only 11 miles a week had significantly higher HDL levels than did their inactive counterparts, and that HDL in the blood of the runners was raised to a level that could be expected to make a significant difference in lowering their coronary risk. The message here is that moderate exercise can provide optimal benefit. According to Dr. Ken Cooper, if one runs no less than 2 miles four times a week, and no more than 3 miles five times a week, the HDL effect is equal to running 80 miles per week. "I've gone from being an extremist to taking a much more moderate view," says Dr. Cooper. "I used to say, run as much as you want. Now I say, if you run more than 15 miles a week, you're doing more than you need for cardiovascular fitness."

OTHER REASONS TO EXERCISE

There are numerous other benefits that occur from exercise. These include strengthening of bones, retardation of aging and increased brain efficiency.

EXERCISE STRENGTHENS BONES

The aging process tends to demineralize bones, causing them to become so brittle and weak that even a moderate fall can produce a break or fracture. This is a particularly serious condition for older women. In light of the large numbers of women with osteoporosis, many physicians are now recommending an increase in calcium intake.

Increased calcium is only part of the solution to the osteoporosis problem. The rest of the answer lies in exercise. Numerous studies have shown that bone, like muscle, tends to get thicker and stronger the more it is used. Weight lifters, for example, have thicker arm bones than runners; runners have thicker leg bones than swimmers. The critical point is that, without exercise, bone density will not be improved and the extra calcium may be useless in reducing the risk of bone disease. The effect of exercise on bone strength is also shown in other cultures. Many African women who are involved in regular physical activity do not suffer from bone deterioration later in life, even though their average calcium intake is only 300 milligrams per day—one-third of the recommended level for American women.

The more exercise, the stronger the bones will be and the less prone to fracture. Taking this one step further, to keep bones strong and protect against osteoporosis, regular exercise is a necessary, even critical need.

EXERCISE RETARDS AGING

This is not to say that exercise can smooth wrinkles or turn gray hair into black. From the standpoint of the cardiovascular system, wrinkles and gray hair are not the most significant signs of aging. Rather, the outstanding result is a decline in the ability to process oxygen, called "maximal O_2 uptake." According to Dr. N. Shock, this decline takes place at a rate of 1% a year after age 25 and accelerates to

2% after age 55. Research shows that exercise can prevent or slow down this process. In one study, conducted at San Diego State University by Dr. Fred Kasch, participants in an adult exercise program had their oxygen-processing capabilities measured over 10 and 15 years. The study found that for those who exercised regularly, there was no difference in maximal uptake between ages 45 and 55. Externally, the 55-year-olds looked older than their 45-year-old counterparts. From the standpoint of cardiovascular performance, however, the two groups showed the same oxygen-processing capabilities. In effect, exercise had retarded the aging process for the older group.

Another study, by Dr. Herbert deVries at the University of Southern California, noted that the average person loses 15% of muscle strength between ages 45 and 65. This is due not to aging but to inactivity. Dr. deVries' study demonstrated that people who continued to exercise in their senior years experienced no decrease in muscle strength through age 60.

Exercise is important for quality of life as well as longevity. "Age is where all the good stuff starts," says Dr. George Sheehan. Citing the result of a study in which the participants were asked to pick the prime of their lives, he says: "No one picked their teens. Only a handful selected their 20's or 30's—who wants to go through raising a family again? Most said ages 50 to 60. If a person exercises, he will not be thought of as emeritus at age 45."

EXERCISE IMPROVES BRAIN EFFICIENCY

Research shows that a long-term exercise program can improve the body's biochemistry and, in doing so, improve brain efficiency. According to Dr. A. H. Ismail at Purdue University, "Exercise not only makes you fitter, it can sharpen your ability to process information; consequently, you'll have enhanced learning capabilities." The left brain in particular improves efficiency as the result of physical fitness. It is the part responsible for logical reasoning and verbal and numerical skills.

WHAT EXERCISE WILL NOT DO

The popular misconception that long-distance running provides immunity from heart attack was based upon an autopsy of the famed marathon runner Clarence DeMar, who died at age 70 of cancer. Medical findings described the diameter of his coronary arteries as two to three times normal size, with only minimal narrowing from cholesterol deposits. Out of this came the "exercise and immunity theory" put forward by Dr. Thomas Bassler, a pathologist and marathon runner, and the American Medical Joggers Association. Their position was overzealous and was shown to be incorrect by Dr. Timothy Noakes in 1979. Dr. Noakes provided autopsy documentation that severe and fatal coronary heart disease and heart attack did indeed develop in select marathon runners.

Exercise can reduce the risk of coronary heart disease and heart attack, and can improve the survivability of those experiencing heart attacks, but it does not provide immunity from heart disease. The causes of coronary heart disease are complicated. A lifestyle that includes a prudent diet, no smoking, stress management and aerobic exercise is the best way to protect against it.

EXERCISE AND CHILDREN

An additional reason to become involved in exercise is your children's health. Children tend to follow their parents' lead, to do what they do. And because so many parents don't do anything, neither do the children. According to Anthony Annarino, a physical education professor at Purdue University, the sedentary lifestyle unconsciously mimicked by many American children puts them at high risk for serious health problems later in life. "Unless their behaviors, values, and lifestyles change," he says, "this trend will have a negative influence on their lifelong health and physical fitness."

Recent studies of school-age children confirm Professor Annarino's worst fears: today's kids are more out of shape and flabbier than were the kids of two decades ago. A 1985 study sponsored by the President's Council on Physical Fitness and Sports showed that fitness levels had declined from 1975 and 1965, and findings of the Health and Human Services Department illustrate that today's adolescents have significantly more body fat than their counterparts in 1965. This trend is leading to future problems with heart and blood vessel disease. In fact, they're already showing up. Researchers at Louisiana State University have found that teenagers with high blood cholesterol levels are exhibiting signs of atherosclerosis.

There are three major reasons for America's children being out of shape: changes in physical education programs, television and parental lifestyle. Many physical education programs teach athletic skills—how to throw a football, for example—rather than conditioning. Other programs are unavailable to all school children. Only one-third of children and adolescents aged 10 to 17 currently participate in a daily physical education program at school. Television, which some kids watch over 50 hours a week, also plays a significant role, as do fast food and junk food. But ultimately it may be the lifestyle of the parents that is most significant. They are the role models that children most often imitate.

UNDERSTANDING AEROBIC EXERCISE

All types of exercise or physical activity have a beneficial effect on cardiovascular health, weight and appearance.

From a cardiac standpoint, it improves circulation, increases the efficiency of the heart and the respiratory system, and positively alters blood chemistry. Regular exercise promotes fat loss and weight control, tones muscles and increases strength. It promotes better digestion, stronger bones, sounder sleep, less tension and a renewed sense of well-being.

All physical activity is beneficial, but one type—aerobic exercise—is the most effective in promoting weight control and cardiovascular health.

WHAT IS AEROBIC EXERCISE?

Basically, there are two types of physical activities: anaerobic ("without oxygen") and aerobic ("with oxygen"). Anaerobic activities are not long-lasting or vigorous enough to give the heart and lungs a workout. They can help the body in many ways—strength, flexiblity, muscle tone—but they do not do much for the cardiovascular system.

Examples of anaerobic activities include:

Tennis (doubles)	Sprinting
Football	Softball
Bowling	Volleyball
Weight lifting	Golf
Calisthenics	Horseback riding
Judo	Yoga
Badminton	Karate
Wrestling	Table tennis
Fencing	Horseshoes
Tobogganing	Scuba diving
Water skiing	Downhill skiing
Surfing	Archery
Croquet	Sledding
Ballet	Isometrics

These activities are classified as "stop and go," of limited duration or of low intensity. Football is a good example of a "stop and go" activity. After each play, activity is stopped. Because the movement in a football game is "stop and go," there is not enough continuous activity to classify it as aerobic. Other good examples are badminton, downhill skiing and calisthenics.

Sprinting exemplifies an exercise of limited duration. Such activities often call for great bursts of energy, but the time involved is too brief to produce a benefit for the cardiovascular system. Weight lifting and isometrics are other limited-duration exercises.

Low-intensity activities include golf, table tennis and archery. These do not produce an intensity of effort sufficient to be classified as aerobic.

Weight lifting is a good example of an anaerobic exercise that strengthens specific muscles but does little to condition the cardiovascular system. A study at the University of California involving 10 body builders (including a Mr. America and a Mr. World) illustrates this point. The weight lifters were exercised on a treadmill. Although they were lean (an average of 9.9% body fat), their lung power was equal to that of non-athletic men of similar weight. The study shows that weight lifting, like other anaerobic exercises, does not produce cardiovascular fitness.

Anaerobic activities are enjoyable and certainly can be a valuable part of a personal fitness program, but their role in cardiovascular health is such that they should be used as a supplement to a regular program of aerobic exercise. What, then, is aerobic exercise? Too often people identify the word "aerobic" with exercise in the extreme, such as the Boston Marathon or the Tour de France bicycle race. Even those who greatly enjoy exercise have little interest in committing to the time and effort needed for such activities. Fortunately, however, aerobic exercise is more than just long-distance competition involving world-class athletes. There are many aerobic activities that can be used by everyday people of all ages and physical conditions to improve appearance and cardiac health.

"Aerobic" describes activities and exercises that cause

the heart and lungs to process oxygen at a steady rate over a period of time. Such activities are designed to enhance stamina and endurance, an ability to keep on going without placing undue strain on the cardiovascular system.

Aerobic exercise is simply exercise that makes the muscles work hard—but not so hard that the heart and the lungs can't keep up with the oxygen demand. For this reason, aerobic exercise can be done continuously and steadily, allowing for an increased heart rate to be sustained over a period of time. Some of the best aerobic exercises include:

Brisk walking	Jogging
Cycling (indoor)	Running in place
Skipping rope	Swimming
Rowing (indoor)	Cross-country skiing

There is also a group of activities that can be aerobic if done at a vigorous pace continuously maintained for a period of time. These activities include:

Basketball	Handball/squash/racquetball
Hiking	Skating (ice or roller)
Soccer	Rowing (outdoor)
Tennis (singles)	Aerobic dance/aerobicize
Cycling (outdoor)	

In order to be classified as aerobic, the exercise must meet a certain criterion, involving frequency, intensity and time (F.I.T.). How often, how hard, how long—these are the three key elements necessary for building fitness.

Frequency

Many health professionals counsel an aerobic exercise program of four days a week, once every other day. This takes into account the recommendations of the American College of Sports Medicine, which suggest that:

■ Fitness is *improved* if you exercise more than three days a week.

■ Fitness is *maintained* if you exercise three days a week.

- Fitness is *lost* if you exercise less than three days a week.

Getting more than five days of exercise a week may overwork a specific muscle group and cause strain or other injury. Anyone who chooses to exercise this often should alternate activities—walk one day, swim the next.

Many health professionals suggest exercising every other day. With this schedule, the cardiovascular system is exercised and the body has time off to rest and recuperate, thus minimizing the potential for injury. A lot, of course, depends on the exercise and the goal involved. Cardiovascular conditioning may be attained by exercising four times a week, but daily exercise may be needed if weight loss and control are also a goal. This is because the more days that exercise can be used to burn 250 calories, the more efficient the body becomes at reducing fat. As part of the 500-Calorie Solution, moderate exercise is a daily affair.

The importance of regular exercise has been borne out in studies of long-distance athletes. One such study compared training levels and body fat percentages in bicycle racers. When training for a race, the cyclists rode every day; on average, their body fat percentage was around 4%. Once the race was over, however, the training schedule lost some frequency; the cyclists rode for two or three days a week only, and almost immediately their body fat percentages increased to about 8%.

Frequency is a key to the effectiveness of exercise. When physical activity is made a regular part of the daily routine, like brushing your teeth, weight control and cardiovascular health benefits are maximized.

Intensity

How hard you should exercise is important because of the relationship between intensity and cardiovascular fitness. Research indicates that exercise done at a moderate rate provides the best cardiovascular and weight control results. This flies in the face of the "no pain, no gain" school of exercise. Current thinking is that "going for the burn" may cause a person to exercise too hard or too fast. You can end up with an injury or just wear yourself out. Either way you get nowhere. Unless you're a competitive athlete, intensity of effort should be moderated for best results. Indeed, today there is a new respect for the effectiveness of moderately intensive exercise.

Just as one can exercise too hard, the other extreme—very light exercise—has not proved to be effective. Exercising too casually will generally not produce significant weight reduction or cardiovascular benefit; however, an "in between" point provides a happy medium between not exercising enough and overdoing it. This is the "aerobic pace," which produces a slight sweat but does not cause breathlessness. There are two ways to determine if an activity or exercise is being done at an aerobic pace. The first is the "Talk Test." If the pace is such that your forehead feels "dewed" but you can still carry on a conversation with a fellow exerciser, your pace is probably just about right. If you can't exercise and talk at the same time, you're probably going too fast.

A more scientific measurement of pace involves monitoring the pulse rate during exercise. The pulse is an indication of how many heartbeats per minute it takes for blood to be pumped through the body. There are many places where a pulse can be taken: chest, neck, temple, wrist, groin and inside of the elbow. The easiest place is the neck. By placing your thumb on your chin, you can press the other four fingertips into the vertical groove on one side of the Adam's apple. Pressing in gently, you can feel the "throb" of rushing blood. Each "throb" is one beat. Count the beats for one minute, and you have your resting pulse. A "normal" resting pulse is between 60 and 90 beats per minute—usually a mean of 72.

Each person has a maximum pulse, a limit on how fast the heart is capable of beating. This is determined by age, not by level of fitness. A 40-year-old fit runner, for example, has a maximum heart rate of 180, while a sedentary 24-year-old has a maximum heart rate of 196; the 40-year-old may be more fit, but, being older, has a lower maximum heart rate. The formula for estimating maximum heart rate is:

$$\begin{array}{l} 220 \\ - \underline{\text{Age}} \\ = \text{Maximum heart rate} \end{array}$$

Figuring out maximum heart rate is easy:

For the 40-Year-Old	For the 24-Year-Old	For You
220	220	220
− 40	− 24	− Your age
180	196	Your maximum heart rate

The Target Zone. When exercise is done at a pace that is in the Target Zone, between 60% and 85% of the age-determined maximum heart rate, it is aerobic. This is the optimal intensity for cardiovascular fitness and weight control. If the heart rate does not come up to the Target Zone during exercise, the activity is not as effective. It must be sped up and performed with more intensity. On the other hand, if the heart is beating faster than the Target Zone during exercise, the intensity of the activity could cause injury. The pace should be slowed down. Staying within the parameters of the Target Zone is vital to effective aerobic exercise.

Historically, the Target Zone has been 70% to 85% of maximum heart rate. This range has worked well for intense aerobic activities such as running and jumping rope. Recent studies, however, indicate that a range of 60% to 75% of maximum heart rate is just as effective. According to Dr. Victor F. Froelicher, chief of cardiology at the Long Beach Veterans Administration Medical Center, "The lower range allows for less intense activities such as walking or low-impact aerobics. They provide cardiovascular benefit without as much physical strain."

The calculation for establishing the Target Zone is as follows:

High-impact Target Zone

Maximum heart rate × 70% = low end of Target Zone
Maximum heart rate × 85% = high end of Target Zone

A 40-year-old runner with a maximum heart rate of 180, therefore, would have a Target Zone of from 126 to 153 beats per minute using the high-impact formula:

180 Maximum heart rate	180 Maximum heart rate
× .70	× .85
126 Beats per minute	153 Beats per minute
(Low end of Target Zone)	(High end of Target Zone)

Low-impact Target Zone

Maximum heart rate × 60% = low end of Target Zone
Maximum heart rate × 75% = high end of Target Zone

A 40-year-old walker would have a Target Zone of 108 to 135 using the low-impact formula:

180 Maximum heart rate	180 Maximum heart rate
× .60	× .75
108 Beats per minute	135 Beats per minute
(Low end of Target Zone)	(High end of Target Zone)

The following is a quick way to determine maximum heart rate and Target Zones by age group:

Age	Maximum Heart Rate (beats per minute)	Low-impact Target Zone (beats per minute)	High-impact Target Zone (beats per minute)
20 to 24	200	120 to 150	140 to 170
25 to 29	195	117 to 146	137 to 166
30 to 34	190	114 to 142	133 to 162
35 to 39	185	111 to 138	130 to 157
40 to 44	180	108 to 135	126 to 153
45 to 49	175	105 to 131	123 to 149
50 to 54	170	102 to 127	119 to 145

Age	Maximum Heart Rate (beats per minute)	Low-impact Target Zone (beats per minute)	High-impact Target Zone (beats per minute)
55 to 59	165	99 to 123	116 to 140
60 to 64	160	96 to 120	112 to 136
65 to 69	155	93 to 116	109 to 132
70 and over	150	90 to 113	105 to 128

Obviously, these figures are averages; individual ranges may differ from 10 to 20 beats per minute. An exercise stress test can determine true maximum heart rate—another good reason for seeing a doctor before starting to exercise, especially for cardiac patients or people who have other health problems such as severe overweight.

Heart rate should always be used in conjunction with the perception of how a person feels when exercising. If you're very tired during the exercise or it takes more than an hour to recover after finishing, you may be working too hard regardless of your heart rate. (If the exercise doesn't take any effort and there's no sweating or hard breathing, then the pace should be increased.) It's also important to note that many medications change heart rate. If you're taking medication for heart disease or high blood pressure, check with a physician regarding exercise heart rate. People on such medications should *not* use the Target Zone guide.

The Target Zone will not change as you lose weight and get in better shape. Remember, it's geared to your age, not to your level of fitness. What does change is the amount of effort you need to reach the Target Zone. People who are overweight and out of shape have an easier time reaching the Target Zone than those who are slimmer and in shape. As level of fitness improves, the pace may have to be stepped up in order for the activity to remain aerobic. If you're first starting a program, for example, you might walk one mile in 20 minutes and this could be enough to move you into your Target Zone. As you get into better shape, however, you may have to increase the intensity and walk that mile in 15 minutes to reach your Target Zone. If it's necessary to increase pace in order to keep the heart rate up, this is a good indication that the heart is becoming more efficient and the body better at burning fat.

Taking an exercise pulse. Shortly after the start of exercise, the pulse rate goes up very quickly and then levels off. By the time you're about four or five minutes into the activity, a consistent pulse rate should be established. This is when you should stop and immediately find your pulse, either at the wrist or at the throat. Using a watch with a second hand, you can count the heartbeats for six seconds. Then, multiplying the count by 10, you know your exercise pulse for 60 seconds, or one minute.

An easy way to measure your exercise pulse is to use the following as a guide:

	Your Target Zone	
Your Age	**Low-impact**	**High-impact**
20 to 29	12 to 15 beats in 6 seconds	14 to 17 beats in 6 seconds
30 to 39	11 to 14 beats in 6 seconds	13 to 16 beats in 6 seconds
40 to 49	10 to 13 beats in 6 seconds	12 to 15 beats in 6 seconds
50 to 59	10 to 12 beats in 6 seconds	12 to 14 beats in 6 seconds
60 to 69	9 to 11 beats in 6 seconds	11 to 13 beats in 6 seconds

It's recommended that you take your exercise pulse at 10-minute intervals, especially when first beginning an exercise program. This will ensure exercise within the Target Zone. After a while, you'll get used to the pace and won't need to monitor it as frequently.

Time

Clinical studies have shown the necessity of keeping the heart rate in the Target Zone for at least 20 continuous minutes in order to promote cardiovascular fitness. This is the *minimum* amount of time that should be spent in non-stop, aerobic exercise. An ideal amount would be closer to one hour. This is why stop-and-go exercises are not beneficial for the heart and blood vessels: they don't have the ability to keep the heart rate in the Target Zone for 20 continuous minutes, and therefore they can't offer cardiovascular benefit.

Time spent exercising is particularly important for fat loss. Nonstop exercise for at least 20 minutes is necessary to rev up metabolism and increase fat-burning capabilities. During the first 20 minutes of exercise, glucose is the primary fuel. As the activity continues past that point, fat takes over as fuel. Thus, the more time spent in continuous aerobic exercise, the greater the opportunity to burn fat.

Actually, not very many calories are burned up in 20 minutes of exercise. If you're serious about weight reduction, the activity needs to be lengthened out. Plan on taking whatever time is necessary to burn 250 calories—generally between 30 minutes and an hour. Studies indicate that weight loss is directly connected to the total time spent exercising.

A nonstop nature is basic to an exercise being aerobic. Walking for 10 minutes, stopping to chat with a friend, and then walking for another 10 minutes does not constitute aerobic activity. To be aerobic, the activity must be performed continuously and steadily within your Target Zone for at least 20 minutes.

SELECTING AN AEROBIC EXERCISE

There are many aerobic activities that benefit cardiovascular fitness and well-being. The key is to select one or two that suit your unique needs and interests. Some considerations in selecting an aerobic exercise include:

- Present level of health and fitness
- Time available
- Interests
- Equipment needed

The best motivator for exercise is the pleasure principle: the activity has to be enjoyed. Pick an activity or a combination of activities that you like and can stick with indefinitely—ideally, for the rest of your life.

Fortunately, today there are many books, tapes and classes that instruct in detail. The following descriptions of specific aerobic exercises are offered as an overview and are not intended to take the place of those in-depth resources.

BRISK WALKING

Brisk walking, also called "power walking" or "striding," is one of the simplest and easiest aerobic activities. It can be done anywhere, virtually by anyone, and takes no great expertise.

Walking offers three primary benefits in addition to ease of entry: it doesn't cause injuries, it aids weight control and it promotes cardiovascular conditioning. Since the weight of the body is shared by the legs between steps, walking does not jar joints or strain muscles as much as jogging does and therefore results in fewer musculoskeletal problems. By allowing for gradual conditioning, walking is especially appropriate for out-of-shape and overweight people. In addition, brisk walking provides the same cardiovascular and weight control benefits that jogging offers.

The single disadvantage to walking is that it may take longer to provide the cardiovascular benefits associated with jogging. A generally accepted standard is that 12 miles of aerobic walking per week is the minimum required for cardiovascular fitness. This equates to four 45-minute walks per week. By comparison, the minimum standard for running is 9 miles per week.

From the standpoint of weight control, brisk walking is a premier exercise. A person can burn almost the same amount of calories walking a mile in 20 minutes as a jogger burns running a mile in 10 minutes. This is due to the fact that the walker and the jogger are using almost the same amount of energy. The amount of work performed (and thus of calories burned) is determined by multiplying body weight times the distance moved. The farther you walk, the more calories you burn. The following comparison for a 150-pound person illustrates how well walking works for weight control:

Exercise	Pace	Minutes	Total Calories Burned
Jogging	11-minute mile	25	228
Walking	4 mph	45	261
Walking	4 mph	60	348

Intensity also counts. Many race walkers cover the same distance in the same time as runners, but because their intensity is greater (race walking takes more steps to cover a mile than jogging), more calories are burned. For example, a jogger at 12 minutes per mile burns 480 calories per hour; a race walker, 530 calories.

The effectiveness of brisk walking as a weight control device is dependent upon frequency and intensity. The more frequently you walk, the more calories burned. Anyone wishing to lose weight and keep it off should consider walking every day, perhaps even twice a day (morning and evening). This will also stoke metabolism so that increased calories are burned at rest.

Whether for cardiovascular or weight control purposes, intensity is what produces results. Casual walking is virtually useless. The key to walking briskly is arm movement, which can have the effect of propelling your body forward so that the pace is aerobic. Begin by walking slowly, increasing the pace over a 5-to-10-minute period and gradually swinging your arms faster. This action forces your legs automatically to keep pace with your arms. Pumping your arms frees your hips for longer, faster steps—for "brisking."

In addition, it's important to walk with a straight spine and a high center of gravity. Don't lean forward too much. "Walking tall" will aid breathing and promote a comfortably long stride.

Although there are no special rules, courses or equipment for a walking program, a comfortable pair of shoes is a necessity. Many people like to wear sneakers, jogging shoes or walking shoes because of the comfort, but any cushioned, sturdy shoe will do. Clothing should be comfortable and not binding. Loose clothing can "breathe" and can be stripped in layers if one becomes too warm.

Start by picking out a pleasant place to walk. If weather is a factor—rain, freezing cold, blistering heat—consider walking indoors. Most YMCAs and health clubs have indoor tracks; in many parts of the country, covered shopping malls have walking paths (including mileage) marked on the floor. Before setting out, do some stretching and flexibility exercises.

It's essential to start slowly. After about 10 minutes, you should be in full stride, arms swinging, and at your aerobic pace. At this point, you should feel "dewed" but not breathless. This is the proper time to take an exercise pulse. Depending upon the Target Zone, the pace may need adjusting. An aerobic pace should be continued for a minimum of 20 minutes, or longer if possible.

It's not necessary to be concerned with aerobic pace during the first few weeks of walking, especially if you've been away from exercise for a period of time, have medical problems or are overweight. It makes more sense to be concerned with building and conditioning the leg muscles. Cardiovascular benefit will come later. Gradualism is the key to success.

Plan for aerobic walks at least three or four days a week for about 45 minutes. Remember, they must be nonstop and at a brisk, aerobic pace if they're to provide maximum cardiovascular and weight control benefits.

JOGGING/RUNNING

Jogging and running are perhaps the most popular of all aerobic activities. The two are essentially the same except that running is done at a faster pace. According to Dr. Ken

Cooper, those who run faster than nine-minute miles are runners; those who run slower are joggers.

Jogging and running present a number of benefits and one major disadvantage. One of the principal benefits is ease of entry. Like walking, these activities require no particular skill. (Other aerobic exercises, such as swimming or cross-country skiing, take a higher degree of expertise.) In addition, both are relatively convenient. You can walk out the door and find a park or street in which to jog or run. It's even easy to take basic running equipment on a trip.

Effectiveness is also of particular importance. From a cardiovascular and weight control standpoint, jogging/running provide positive results in a shorter period of time than many other aerobic activities. The minimum for cardiovascular fitness is 9 miles spread over four days per week. At a 10-minute-per-mile pace, this equates to an hour and a half of running during a week. This makes running very effective from a time/benefit viewpoint. Remember, this is the *minimum*. Greater cardiovascular and weight control benefits accrue with more mileage, perhaps 12 to 15 miles per week.

The downside of running is the potential for injury. The ankles, knees and feet are subjected to intense pounding in this exercise, and orthopedic injury can result. According to the National Centers for Disease Control, one-third of those running at least 6 miles per week are injured. Recreational runners have a 1 in 6 chance of sustaining knee injuries, a 1 in 10 chance for foot problems, and a 1 in 20 chance for ankle or shin injury. Runners are especially susceptible if their warmup is insufficient or if the mileage is excessive. Twenty-five miles a week seems to be the breakpoint. Once that threshold is crossed, the opportunity for injury rises dramatically. This is not to say that all long-distance runners suffer orthopedic injuries, for they do not. But it's essential to listen to your body when you run and to be aware of the fact that excessive mileage does increase the risk. This is particularly important in

light of the fact that significant increases in HDL cholesterol—one of the primary reasons for aerobic exercise—can
occur from running just 9 to 12 miles a week.

Exercise gear is at a minimum, but what you use must
be of good quality. Function, not fashion, is important
here. If jogging in a red velour exercise suit and hand-
stitched shoes makes you feel better, so be it. But expensive clothing is not a necessity; as long as it's comfortable
and offers protection from the weather, it will do. Shoes
are the most crucial equipment in running. They're needed
to protect ankles, knees and feet from pounding, so they
should be of the highest quality. A bad pair of shoes can
ruin a good pair of legs. The shoes should be *running*
shoes—not sneakers, gym shoes or all-purpose shoes. The
best selection, and often the most knowledgeable people,
are found in athletic stores.

When you first start to jog, it may be appropriate to
alternate walking with very slow jogging, slowing to the
point of walking whenever breathlessness is reached. As in
walking, it may take time to work your legs into shape.
Again, gradualness is the key to success. Over time, increase the proportion of jogging to walking until you're
jogging on a nonstop basis. Once your legs are in shape,
concentrate on exercising in the Training Zone. The proper
sequence should be stretching for 5 to 10 minutes; slow
jogging for 5 to 10 minutes; a minimum of 20 minutes
of jogging at the Target Zone; and 5 to 10 minutes of slow
jogging or walking to cool down.

The key to a successful jogging program is to understand
that time, not distance or speed, is the main determinant
of beneficial effect. Thirty minutes of exercise is better
than 20 minutes. Intensity is important. If you're jogging
too fast to keep up a conversation, then you're working too
hard. If you're jogging such distances that chronic fatigue
or injury is occurring, you're jogging too far. Jogging
within the Target Zone for 20 to 45 minutes, three or four
times a week, is all it takes.

Obviously, some people should *not* jog. If you're seriously overweight, with a heart condition or with leg, feet or hip problems, you might consider less stressful activities. Be sure to consult a physician before beginning a jogging/running program.

CYCLING

Both indoor and outdoor cycling are excellent exercise. Cycling strengthens the back, abdomen and leg muscles, and, if aerobic, can provide cardiovascular conditioning as well. It's not a weight-bearing activity, so there is less stress on the joints and muscles than in running or jogging. Like walking, cycling is a particularly good exercise for older people, for overweight individuals or for those who have joint problems.

Both types of cycling have their proponents, and both offer certain benefits. Indoor cycling protects from the weather, provides for a steady pace and allows other activities to go on simultaneously—reading, watching television, listening to music. It's a particularly good activity if you need to squeeze exercise into a busy day—you can cycle while watching the 11 o'clock news.

Outdoor cycling, on the other hand, allows for exercising in the fresh air and the environment. This is certainly a benefit if you live in the country or the suburbs. (In the city, where the air may be polluted and the environment replete with traffic, this may not be a benefit at all.) Outdoor cycling also provides cardiovascular benefit with less effort than indoor cycling. The cardiovascular effect of cycling derives from overcoming the resistance of the bike. With outdoor cycling you must also move your body weight, an additional task that is sufficient to elevate the heart rate so that the Target Zone is reached more easily. On an indoor bike, the only way to elevate heart rate is to increase tension or speed, which may simply take too much out of the legs and force curtailment of the activity. Some indoor bikes, such as the Schwinn Air Dyne, require a pumping action of the arms; this design can provide substantially better aerobic benefits than the normal indoor bike.

According to Dr. Thomas Dickson, Jr., an orthopedic surgeon specializing in sports medicine, it's a mistake to think that pedaling in a harder gear will provide a better aerobic workout. A harder gear will reduce the rpm's (revolutions per minute) and make it harder to pump. Increased resistance could cause injury—and it provides no better exercise aerobically. A better aerobic effect, one with less wear and tear on the knee, comes from riding in a gear that allows for 60 to 100 rpm's.

The minimum required for cardiovascular fitness is 24 miles of cycling a week at an aerobic pace; as with other aerobic exercises, more is necessary if weight control is the goal. Five to 10 minutes of stretching should precede outdoor cycling. Start at a slow pace for another 5 or 10 minutes to warm up the leg muscles, progressively increasing your speed until you find a nice rhythmic pace within your Target Zone. Stay in the Target Zone for at least 20 minutes. Since the nature of aerobic exercise is to be continuous, stoplights and "coasting" can be a problem for outdoor cyclists. A bike path or a straight stretch of road is often the best solution. In addition, a protective helmet should always be worn. After a proper amount of time in the Target Zone, be sure to spend 5 or 10 minutes peddling slowly to cool down.

Indoor bikers should follow the same basic program. After stretching, there should be a warmup period of pedaling slowly with low tension resistance. After about 5 minutes, the tension should be slightly increased until the Target Zone is reached. A cool-down period should follow 20-minutes of cycling at an aerobic pace.

SWIMMING

Swimming is a great way to condition the heart and lungs and to reduce weight. It involves all the major muscles and therefore offers more of a total conditioning effect than many other activities. It's also highly recommended for older people and those with back or joint problems because no weight bearing is involved.

The equipment needed for swimming is minimal: a suit and, if desired, eye and ear protection. The greatest hassle for many people is simply finding a pool sufficiently convenient to allow swimming to become a part of their lifestyle. Check with private swim clubs, health clubs and your local YMCA or YWCA. Many universities and schools also open their pools to the public. If the pool is not conveniently located or the hours are restrictive, consider balancing swimming with other aerobic activities—perhaps walking on two days and swimming on two days.

The minimum needed for cardiovascular fitness is to swim (crawl) for 900 yards per week. The procedure here is the same as that for other aerobic exercises: stretch, warmup, 20 minutes of nonstop exercise in the Target Zone, and cooldown. Take sufficient time to work up to nonstop swimming. If tired or winded, switch to an easier stroke until recovered, then pick up the pace once again.

Because of the prone position used in swimming, blood flow does not have to fight gravity as much as it does in other exercises. For this reason, the Target Zone formula is based on a maximum heart rate of 205, not 220. The formula for swimming is:

$$
\begin{array}{rl}
& 205 \\
- & \underline{\text{Age}} \\
= & \text{Maximum heart rate} \\
\times & 60\% \text{ for low end of Target Zone} \\
\times & 85\% \text{ for high end of Target Zone}
\end{array}
$$

AEROBIC DANCE/AEROBICIZE

Aerobic dance and aerobicize classes have many positive points. They're upbeat activities that offer significant weight control and cardiovascular benefits. They're easy to start and stick with, and no expertise is required. They exercise the whole body. And, for most people, they're a positive experience. Many experts believe the group dynamics and the music combine to make exercising fun, rather than a grind, thus encouraging people to exercise as a regular part of lifestyle.

Normally, an aerobics class will last 45 minutes. An exercise routine that contains at least 20 minutes of nonstop exercise will provide aerobic benefit. Done three to four times a week, a minimum for cardiovascular fitness will be achieved. A number of aerobic classes meet only twice a week, which isn't sufficient to produce aerobic or weight control benefits, so it may be necessary to join more than one class to aerobicize every other day. Another approach is to supplement classes with other aerobic activities, such as walking or swimming. In addition, many good video-tapes are now on the market; often a combination of home/class exercise will provide a sufficient workout.

A word to men: aerobic dance is not an exercise just for women. A study in *The Physician and Sports Medicine* reported on a group of men aged 33 to 72 who attended aerobics classes three times a week for 45 minutes. After six weeks, they had lost weight, lowered resting heart rate and reduced cholesterol.

The effectiveness of aerobic dance and aerobicize classes depends on the instructor and on the routines, the site and the shoes. The instructor is critical, not only in deriving cardiovascular benefit but in avoiding injuries. Dr. Jean Rosenbrum, in an article in *Medical Selfcare,* reported that over 55% of the aerobic dance instructors he surveyed experienced significant injuries and over 80% of the programs he observed contained dangerous stretching or workout elements. When selecting a class, be sure to find out from the sponsoring agency (YMCA, private club, community program) whether or not the instructor is properly qualified. Sit in on a class. The routine should provide for stretching and warm-up time, build gradually to 20 minutes of nonstop exercise at an aerobic pace and provide a cool-down period. The floor is also critical: concrete and linoleum or hardwood over concrete have no "give" and should be avoided; the best floor is cushioned hardwood, as used for basketball courts.

Shoes are the final ingredient. Use a shoe specifically designed for aerobic routines. Don't use running shoes—they're not designed for side-to-side movement. Aerobic shoes absorb shock, stabilize the foot and minimize twisting. Never use worn shoes or exercise barefoot.

THE BEST TIME TO EXERCISE

Anytime you can exercise is the "best time." Morning, noon, evening—it's strictly up to you, your schedule, interests and, some would say, your biorhythms. If you're a "morning person" who springs out of bed and can't wait to get going, there are many advantages to early-morning exercise: it provides alertness to face the day; it allows a sense of control that carries through the day; and it's easier to schedule. In addition, studies show that morning exercise is the most effective for burning fat.

But not everyone is a morning person. Some people like to exercise at noon. It helps them to dissipate morning stress, provides a refreshed feeling and helps to control luncheon appetites. People who exercise before dinner often like the feeling of tension release. The day is done, and exercise helps them to relax.

More important than time of day is making exercise a priority—a daily or an every-other-day event—so that it will produce significant cardiovascular and weight control benefits. One of the best ways to do this is to schedule exercise on a weekly calendar as if it were a business meeting or a doctor's appointment. This action often keeps exercise from falling to the bottom of priority lists ("I'll get to it when everything else is done"). On my calendar is written "Appointment with Mr. Nike." Nike, of course, is a brand of jogging shoes. Should someone want to meet with me during that time, I tell them, "I have a previous appointment.'' Remember, exercising regularly is a lifestyle choice that you make for yourself.

SLOW AND STEADY PROGRESS

As often mentioned, *gradual* progress is the key to long-term success. The best way to kill an exercise program is to go at it too hard and fast. It's important to monitor your pulse rate and to use the Target Zone, but the ultimate criterion should come from listening to your body. If your muscles are sore and your breath is short, slow down or stop. If there are threatening symptoms, see a doctor.

Building up exercise capability slowly, over time, will ensure that the progress you make is once and for always. That's why it takes a minimum of six to eight weeks, depending on age and condition, to work into a true aerobic program. According to Dr. Steve Van Camp, director of the Adult Fitness Program at San Diego State University, it takes about one month to get in shape for every year that you've been out of shape. Obviously, a 30-year-old might do it in less time, a 60-year-old in more time. The point here is that it isn't a race. The time spent conditioning the body will allow for much better long-term results. Cardiovascular fitness doesn't come in one day.

GETTING STARTED

Once you begin, exercising often becomes so enjoyable that it's easy to do regularly. But overcoming a negative attitude is the first hurdle. A person who is open to change, who understands the benefits of aerobic exercise and is motivated, can overcome the following objections to getting started.

■ ''It's too hard.'' It doesn't have to be. If you exercise at the right pace, you won't get tired and out of breath. Aerobic exercise is geared to what the body can do steadily.

Starting out slowly and attaining fitness over time takes the "work" out of exercise.

- "I don't have the time." An effective aerobic exercise program takes no more than 30 or 40 minutes, including warmup and cooldown, every other day. It's certainly possible to find that time just from the hours spent in front of the television set.

- "I'm too tired." The feeling of fatigue often is the result of a lack of exercise. Regular exercise promotes blood circulation, provides more oxygen to the brain and dissipates stress. It can provide the excess energy needed to overcome chronic fatigue.

Zero in on the positive aspects of an exercise program: you'll lose weight and keep it off; your muscles will be shaped and toned for better appearance; you'll gain self-confidence; you'll meet new people with similar interests; your cholesterol and blood pressure will be reduced; stress will be dissipated; and your heart will be strengthened.

Getting started is aided by following a few simple guidelines.

1. Get an okay from your doctor. This is particularly critical if you haven't had a checkup recently, are over 35 years of age, are severely overweight or have a family history of heart disease or high blood pressure.

2. Determine your present level of fitness. A good test to approximate fitness is to check your resting pulse. Find a quiet place and relax for 5 minutes before taking the pulse. (Be certain that at least an hour has gone by since you've eaten, had coffee or smoked a cigarette.) Find your pulse and count it for 60 seconds. The lower the rate, the more efficiently your heart is pumping blood.

Heartbeat per 15 Seconds

Men under 45	Men over 45	Women under 45	Women over 45	Fitness Rating
Below 18	Below 19	Below 20	Below 21	Excellent
18 to 20	19 to 21	20 to 22	21 to 23	Good
21 to 25	22 to 26	23 to 28	24 to 29	Average
Above 25	Above 26	Above 28	Above 29	Poor

3. Select an activity that matches your fitness level and interest. It should be enjoyable, not a punishment. Exercise isn't retribution for "porking out." If you hate jogging, don't do it. Try something else, and keep trying until you find an activity that you really enjoy. Plan exercise to keep interest high. Vary the route for walking or jogging, or use headphones or the TV while exercising on an indoor bike. Exercise should be a good time, not a grind.

4. Look for activities that can be done with a friend or a family member. This can make exercising a social time and add a new dimension to the experience. Making a date with someone to exercise makes it harder to cancel.

5. Commit in writing to an exercise program for six weeks. Base activities on 250 calories burned per day. Six weeks is not an eternity, but it's long enough to see some results. Schedule exercise time on the calendar, preferably the same time each day so that a routine is developed. Write down the chosen activity and when it will be performed—there's something about the act of writing that makes it "real." When you make an appointment with yourself to exercise, chances are you'll schedule other activities around it.

6. Learn how to take an exercise pulse and determine the Target Zone. Always listen to your body. Don't "go for the burn."

7. Be sure to spend sufficient time warming up and cooling down. At rest, about 85% of the blood is in the chest and abdomen. As activity begins, it takes 6 to 10 minutes for the blood to reach the extremities. Stretching followed by slow activity can prevent nagging injuries. Don't simply stop when the exercise is over. Take time to cool down by tapering intensity for the last 10 minutes of exercising.

8. Go slowly, easily. Don't overtax. Build into fitness gradually. Remember, exercise is a lifetime program. Don't expect overnight miracles.

9. Keep a record of exercise activities. As the minutes and miles start to accumulate, you'll feel a renewed sense of accomplishment and commitment.

10. Most important, have fun with it. Make exercise an enjoyable part of everyday life.

The benefits of exercise are numerous, but they'll have no effect until you take the first necessary action—choosing to be physically active. The rest will follow once this is done, but *you* are responsible for taking the first step.

Exercise, like good health, is a choice.

CHAPTER 6

STRESS

*The Bane of a
Healthy Lifestyle*

S tress may be the single greatest contributor to illness in the industrialized world. It may also be the most misunderstood. Linked to high blood pressure, peptic ulcers, migraine headache, backache, certain cancers, allergy and alcoholism, stress is also a primary factor in the twin plagues of obesity and cardiovascular disease. It is seldom listed as the official cause of death, but its negative role is now undisputed; in fact, one researcher has estimated that mental stress has either caused or aggravated the symptoms of from 50% to 90% of all hospital patients in the United States.

The impact of stress on cardiovascular health and weight control is twofold. On the surface level, stress produces direct, deleterious effects: it injures artery walls, raises blood pressure, elevates cholesterol levels and causes coronary artery spasms that can lead to sudden death. But stress also works on an indirect, insidious level to produce disastrous health consequences. People under chronic stress often choose poor lifestyle habits. In trying to cope, they smoke, neglect exercise, eat too much and too often, make poor food selections, and abuse alcohol and/or tranquilizcrs. The effect is a double blow to the heart.

Stress is thought of as a modern problem, but its impact upon health has been recognized for hundreds of years. Medical observations from the eighteenth century describe people "paled with fear, reddened with rage, or weeping with joy or sorrow." Such observations also noted that people under extreme stress could go mad or pine away from maladies without clear cause. In 1813 James Johnson, a London physician, was the first to note the relationship between "wear and tear" of life and premature old age. Documentation of the impact of stress on cardiac health goes back even further. Dr. William Harvey, the discoverer of blood circulation, wrote in 1628: "Every affection of the mind that is attended with either pain or pleasure, hope or fear, is the cause of an agitation whose influence extends to the heart."

Never has this "agitation" been more evident than in a contemporary American lifestyle characterized by pressures, time demands and materialism. The resulting stress pervades all walks of life. It can be seen in the harried housewife at home with young children; the assembly-line worker who feels like a cog in a machine; the elderly couple dealing with extensive medical bills; the 20 schoolgirls trying out for 10 cheerleading positions; the Silicon Valley executive attempting to manage a business whose technology changes weekly; the student who "must" get all A's.

The presence of "agitation" is also apparent in more quantitative information:

- Painkillers are the leading over-the-counter drug in the United States. Valium, a calmative, is the most commonly prescribed drug in the world.

- The popularity of cocaine, in the opinion of many health professionals, is due to its use as a stress reducer. It often provides a feeling of accomplishment that is missing in real life.

■ Rampant alcoholism is linked to stress. There are 13 million alcoholics in the United States, many of them children and adolescents.

■ Teenage suicide is on the upswing.

■ Over 25% of adult Americans have high blood pressure, caused or aggravated by stress.

■ Heart attack, the nation's number one killer, is caused or aggravated by stress.

■ According to the American Medical Association, 50% of the annual $380 billion national medical bill is due to an unhealthy, stressful lifestyle.

Society today is concerned about Type A behavior, the effect of stress on the modern woman, burnout and dropout. Virtually everyone has felt stress, and many confront it daily. The pressure of schedule ("I'm late!") or performance ("I should have done better") is a common experience. More people are aware of stress as a legitimate lifestyle problem. In a poll conducted by National Family Opinion, 80% of Americans interviewed stated that they "need less stress in their lives."

WHAT IS STRESS?

Stress is any situation that places special physical or psychological demands on a person, anything that can unbalance an individual's equilibrium. Says Dr. Wayne Lesko of the Center for Stress Management in Arlington, Virginia, "Stress is anything that causes us to change."

The physical responses to stress are surprisingly consistent—tightness in the neck, a knot in the stomach—but the situations that cause stress differ greatly. Divorce is usually stressful, but marriage can be also. The death of a relative produces stress; so does birth. Indeed, not all stress is negative, or what noted stress researcher Dr. Hans Selye calls "distress." Positive stress, called "eustress," is often reflected in a confident attitude and a superior performance; athletes, for example, may use it to "get up" for competition and control tension so that their performance is enhanced. A certain amount of stress is necessary to make life interesting. It can be thought of as a challenge: too little, and life becomes boring; too much, and it becomes overloaded and out of control. It's been compared to adjusting the strings on a violin: too loose and the music is poor; too tight, and the strings might break.

Unfortunately, modern society tends to produce excessive negative stress. From morning to night (and sometimes through the night), many people experience a continuing series of stressful events. Not all are as overwhelmingly serious as divorce. Others are trivial, like being delayed in a bank line or traffic jam, or having a shoelace break when already late for an appointment. Some stress is even associated with positive events, such as shopping for the "perfect" Christmas present. Research shows that the cumulative effect of the trivial hassles of life often is the most difficult to deal with, produces the greatest hostility and may have the most negative health consequences. Parking tickets and traffic jams, it seems, can be harder on our health than a life-threatening medical crisis.

PHYSICAL RESPONSES TO STRESS

The body reacts to stress by adjusting and adapting through a series of physiological changes. These were first noted by Dr. Walter B. Cannon of Harvard University, who labeled them the "Fight or Flight Syndrome."

Consider the following scenario commonly used to explain this adaptation. The year is 20,000 B.C. The place is a cave, in the middle of the night. Inside is a sleeping caveman. He is awakened suddenly by the low growl of a saber-toothed tiger. Long before he is fully awake, his brain has sent a biochemical message to his body in the form of stress hormones—norepinephrine, adrenaline and cortisol—to put it on notice that quick action will be taking place soon. Stored fats and sugars immediately pour into his bloodstream to provide quick-energy fuel. His breathing rate increases to meet the anticipated oxygen needs. In order to carry that oxygen, his heart rate and blood pressure have jumped. The activity of the digestive system and other internal organs has been slowed to make extra blood available to the muscles and the extremities. His blood-clotting mechanisms have been activated in the event of an injury. In short, all senses are primed, all muscles are tensed—he is ready for action. He will either take a stand and fight the tiger—or take flight by running away. His body is ready for either event.

This is a very appropriate response to external physical danger, one that man has used successfully for over three million years. It is not, however, a healthy response to the emotional stress we face in modern society. The problem is this: contemporary life has changed greatly from prehistoric times, but physiology has not. The stress caused by a parking ticket can produce the same bodily response as a confrontation with a saber-toothed tiger—a response that is no longer appropriate to the stimulus.

Stress gets the body all worked up, heart racing and muscles tensed, but in modern society there are few ways for the stress to be released. "Fight or flight" is no help with a jangling telephone or a vaguely threatening note from the IRS. In the modern world, we do not respond to a nagging boss or spouse with a spear; we grin and bear it. In the modern world, stress is not a situation that is soon over; it is continual. The same response that served ancient man so well is detrimental to the health of modern man. The brain has been taught to write the body a prescription that is an overdose of stress chemicals. What once was survival has now become suicidal.

EMOTIONAL RESPONSES TO STRESS

When one is under stress, two emotional responses are produced. The first is *acute alarm,* what the fireman feels while sliding down the pole or the mother while dashing into the street to rescue her toddler from traffic. This is the emergency system that prepares the body to fight or take flight.

Today, acute alarm is often the response used against less severe stressors such as nervous irritation stemming from a red light, a television program or a telephone call. Indeed, acute alarm is the result of any situation or perceived situation that threatens a loss of control, setting off internal alarm bells and provoking an active response such as anger or aggression. The body is prepared to fight, but how can you punch a traffic light? Instead, the blows are internalized. Acute alarm can occur up to 40 times a day. Each time it happens, powerful stress hormones are secreted and the body ends up literally stewing in its own juices.

The second emotional response to stress is *long-term vigilance,* or mentally projecting the future and adapting to that projection. This is what separates man from other animals, yet many people look into the future with fear— watching and waiting for something disastrous to happen. Vigilance is a response to lack of control. It can occur on a temporary basis, as in the case of accountants who face a tax deadline. Or it can occur as a way of life, as with air-traffic controllers. Chronic vigilance can lead to a passive outlook, an "It's out of my hands" mentality that is responsible for self-doubt, a sense of failure, depression and feelings of entrapment.

The emotional response to stress dictates how people see the world and how they think it sees them. Man, programmed as a predator, winds up preying on himself. At best, the result is chronic tension; at worst, damage to the cardiovascular system can lead to serious physical and psychological disorders and, not infrequently, to premature death.

WARNING SIGNS

There are emotional, behavioral and physical signs that can be used to warn about an overabundance of stress. Some of the signs that indicate a person may be under too much stress include:

- Increased muscular tension
- A loss of self-esteem, a feeling of worthlessness
- Difficulty in making decisions
- A feeling that there "just aren't enough hours in the day" to get things done
- Trouble meeting important deadlines
- A sense of paranoia and an increased sensitivity to criticism
- Feelings of fatigue and boredom, unhappiness and sadness
- A harder time being productive or creative, an inability to concentrate
- A tendency to criticize others and be argumentative
- Problems with moodiness or depression
- A desire to experiment with drugs such as marijuana and cocaine
- Poor lifestyle habits—overeating, abusing alcohol, being too tired to exercise, smoking

Often a person can have many signs at the same time. The cruel irony is that the reaction to stress may itself produce more stress. It can become a vicious spiral of increasing signs and increasing stress.

THE IMPACT OF STRESS ON CARDIAC HEALTH

A number of specific physical responses come into play when the body is under stress. Many have a devastating effect on cardiovascular health by causing injury to the coronary arteries, producing unhealthy changes in blood chemistry and straining the heart.

Injury to Artery Walls

Powerful hormones travel through the bloodstream every time the body reacts to stress. These hormones have the ability to injure the walls of the coronary arteries, creating places for cholesterol to collect. The more stress experienced, the greater the chance for arterial injury—and the greater the risk for artery blockages.

Recent research also indicates that stress may be a significant determinant of whether or not blood fat and cholesterol collect to form a blockage. In a study conducted by Dr. Jay Kaplan of the Bowman Gray School of Medicine in Winston-Salem, North Carolina, one group of monkeys was fed a low-fat, low-cholesterol diet but was subjected to constant social stress while another group was fed the same diet but was not subjected to stress. The study showed that the stressed monkeys developed extensive blockages of the coronary arteries whereas the unstressed group did not—even though both groups ate the same low-fat diet and even though both groups had similar blood cholesterol levels. Stress, not diet, was thus the key factor in causing artery blockages to form.

Elevated Blood Pressure

The "Fight or Flight" response causes a temporary increase in blood pressure. When stress is occasional, such an increase does not usually present a health problem because blood pressure returns to its normal level. When stressful events take place too frequently, however, stress hormones continuously push blood pressure up. The result may be the permanent establishment of a new and higher blood pressure level.

According to studies done by stress expert Dr. Robert S. Eliot, about 20% of Americans are "hot reactors" whose response to even mild stress is skyrocketing blood pressure. Each time stress is encountered, their blood pressure rises—and this can happen 30 to 40 times a day. Over time, it settles permanently at a higher level, elevating heart attack risk significantly.

Increased Blood Clotting

Stress increases the stickiness of blood platelets and promotes clotting. As part of the prehistoric protection pattern, this makes good sense in light of a physical threat that could produce a wound. The clotting mechanism would help to minimize blood loss. But an excess of sticky blood platelets may also promote internal clotting, which, particularly in combination with an existing artery blockage, could totally occlude the artery channel, deny blood to the heart or brain and result in a heart attack or stroke.

Increased Cholesterol Levels

Medical research shows that people under stress often have more cholesterol in their blood. This is illustrated in tests of accountants, who show much higher cholesterol levels in April when facing tax deadlines than in August when on vacation. Studies of auto racers produced similar results: cholesterol levels were twice as great on the day of a race as on the day after.

Some researchers believe this is caused by a reduction of the liver's capacity to prepare cholesterol for excretion. One of the physical responses to stress is to shunt blood to the arms (to fight) and legs (to take flight) and away from the internal organs. Reducing blood supply to the liver causes a slowing down of its function, impairing its ability to rid the body of cholesterol and thus raising the cholesterol level. This may be the reason that some people with intense Type A personalities, under stress continuously, have problems lowering cholesterol. They do not produce more cholesterol than others; they simply have more difficulty in its orderly elimination.

"Sudden Death"

Coronary arteries are often pictured as passive, rigid tubes. They are not. They expand and contract regularly, aided by muscle cells in the artery walls. Powerful stress hormones can cause muscle cells to contract excessively, producing an artery spasm and denying blood to the heart. "Sudden death" from a heart attack can result.

There are many examples of stress-induced "sudden death":

- Ten days after the assassination of President John F.

Kennedy, the 27-year-old army captain responsible for the ceremonial troops at the funeral died of a heart attack.

■ A 56-year-old man collapsed and died of a heart attack while celebrating his first hole-in-one.

■ A man watching his favorite baseball team lose on television got so wrought up that he suffered a heart attack.

Of more than over 5,000 male heart attack fatalities examined in a study at Peter Bent Brigham Hospital in Boston, 30% did not have significant coronary artery blockages at the time of death. Their heart attacks were attributed primarily to stress.

Overweight

Genetics aside, excessive body fat is a product of eating too much and exercising too little. Unfortunately, stress often results in poor lifestyle choices—overeating, avoiding exercise—that can result in overweight.

Anger, depression, loneliness, nervousness—any of these negative emotions can be caused by stress and can motivate a person to eat. In this case, food isn't eaten because of hunger; instead, it has become a reward or a consolation, good for whatever ails. Stressed people are unconcerned about the quality of food. They eat because of nervous energy, often "losing track" of calories and not even tasting the food.

Stress is a particularly severe problem for many overweight people. They feel stress because they hate being overweight—and it's their excess weight that causes their stress. They're caught in a vicious cycle. Many suffer from low self-esteem, actually despising their bodies. No matter what, they never seem to lose weight. Consequently, they see their lives and their appearance as being out of control. Tension and unhappiness, the stress of the situation, drive them to overeat often to the point of binge eating. Feelings of guilt, accompanied by even lower self-esteem, soon result and the cycle begins anew.

The problem is compounded by a lack of exercise. Stress causes mental fatigue, a chronic feeling of tiredness, which keeps many overweight people from participating in physical activities that would actually dissipate stress and renew energy levels. As a result, these people make the poor lifestyle choice to remain sedentary. They restrict activities that would burn fat, control weight and give them a sense of being in charge of their lives. When stress produces a cycle of overeating and underexercising, extra weight becomes a predictable result.

THE CAUSES OF STRESS

Virtually everything that happens, or is perceived to be happening, can subject a person to harmful stress. One of the keys to managing stress, then, is an understanding of its causes.

CULTURAL CAUSES

Although stress has been around since the dawn of man, its intensity and frequency have increased dramatically in this century, especially since the end of World War II. One reason is that life has become more complicated. Multidimensional issues today raise wrath, consume energy and seem to go on forever. Divorce, juvenile crime, the homeless and the hungry, nuclear arms, the changing male-female roles, terrorism, abortion, inflation, drugs—there are few simple answers to these and other problems of modern society.

Support organizations of the past, particularly organized religion and the educational system, have their own problems today. The extended family, once a bulwark against the world, has broken up and moved to the suburbs. Feeling alone and helpless against such overwhelming issues, many people experience chronic stress.

The pace of contemporary life has accelerated to warp speed. Modern man encounters a thousand more events every year than did his great-grandparents, yet he has the same or less time for making decisions, for relaxing or enjoying. Swedish economist Staffan Linder, in *The Harried Leisure Class,* states that the time needed in modern society to produce and to consume has by necessity reduced the amount of "free" time, which has become too valuable to use for doing "nothing." The growing speed and complexity of life on the one hand, plus diminished time for decision making on the other, have created an "out-of-control" feeling that for many people has become a permanent condition.

The high-speed American lifestyle produces a great number of social contacts in the course of a single day, a condition described by John B. Calhoun of the National Institute of Mental Health as "social velocity." Tests on animals show that social contact takes two forms: positive contact, as in a courtship dance, and negative contact, as in a battle for territory. A second social encounter coming too quickly on the heels of the first, however, is *always* perceived as negative. The more total encounters the animals experience, the more negative encounters result, until even a friendly or a neutral approach is seen as aggressive.

Human social velocity produces the same results. Take the harried working wife who, strung out from an excess of stressful contacts (children, carpool friends, boss, co-workers, grocery store checkout clerk, etc.), greets her husband that evening with a growl. It isn't that she doesn't want to see him, but the sheer number of contacts in her day has taken its toll. She is tired and stressed, and he is just one more contact.

Overabundant social contact is heightened by two modern devices: the telephone and the television set. Social velocity—and stress—increase with a telephone that rings constantly. The problem is increased dramatically by television, with its daily inundation of over two thousand advertising messages, each one a social contact. Television causes an additional problem by telling us how to look, what to drive and where to go. Some people are particularly susceptible to these messages and accept them as real-

life standards. When advertising and reality become confused, confidence, goals and self-esteem are the victims.
Comparisons with what is seen on television make some
people feel they're losing the game of life. Happiness and
self-worth are seen as the result of "things," or posses-
sions. "I'd be truly happy," a man tells himself, "if only
I had . . . (fill in the blank)." If he falls short of his goal,
he becomes frustrated. If it is achieved, he may experience
the Peggy Lee Syndrome: "Is that all there is?" Dissatis-
faction then turns to frustration and anxiety.

The modern American lifestyle—fast-paced, aggressive,
consumption-oriented—has produced more benefits for
more people than any other culture in the history of the
world. Unfortunately, one of its principal by-products is
chronic stress.

CHANGES IN LIFE EVENTS

Life is constantly changing. People move, change jobs, get
married or divorced, buy/sell houses, have children and
watch them grow up. There is birth; there is death. Whether
trivial or significant, happy or sad, planned or unplanned,
all change stresses the body by causing it to adapt. It is the
process of adaptation that the body finds stressful. Change,
adaptation, stress—these elements always go together.

The body adapts to most changes fairly well; however,
when change occurs too often or too rapidly and produces
an excess of stressful events happening at one time, there
can be a problem. The body's adaptation mechanism over-
loads, stress increases and illness can result.

The relationship between the amount of change in life
and the risk of illness was first studied at the turn of the
century. Researchers proposed then that the more changes
involved, the greater the incidence of illness. Work by
Dr. Thomas H. Holmes, a University of Washington researcher, corroborated what earlier studies had suggested:
hospital patients, regardless of the nature of their illness,
had one major thing in common—the occurrence of a sig-

nificant number of life changes just prior to their hospitalization. Carrying his findings forward, Dr. Holmes developed the Social Readjustment Rating Scale, which ranks specific life events in terms of their relationship to illness. Some events are significant, such as divorce; some are less so, such as being handed a traffic ticket. This scale is important because it shows that stress is cumulative. It takes only a few significant events, or a number of smaller events, to overload the adaptive system of the body. In addition, it illustrates that the event need not be negative to cause harmful stress. Vacations, Christmas and marriage are positive but still stressful events.

Use the Holmes Scale to evaluate changes in your life. Obviously, the scale cannot predict with certitude, but it's a good tool for raising awareness about the potential external sources of stress in contemporary life.

THE SOCIAL READJUSTMENT RATING SCALE

Read the list of Life Events and enter the score for each event that has occurred in your life over the past year. If any event occurred more than once, multiply the Point Value by the number of times the event occurred. Then total your score.

Life Event	Point Value	Your Score
1. Death of spouse	100	_____
2. Divorce	73	_____
3. Marital separation	65	_____
4. Detention in jail or other institution	63	_____
5. Death of a close family member (other than spouse)	63	_____
6. Major personal injury or illness	53	_____
7. Marriage	50	_____
8. Dismissal from job	47	_____
9. Marital reconciliation	45	_____
10. Retirement	45	_____

11. Major change in health/behavior of a
    family member   44   _____

12. Pregnancy   40   _____

13. Sexual difficulties   39   _____

14. Gain of a new family member
    (through birth, adoption, mother
    moving in, etc.)   39   _____

15. Major business readjustment (merger,
    reorganization, bankruptcy, etc.)   39   _____

16. Major change in financial status   38   _____

17. Death of a close friend   37   _____

18. Change to a different line of work   36   _____

19. Major change in number of
    arguments with spouse   35   _____

20. Taking out a mortgage/loan for a major
    purchase (home, business, etc.)   31   _____

21. Foreclosure of mortgage/loan   30   _____

22. Major change in responsibilities at
    work   29   _____

23. Son or daughter leaving home
    (college, marriage, etc.)   29   _____

24. Trouble with in-laws   29   _____

25. Outstanding personal achievement   28   _____

26. Wife beginning or ceasing work
    outside the home   26   _____

27. Beginning or ceasing formal
    schooling   26   _____

28. Major change in living conditions
    (new home, remodeling, moving)   25   _____

29. Revision of personal habits (dress,
    manners, etc.)   24   _____

30. Trouble with boss   23   _____

31. Major change in working hours/ conditions 20 _____

32. Change in residence 20 _____

33. Change in schools 20 _____

34. Major change in usual type/amount of recreation 19 _____

35. Major change in church activities 19 _____

36. Major change in social activities 18 _____

37. Taking out a loan for a lesser purchase (car, TV, freezer, etc.) 17 _____

38. Major change in sleeping habits 16 _____

39. Major change in family get-togethers 15 _____

40. Major change in eating habits 15 _____

41. Vacation 13 _____

42. Christmas/holiday season 12 _____

43. Minor legal violations (traffic or jaywalking ticket) 11 _____

TOTAL _____

WHAT YOUR SCORE MEANS

The higher your score (the more changes in your life in the past year), the more likely you are to experience a significant illness in the near future. This is because the effect of stress on health is cumulative.

Below 150 Points
Statistically, you have a 30% chance of experiencing a significant health problem in the near future.

Between 150 and 300 Points
This represents a 50% chance of experiencing a significant health problem in the near future.

Over 300 Points
This represents an 80% chance of experiencing a significant health problem in the near future.

A number of other studies show a relationship between life events and the onset of disease. One demonstrated that the death rate for widows and widowers was highest during the first six months following the death of a spouse; considering that this event is thought to be the greatest change in life, the finding was no surprise. Another illustrated that the death rate from cardiovascular disease is two to three times higher for divorced women than for married women. Psychologist James J. Lynch, in his article "The Broken Heart: The Medical Consequences of Loneliness," links the stress from divorce to an increase in asthma, cervical cancer, peptic ulcer, disruption of menstrual cycle, headaches and depression.

Even Mondays are stressful! Most people know this intuitively, but research by Dr. Simon Rabkin of the University of Manitoba lends medical credence. Dr. Rabkin studied 3,983 men with no previous history of heart disease from 1948 until 1977. Of the fatal heart attacks suffered among this group, 75% were "sudden deaths" that occurred at work on a Monday—following reintroduction to occupational stress after a weekend respite.

A new area of investigation involves the impact of environmental and cultural changes on the risk for illness. Some areas of the country are undergoing many significant changes, such as population shifts or economic fluctuations. While no single change may conclusively impair health, the cumulative impact can be a threat. A good example is the state of Washington, located in the pastoral Pacific Northwest. Its lifestyle is perceived by many people as being more relaxed and less stressful than other areas, notably California and the East Coast. According to a study by University of New Hampshire sociologists, however, underneath the thin veneer of tranquillity is a tension storm. Using an index with 15 indicators to assess the degree of statewide stress, the study ranked Washington as the fourth most stressful state in the country (behind Nevada, Alaska and Georgia). It received its position because of high rankings in environmental and cultural changes. At the time of the study, Washington led the nation in business failures and was fifth in unemployment, eighth in divorce, fifth in abortion and third in moves to a new house. "Stress is not only an individual event," stated Dr. Murray Strauss, a partner in the study, "but grows out of social living. It happens a lot more in some states than in others."

This study also illustrates the effect of stress on poor lifestyle habits. It found a correlation between states with high levels of social stress and those with high rates of cigarette sales. According to Dr. Arnold Linsky, the link between stress and cigarettes is "much stronger among females than among males" because certain stress factors—divorce, abortions—seem to have a greater effect on women than on men.

TYPE A PERSONALITY

Type A personality is the term used in connection with those individuals whose behavior pattern makes them prone to coronary heart disease and heart attack. It was first identified over 20 years ago by San Francisco cardiologists Meyer Friedman and Ray Rosenman, who saw it as an external manifestation of internal stress. Characteristically, Type A people want to do everything themselves, never have enough time, are bossy, impatient and aggressive.

While described as a "personality," in reality Type A refers to a behavior pattern based on a way of viewing the world that calls for high achievements, competitiveness, time urgency and ambitiousness. Type A people are involved in an incessant struggle to achieve more and more in less and less time against the opposition of other people or things. They are combative, relentless "doers," impatiently steamrolling over any obstacles that may appear. Someone once described the perfect Type A coat-of-arms: a clenched fist wearing a stopwatch!

Often, Type A people are society's heroes and leaders, the "people who get things done." Recently, however, this perception is being questioned. First, there is the issue of price. Type A's may run the world, but often they do it at the cost of cardiovascular health. The risk of heart attack for a Type A is five to seven times greater than for a more relaxed Type B, a fact that moved the American Heart Association to include Type A personality as a cardiac risk factor. Indeed, studies at Mt. Zion Medical Center in San Francisco and at Boston and Stanford universities have shown Type A personality to be an independent risk factor in the development of coronary heart disease.

Second, the effectiveness of Type A efforts are being questioned. Corporate profiles of top executives show that many are Type B's. Calmer, less impulsive, less angry than Type A's, these executives make cooler decisions. They are not easily upset by change, and they are able to adjust more easily, manage their business more efficiently and enjoy life more fully. To a great extent, the linking of Type A personality with corporate success is a myth.

Characteristics of Type A Behavior

Type A behavior is not simply a reaction to stress, but a persistent pattern of behavior evident in both pleasant and unpleasant life situations. The key factor is that Type A individuals see *all* situations as a challenge to control and will react to them as if under great pressure to "win." According to health professionals, this view is often based on deep-seated insecurity and low self-esteem. While a Type B woman might regard the tardiness of a friend for a lunch date as an opportunity to read the newspaper, the Type A sees it as an affront—a challenge to who and what she is. The Type B remains calm; the Type A fumes and stresses herself.

Over 50% of American men and women demonstrate the Type A behavior pattern. Many readers may recognize in themselves the characteristics of Type A people, who are always:

■ Feeling a great sense of time urgency. Time always seems to slip away; there's never enough of it. When the end of the day comes, Type A's almost never have completed all of the 30 or 40 items on their "to do" list. They're always in a hurry, making a fetish of being punctual, and are greatly annoyed if kept waiting. Type A's will actually set their watches ahead, making themselves constantly behind schedule, in order to induce more self-pressure to be on time.

- Maximizing their time by doing two or more things at once. They talk on the phone while signing letters, watch TV while reading a book, converse with someone while carrying on a completely different train of thought.

- Acting as if they're behind a deadline. They walk, talk and eat rapidly. Type A's will not linger at the table after dinner. They dislike routine jobs at home because their time is too valuable. In their impatience, Type A's will interrupt to answer a question before it's asked. They do not delegate well. If the job is not being done precisely as they would do it, Type A's step in and take over.

- Demonstrating excessive motor energy in rapid speech, clipped words and gestures, tense, tight smiles, and repetitive tapping, drumming or shaking of hands and feet. Type A's can't sit still, drive fast and are workaholics.

- Measuring success in terms of numbers—dollars, sales calls, size. A Type A's first thought upon seeing a Michelangelo painting will be: *How much is it worth?*

- Turning hobbies into competitive events. A Type A person who builds model cars to relax, for example, enters a competition—and wins! Soon he's building more and more cars and competing every weekend. This competitiveness extends to games also. Type A's always play games to win—even with children. Some sons of Type A's reach adulthood without ever having beaten their father in a single game of backyard one-on-one basketball! Winning is success; losing is disaster. As one psychologist observed, "Type A's will kill for a blue ribbon or a T-shirt." Type A's do not enter 10-K runs for fun; they do it to win or at least to beat their best time. Research shows that competition to this degree may be harmful or even lethal. Psy-

chologist Kenneth France at Shippensburg State College
found that when people are competitive in workouts, mentally pushing harder and faster, stress hormones such as
norepinephrine are raised. With the rise in hormones comes
an elevation of heart attack risk.

■ Feeling guilty about relaxing and doing nothing. They
take a briefcase on vacation or climb into a hammock with
a sheaf of PTA projects. Take Type A's to the beach or the
top of a mountain, and they'll overlook the beauty in favor
of an overwhelming concern to start back by a certain time.

■ Feeling insecure and lacking self-esteem. They constantly fear that sooner or later they'll be unable to cope in
a situation and lose status in the eyes of their peers. Fear
of failure keeps Type A's struggling to achieve more without taking time to savor their accomplishments.

Some experts believe this behavior pattern to be a conditioned response to the competitiveness of capitalism and
free enterprise. Others, such as Dr. Friedman, see it as the
result of inadequate parental love. Parents who lavish love
and affection only when a child accomplishes something—
wins the spelling bee, for example, or hits a home run—
create a sense of diminished self-esteem. The child feels a
need to achieve in order to win parental love. In an adult,
this feeling produces a frantic attempt to accomplish more
and more.

Women and Type A Personality

Until recently, Type A personality was viewed as an exclusively male problem. It is not and never has been. This
misconception was due to the fact that most early Type A
research involved males. Furthermore, this research was
concerned with a link between Type A behavior and stressful, traditionally male jobs. Today, Type A behavior is
clearly identified as a problem for females as well, affect-
ing both employed women and homemakers.

A study at UCLA shows that Type A women under stress
act no differently from Type A men and suffer similar health
consequences. Type A women have from four to seven

times the risk of heart attack as do Type B women. According to psychologist Margaret Chesney, the Type A reaction "may be part of an overall coping style for challenge, a catalyst in a set of negative health behaviors that increase risk not only for heart disease but for other diseases as well." She found that Type A women made lifestyle choices that fostered poor health habits: they tended to smoke more, exercise less, be more overweight, consume more caffeine, feel angry more often and get less sleep than Type B women.

The link between Type A personality and overweight may be surprising to many people because it upsets the stereotype of the continuously active Type A, frantically burning off calories at all hours of the day or night. In reality, Type A lifestyles are characterized by inadequate exercise and excessive caloric intake—factors that combine to make Type A a risk for overweight as well as for a coronary. Apparently, the Greyhound-thin "supermom," able to balance home, career and her figure, is as much a myth as the relaxed, jolly fat lady.

Though evident in a cross-section of American women, Type A characteristics are particularly noticeable in women who work outside the home. Not only are these women under the same career pressures as males, but many are breaking new ground, performing in arenas once classified as "male only." Often they feel more pressure than their male counterparts to succeed at their jobs. Much of the tendency toward Type A personality in working women may be the result of a drastic change in the social order, according to psychiatrists Dr. Susan Wooley and Dr. O. Wayne Wooley at the University of Cincinnati Medical College. Before adolescence, girls and boys are raised very differently. Girls are taught to value relationships and usually form strong bonds with their mothers; boys are raised to compete and achieve. In modern society, however, girls in adolescence are being told to become more like boys— to break the ties and become independent self-achievers. Having motherhood and homemaking as a goal is no longer enough; they must aspire to succeed on male terms—independence, self-reliance and important jobs. In the new order, many women find themselves in stressful conflict because they have no role models.

An additional problem for many working women is that they are also primarily responsible for running the home. They "punch out" of their regular job, only to "punch in" at a second one as homemaker. Even in this day of the sensitive, empathic male, studies show that women still perform the vast majority of household tasks. This is further complicated by female child-raising responsibilities, an aspect of society that has remained unchanged. The mother is still seen by males and females as having the primary role in child-rearing. It is estimated that nearly 60% of women employed outside the home have children under six years of age. Even with good child care—not always easy to find—working women often feel guilty about leaving their children with someone else. This problem is even greater for single mothers. Many women, attempting to build two "perfect" worlds with limited time and energy, run themselves ragged—and into Type A lifestyles.

Although employed women are more A-prone than homemakers, research has shown that housewives are not immune. A study by University of Kansas psychologist B. Kent Houston showed that housewives structure their home environments to be as stressful as some work environments, attempting to "do it all themselves." Many found housework more taxing and reported less satisfaction in their marriages. These traits—taxing work and lack of marital satisfaction—are the same as those reported in other studies on Type A men and career women.

Testing for Type A Personality

Whether or not a person exhibits Type A behavior can be determined by means of a self-scoring test such as the one on the facing page, based on research by Drs. R. W. Bortner and Ray Rosenman. This test asks you to describe yourself and your feelings on a rising scale. The higher the number, the greater the Type A tendency. For example, if you're very concerned about punctuality (you're *never* late), your score might be 24—the highest point of the scale. If, on the other hand, you're casual about appointments, you

TYPE A BEHAVIOR TEST

The following scale represents a range of emotions from 3 to 24. Find yourself on each scale and record your score. Then total your score.

3 6 9 12 15 18 21 24

You have a variety of interests	You're a workaholic
You do things at a slow or moderate pace	You're fast in all things—eating, talking, actions
You do one thing at a time	You do many things at one time
You seldom feel pressured or rushed	You always feel behind schedule
You are not competitive	You're highly competitive in everything
You describe things with words	You describe things with numbers
You're casual about appointments	You're never late

YOUR SCORE _____

Score	Personality Type
120 and over	A-plus
106 to 119	A
100 to 105	A-minus
90 to 99	B-plus
Less than 90	B

Adapted from R. W. Bortner and R. H. Rosenman in *Journal of Chronic Diseases* (July 1967).

might score a 3—the lowest point of the scale. If your feelings fall somewhere in between, your score will fall between 6 and 21. While not clinically exact, the test gives a fair representation of whether or not you have Type A tendencies.

Can Type A Be Changed?

Most health professionals do not believe that Type A behavior can be totally changed. It is seen as endemic to the American culture, which teaches that it's better to wear out shoes than sheets, the early bird gets the worm, a man's reach should exceed his grasp. As long as society views Type A behavior as desirable, it will be encouraged. The basic problem, as Emerson said, is that "solitude is impracticable and society is fatal."

While total change may not be possible, however, a decrease in the intensity of Type A behavior *is* attainable. A four-and-a-half-year study of 1,102 cardiac patients conducted by Dr. Carl Thoresen of Stanford University showed that Type A personalities can be counseled and learn to modify behavior. Almost 600 of the group received intensive behavioral training to change Type A habits—how to slow down, be more patient and have a more positive outlook—and were also given advice on diet and exercise. Only 12.9% of this group suffered a second heart attack. Some 270 patients received advice on diet and exercise only, with no instruction on Type A behavior modification; second heart attacks hit 21.2% of this group. A third group of 90, who got no instruction, had a 31.8% rate for second heart attacks. "This study," says Dr. Thoresen, "clearly tells us that changing these destructive Type A habits can affect the chances of a second heart attack."

A similar project, headed by Dr. Meyer Friedman, illustrated the effect of such behavior modification on 1,000 patients: after three years, only 9% of those who modified their Type A behavior had suffered a new heart attack, compared with 20% of those who did not modify their behavior. Psychologists say that Type A's try to become Type B's when convinced that Type A behavior is "inefficient" and reduces productivity. Type A values often can motivate Type A's to become Type B's.

The fact is that Type A behavior produces a lifestyle that is conducive to coronary heart disease and excessive weight. But it doesn't have to be that way. Type A behavior *can* be modified: stress can be managed, weight can be controlled and cardiac risk can be lowered.

HOW TO MANAGE STRESS

It is not my intention to provide detailed information on all the techniques used to dissipate stress. Indeed, entire books have been devoted to techniques of stress management. It *is* my intention to provide a perspective, a view of the damaging effects of stress on a healthy lifestyle— and to highlight stress management from the vantage point of personal experience.

The management of stress is essential to a healthy lifestyle. Whether stemming from changing life events or from Type A personality, chronic stress directly increases the risk of cardiovascular disease. Its most devastating effect, however, often is to pressure a person into an unhealthy lifestyle involving cigarettes, excessive calories and alcohol, and lack of exercise. As Woody Allen is reported to have said, "Death is nature's way of telling us to slow down." Stress is a characteristic of modern life, but we don't have to succumb to it. There are alternatives. If we "slow down" and assess stress in terms of causes and reactions, we can see many opportunities for managing it.

A number of valid, tested techniques are available to anyone interested in stress reduction. In my opinion, three of the best techniques are: creating a realistic perspective, clarifying goals and dissipating stress through exercise.

CREATE A REALISTIC PERSPECTIVE

The Chinese character for crisis means "danger," but it can also be translated as "opportunity." This illustrates a tenet basic to an understanding of stress and stress management: it's not the event that is stressful but the perception of the event. What may be "danger" to one person is seen as "opportunity" by another. Situations—events, people, workloads—are essentially neutral. Of and by themselves, they do not cause stress; instead, it's one's viewpoint that can make a situation stressful.

A good example is a man caught in a traffic jam on the way to an important meeting. He thinks to himself: *It's already eight o'clock. I'll never make it on time. Jim will tear my head off for being late.* He reacts by shouting at the driver ahead: "Move it, you jerk!" His heart rate and blood pressure increase; he feels stiffness in his shoulders and tightness in his stomach, and his thoughts become overwhelmingly self-critical. What really stresses him is not the event itself, but his judgment of the event.

Stress—or lack of stress—is the result of perception. Each of us sees the same event differently, and this difference dictates whether or not the event is stressful. In other words, one person's stress can be another person's pleasure. This is illustrated by a story about a wealthy woman who lives in a rooftop suite of an elegant hotel in New York. About one o'clock in the morning, she was awakened by a piano in the adjoining suite. Boiling mad to be hearing "noise" at that hour, she vented her stress on the front-desk manager, who apologized and explained that the occupant of the adjoining suite was world-renowned concert pianist Artur Rubinstein. Mr. Rubinstein was disappointed in his performance that evening at Carnegie Hall, and though the audience loved it, he had returned to his suite to replay the entire concert. Upon hearing the explanation, the woman promptly forgot her complaint, pulled a chair next to the wall—and spent the next two hours listening to Mr. Rubinstein play.

Had a change of events reduced her stress? No. What had changed was her perception. She herself had taken a highly charged, stressful event and turned it into one of deep pleasure. The "noise" had become beautiful music.

I heard this story in a seminar, so I can't verify its veracity. But even if untrue, it's a tremendous illustration of how a change in perspective can help to defuse stress.

"Concern" vs. "Worry"

De-stressing events through perspective is called "straight thinking." It comes about when we see events in realistic terms and talk positively to ourselves about them. Straight thinking helps to differentiate a "concern" from a "worry." A concern is something that can be impacted or changed—that a person can come to grips with. Concerns are characteristically centered in the present. For example, habitually being late for work or car pool in the morning is a legitimate concern. It's a problem, but action can be taken to address it, such as setting the alarm 15 minutes earlier and laying out clothes the night before. In this way the concern is dealt with realistically, the problem is solved and the situation is de-stressed.

A worry, on the other hand, is immune to direct action. A good example is provided by a friend of mine who has been working to reduce weight by using the 500-Calorie Solution. She was eating fewer calories, exercising regularly and making steady progress—until one day, in a moment of weakness, she ate a dozen Oreo cookies. Her body is a realist; it lives in the present. It knows that the Oreos will create some excess fat. But her mind has the ability to make this relatively minor slip-up into a major event. It time-travels to unlock unpleasant images of the past or to bring up potential dangers in such future "foul-ups." In doing so, the mind promotes worry—as if by dwelling upon the incident, it could be changed. It cannot, but nevertheless she feels guilty and depressed, and her self-esteem suffers.

A better perspective is to zero in on the present. Why

worry about the event? It's over. It can't be undone. So what? There's no rule that says my friend—or anyone—has to be perfect. Her true concern should be to get back on track for weight control. Taking action to eat prudently again and to exercise regularly will provide a positive outlet for feelings and de-stress the event.

Unfortunately, concern is often confused with worry. A worry is something that is out of a person's control. Worrying does not affect the outcome. Why worry when you're flying cross-country? It doesn't help the situation. The fact is that the safety and the timeliness of the flight depend on a number of things—all beyond your control. Sometimes worrying can be brought into perspective if you ask the question "What's the worst thing that can happen?" Once this is determined, you can make plans to cope with the scenario. Applied to the Oreo example, "the worst thing" is that body fat could increase. In this case a plan to reinstitute a healthy diet and exercise program, and the action that follows, can prevent unnecessary additional stress.

Positive Self-Talk

De-stressing events in the mind with straight thinking is aided by a technique called positive self-talk. Each of us is continually involved in running internal conversations that interpret events and actions. Psychologists call these conversations "self-talk." Most people are generally aware of self-talk, although a great deal of it occurs beyond conscious awareness. It takes place in somewhat automatic fashion, much like riding a bicycle. If you tune in to self-talk, however, you can become more aware of what you're telling yourself and of how self-talk influences your perspective—and your feelings.

Some self-talk is positive, such as planning priorities for the next day. Some is neutral, like wondering how long the sermon in church will last. But much self-talk consists of negative, harmful putdowns. If corrected by a boss or parent, we might say to ourselves: "Can't I do anything right?'' or "I'm always fouling things up.'' These messages create a self-perception that increases stress.

Stress is normally viewed as the result of a disturbing event or situation. As seen in the example of the woman and Mr. Rubinstein, however, situations per se are neutral. What really happens when a disturbing event occurs is that we tell ourselves about it: "This is terrible!'' . . . "How could they do this to me!'' . . . "The workload is killing me!'' It is this self-talk that triggers the emotion. The process takes place in a step-by-step sequence of events:

$$A \qquad\qquad B \qquad\qquad C$$
$$\text{SITUATION} \longrightarrow \text{BELIEF} \longrightarrow \text{EMOTION}$$
$$\text{(the event)} \qquad \text{(self-talk)} \qquad \text{(the result)}$$

Suppose you're scheduled for an important job interview. You jump in your car, turn the key and—it won't start. The meeting is scheduled for 10 o'clock, and there's no way that you'll make it. This is the situation (A). The belief you have about the meaning of the event, your interpretation, takes the form of self-talk (B). In this instance, the talk is negative: "Mr. Brown will be disappointed in me. He'll think I'm rude and that I don't care about the job. Why does this always happen to me? I'll never have such a great opportunity again.'' The result of this self-talk, of course, is mushrooming stress (C).

But what if the self-talk is positive? "Mr. Brown is going to be unhappy because I'm late, but the battery is dead. Getting upset won't help. I'll call him to say I have to come by taxi. I won't be there on time, but I'm sure he'll understand. He's probably been caught in the same situation himself. And besides . . . he wants to talk to me. He knows I'll be a great addition to his company.'' This self-talk produces a very different perspective of the event and keeps it from generating stress.

The A-B-C concept illustrates how thinking influences feeling and explains why two different people can respond to the same situation with far different emotional reactions. It also suggests that by altering self-talk (B), the resulting emotion (C) can be changed. This is known as "cognitive restructuring." It calls for being aware of negative self-talk (B), challenging those self-defeating comments and replacing them with positive statements that decrease or prevent a stressful emotional response.

Controlling Feelings

The first step in taking control of feelings is to determine the kind of self-talk that is communicated in times of stress. In most instances, the self-talk is terribly distressing: "Isn't it *awful* that . . ." or "Wouldn't it be *terrible* if . . ." or "What an *(awful) (lousy) (rotten)* thing for (me) (him) (her) (them) to do." We're either telling ourselves how awful it is that things aren't the way we want them to be or we're condemning ourselves/someone else because of the way things are. Most of the time we're dealing with a worry— an event over which we have no direct control.

Relatively minor frustrations, inconveniences and concerns are mentally blown up so that they become, for the moment, catastrophes. The reaction to them produces stress and emotional disturbance. It is precisely at this point that one needs to deal with reality. How is it so terrible that this event has occurred? Why is it awful? Can any control over the situation be exerted? By examining these questions, we often can readily see the irrational aspects of negative self-talk and can recognize it as being self-defeating and stress-producing.

By systematically tuning in to internal statements about troublesome situations, the thoughts that are stress-provoking will quickly be illuminated. This not only places things in proper perspective but causes us to focus on our own stress-producing thoughts and to consciously trade them for stress-reducing thoughts. It's also a signal that stress management techniques may be needed.

Replacing Negatives with Positives

Replacing negative with positive self-talk can provide more control over stress. A great deal of stress comes from the difference between the way things or people are and the way we want them to be. The idea that things/people should or must be the way we demand creates an emotional catastrophe. These feelings can be counteracted with positive statements that defuse the irrational demands and stop stress from developing: "Okay, so I don't like this. It's not the end of the world. I can live with it." Or: "I don't have to be perfect. I can make mistakes, too. I don't have to please everyone."

Positive self-talk statements can help to short-circuit unpleasant emotions by placing things in a non-crisis perspective. In doing so, they cause us to deal with the present. We can become so bound up in self-defeating thoughts about how terrible the situation is or will be that we don't give our full attention to what should be done to cope with the situation. Positive self-talk can keep the mind focused on the task at hand: "Relax. You're in control. Take a deep breath and concentrate on what you have to do."

When the essence of stress is examined, it often comes down to one message: "I have no control. Other people and other things dictate my life." This message is reinforced by negative self-talk that erodes self-esteem. A mistake calls for a response such as "You dummy! You never do anything right." Such messages impact self-confidence, attitudes, expectations and interpretations so that events or situations result in feelings of ineptness and unworthiness. We feel as if we have no power over life's events or, we think, over ourselves.

Positive self-talk is an advertising message for worthiness and control. Like any successful advertisement, repetition is the key—the more often it's repeated, the easier it's remembered. This is because the brain is essentially a computer. The information fed into it is what comes out in terms of actions. Behavioral scientists teach that negative self-talk causes people to view themselves in a negative light and program their behavior to act accordingly. On the other hand, by being positive in self-thought, they feed affirmative data into their mental computer. The response is to create feelings of control and self-worth—and positive actions. A self-confident person who is in control is not easily stressed.

A Stress-Resistant Attitude

Outlook and attitude can play a tremendous role in whether or not life is stressful. Differences in the perception of events explain why some people are vulnerable to stress and others are not.

Research by psychologists Suzanne Kobasa and Salvatore Maddi indicates that some people are stress-resistant because of "hardy" personalities. In a study of Bell System executives during the 1983 breakup, they found that some executives flourished under the change while others wilted. The stress-resilient people demonstrated three attitudinal characteristics: a sense of control, commitment and challenge. Drs. Kobasa and Maddi found that stress-resilient people have a feeling of being in control while those vulnerable to stress are likelier to feel helpless. Hardy people believe in their ability to influence and shape events—to turn situations to their advantage. In contrast, stress-prone people feel powerless and act as if they're the victims of forces beyond their control. Some displaced Bell executives for example, looked at the breakup as a fresh chance to find a better position; they were not stressed by the situation. Others felt that being fired was a ruination and that they might never be hired again.

Hardy people demonstrate a feeling of commitment to life, to going at what they're doing at full tilt, because they believe their actions are worthwhile and useful to themselves, their families and society. In addition, their lifestyles are in balance and contain diverse interests. They do not allow one aspect of life to become an obsession. When changes or setbacks in one area occur, they have other places to turn for the psychological uplifts needed to help them over a hurdle. Stress-vulnerable people, by comparison, often believe that many of the things they do are meaningless—done only because they feel they have to.

Finally, the study showed that stress-resilient individuals have a sense of challenge and a willingness to deal with new experiences. They accept and anticipate changes as natural and useful, instead of threatening. Life for them might be difficult at times, but it's always exciting.

One of the most important benefits of hardiness is that it helps to provide a perspective for failure, one of life's greatest stresses. No one can be successful in everything. Failure is a product of the human condition. But failing does not have to be a weakness—it can provide for tremendous growth. It isn't the failure that's important; it's how the failure is handled. There are classic examples throughout history: Albert Einstein's poor performance in all classes except math prompted a teacher to predict failure for him and ask him to leave school; Thomas Edison's father called him "a dunce" and his teachers described him as "addled," warning that he "would never amount to anything"; Sir Winston Churchill, who twice failed the entrance exams to Sandhurst, was considered "dull" by his father. But these men demonstrated hardiness—and turned roadblocks into stepping stones.

Can a person become hardier? According to Drs. Kobasa and Maddi, three techniques can help. The first is to focus on signals from the body that something is wrong, then mentally review the situations that might be stressful. Focusing increases a sense of control and puts a person in a better position to cope. The second is to mentally reconstruct stressful situations—to think about how it could have gone better or gone worse. This often illustrates that things did not go as badly as they might have. The third is to compensate for stress through self-improvement. When life seems out of control, taking on a new challenge can result in regaining self-esteem and a sense of accomplishment. The source of the stress—loss of a job, divorce—may be impossible to avoid. But by taking on a new task, a person is assured that he or she can still function.

CLARIFYING GOALS AND VALUES

Stress resiliency is a product of lifestyle attitudes and actions that mesh with personal goals and values. Those who are under the greatest stress, say many psychologists, are those who drift through life without direction. They have no standard against which to measure their lives, so the act of living itself carries no reason and little joy.

Stress-resistant people, on the other hand, exhibit goals that concern quality of life as well as material success. They concentrate on what is worth being, not just worth having. People who choose lifetime goals, and a lifestyle pattern commensurate with those goals, put themselves under pressure to achieve them. However, these goals are what make life meaningful and provide a means of attaining satisfaction and self-esteem. Goals work when we work toward them—and we only do that when they're our own.

It's the same with values. Too many people live a stressful existence because their lives and values are out of sync— they declare one set of values and interests but live life with another set. A good way to get this into perspective is to write your own epitaph based on how you're living. Is it how you would like to be remembered? If not, you may need to clarify your values and adjust your lifestyle. An example of how this technique works involves a friend of mine—a hard-working, perpetually "stressed-out" man who takes a deep interest in his family but, because his work calls for constant travel, simply isn't home very much. He went through the epitaph exercise and was disappointed. Based on the way he was spending his time, it would read: "Here lies the best widget salesman in the 11 Western states." He would have preferred: "Here lies a great father and a wonderful husband." When it dawned on him that his real values, priorities and goals were inconsistent with how he was living, he toned down his travel. In doing so, he gained a balance that produced self-satisfying tranquillity and reduced his stress.

There are many other exercises that can be used to

clarify and crystallize priorities. Among the best is one proposed by stress expert Dr. Robert Eliot, which he calls the "Six-Months-to-Live" Test. Suppose you had just six months to live and had to decide how to spend the time. You make three lists to identify 1) the things you have to do, 2) the things you want to do, and 3) the things you neither have to do nor want to do. Dr. Eliot recommends forgetting about the third list, even throwing it away. It contains the things that prevent you from doing what you really want to do. The first list should be taken care of, but once that's out of the way the rest of the time should be spent on the second list—those things that give life meaning for you. It's important to select goals that are genuinely important and that reflect personal values, interests and talents.

DISSIPATING STRESS THROUGH EXERCISE

Exercise, nature's own tranquilizer, may be the best technique for dissipating stress on a regular basis. The physical act of exercise itself allows the body to "throw off" tension. Anyone who runs, walks or swims regularly knows that post-exercise feeling—the body feels tired, even drained, but good.

But this may not be the real reason for exercise's calming effect. According to a study conducted by the National Center for Health Statistics, frequent exercisers have more positive moods and less anxiety than those who exercise little or not at all. "The relationship is clear across the board," says psychologist Thomas Stephen. "The more you exercise, the better your mood is and the less likely you are to be anxious or depressed." Anxiety, depression, anger and other stressful emotions are banished through physical activity.

One of the reasons for the positive impact of exercise on mood is the dissipation of excessive stress chemicals. This is particularly important for those who suffer from chronic stress. These people generally have a high level of stress chemicals constantly circulating in the bloodstream, a "fight or flight" reaction that gears the body to do something physical. If no physical activity is forthcoming, the stress hormones bombard the heart and the coronary arteries, causing injury and, in some instances, sudden death. Exercise appears to burn up excess stress chemicals by using them for energy expressed outwardly. Obviously, the next time stress appears, the stress chemicals will reappear. But when a person exercises regularly, the body learns to metabolize these chemicals more easily, and fewer are available to injure the heart and the blood vessels.

Other scientific studies support the notion that exercise can have a positive effect on emotions and moods. A University of Southern California study found the effect of a 15-minute walk to be that of a strong tranquilizer; indeed, it was more effective than the tranquilizer in reducing tension. A study at Duke University illustrated that Type A behavior, characterized by aggressiveness and impatience, can be modified with aerobic exercise. In this study, 50 men and women aged 25 to 61 were tested to determine A or B types, then put on an exercise program (45 minutes, three times per week). After 10 weeks, the Type A's were found to be substantially calmer and more relaxed.

One theory on why exercise dissipates stress involves the stimulation of endorphins by the brain. These are chemicals that produce a positive feeling and a happy, self-satisfied attitude. Exercise causes endorphins to be released in the body, so the person who exercises feels better about life. The result is a decrease in stress.

The bottom line, perhaps, is that exercise provides a sense of self-reliance, power, control and greater self-esteem. Since much stress is the result of low self-esteem and a perceived lack of control over life, exercise can reduce stress by reversing those conditions. If you have the discipline to commit to a regular program of exercise, you *are* in control and you feel good about yourself. As clinical psychologist Dr. Kenneth R. Pelletier observes, "When people begin to pay attention to their health, they seem to have a much better ability to look at things that used to bug them and simply be more detached. If you are taking time out of your life to exercise, you're taking a psychological stance that in itself is going to have you reacting differently to your job, your office, your sense of achievement, your career.''

OTHER WAYS TO DISSIPATE STRESS

While straight thinking, self-talk, goals and attitudes, and regular exercise are critical in reducing tension, fear, anxiety and anger, there are many additional stress management techniques.

Repetition

This centuries-old technique, also called meditation, involves the repeating of a single word for a concentrated but brief period of time. It is designed to clear the mind and, in doing so, to produce an immediately calming effect on the nervous system. Studies at UCLA and at Harvard University show the physiologic effect of repetition. When you're asleep, for example, your oxygen consumption is decreased by 8%; with repetition, however, it's down by 12%, an indication that your body is more deeply relaxed. These studies also illustrate that repetition can decrease blood pressure significantly.

To use repetition, select a quiet environment that is both pleasant and comfortable. Loosen your clothing if it's tight or uncomfortable and remove your shoes. Assume a comfortable position, either sitting or reclining, close your eyes and empty your mind of all thought. Take a deep breath and slowly repeat a single word. Dr. Herbert Benson, author of *The Relaxation Response,* recommends using words or sounds that end in *m* or *n*, such as ''calm'' or ''ocean,'' but any word will do. Slowly repeat the word mentally, over and over again. Other thoughts will occasionally interfere, but just let them pass through your mind. After a while, repetition will have an almost hypnotic effect and create a state of deep rest and relaxation. In a few minutes, you'll feel renewed energy and new hope.

Deep Breathing

This simple exercise can be done once or twice a day to break tension's hold. Most people tend to breathe incorrectly, by expanding the rib cage. This is called chest breathing and results in short, shallow breaths. Chest breathing is most evident when a person is under stress. Unfortunately, it is constricting and has the effect of heightening stress.

A better form of breathing is deep, or abdominal, breathing. The technique is easy to practice and can be done standing, sitting or lying down. Find a comfortable position and take deep breaths. As you inhale oxygen, push out your stomach. This lowers the diaphragm. Hold the breath for a few seconds, then expel it slowly and easily. Both intake and expulsion should be rhythmical. Deep breathing results in slow, regular breaths and creates a state of calmness. Do it for just two or three minutes, and tension will dissolve.

If you're unfamiliar with this technique, a good way to learn it is to lie on your back and place a weight on your stomach. Two or three books are usually sufficient. When you breathe in and push out your stomach, the books will rise; when you exhale, their weight should press in. This exercise will give you a good feel for how deep breathing is practiced.

Modified Progressive Muscle Relaxation

This is one of the best techniques to clear tension from the body. By concentrating the mind on groups of muscles, you can imagine them relaxed, which in turn causes an actual relaxation to take place.

Begin by finding a quiet environment where a half-hour can be spent without pressure. Lie on your back in a comfortable position with arms at your sides and legs uncrossed. Loosen any restrictive clothing. Close your eyes and adjust your body position to be comfortable. Focus your attention on breathing. Notice the inhalation of air through the nostrils down into the lungs, filling them up, and then back out again. Breathing should be deep and easy, rhythmic and smooth. Bring attention to the muscles of the scalp and forehead. Tune in to feelings of tension there. Tighten the scalp and forehead muscles. Squeeze and hold the tension, then release it, relaxing the area.

Repeat this cycle—awareness of an area, tightening of the area, relaxation—with all parts of the body. Start with the head and move systematically to the feet. Go slow. Try to focus on only one part at a time, letting go more and more, until your whole body is in a state of deep relaxation. Let every muscle relax. Allow the tension to flow out with each breath. After you've gone through these steps, you'll be very relaxed and will feel calm, refreshed and rejuvenated.

Laughter

An often overlooked stress reduction technique is laughter. According to Dr. William F. Fry, Jr., of the Stanford Medical School, a good laugh—like a good workout—produces an overall sense of well-being. Laughter flexes the diaphragm, chest and abdominal muscles, causing deep breathing to take place. It exercises the shoulders, neck and face, allowing muscles to release tension. The humor involved also can help create a different perspective on life and its problems. As cardiologist Dr. Steve Yarnall says, "Laughter is the shortest distance between two people."

Until recently, many medical professionals discounted its therapeutic effect, but now laughter is taken seriously as a health management technique. Much of this understanding has come as the result of work done by Norman Cousins, former editor of *Saturday Review* and now a professor at the UCLA Medical School. In an article in the *New England Journal of Medicine,* and later in his bestselling book *Anatomy of an Illness,* Mr. Cousins recounts how laughter helped to cure an unexplained sudden illness.

The illness, which hospitalized him, seemed to be immune to traditional medical therapy. After a period of time with no progress, he abandoned conventional thinking, stopped taking medication and ordered in reel upon reel of Marx Brothers films and *Candid Camera* reruns. According to Mr. Cousins, the resulting laughter, sustained and heavy, caused the illness to disappear and was the key to his recovery.

While many medical experts remain skeptical of laughter's role in treating disease, more are coming to understand its benefit in reducing the stress that underlies so many diseases and are recommending laughter-provoking activities such as cultivating friends and acquaintances who smile and joke, putting playfulness into relationships, leaving work concerns at the office. Laughter can provide a needed sense of balance to the serious business of life.

Assertiveness

For many people, stress can result simply from not knowing how to say no. These people feel put upon yet powerless to change the circumstances.

Learning how to be more assertive, to express feelings and needs to others forcefully, honestly and politely, can significantly reduce the level of stress. If you don't express feelings and needs when it's your right to do so, or if you discount your feelings as being unimportant or less worthy than someone else's feelings, emotions get bottled up inside and you feel miserable. On the other hand, if you're aggressive to the point of insult or criticisms, neither good communication nor good relationships are fostered. Assertiveness involves the stating of feelings and the request for an appropriate change. If a meeting is scheduled for a time convenient for others but not for you, an assertive response can avert later feelings of stress: "This isn't a good time for me, and I'd really like to be at the meeting." (Statement of feelings.) "I know we've tried to find a time good for everyone, but let's give it one more effort." (Request appropriate change.)

Assertiveness is not rudeness. It's simply taking your own needs and desires into consideration. Often the mind has to overcome the heart in order to be assertive. The mind knows that you have a right to put yourself first sometimes, but the heart feels that old childhood programming that "nice people always put others first." Assertive thinking and action place a person in control and can be instrumental in managing stress.

CHOOSING TO MANAGE STRESS

Stress is a fact of modern life. It is particularly so in the United States, where a fast-paced lifestyle and a Type A-fostering culture combine to induce high levels of frustration, anxiety and anger. Whether external (life events) or internal (Type A personality) in source, stress can build to a lethal point. Its harmful effect on cardiovascular health is evident in heart attack and stroke statistics, and its impact on habits leading to obesity is direct. But stress does not have to waste health, impair longevity and lead to overweight. There is a choice. Not many of us can avoid the events that make life stressful, but each of us has control over our perception of and reaction to those events. We each choose our own goals and values.

A choice exists: we can manage stress successfully—or we can allow it to dictate life and impair health. Stress may never go away altogether, but it can be minimized.

Managing stress, like good health, is a choice.

CHAPTER 7

SMOKING

*The Habit
That Kills*

No aspect of lifestyle choice has a greater impact on health than cigarette smoking. Medical professionals consider it to be the worst health hazard in America today. In addition to increasing the risk of lung cancer by a factor of 20 and being the principal cause of emphysema, it is one of the three major risk factors for heart attack and stroke. Other results of cigarette smoking include chronic bronchitis, high blood pressure, and cancer of the larynx, mouth, kidney, pancreas, stomach, esophagus and bladder. In every annual report since 1964, the U.S. Surgeon General has cited cigarette smoking as the largest preventable cause of death in the United States.

Smoking clearly is a health hazard, a killer habit, yet it is a fixture in the national lifestyle. Americans spend $23.4 billion to purchase 607 billion cigarettes each year, or about 206 packs for every adult. With cigarettes pervading lifestyle to such a degree, it should come as no surprise that smoking causes about 500,000 American deaths annually.

It is responsible, according to World Health Surveys, each year for:

147,000 cancer deaths
240,000 heart disease deaths
61,000 respiratory disease deaths
4,000 deaths from injuries such as those caused by fire
4,000 infant deaths

A half-million deaths a year is a staggering figure yet one that may actually be understated. Extensive analysis of data on smoking by the Department of Agriculture indicates that the true impact on mortality is much higher.

One of the problems in understanding the impact of smoking on mortality is that the numbers are too large to relate to everyday life. More graphic descriptions better illustrate the true scope of the problem. Deaths caused in one year by cigarette smoking are:

- More than the total U.S. casualties in World War II.
- Twelve times the annual deaths from auto accidents.
- Equal to 1,315 fatal crashes of fully loaded 747's—about four a day.

Indeed, the connection between cigarette smoking and death is so direct that scientists have been able to calculate a figure for "loss of life per cigarette." The death rate increases proportionately with the number of cigarettes smoked per day and the length of time a person has smoked. According to the American Lung Association, it is not the number of years lived but the number of cigarettes smoked that ultimately predicts mortality. A man who started smoking at age 15, and smoked one pack a day, will have smoked 109,000 cigarettes by age 30. Each cigarette will cost him an average of 20 seconds of life. If he didn't start until age 20, he'll have smoked 36,500 fewer cigarettes by the time he's 30—which on average will be worth 15 seconds of life apiece. A two-packs-a-day smoker, who will take 100,000 to 140,000 puffs of cigarette smoke a year, on average throws away 8.3 years of his life. If he has coronary heart disease, the years of life lost are even greater.

CORONARY HEART DISEASE MORTALITY RATES BY NUMBER OF CIGARETTES SMOKED PER DAY

(Men Aged 35 to 44 and 45 to 54)

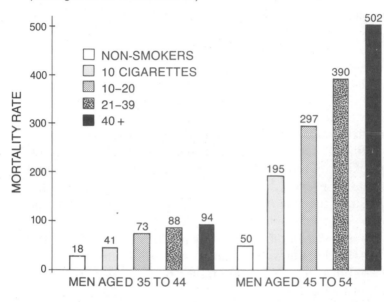

The negative impact of smoking on longevity is evident from research involving lifespan differences between males and females. As a group, females live longer than males (currently, the difference is about 7.5 years). Now researchers believe they have found a main reason: cigarette smoking. A study conducted by Edinboro State College in Pennsylvania and the National Research Council examined the smoking habits of over 4,000 men and women who died between 1972 and 1974. The study found that non-smoking men, defined as having smoked fewer than 20 packs in their entire lives, lived as long as non-smoking women and therefore illustrates that the difference in longevity is less a product of gender than of a lifestyle choice.

Does all smoking have the same effect? While ''full-flavored'' cigarettes are plainly the greatest hazard, a threat is also posed by pipes, cigars and filter cigarettes. Provided they don't inhale, pipe and cigar smokers generally suffer fewer negative effects than do cigarette smokers. The problem is, according to studies at St. Bartholomew's Hospital in London and the Tampa Veterans Administration Hospital, that they *do* inhale. This is especially true of those who at one time smoked cigarettes: research indicates that these smokers may actually have a greater risk of lung cancer and heart disease than cigarette smokers. In addition, cigar and pipe users' smoky environment, or "sidestream exposure," may do almost as much damage to the lungs over the long run as conscious inhaling.

Filter and low-nicotine cigarettes have fared no better. A study by Dr. David Kaufman of the Boston University Medical School shows that the heart attack risk for smokers is the same whether they smoke low- or high-nicotine brands. As Dr. William Castelli, director of the Framingham Study, points out, "Filters are not doing what they are reputed to be doing. You're still getting the poison."

UNDERSTANDING THE IMPACT OF SMOKING

While most people are aware of the relationship between tobacco and lung cancer, many do not realize that an even stronger link exists between cigarette smoking and coronary heart disease. Smoking is in fact the major preventable cause of heart disease.

Heart disease, not lung cancer, is the principal cause of death among cigarette smokers. Of the 600,000 to 800,000 annual heart attack deaths in the United States, it is estimated that over 40% are attributed to cigarette smoking. Smokers are twice as likely to have a heart attack as nonsmokers and are five times more likely to die a sudden death from heart attack.

Autopsy studies illustrate that coronary heart disease is far more severe and extensive in smokers than in nonsmokers. The message from these studies is: "The more you smoke, the more severe your coronary heart disease is

CIGARETTE SMOKING AND FIRST MAJOR CORONARY EVENT*

(Men Aged 30 to 59)

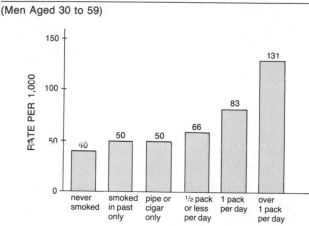

* A coronary event is defined as any clinically significant manifestation of coronary artery disease, such as heart attack or angina.

Source: American Heart Association.

likely to be.'' This is especially true when smoking is combined with other risk factors, such as hypertension or high cholesterol. The effect of smoking, then, is not additive but compounded and lethal.

HOW SMOKING CAUSES HEART DISEASE

A lighted cigarette gives off several hundred compounds, some in gaseous form and others in the form of particles, or tar. The gases, which constitute about 60% of cigarette smoke, include carbon monoxide, cyanide, ammonia, nitric acid, acetone and acrolein. The tar inhaled produces ammonia, benzpyrene and at least 10 other known carcinogens as well as nicotine, a toxic chemical. A pack-a-day smoker will pour one cup of tar into his or her lungs in the course of a year.

Scientists are not certain how these compounds work to produce coronary heart disease and heart attack, but the consensus is that the chief culprits are nicotine and carbon monoxide. Nicotine increases the workload of the heart, causing it to require more oxygen. At the same time, carbon monoxide enters the bloodstream (smokers have up to 10 times more carbon monoxide in their blood as nonsmokers) and displaces oxygen, making it less available to the heart at the precise moment when it is most needed. The result is a "Catch-22" situation in which the heart cannot win.

Nicotine and carbon monoxide work in three ways to produce heart disease: by injuring the walls of the coronary arteries, by producing an unhealthy blood chemistry and by placing extreme strain on the heart.

Injury to Artery Walls

The internal lining of the coronary arteries is made up of delicate tissue that is susceptible to irritation and injury. Such injury is often caused by an excess of carbon monoxide in the blood. A single cigarette contains 640 times the amount of carbon monoxide as would be allowed in any industrial plant in the country by OSHA, the government department charged with occupational safety and health. As carbon monoxide moves through the bloodstream, artery walls can become pitted and cratered, providing a repository site for cholesterol and other blood fats. Arterial injuries often result in clogging blockages that lead to heart attack.

The injury process is illustrated in a UCLA study by Dr. George Sieffert and Dr. Wesley Moore, who placed laboratory rats in airtight chambers and exposed them to tobacco smoke roughly proportional to human intake of one pack of cigarettes a day. After 12 weeks of "smoking," the rats were found to have severely pitted arteries. Thus, the more a person smokes, the more opportunity carbon monoxide has to create sites for cholesterol deposits.

Unhealthy Blood Chemistry

The more fat in the blood, the higher the risk of cardiac disease. Excessive fat in the bloodstream provides an increased opportunity for a "fatty streak" to develop and clog the artery. Cigarette smoking can increase the fat level of the blood. This happens when nicotine frees fatty acids in the bloodstream, thus accelerating the atherosclerotic process.

Cigarette smoke also affects blood viscosity. When blood is "thin," the tendency to form clots is reduced. This is one of the reasons that fish oil is recommended in a heart-healthy diet—it keeps blood thin. Carbon monoxide works in just the opposite manner, causing blood platelets to become "sticky" and increasing clotting within the blood vessels. Clots can seal off blood supply to the heart and promote a heart attack.

Strain on the Heart

Nicotine is a stimulant. The "lift" a smoker feels with the first puff is real. Nicotine quickly causes an increase in cardiac workload; the heart rate is increased by 15 to 25 beats a minute and the blood pressure rises by 10 to 20 points. In order to maintain the increased workload, the heart needs more oxygen. This is precisely where the "Catch-22" situation develops. As the heart cries out for oxygen, nicotine and carbon monoxide restrict its delivery.

Studies at the University of Southern California Medical School show that nicotine alters the production of two critical hormones: it inhibits the hormone responsible for blood vessel expansion and enhances the hormone that constricts blood vessels. The net effect is to slow down the delivery of oxygenated blood to the heart. The impact of carbon monoxide is even more direct: it displaces oxygen in the bloodstream. Carbon monoxide has 210 times the affinity for red blood cells that oxygen has, so replacement is rather easy. Oxygen decreases by about 20% in the presence of carbon monoxide, so that a smoker at sea level gets as much oxygen as a non-smoker at the top of an 8,000-foot mountain.

While nicotine is forcing the heart to work harder, carbon monoxide is taking away needed oxygen. The result is enormous strain on the cardiac muscle, which can lead to a heart attack.

THE EFFECT OF SMOKING ON WOMEN

The disastrous health effects of cigarette smoking are well documented. The numerous studies have generally involved males, with the results clearly showing men who smoke to be at greater risk for cancer and heart disease than non-smokers. Because women did not begin to smoke heavily and in large numbers until recently, they were not included in much of the data. With the horrifying statistics covering men only, some women have been lulled into a false sense of security, as if they were immune from the health hazards of cigarettes. This misconception is characterized in a comment from Dr. N. Stoehr of Washington Adventist Hospital: "As a med student, whenever I looked at a chest X-ray of an individual with a mass in the lung, the first question was, 'male or female?' If male, it was cancer of the lung. If female, it was probably something else. With one-third of American women now smoking, and lung cancer overtaking breast cancer as the number one cancer killer of women, this is no longer true."

Scientific findings now clearly demonstrate that there is no immunity from the ravages of smoking. Women are as susceptible to smoking-induced diseases as males. The research shows that 75% of the heart attacks suffered by otherwise healthy women under the age of 50 are related to cigarette smoking. Medical scientists, aware of the increase in women smokers and the earlier ages at which girls begin to smoke, project that lung cancer and not breast cancer will become the leading cause of malignant death among American women.

Actually, the number of smokers in the adult population has dropped since the first Surgeon General's Report in 1964 linked smoking to lung cancer and heart disease. Today, about 33% of American adults smoke: 35.4% of this group are men; 29.9% are women. Back in 1964, 52.1% of men smoked, compared to 34.2% of women. While the overall trend is downward, the one segment of the population that has not responded to the message is women between the ages of 17 and 35. The number of smokers in this group has increased.

Why has this segment continued to smoke in the face of overwhelming evidence of health erosion? Some health professionals attribute it to cigarette advertising, which has portrayed smoking as a profeminist issue, as a weight control device and as a necessary component of a chic image. This theory seems to be shared by the tobacco industry itself. According to an article in *TR*, a tobacco industry magazine, women are being targeted as an increasingly important market segment by cigarette companies. This is because women are adopting more dominant roles in society, have increased spending power, live longer than men and are less influenced by anti-smoking campaigns.

The Impact of Advertising

Going after the women's market is not new for cigarette companies. In 1919, the Helman brand was the first to show women smoking. Lucky Strike's motto in 1928 was "Reach for a Lucky instead of a sweet"—perhaps the first "smoke and get thin" advertisement. One company even introduced a red-filtered cigarette that wouldn't show lipstick marks. Yet attempts to penetrate the female market were unsuccessful until Virginia Slims appeared in 1968 and won a 2.5% share of the American market. Their link to women's professional tennis and their "You've Come a Long Way, Baby!" campaign has had great appeal for women in the 17-to-35 age group.

Unfortunately, any link between smoking and athletics, glamour or female equality is an illusion, just as the Marlboro man's macho image is for men. Cigarettes are not a societal issue but a health issue. The devastating effects of cigarettes cut across gender, thus producing the ultimate equality. How far has "Baby" come? In 1963, only 6,500

American women died of lung cancer. In 1984, over 36,000 women died of lung cancer. In 10 states—California, Florida, Kentucky, Washington, West Virginia, Texas, Vermont, Nevada, Alabama and Hawaii—lung cancer has overtaken breast cancer as the number one cancer killer of American women. The so-called "equality" promoted by cigarettes is chiefly in cancer and heart disease deaths.

The media image of cigarette smoking as sexy, sporty and savvy has also had an impact on the smoking habits of American women. Chic, glamorous models adorn the pages of *Vogue, Cosmopolitan, Mademoiselle* and *Ms.*, cigarette in hand, exuding camera-ready beauty and self-assurance. In fact, so many women identify smoking with a fashionable image that Calvin Klein, Yves Saint Laurent and others now market "designer cigarettes," complete with fashion logo. Lynn Newman of the American Lung Association responds by asking a critical question: "Do designer cigarettes give you designer lung disease? They're trying to make it a mark of quality for a cigarette to be endorsed by a famous person," she states. "I think it is an injustice for people to use their recognition or fame to endorse a product that's harmful to your health."

Many health professionals also see an inconsistency in the promotion of cigarettes by magazines supportive of women and women's issues. A number of these magazines offer valuable health articles and tips, ranging from nutrition to breast self-exams. But few run articles that speak to the issue of smoking and health. One study, comparing health articles and references to smoking in women's magazines over a two-year period, reported that *Cosmopolitan,* for example, published 300 articles on health but that only 2% of the stories mentioned smoking even vaguely. The same relationship exists with other magazines: *Mademoiselle* published 310 stories on health, but only 1.9% mentioned smoking; *Ms.* offered 60 health articles, not a single one of which dealt with smoking. A reason for this lack of concern may well be the tobacco industry's $1 billion annual advertising budget. Women's magazines are not alone in catering to cigarette companies. A 1981 *Time* article on heart attack devoted just three sentences to cigarette smoking—and was positioned adjacent to a six-page pull-out advertisement for Vantage cigarettes.

The Weight Control Factor

Perhaps the greatest appeal of cigarettes for many women is their use as a weight control device. While substituting them for food at breakfast or lunch does restrict calories, it also creates an unhealthy nutritional imbalance.

Smokers have another weight concern: "If I quit, I'll look like a blimp." Researchers have known for some time that about one-third of smokers who quit experience temporary weight gain—an average of eight pounds. The popular explanation is that smokers are jittery types who eat less than others and, when they quit, compensate by devouring every candy bar and cookie in sight. New information has shown that there's more to the story. Swiss researchers have discovered that under constant conditions of diet and activity, smoking 24 cigarettes daily at half-hour intervals can cause the body's metabolic engine to accelerate. On days when subjects smoked, they burned about 200 calories more than on days when they didn't.

What bumps the metabolic rate is the nicotine, which appears to stimulate the "Fight or Flight" response and causes the adrenaline level, heart rate and metabolism to rise. As a method of staying svelte, this is a markedly poor bargain. The same 200 calories could be burned with a 30-minute walk. The answer is for the quitter to know that weight gain is a probability and to compensate for it with low-fat, low-calorie foods during the first few weeks and with an increase in aerobic exercise.

Smoking is a double threat for women, not only to their own health and life but to their ability to bear healthy children. Pregnant women who smoke have more miscarriages and premature births, and have more of their babies die in the first few days after delivery, than do mothers who do not smoke. A pregnant woman who smokes two packs a day reduces oxygen to the fetus by 40%, causing increases in respiratory diseases, birth defects and stillbirths. Women who smoke also have smaller babies, weighing an average of a half-pound less than the babies of non-smokers, and their babies suffer more health problems.

CHILDREN AND SMOKING

Despite an increasing awareness of the health hazards of smoking, teenage children have continued to smoke. According to data reported by the Surgeon General, the smoking level of teenage boys has not decreased from that of the past, while that of teenage girls has actually risen. Overall, the percentage of smokers between the ages of 12 and 14 has doubled. This is significant in light of the fact that death rates from all causes are much higher among people who start smoking earlier in life.

It isn't ignorance that moves teenagers to smoke. By the time they're in junior high school, most know that smoking is dangerous. Why, then, do they get started? One reason may be that teenage children do not identify with illness and death, viewed as "old people" problems. At age 14, one thinks that life will go on forever. Another reason may be peer pressure. No teenager wants to appear different or strange; the group mentality is very strong during these years. For many teenagers, smoking is a means of becoming an accepted part of the group. Some teenagers simply follow in the footsteps of their parents: if the mother and father smoke, chances are good that the children will also.

And finally, teenagers are taken in by tobacco advertising that uses athletic, attractive models who are shown smoking yet who look terrific and always seem to be having fun. Critics claim the ads entice children to smoke. Tobacco companies respond that their advertising features adults—models generally in their early twenties—and that they do not direct the ads toward children. It is true that adult models are used, but this just makes smoking more enticing to a teenager. How many 16-year-olds want to look or act their own age?

Advertising also takes place on a more subliminal level. The movie *Superman II,* for example, contained 22 specific references to Marlboro cigarettes. An article in the Reno *Gazette-Journal* stated, "Lois Lane smokes them, billboards proclaim them, and Clark Kent is thrown into a van with the Marlboro Man advertised on the outside."

Tobacco industry spokesmen continue to deny that they're out to hook young people on cigarettes, but the evidence shows that they are. The industry's future depends on it. As James Swomley of the American Lung Association says, "Cigarette companies are in the disadvantageous position of killing off their best customers."

PASSIVE SMOKING

Non-smokers exposed to cigarette smoke suffer more lung cancer and severe illnesses than do people who don't breathe smoke-contaminated air. According to the National Academy of Sciences, "passive smoking" is especially harmful to children and poses an alarming cancer risk for adults.

What is passive smoke? A burning cigarette produces two kinds of smoke: *mainstream smoke,* inhaled into the lungs of the smoker and then exhaled, and *sidestream smoke,* the smoke coming off the burning end of the cigarette. Both produce a wide variety of gaseous and particulate compounds, such as tar, nicotine and carbon monoxide, which pollute the surrounding air. In fact, the concentration of these pollutants is greater in the air around the smoker than in the smoke inhaled with a drag. When the non-smoker breathes contaminated air, it amounts to passive smoking.

The effect of passive smoking can be significant and in some cases lethal, often depending upon the amount of exposure. Research has shown that non-smokers who work in smoky offices for 20 years have the same degree of lung damage as non-inhaling pipe and cigar smokers and as smokers who smoke less than 10 cigarettes a day. Their risk of lung cancer was 14% to 30% greater than workers in smoke-free environments. For this reason, the Surgeon General has branded workers who smoke a "health risk" to their colleagues.

Studies in Greece and Japan identified an increased cancer risk for non-smoking wives living with husbands who smoke. The Greek study showed that the risk of developing lung cancer for a woman whose husband smokes one pack of cigarettes a day is 2.4 times greater than for a woman married to a non-smoker. The risk for a woman married to a heavy smoker (more than one pack a day) is 3.4 times greater. A similar study, concluded in 1986 at the University of California Medical School in San Francisco, found that the wives of cigarette smokers are three times more likely to suffer heart attacks than women whose husbands have never smoked. The same is true for a non-smoking man married to a woman who smokes.

According to the Environmental Protection Agency, passive smoke is "the most dangerous airborne carcinogen" in the United States. The agency estimates that from 500 to 5,000 Americans die every year from someone else's cigarette smoke.

Nowhere is the effect of secondary smoke more devastating than in the case of children. It has been known for several years that infant children of smoking parents are twice as likely to suffer attacks of pneumonia, bronchitis and respiratory infections as are children of non-smokers. A seven-year study in Boston of 5,000 children illustrates that the damage can be more permanent. In a comparison of children raised in a smoke-free environment with those in homes where the mother smoked (even as little as one cigarette a day), researchers found that lung development in the children of smoking mothers had been permanently impaired by as much as 7%.

New infants are denied oxygen because of passive

smoke, which, according to Dr. Richard Naeye of the Pennsylvania State University College of Medicine, may affect behavioral and mental development. In a comparison of seven-year-old children of smokers with those of non-smokers, the children of smokers scored 3% to 4% lower on spelling and reading tests, 2% lower on attention span.

THE DANGERS OF SMOKELESS TOBACCO

The popularity of chew and snuff, so-called smokeless to-bacco, has gained tremendously over the past five years, especially among teenage boys. Currently, over 22 million Americans use smokeless tobacco regularly, the largest per-centage of whom are under 24 years of age.

Young men in particular are attracted to these products for many reasons. Some associate smokeless tobacco with a macho, cowboy image. Others see it as being less harm-ful than smoking. Neither view is correct. The "image" that rough, tough men chew tobacco is an advertising ploy. Tobacco doesn't make a man tough; lack of tobacco doesn't make him a wimp, either. By creating this image, however, the advertising attracts many males on the verge of adult-hood. Chewing tobacco becomes a rite of passage. What the teenagers don't understand is that tobacco companies would use ballet dancers if their image would sell more product!

Misunderstanding the claims of advertising is a prob-lem; misunderstanding the health issues involved can be a tragedy. Some people use smokeless tobacco to avoid the nicotine found in cigarette smoke—no smoke, no nicotine. This is untrue. Snuff and chewing tobacco do contain nic-otine, usually in more concentrated levels than found in cigarette smoke. It is absorbed by the body through the nasal passages and the lining of the mouth, rather than the lungs, but the result is the same: a kick in heart and blood pressure rates, producing strain on the cardiac muscle. Smokeless tobacco increases the risk of heart attack, oral cancer, gum disease and tooth decay.

HOW TO BREAK THE SMOKING HABIT

The alarming health consequences of smoking provide a multitude of reasons not to smoke. The evidence linking cigarettes to heart disease, cancer and increased mortality is conclusive: cigarettes destroy health and longevity.

The arguments for not smoking are logical and persuasive. If smokers responded to such arguments, the cigarette industry would close its doors today. But smoking is less an intellectual than an emotional act, so logical arguments and scary statistics do not motivate many smokers to quit. People smoke because it makes them feel alert, quiets their nerves or helps them control their appetites—or just because smoking feels good and not smoking doesn't.

In the final analysis, no one can make anyone else stop smoking. People must make their own decisions, their own choices. It is not my intent to nag, scold or preach . . . that won't help. It is also not my intention to present a failsafe method to stop smoking in a few pages . . . that's impossible. My purpose is simply to put the smoking habit into perspective, to let the reader see that the decision to smoke is a lifestyle choice that impacts health, longevity and the quality of life.

In addition, I'd like the reader to know that positive choices in other lifestyle areas—diet, exercise, stress management—can support non-smoking behavior.

FOLLOW THE 500-CALORIE SOLUTION

Gaining weight is perhaps the single biggest reason cited by people who don't want to stop smoking—or who go back to smoking. Research shows that a reduction in nicotine intake will also reduce basal metabolism, sometimes by as much as 200 calories a day. This means that at the same rate of activity, the body needs fewer calories to survive. To further complicate the situation, many smokers increase food consumption. Sometimes this is the result of the stress involved in quitting, but often it's because many smokers experience an intense craving for high-calorie sweets. The combination—fewer calories needed, more calories coming in—can be devastating for weight control.

The 500-Calorie Solution provides relief from this problem. Many smokers begin to change their diet pattern before they quit smoking, thus allowing themselves to work on one lifestyle change at a time. It also means that a new diet pattern will be in place when smoking reduction efforts are started. The 500-Calorie Solution—low in fat and sugar, high in complex carbohydrates—provides taste and satisfaction, so that the person experiences fewer cravings for high-calorie treats. Also, by taking in fewer calories, the change in metabolic rate doesn't penalize. Many smokers find that crunchy foods such as apples, carrots and celery help to dissipate the craving to smoke. Mouth, jaws and hands are kept occupied, and the chewing burns up nervous energy. Research also shows that drinking plenty of fluids—at least six glasses of water a day—keeps down the craving for nicotine.

A regular program of aerobic exercise can be critical to the success of an effort to stop smoking. Smokers generally like what nicotine does for them; they smoke to feel alert and relaxed. Nicotine is responsible for these feelings. Shortly after being inhaled, it causes an adrenaline reaction that raises the heart rate and blood pressure, and stimulates the electrical activity of the brain. The smoker immediately feels sharp and focused. As more nicotine enters the bloodstream, it stimulates the release of endorphins, natural opiates that produce feelings of calmness, relaxation and well-being.

Exercise can bring about the same results. Regular exercise drives additional oxygen to the brain, producing mental alertness and creativity. In addition, by causing the release of endorphins, it produces feelings of well-being and relaxation. Even small bouts of exercise are effective in replacing nicotine to create positive psychological and physiological changes without damaging health. Exercise also dissipates stress and burns up nervous energy, giving a person less reason to light up. By dissolving anxiety and depression, exercise creates feelings of self-confidence and control that can help a person to remain smoke-free.

INSTITUTE BEHAVIOR MODIFICATIONS

Smokers are more likely to remain off cigarettes if they've given some thought to their behavior and have planned in advance how to cope with situations that have triggered smoking in the past. If coffee is a signal to light up, for example, juice can be substituted at the morning break.

Small changes in behavior can be instrumental in helping to foster a non-smoking lifestyle:

- Each day, postpone the first cigarette by 30 minutes.
- Establish a quota of cigarettes for the day, then hand them over to a co-worker who moves around a lot or who is removed from your work area. This will cause second thoughts about making the effort to smoke.
- Avoid those situations that call for a cigarette. Get up from the table after dinner and take a walk; stay away from cocktails that call for a cigarette.
- Celebrate "quit day" each week with a reward.
- Get help from the American Cancer Society, the American Heart Association, the American Lung Association and other organizations.

Thirty-three million Americans have quit smoking, and more are choosing to do so every day. They all took the same first step: making a lifestyle decision to be smoke-free. This decision is fundamental to viewing the process as an opportunity for self-improvement rather than a painful ordeal of deprivation.

Breaking old negative habits, and instituting new, positive habits is difficult—but it can be done. Not smoking is an essential component of a healthy lifestyle. In the final analysis, a person who controls weight, eats a healthy diet, exercises regularly and manages stress but still smokes is a long way from wellness.

Not smoking, like good health, is a choice.

CHAPTER 8

POSITIVE MENTAL ATTITUDE

*The Key to Making
Healthy Choices*

Too many people, after completing a health question-naire, listening to an inspiring speaker or reading a great article on weight control, set out with high resolves to make healthy changes ("Starting tomorrow I'm going to take control of my life, lose weight, begin exercising, stop smoking") but abandon their new program after a few days or weeks. They start strong, but soon their efforts become sporadic and wane, yielding few noticeable results—so they quit. They return to their old, unhealthy habits. Nothing has really changed.

This scenario takes place often. Many people institute healthy choices in fits and bursts but fail to make them a way of life. They understand the "why" and the "how" of a healthy lifestyle, but these aren't enough to ensure success. According to Thomas Dybdahl, executive director of the American Prevention Council, people who know that their habits may be unhealthy, and even know what to do, fail to make changes because ". . . it's hard. The pay-off for losing weight or exercising is way down the road.''

The missing ingredient for many people is a positive mental attitude, a basic decision to take action and to persevere until permanent change occurs. Positive mental attitude is an outlook that fosters commitment and success. It's a mental resolve that says: ''I've had enough of failure. This time I'm going to succeed.'' A good example is a woman I know who had lost 100 pounds—20 pounds five different times! Each time she'd gain them back. She had good reasons for losing weight; she even knew how weight was lost and controlled permanently. What was missing was a positive mental attitude, a determination to see change through. ''When I saw losing weight as a problem,'' she said, ''I failed. When I saw it as an opportunity, I succeeded. The difference between failure and success was a positive mental attitude.''

Positive mental attitude is a perspective that centers on what can be done rather than on what cannot be done. Its importance was illustrated to me recently at a talk I gave to cardiac patients at a large California hospital. After the program, the medical staff introduced me to many people. Two men, Jim and Tom, were neighbors who worked for the same company and who, ironically, had each undergone bypass surgery in the same month. But that's where the similarity ended. Jim was doing wonderfully in his recovery. He viewed the changes in his life—healthy eating, regular exercise, no smoking—as discoveries. He was thankful the surgery had worked so well, providing him with a second chance, and he was determined to live life to the fullest. For Jim, lifestyle change was a beginning.

Tom, on the other hand, viewed change as an ending. He had become a cardiac cripple. Soon after the operation, he had mentally crawled into a fetal position and said, ''My life is over.'' He was a young man, but in his mind he was old and frail. His viewpoint centered on what he couldn't do. The difference between these men was their mental outlook. For Jim, change was a steppingstone; for Tom, it was a roadblock.

THE THREE DIMENSIONS OF POSITIVE MENTAL ATTITUDE

Making healthy lifestyle change is hard. A positive mental attitude is what helps a person to stay committed and to persevere one day at a time, to keep practicing healthy habits until they become a way of life. The key elements in a positive attitude are motivation, receptiveness to change and self-responsibility.

MOTIVATION

Motivation is fundamental to success because people who don't want to change, *won't* change. It's that simple. Telling them why healthy change is positive ("You'll look more attractive with a slim, toned body . . . You'll have more energy . . . You'll live longer and have a better quality of life") won't make it take place. All the logical arguments in the world won't make an impact on someone who is not motivated to change.

A good example is a man I met about six months after his heart attack and bypass surgery. At the time of the attack, he was 50 pounds overweight with a cholesterol count of 350. Now, a half-year later, he was in even worse shape. At the request of his concerned wife, I agreed to talk with him about the importance of lifestyle change. By the time I arrived for our breakfast appointment at a local restaurant, he had already ordered ham and eggs, fried hash brown potatoes, toast with butter, coffee with cream—and, just to make sure he wouldn't starve until lunch, a side order of pancakes with butter and syrup. It was obvious that he had no interest in dietary change, and he rationalized his behavior by telling me: "It took 60 years for my arteries to get blocked up. If it takes another 60 to happen again, who cares?" Down deep, he knew this was not the way coronary heart disease worked. The simple truth was that he wasn't motivated to make the effort, to do the hard work required, so he made no changes in his lifestyle.

What a contrast to another man I met in a similar situation. A busy executive, this man had grappled with stress for years. His hours were long, so there was never time for exercise. He had clients to entertain, which meant a lot of restaurant eating and drinking that resulted in an overweight problem. He smoked to relax. And he had high blood pressure. The man was a walking time bomb, and one day the bomb went off. He had a heart attack. I met him about a month after his attack. He was recovering at home and experiencing mental anguish sorting out all the lifestyle changes recommended by the doctors: lose weight; eat a low-fat, low-salt diet; start exercising; stop smoking; reduce stress at work. Just thinking about these changes put him on the verge of an anxiety attack. My advice to him was to concentrate less on *what* had to change and more on *why* he wanted to change. My feeling was that if the reasons to change were significant, he would become motivated and find it easier to take the correct action.

I saw him a year later—buying equipment for climbing Mt. Rainier with his teenage son! He had lost 30 pounds, was exercising regularly and eating healthfully. He had stopped smoking, and he was more relaxed. He was spending less time at his job—but he was doing so well that he'd been promoted. He had fundamentally altered his lifestyle. The key, he told me, was his young family. As he thought of life for them without him, his focus changed. He dwelled less on the unfairness of the situation and became more concerned about what he could do. In a word, he became motivated to change. "I discovered," he said, "that life is difficult. It's a series of problems to be solved. You can either moan about them or you can welcome the challenge. If the reasons for solving them are important enough, you'll find the solution—and stick with it. But you have to want it. No one else's desire is sufficient. It's your own motivation that puts you on the road to realizing a healthy lifestyle."

RECEPTIVENESS TO CHANGE

The second dimension of a positive mental attitude is receptiveness to change. As discussed in the chapter on stress (pages 240–245), any type of change can be hard. Change deals with the unfamiliar, so it tends to breed resistance. Doing things differently takes thought and effort, and forces many people out of their comfort zone—the self-image that says, "I am what I am, and I can't change." When faced with a new way of living, reasons not to change are easily found: "I'd like to exercise, but I just don't have the time," or "I know I should eat a better breakfast, but my friends meet for coffee and doughnuts every morning and I like being there," or "I'm too busy at work to think about stress reduction."

Resistance to lifestyle change often is a product of a particular view of life. What must be understood, however, is that many adult viewpoints are rooted in childhood experiences. For example, most people choose the vegetables they like and dislike at about age 10—by then, they've learned to like corn and hate brussels sprouts. That viewpoint may never change. Favorite colors, for example, are most often chosen at about age 10 for boys and age 13 for girls; these colors tend to stay as favorites throughout their lives. Psychologist Dr. Jennifer James illustrates the impact of early defined views with what she calls the "spaceship test." Suppose a flying saucer lands in the middle of town. A crowd soon grows around it. The saucer is shrouded in mist, has eerie blinking lights and makes strange noises. Suddenly a staircase is dropped, inviting everyone to climb into the saucer. Would anyone go? Certainly not many of the people raised on *War of the Worlds* or *The Monster from the Black Lagoon* would venture forth; they know that aliens are dangerous. But what about the people brought up on *E.T.*? Most of them, Dr. James believes, wouldn't hesitate; they have a different viewpoint concerning aliens.

Receptiveness to change is a product of perspective and

attitude, an understanding that doing things differently may break a comfortable pattern of life but can result in growth and improvement. A closed attitude, on the other hand, acts as a barrier and prevents the implementation of healthy lifestyle changes. Self-imposed barriers restrict the possible, limit expectations and impair the ability to change for the better. People have to overcome them in order to see themselves as individuals who *can* live a healthy lifestyle.

This is pointed up by a story that takes place in Australia where every year a 550-mile endurance race is run from Sidney to Melbourne over rugged terrain. As race day dawned a few years ago, the starting line was elbow to elbow with world-class runners decked out in stylish gear and state-of-the-art shoes. Also waiting for the starting gun was Cliff Young, a 61-year-old sheep rancher, wearing boots and bib overalls. Being a very polite people, the Australians didn't laugh at him. "He paid his entry fee, he gets to run" was the sentiment. The accepted wisdom in such a race is to run about five hours, then rest, then run again a few more hours, then stop to rest and to sleep. Not being a trained runner, Cliff knew nothing of how races were run. In fact, no one told Cliff he had to stop to sleep— so he didn't! He just kept on going at a trotting pace and won the race—by two days!—instantly becoming a national hero.

Cliff Young wasn't limited by a view of himself that said, "You can't do this" or "You can't do it this way." He had an open attitude, and that is what allowed him to achieve his goal.

Why did it take until 1954 before the four minute-mile mark was broken? Perhaps it was because no one before Roger Bannister *believed* it could be done. Today there are thousands of sub-four minute miles recorded, and the world mark is somewhere in the 3:40's. Certainly technique, training methods and equipment have improved. But the most significant factor is that the barrier had been removed. Once Bannister showed it could be done, everyone knew it was possible for a human to do it again.

This also holds true in making healthy lifestyle changes. If people are locked into the way they've always lived ("I am what I am"), their comfort zone becomes a psychological rut . . . and any attempt to change is met with a constant struggle. At best, temporary results are achieved. But if lifestyle change is approached with an open attitude, what "I can become," the chances for long-term success are greatly increased.

SELF-RESPONSIBILITY

The third dimension of a positive mental attitude is self-responsibility, the knowledge that we alone are responsible for our health. Too often, the answer to the question "Who is responsible for your health?" is "The doctor" or "My spouse" or "My family." Too often, being overweight is blamed on other people or outside circumstances. Other people do impact our lifestyle, of course, but in the final analysis they are *not* responsible for our decisions and actions. This is as true for a person counting calories to lose weight as it is for a person exercising for cardiovascular benefit. What we do to and for our body is a personal responsibility.

An understanding of self-responsibility was driven home to me soon after my surgery during a visit with my cardiologist. I had done some reading about coronary heart disease, and I knew that diet was a factor.

"My diet is a problem, isn't it?" I asked.

"Yes, it is," he said. "Your cholesterol and triglycerides are too high, and you need to lose weight."

"What are we going to do about it?" I inquired.

"Darned if I know," he replied. "I'm the physician," he continued, "and I understand disease. If you have another blockage, come back and see me. But what you're talking about is not disease, it's health. And frankly, health is not my field."

I was stung by his words and was so angry that I could hardly speak. Fortunately, he had to leave the room for a call, which gave me a minute to cool down and think about what he had said. Soon his true meaning began to sink in. The fact was, he could help. He could provide resources such as books and tapes, direct me to classes and to counseling dietitians, and give me his support. What he could not do was make positive lifestyle changes for me. He knew I had come to his office looking for a prescription or a pill—a quick fix for my dietary problem. He knew I wanted to make him responsible for my health. His message, though shocking, moved me to a fundamental understanding of who was responsible for the way I lived. It was my heart, my life, my diet—and ultimately my health. The decisions and actions also had to be mine.

That message was reinforced the following week when I attended a healthy-eating class conducted by the hospital dietitian. Of the 12 male bypass patients who had been invited, I was the only one who showed up. The others sent their wives! These men did not see themselves as being responsible for what they ate. Instead, they saddled their wives with that responsibility. No one can assume responsibility for another's health. Not only is it unfair, but it doesn't work.

TURNING ATTITUDE INTO ACTION

Positive mental attitude involves a decision to take action— and to convert that action into a daily habit. Positive action involves two additional dimensions of mental attitude. The first is establishing health goals. Whether you're developing a financial strategy or planning a vacation, to get what you want you must first *know* what you want. You must have a goal and know where you're headed.

According to Dr. Denis Waitley, too many people fit the following description: "If you don't know where you're going, you'll end up somewhere else, but it doesn't matter, because you won't recognize where you've been or where you are anyway." It's the same in constructing a healthy lifestyle. Establishing explicit health goals ("I'm going to lose 20 pounds" rather than "I'm going to lose some weight") provides direction and a sense of purpose.

It's particularly important to commit goals to writing. Writing demands clarity, conditions, a time frame and a strategy—a process that often serves to make the goals "real." It allows a person to prioritize goals so that time and energy can be focused on what is important. It also provides a means to review goals often and to measure results. Goals must be realistic. If losing 20 pounds is in order, that is a proper goal. But if a person expects to do it in 30 days, or is planning to shed the weight by running in next week's marathon, it isn't realistic. Goals should reach—yet be reachable.

The second aspect is a sense of timing. Instituting a healthy lifestyle may require changes in a number of key areas. No one should expect to change everything at once. Starting a healthy diet pattern, beginning an exercise program, reducing stress, giving up smoking—to try to accomplish all this at the same time is to invite frustration and failure.

A better way is to view change as a steady progression. Walking today *will* lead to running tomorrow. It takes about six months to accomplish significant changes in lifestyle habits. During that time, a person shouldn't feel pressured to rush or to succeed. It isn't a race. The important thing to keep in mind is not the speed of the progress, but the continuance of it . . . not quick results, but permanent change.

Realistic timing also recognizes that there will be setbacks. They shouldn't be dwelled on as "mistakes" or "failures." They should be treated for what they are: learning experiences. When asked what he had learned after years of inventing, Thomas Edison replied: ". . . one way to produce electricity . . . and 25,000 ways not to." People should focus on successes, not failures. A candy bar doesn't mean they "blew it." It isn't the end of the world—

it's just a temporary setback to their normal, healthy diet pattern.

Small changes made over time add up to major differences. This is well illustrated by the performance of two professional golfers a few years ago. Tom Watson was the number one golfer in the country then, earning more than $400,000 in tournament play; according to *Sports Illustrated,* his average score for 18 holes of golf was 70.05 strokes. Craig Stadler, another top professional, was ranked tenth; he earned about $200,000, or one-half of Watson's earnings. Craig Stadler's average for 18 holes? Four-tenths higher than Watson's, or 70.09 strokes. A difference of less than one-half stroke per round produced a number one ranking and an additional $200,000 that year for Tom Watson.

The lesson here is that the small things count, both in professional golf and in healthy lifestyle changes. A minuscule difference today—10 more minutes of walking, an apple rather than a doughnut, reducing stress with a workout instead of a drink—can produce enormous changes tomorrow in health, longevity and appearance. Realistic timing allows small changes to add up and makes healthy habits a way of life.

At the beginning of this book is a quote by Dr. Robert Hoke, who talks of health as "not something to have, but something to become." It recognizes that "becoming" healthy is a process—one in which choices are made and, over time, habits are changed. The information in this book is designed to help with that process. The key ingredient, however, is *you.* Only you can use the information, only you can institute the process, only you can make the choices and changes necessary for good health.

Good health is yours for the choosing. It *is* a choice.

COOKBOOK

COMMENTS FROM THE COOK

by Bernie Piscatella

Eating healthfully is a way of life for our family, but this wasn't always so. After open-heart surgery almost 10 years ago, Joe presented us with a list of foods he was to avoid: bacon, sausage, hot dogs, spareribs, luncheon meats; eggs, avocados, olives, whole milk, cheese made from whole milk and cream, sweet cream, sour cream, ice cream, chocolate, butter, lard, hydrogenated margarine, hydrogenated peanut butter; most frozen dinners, commercially baked goods, French fries, crackers, most sauces and gravies; and fast foods such as hamburgers, fish, chicken, tacos and pizza. In addition, red meat was to be limited. The forbidden list seemed to contain most of the best-tasting foods on the market and the foods we liked most to eat. I was not sure what foods, if any, were left!

Meal preparation was further complicated because our children, who had definite likes and dislikes, weren't about to forgo pizza, Big Macs, French fries and milk shakes graciously.

Suddenly being thrust into the world of reduced fat, salt, sugar and cholesterol was overwhelming. I felt as if I had to learn how to cook and eat all over again. But I decided the key was to learn how to *eat,* not how to *diet;* otherwise, we could never stick with it. I chose to concentrate on what we *could* have and not on what we could *not* have.

Since the foods we *could* have needed to stand on their own and not be masked by heavy sauces or extra salt, I learned to buy the freshest of fish, the leanest of meats, the lightest of dairy products. The trick was to make healthy foods so satisfying that the unhealthy foods would not be missed. Who could yearn for prime rib, for example, when there was seafood fettuccine? Who could miss store-bought apple pie when presented with an array of the freshest fruits of the season?

Changing our eating pattern was a lifestyle change that

did not come about overnight. It was the result of slow but steady progress, of trial and error, of success and failure. When we "blew it," we started over again the next day with renewed commitment. We often had to remind ourselves that small changes over time add up to large ones. Habits change slowly, but they do change. You *can* prepare and enjoy food that is both delicious and good for you.

My intent in the following pages is to share information, experience and perspective to help with making changes. In combination with the suggested meal plans and the recipes, I hope to help the reader to achieve a more positive, healthful way of eating. In particular, there are two major concepts that need to be understood: how to modify a recipe and how to reduce the fat in a meal.

HOW TO MODIFY A RECIPE

There are a number of books on the market that offer healthful recipes, and some of them are quite good. Using someone else's recipes is a good way to begin preparing wholesome foods, but lasting change takes place only when you learn to make your own recipes more healthful.

It's unrealistic to throw away all your old recipes. Rather, a better way is to analyze the recipe, remove the unhealthy ingredients and replace them with healthier choices. Then you have the best of both worlds—healthy food that tastes familiar and that tastes good. To modify a recipe, you first have to identify the dietary elements that contribute to overweight and heart disease. These are excessive fat, calories, salt, sugar and cholesterol. The key question to ask is "Why are these ingredients in the recipe?" Many of us learned to cook by following instructions from a mother or grandmother, or from a book. Ingredients or cooking methods were never questioned. Today, such inquiry is necessary to determine whether or not the food is as healthful as it can be. Is the ingredient really needed? Should it be reduced . . . or a substitute used? Is there a healthier cooking method?

On the next few pages, you'll find a number of recipe modification examples. Each example provides the original recipe (with questionable ingredients and cooking methods circled) and the modified version. In addition, the benefits of modification are shown in comparisons of calories, fat, sodium, cholesterol and percentage of calories from fat.

ITALIAN VINAIGRETTE

(ORIGINAL RECIPE)
1 cup

¾ cup olive oil
¼ cup cider vinegar
¾ teaspoon salt
¾ teaspoon black pepper

Combine ingredients in a covered jar. Shake well.

Approximate Nutritional Content per 2 Tablespoons

Total calories: 180
Sodium: 206 mg
Cholesterol: 0 mg
Fat: 20 g
Percentage of calories from fat: 99%

ITALIAN VINAIGRETTE

(MODIFIED RECIPE)
1 cup

¾ cup water
¼ cup cider vinegar
¾ teaspoon salt
¼ teaspoon black pepper

Combine ingredients in a covered jar. Shake well.

Approximate Nutritional Content per 2 Tablespoons

Total calories: 2
Sodium: 274 mg
Cholesterol: 0 mg
Fat: Trace
Percentage of calories from fat: 1%

EFFECTS OF MODIFICATION ON THE RECIPE

Instead of	Change to	Benefits	Approximate Calories Saved
Olive oil	Water	Less fat	180

FRENCH TOAST
(ORIGINAL RECIPE)
9 slices

¹/₂ cup whole milk
4 eggs, slightly beaten
¹/₂ teaspoon salt
¹/₂ teaspoon sugar
9 slices bread
1 tablespoon hot fat or butter

Combine milk, eggs, salt and sugar. Dip bread into egg mixture. Fry in hot fat until brown.

Approximate Nutritional Content per Slice

Total calories: 158
Sodium: 371 mg
Cholesterol: 122 mg
Fat: 5.3 g
Percentage of calories from fat: 31%

FRENCH TOAST
(MODIFIED RECIPE)
9 slices

¹/₂ cup non-fat milk
1 whole egg plus 3 egg
  whites, slightly beaten
¹/₄ teaspoon vanilla
¹/₄ teaspoon cinnamon
pinch of turmeric (for color)
9 slices bread

Combine milk, eggs, vanilla, cinnamon and turmeric. Dip bread into egg mixture. Fry in nonstick skillet until brown.

Approximate Nutritional Content per Slice

Total calories: 121
Sodium: 233 mg
Cholesterol: 30 mg
Fat: 1.7 g
Percentage of calories from fat: 13%

EFFECTS OF MODIFICATION ON THE RECIPE

Instead of	Change to	Benefits	Approximate Calories Saved
¹/₂ cup whole milk	¹/₂ cup non-fat milk	Less fat	30
4 eggs	1 egg and 3 egg whites	Less cholesterol	193
¹/₂ teaspoon salt	No salt	No sodium	
¹/₂ teaspoon sugar	¹/₄ teaspoon vanilla and ¹/₄ teaspoon cinnamon	No refined sugar	20
1 tablespoon hot fat or butter	Nonstick skillet	Less fat	100

SAUTÉED MUSHROOMS

(ORIGINAL RECIPE)
4 servings

3 tablespoons butter
1 pound fresh mushrooms
salt and pepper to taste

Melt butter in skillet; add mushrooms and toss until coated. Cover and cook over low heat until tender, about 8–10 minutes, turning occasionally. Season to taste.

Approximate Nutritional Content per Serving

Total calories: 131
Sodium: 120 mg
Cholesterol: 31 mg
Fat: 12 g
Percentage of calories from fat: 78%

SAUTÉED MUSHROOMS

(MODIFIED RECIPE)
4 servings

3 tablespoons chicken stock
1 clove garlic (optional)
1 pound fresh mushrooms

Heat stock and garlic in non-stick skillet; add mushrooms. Cover and cook over low heat until tender, about 8–10 minutes, turning occasionally.

Approximate Nutritional Content per Serving

Total calories: 27
Sodium: 28 mg
Cholesterol: Trace
Fat: .6 g
Percentage of calories from fat: 15%

EFFECTS OF MODIFICATION ON THE RECIPE

Instead of	Change to	Benefits	Approximate Calories Saved
Sauté in butter	Sauté in broth	Less fat; less cholesterol	104
Salt	Garlic	Less sodium	

CHICKEN DIVAN

(ORIGINAL RECIPE)
6 servings

3 chicken breasts, halved and
  boned
1/3 cup butter
2 10-ounce packages frozen
  asparagus spears
1 10-ounce can cream of
  chicken soup
2/3 cup mayonnaise
1/3 cup evaporated milk
2/3 cup grated Cheddar cheese
1 teaspoon lemon juice
1/2 teaspoon curry powder
1/2 cup bread crumbs
1 tablespoon butter

Brown chicken breasts in butter. Cook asparagus according to package directions; drain and arrange in casserole dish. Top with chicken. Combine cream of chicken soup, mayonnaise, milk, cheese, lemon juice and curry. Pour over chicken. Top with bread crumbs. Dot with butter. Bake at 350°F. 25–30 minutes.

Approximate Nutritional Content per Serving

Total calories: 647
Sodium: 865 mg
Cholesterol: 155 mg
Fat: 48 g
Percentage of calories from fat: 67%

CHICKEN DIVAN

(MODIFIED RECIPE)
6 servings

3 chicken breasts, halved,
  skinned and boned
1 pound fresh asparagus
  spears
1 1/2 cups homemade chicken
  stock
2 tablespoons cornstarch
1/3 cup safflower mayonnaise
1/3 cup plain non-fat yogurt
2/3 cup skim-evaporated milk
1/3 cup grated part-skim
  Cheddar cheese
1 teaspoon lemon juice
1/2 teaspoon curry powder
1/2 cup bread crumbs

Brown chicken breasts lightly in a nonstick skillet. Steam asparagus until crisp-tender. Arrange in baking dish; top with chicken. Bring 1 cup of stock to boil. Combine remaining 1/2 cup stock with cornstarch; gradually add to boiling stock. Cool slightly. Add mayonnaise, yogurt, milk, cheese, lemon juice and curry powder. Pour over chicken. Sprinkle with bread crumbs. Bake at 350°F. 25–30 minutes.

Approximate Nutritional Content per Serving

Total calories: 363
Sodium: 368 mg
Cholesterol: 82 mg
Fat: 16 g
Percentage of calories from fat: 37%

EFFECTS OF MODIFICATION ON THE RECIPE

Instead of	Change to	Benefits	Approximate Calories Saved
Chicken with skin	Chicken without skin	Less fat	360
Fry in butter	Nonstick skillet	Less fat	535
Packaged asparagus	Fresh asparagus	Better flavor; increased nutrition	
Cream of chicken soup	Homemade stock, thickened	Less fat; less sodium	75
2/3 cup mayonnaise	1/3 cup mayonnaise and 1/3 cup non-fat yogurt	Less fat	480
1/3 cup evaporated milk	1/3 cup skim evaporated milk	Less fat	50
2/3 cup cheese	1/3 cup part-skim cheese	Less fat	100
Dot with butter (1 tablespoon)	No butter	Less fat	100

EASY RECIPE MODIFICATIONS

Instead of	Change to	Benefits	Approximate Calories Saved
Whole milk	Non-fat milk	Less fat	60 per cup
Frying in oil	Nonstick skillet with stock	Less fat	125 per tablespoon of oil
2 eggs	1 egg and 1 egg white	Less cholesterol	60
3 eggs	1 egg and 2 egg whites	Less cholesterol	110
4 eggs	2 eggs and 3 egg whites	Less cholesterol	125
Mayonnaise	Mustard	Less fat	95 per tablespoon
Oil-packed tuna	Water-packed tuna	Less fat	220
Whole sandwich	Open-faced sandwich	Fewer calories	70–125 per slice of bread
Butter/syrup on pancakes, waffles, French toast	Puréed berries	Less fat; less refined sugar	90 per teaspoon of butter; 40 per teaspoon of syrup
Butter on toast	Dry toast or half the butter	Less fat	50–100
Tuna made with 5 tablespoons mayonnaise	Tuna made with 3 tablespoons mayonnaise	Less fat	200
Chili with 1 pound ground beef	Chili with ½ pound ground beef	Less fat	400
Grapefruit juice (8 ounces)	½ grapefruit	Less sugar; more fiber	60
Oil dressing on green salads	Oil-free dressing or fresh lemons	Less fat	125 per tablespoon

EASY RECIPE MODIFICATIONS

Instead of	Change to	Benefits	Approximate Calories Saved
Oil dressing on pasta salad	Reduce by ¼ cup	Less fat	600
Untrimmed steak	Trimmed steak	Less fat	55 per ounce
Cereal with 3 teaspoons refined sugar	Cereal without sugar added	Less sugar	46
Buttered, salted popcorn	Plain popcorn	Less fat; less sodium	30 per cup
Salted peanuts	Unsalted peanuts	Less sodium (120 mg per ounce)	
Mayonnaise in dressing	Yogurt in dressing	Less fat	480 per ⅓ cup
Mayonnaise in dressing	Buttermilk in dressing	Less fat	500 per ⅓ cup
1 bouillon cube	1 cup homemade chicken stock	Less sodium (685 mg)	
Regular soy sauce	Reduced-sodium soy sauce	Less sodium (1,900 mg per tablespoon)	
Cream	Plain non-fat yogurt	Less fat	720 per cup
Sour cream	Plain non-fat yogurt	Less fat	360 per cup
Full-fat cheese	Part-skim cheese	Less fat	10–25 per ounce
Ground round in tacos	Diced chicken in tacos	Less fat	300 per pound
Bologna	Sliced chicken	Less fat	40 per ounce

HOW TO REDUCE FAT IN A MEAL

Since fat is so high in calories, it's important to restrict its intake for weight control and cardiac health. Many health professionals counsel that no more than 25% of daily calories should come from fat. In a number of foods, especially red meat and whole-milk dairy products, considerably more than 25% of the calories are supplied by fat. How, then, can these foods be included in a healthy diet?

The answer lies in the fat content of the *entire* meal. To isolate your concern on a single food isn't meaningful. You need to be concerned about the balance provided by all the foods, including those lower in fat. For example, four ounces of lean roast pork tenderloin is 290 calories and is 52% fat, but look what the accompanying foods can do:

	Calories	% of Calories from Fat
Roast Pork Tenderloin (4 ounces)	290	52%
Green salad with 1 tablespoon blue cheese dressing	100	70
Baked potato	90	1
with 1 tablespoon butter	+ 100	100
with 2 tablespoons sour cream	+ 56	80
with 1 tablespoon Parmesan cheese	+ 31	64
with 1 slice bacon bits	+ 43	82
TOTAL	**710**	**65%**

By selecting high-fat foods to accompany the pork roast, the fat content of the meal is increased to 65%!

The opposite occurs when low-fat foods are chosen:

	Calories	% of Calories from Fat
Roast Pork Tenderloin (4 ounces)	290	52%
Green salad with oil-free dressing	20	1
Snow peas with lemon (½ cup)	58	4
Roast Potatoes with Rosemary (1 cup)	129	16
TOTAL	**497**	**34%**

Not only have the calories dropped, but the fat content has been reduced to 34%. By choosing foods that are low in fat to be served with the pork, the total fat content of the meal is reduced.

It's the same when you plan for the day. If you'll be eating dinner at a restaurant where calories and fat may be high, select foods with less fat and fewer calories for breakfast and lunch. Balance out your food choices. Then your daily calories from fat will not be out of line.

ENTERTAINING WITH HEART-HEALTHY ALTERNATIVES

The thought of entertaining guests generally provokes worry centered on whether or not the guests will find the food appealing. Such worry is unfounded because recipe modification makes it possible to serve healthy food that tastes good. No one who enjoys chicken piccata or French Market soup would confuse these recipes with bland, tasteless dishes.

Even knowing this, however, it's necessary to understand that not all your guests will be interested in healthy food. The key to successful entertaining is to provide a variety of food choices. If tortellini, which is high in calories, is served as an appetizer, balance it out with lower-calorie foods such as grilled clams or mussels. As the salad course, offer both oil dressing and oil-free dressing. And after the main course, balance a sweet dessert with a selection of fresh fruit. In this way, each person makes his or her own decisions and food selections. This is very much appreciated by most guests.

The same is true for more casual dinners. If you want to serve chili for a *Monday Night Football* get-together, offer a variety of choices. You might serve high-fat toppings such as cheese and olives balanced by low-fat toppings of diced jalapeño peppers, chopped onions, tomatoes and salsa. Put out a bowl of salted taco chips, but offer unsalted chips as well. Cold beer could be a choice, but so could bottled mineral water.

People entertain in their own style. With a little fore-thought and planning, healthy food can be made a part of that style. Coupled with a variety of choices, guests will enjoy and appreciate your attempts to please.

AFTER-SCHOOL SNACKS

Avoid junk foods as after-school snacks. If you want your children to eat healthy food, look for alternatives to sugar-rich, fatty, high-sodium snacks. In place of chips or ice cream, keep popcorn, non-fat yogurt or fruit and juice popsicles on hand.

The best after-school snacks are fresh fruits and vege-tables. The key is to have them cut up and ready. If my children ask what there is to eat, and I say "How about an apple or some celery," their reply is a big "YUK!" On the other hand, if they see a plate of sliced apples or pears, or heaping bowls of grapes, strawberries or raspberries, or a tray of vegetables with salsa or heart-healthy dips, they unconsciously start munching while telling about their day. Before they realize it, they've eaten a lot of fruit and/or vegetables, and they're no longer hungry and looking for junk food.

A better choice than cookies, cakes, cupcakes or chips is homemade muffins or breads. Try serving them with homemade apple butter or homemade strawberry pre-serves. What could be nicer than coming home to the smell of bread or muffins still warm from the oven?

Instead of making a special dessert at dinner time, try preparing one earlier in the day. Serve it for a midafternoon or after-school snack. You'll have more of a chance to burn the calories. Some choices from this book might include: Easy Chocolate Pudding, Spanish Cream, Peach Cobbler, Oatmeal Raisin Cookies or Apple Coffee Cake.

Once again, the key is planning. If you expect your fam-ily to eat healthfully, you have to plan for healthy snacks.

A LAST WORD

Good food and good health go together. Changing eating habits is difficult but not impossible. Small changes, made gradually over time, can add up to a tremendous difference. To achieve a healthy diet pattern, you need knowledge, motivation, self-help tools and perseverance. As Calvin Coolidge once said: "Nothing in the world can take the place of persistence. Talent will not; nothing is more common than unsuccessful men with talent. Genius will not; the world is full of educated derelicts. Persistence and determination alone are omnipotent. The slogan 'press on' has solved and always will solve the problems of the human race."

NUTRITIONAL CONTENT ANALYSIS

The following recipes have been analyzed for nutritional content by Evette Hackman, R.D., Ph.D., a registered dietitian in private practice. Dr. Hackman is a member of the American Dietetic Association and of SCAN (Sports and Cardiovascular Nutritionists). She is the nutrition and food editor for *Shape* magazine.

The primary sources for values used in Dr. Hackman's computerized data base are Agricultural Handbook No. 8 and No. 456, and are only as correct and complete as the information supplies.

A nutritional analysis is provided for each recipe on a per-serving basis. The analysis includes: calories; grams of protein, carbohydrates and fat; milligrams of cholesterol and sodium; percentages of calories from protein, carbohydrates and fat.

For the sake of consistency and clarity, certain decisions were made concerning the analyses:

- When a range is given for an ingredient, the midpoint amount is analyzed.
- When the ingredient listing gives one or more options, the first ingredient listed is the one analyzed.

- Figures are rounded off to whole numbers, so there may be slight discrepancies between an analysis for a whole meal and the sum of its parts.
- Salads and dressings are analyzed separately. The amount of dressing, which is an individual choice, can greatly change the calories and the fat content of a salad.
- A recipe calling for a "chicken breast" means one whole chicken breast: 7 ounces uncooked meat; 6 ounces cooked meat.
- Servings are "family-size" and generous. Those wishing to reduce calories further should use smaller servings.
- Some recipes are so low in calories that even a trace of fat causes a high fat percentage. These have been identified with a notation. Do not be overconcerned with the fat content.

The menus and recipes are designed to ensure that a meal falls within the guidelines of the American Heart Association for fat, cholesterol and sodium. Sometimes a single recipe may exceed the fat guideline—no more than 30% of calories from fat—but the whole meal is in line when other foods are included for nutritional balance.

Every effort has been made to ensure the accuracy of nutritional data information; however, the authors do not guarantee its suitability for specific, medically imposed diets. Those people with special dietary needs should consult with their physician and dietitian.

NOTES ON INGREDIENTS

All the ingredients described below are available in most supermarkets. Often, it's a case of knowing where to look: some foods, such as whole spears of small baby corn, will be found in the Oriental section with the water chestnuts and soy sauce; in the gourmet or international food sections, you may discover Oriental noodles and rice, Mexican pure ground chili powder, and various spices and flavorings. Check spices and condiments, canned goods, rice, grains and frozen-food sections. If you don't find what you're looking for, ask the manager to order it.

For a delightful adventure, familiarize yourself with Oriental, Italian and other ethnic markets in your area, as well as gourmet and health food stores.

ARROWROOT

is a delicate thickener for sauces and gravies. It's neutral in flavor and does not mask or alter natural flavors. Because it reaches maximum thickening power before boiling, it produces very clear sauces and gravies. Use 2 teaspoons arrowroot in place of 1 tablespoon cornstarch. Use 1½ teaspoons arrowroot in place of 1 tablespoon flour. Combine arrowroot with 2 tablespoons cold water. Gradually add to hot sauces, soups or gravies to thicken.

ARTICHOKE HEARTS

are available packed in water or oil. Unless otherwise stated, all recipes in this book refer to those packed in water. The water must be drained before use. In recipes specifically calling for artichokes marinated in oil, look for brands packed in non-hydrogenated, unsaturated oils such as soy oil or safflower oil.

BABY CORN (WHOLE SPEARS)

is miniature ears of corn that are canned in water. Look for it in the Oriental section of the supermarket near the soy sauce and water chestnuts.

BEAN CURD or TOFU

is available in the produce section of most supermarkets. This high-protein, low-calorie, no-cholesterol product, made from the milk of puréed soybeans, is best in stir-fried dishes and in soups.

BROTH or STOCK

(whether chicken, beef or fish) will have the maximum flavor and quality when it's homemade and then reduced by one-third (see stock recipes). Commercially canned stock or broth can be substituted for homemade broth or stock in most recipes, and is convenient to have on hand. Always buy the best commercial grade of stock available. Remember: using commercially prepared broth instead of homemade will substantially increase the milligrams of sodium.

CHINESE CABBAGE

(Napa Cabbage) is tall, tightly packed, fresh cabbage with white stalks and light green crinkled leaves. It's found in the produce section of most supermarkets.

FLOUR

SEMOLINA FLOUR, available in the gourmet section of most supermarkets, has a high gluten content and a golden color. It's the best flour to use in homemade pasta and makes delightful bread.

WHOLE-WHEAT FLOUR may be substituted for unbleached all-purpose white flour in the following proportions: ¾ cup whole-wheat flour to 1 cup all-purpose flour.

GINGER ROOT

adds a distinctive, spicy flavor to many Chinese dishes. It's especially good on chicken and fish. To use, peel the tan skin and thinly slice the root. To obtain ginger juice, peel the ginger root and grate the root with a fine grater; squeeze the pulp to extract the juice. Look for ginger root in the produce section of most supermarkets.

GRAINS AND RICE

ALA is a cracked-wheat bulgar available in the rice or gourmet section of most supermarkets.

COUSCOUS, a wheat grain, is a delicious alternative to rice. It's available in the rice or gourmet section of most supermarkets.

ORIENTAL-STYLE RICE is the long- or short-grain, sticky type of white or brown rice that is served in Chinese restaurants. Look for it in Oriental markets or in the Oriental section of the supermarket, near the soy sauce and water chestnuts. (Follow the recipe on the package or refer to the recipe in this book.)

HERBS AND SPICES

Fresh herbs and spices are much more flavorful than dried. Substitute three parts fresh herbs for one part dried herbs.

BASIL should be used fresh whenever possible; the flavor is markedly superior to dried. Fresh basil is now more often available in produce markets year round. Preserve fresh basil by standing the stems, with roots intact, in a jar of water; loosely cover the leaves with a plastic bag. Store in refrigerator.

CHILI POWDER for maximum flavor should be made from and labeled pure ground chili powder. Take the time to search for a Spanish or Mexican market or a supermarket that carries pure ground chili powder. Pure ground chili powder is made by grinding dried chilies, and the flavor is far superior to commercial chili powder, which is most often 40% salt and 20% additives. It comes in mild, medium hot and hot.

JUNIPER BERRIES give a distinctive, delightful flavor to poultry and red meat. They're available in gourmet food stores and in the gourmet section of many supermarkets.

PEPPERCORNS. *Green peppercorns,* picked before they're ripe, have more of a bite than white or black peppercorns; for best flavor, buy them freeze-dried rather than packed in brine. *Szechuan peppercorns* are dried reddish berries that are fragrant and mildly hot; look for them in Oriental markets and in the gourmet section of the supermarket. *White peppercorns,* more aromatic than black peppercorns, are best on light-colored foods such as chicken, fish and potatoes; you'll find them in the spice section of the supermarket.

CRUSHED RED PEPPERS are especially good as a topping for pasta dishes. They're available in the spice section of most supermarkets.

SAFFRON, made from the dried stigmas of a type of crocus, adds both color and flavor. A small amount goes a long way. The most costly of all seasonings, it's available in the spice section or gourmet section of most supermarkets.

LEMON JUICE

is most flavorful when it's freshly squeezed. For maximum quality, do not substitute bottled juice or lemon extract in recipes calling for lemon juice.

LIQUID SMOKE

is a natural product made by burning hickory wood. Excellent in homemade barbecue sauce, it's available in most supermarkets near the Tabasco and Worcestershire sauce.

NOODLES

BUCKWHEAT (CHUKA SOBA) NOODLES are curly noodles made with wheat flour. They're available in Oriental markets and in the Oriental section of most supermarkets near the soy sauce and water chestnuts.

MAIFUN BEAN NOODLES or CELLOPHANE NOODLES are dry, thin, transparent noodles. You'll find them in Oriental markets and in the Oriental section of most supermarkets near the soy sauce.

OILS

CHILI OIL (LAYU) is oil flavored with red hot peppers. It can be found in Oriental markets and in large supermarkets.

OLIVE OIL ranges from mild-flavored to rich-flavored. Use a lighter variety for cooking and a stronger one for salads. The finest quality, labeled extra-virgin or virgin, has a more intense flavor, so the amount of oil can be reduced.

SESAME OIL is made from toasted sesame seeds. It's available in Oriental markets and in the Oriental section of most supermarkets near the soy sauce.

SAFFLOWER MAYONNAISE

is mayonnaise made with unsaturated safflower oil. Mayonnaise is high in calories, and most of the calories are from fat, so be judicious in its use.

WHITE ONIONS

(sometimes called Bermuda onions or Walla Walla sweet onions) are the best onions for salads and sandwiches.

PARMESAN CHEESE

should be used only sparingly. Avoid the preground, packaged variety, which is very expensive and almost flavorless. Buy a small wedge of fresh Parmesan and grate as needed. Or have the delicatessen or dairyman freshly grate the amount you need.

SHALLOTS

have a delicate garlic flavor. They're available in most supermarkets near the garlic and onions.

SHIITAKE

(dried forest mushrooms) are available in Oriental markets and in the Oriental section of most supermarkets near the soy sauce. To reconstitute the dried mushrooms, soak them in enough water to cover for about 30 minutes, or until soft. Drain. Squeeze out excess water. Remove and discard stems.

REDUCED-SODIUM SOY SAUCE

contains 46% less sodium than regular soy sauce, with little or no difference in flavor. Reduced-sodium soy sauce has 80 milligrams of sodium per ½ teaspoon. By comparison, ½ teaspoon of salt has 1,150 milligrams of sodium.

CANNED PLUM TOMATOES

are the best substitute for fresh or home-canned tomatoes. It's important to buy the best available. Progresso Plum Tomatoes and S&W Pear Tomatoes are especially good, as are many of the imported brands. The better the grade, the more flavorful the sauce. For recipes in this book that call for diced plum tomatoes, buy the whole plum tomatoes and dice them yourself.

TOMATO SALSA

may be homemade (see our recipe) or a commercially made variety purchased in the gourmet section of most supermarkets. Refer to a good sodium dictionary to ensure buying the brand with the least amount of sodium.

TOMATO SAUCE, TOMATO PURÉE, TOMATO PASTE

should be of the highest grade available. Progresso and Contadina are among the best. Freeze any leftover paste in the can by the tablespoonful on a sheet of waxed paper. Once frozen, remove to a plastic freezer bag and store in the freezer for later use.

TORTILLAS

are available in flour and corn. Always buy flour tortillas that are made with soy bean oil, not with lard. Corn tortillas generally do not contain oil or shortening, so they're more heart-healthy and lower in calories.

TORULA YEAST

(made by Bakon Seasoning) is a bacon-flavored seasoning made from torula yeast. High in B vitamins and protein and low in sodium, it gives a hickory-smoke, bacon flavor to foods. Try it on scrambled eggs, baked potatoes, salads, and lettuce-and-tomato sandwiches for a bacon flavor without the bacon. Look for the seasoning in health-food stores.

VANILLA EXTRACT

will give the best flavor when it's a pure vanilla and not an imitation variety. If you travel to Mexico (or have a friend who does), bring some back; the quality is worth the effort.

VINEGARS

BALSAMIC VINEGAR has a mellow, sweet-and-sour flavor. Good on salads, cold chicken and fish, or drizzled over warm vegetables, it's found in the gourmet section of most supermarkets.

CHAMPAGNE VINEGAR enhances any salad. It's available in gourmet food stores, delicatessens, and the gourmet section of many supermarkets. Buy the best French or American champagne vinegar you can find.

RASPBERRY VINEGAR is good on salads and drizzled over warm vegetables. It's also good for deglazing a pan. (Try it over our Pan-fried Chicken.) Look for it in gourmet food stores, delicatessens and the gourmet section of many supermarkets.

RICE VINEGAR is a mild vinegar made from fermented rice. It's available in the Oriental section of most supermarkets near the soy sauce.

WON-TON or SPRING ROLL WRAPPERS

are a quick and easy way to prepare tortellini and ravioli. (I think the quality is equal to those made with homemade pasta.) Look for them in Oriental markets and in the gourmet frozen-food sections of the supermarket.

COOKING EQUIPMENT

Always use a *nonstick* skillet, griddle, baking sheet or cake pan. Some of out recipes call for bamboo or vegetable steamer baskets. The bamboo baskets, which can be placed over boiling water in a wok, come in single or double tiers at a cost of under $5. The bamboo bottoms are loosely woven to let steam rise to the next tray. A lid on top of the steamer or the wok prevents steam from escaping. (Always make sure the water level is at least 2″ below the steamer.) Bamboo steamers are available at kitchen shops, Oriental markets and Oriental import stores.

The vegetable steamer baskets are metal baskets with perforated holes that adjust to fit into most pots and pans. They work on the same principle as the bamboo steamer (see above). Vegetable steamer baskets are a must for perfectly steamed fresh vegetables.

PANCAKES, WAFFLES & BREADS

BUTTERMILK PANCAKES

20 pancakes

2 cups sifted unbleached white flour
½ teaspoon salt
1¼ teaspoons baking soda
¾ teaspoon baking powder
1 egg
2¼ cups 1% buttermilk
2 teaspoons skim milk
1 tablespoon safflower oil

In a mixing bowl, blend ingredients with a wire whisk, just enough to moisten. Dip up batter with a large serving spoon. Bake on a preheated nonstick griddle. Turn pancakes when top side is bubbly and a few bubbles have broken. Flip only once.

APPROXIMATE NUTRITIONAL CONTENT PER PANCAKE

Total calories: 63
Protein: 2 g
Carbohydrates: 10 g
Cholesterol: 14 mg
Fat: 1 g
Sodium: 149 mg

Percentage of calories from:
Protein: 17%
Carbohydrates: 64%
Fat: 19%

BUTTERMILK WAFFLES

4 large (11" × 6") waffles

3   egg whites
1   egg yolk
2   cups 1% buttermilk
1 ¼ cups unbleached white flour
¾   cup whole-wheat flour
2   teaspoons granulated sugar
2   teaspoons baking powder
1   teaspoon baking soda
¼   teaspoon salt
2   tablespoons safflower oil

In a mixing bowl, lightly beat egg whites and yolks. Add buttermilk. Beat with wire whisk. Add remaining ingredients. Beat until smooth. Bake in a nonstick waffle iron until waffles are golden brown.

SERVING SUGGESTION: In place of high-calorie syrup, serve puréed fresh or frozen strawberries, raspberries, blueberries or blackberries with waffles, pancakes, and French toast.

APPROXIMATE NUTRITIONAL CONTENT PER WAFFLE

Total calories: 243
Protein: 10 g
Carbohydrates: 36 g
Cholesterol: 46 mg
Fat: 7 g
Sodium: 424 mg

Percentage of calories from:
Protein: 16%
Carbohydrates: 60%
Fat: 25%

ENGLISH MUFFIN BREAD

2 loaves (10 slices per loaf)

3 cups unbleached white flour
2 cups whole-wheat flour
1½ teaspoons active dry yeast
1½ teaspoons salt
1 tablespoon granulated sugar
2 teaspoons safflower oil
2 cups very warm water
tub safflower margarine
cornmeal

In a large mixing bowl, combine flours, yeast, salt, sugar and safflower oil; add warm water. Stir with a wooden spoon until ingredients are moistened. Mix with an electric mixer, on low speed, 1–2 minutes, just long enough to mix thoroughly. Place dough in a bowl greased with tub safflower margarine. Cover with a kitchen towel. Let rise in a warm place 6 hours.

Grease 2 loaf pans with tub safflower margarine; sprinkle pans with cornmeal. Divide dough in half; roll each half into a loaf-shaped cylinder. Put dough into pans. Sprinkle top of each loaf with cornmeal. Cover with kitchen towel. Let rise in warm place 2 hours.

Bake at 350°F. 30–40 minutes, or until bread pulls away from edges of the pans. Remove from pans and cool on wire racks.

APPROXIMATE NUTRITIONAL CONTENT PER SLICE

Total calories: 117
Protein: 4 g
Carbohydrates: 23 g
Cholesterol: 0 mg
Fat: Tr
Sodium: 168 mg

Percentage of calories from:
Protein: 12%
Carbohydrates: 80%
Fat: 8%

FOUR-GRAIN BREAD

3 loaves

2	packages active dry yeast
3	cups warm water
2	tablespoons honey
2⅓	cups whole-wheat flour
2½	cups semolina flour
1¾	cups unbleached white flour
½	cup soy flour
¾	cup skim milk powder
1	tablespoon salt
1	tablespoon olive oil
1	tablespoon safflower oil
3	tablespoons wheat germ
	tub safflower margarine

In a mixing bowl, dissolve yeast in 3 cups warm water; stir in honey. Let stand 5 minutes. Combine flours with milk powder; add 3 cups of the flour mixture to the dissolved yeast. Add salt and stir with a wooden spoon to form a soft dough. Stir in olive oil, safflower oil, wheat germ and remaining flour. Knead on a lightly floured surface until smooth and elastic. Turn dough into a bowl greased with tub safflower margarine. Cover and let rise in a warm place until double in size. Punch down. Return dough to warm place; let rest 15 minutes.

Knead lightly. Divide dough into thirds and roll into rectangles; place each in a bread pan greased with tub safflower margarine. Cover and let rise until bread comes over the top of pan.

Bake at 350°F. 30 minutes, or until bread pulls away from edges of the pans. Remove from pans and let cool on wire racks.

VARIATION: Prepare part of the bread as indicated above and the other part as raisin bread (see Four-grain Raisin Bread on the facing page).

APPROXIMATE NUTRITIONAL CONTENT PER SLICE OF FOUR-GRAIN BREAD (15 SLICES PER LOAF)

Total calories: 77
Protein: 3 g
Carbohydrates: 14 g
Cholesterol: Tr
Fat: 1 g
Sodium: 157 mg

Percentage of calories from:
Protein: 14%
Carbohydrates: 71%
Fat: 15%

FOUR-GRAIN RAISIN BREAD

3 loaves

1   recipe Four-grain Bread (above)
3   cups raisins
    tub safflower margarine

Prepare Four-grain Bread according to instructions until the last paragraph. Then divide dough into 3 loaves. Knead 1 cup of raisins into each loaf. Turn dough into loaf pans greased with tub safflower margarine. Cover. Let rise in warm place until dough comes over the top of pan. Bake at 350°F. 30 minutes, or until bread pulls away from edges of the pans. Remove from pans and let cool on wire racks.

APPROXIMATE NUTRITIONAL CONTENT PER SLICE (20 SLICES PER LOAF)

Total calories: 109
Protein: 3 g
Carbohydrates: 23 g
Cholesterol: Tr
Fat: 1 g
Sodium: 155 mg

Percentage of calories from:
Protein: 11%
Carbohydrates: 80%
Fat: 9%

OLD-FASHIONED WHEAT BREAD

2 loaves

$\frac{1}{2}$ cup cornmeal
$\frac{3}{4}$ cup cold water
$1\frac{1}{2}$ cups water
3 tablespoons olive oil
$\frac{1}{2}$ cup dark molasses
2 tablespoons salt
1 package active dry yeast
$\frac{1}{4}$ cup warm water
3 cups whole-wheat flour
3 cups unbleached white flour
$\frac{1}{3}$ cup 1% buttermilk
   tub safflower margarine

Put cornmeal into a small bowl; cover with $\frac{3}{4}$ cup cold water. Soak 5 minutes; stir. Bring $1\frac{1}{2}$ cups water to a boil; gradually add cornmeal. Cook and stir over low heat until mixture comes to a boil. Remove from heat. Add olive oil, molasses and salt. Cool to room temperature, stirring occasionally.

Dissolve yeast in $\frac{1}{4}$ cup warm water; stir into cornmeal mixture. Put whole-wheat flour into a mixing bowl; add cornmeal-molasses mixture and stir with a wooden spoon to blend. Gradually add white flour and buttermilk. Knead on a lightly floured surface until smooth and elastic. If dough seems dry, add additional water, one tablespoon at a time. (This dough has a dry, heavy consistency; however, it will not be that way once it is baked.)

Turn dough into a mixing bowl greased with tub safflower margarine. Cover with a kitchen towel and let rise in a warm place 3 hours. (It may not double in size.) Punch down; knead slightly. Divide dough in half. Roll each half into a cylinder; turn each cylinder into a loaf pan greased with tub safflower margarine. Cover and let rise in a warm place $1\frac{1}{2}$ hours.

Bake at 400°F. 15 minutes. Reduce heat to 350° F. and bake 20–30 minutes longer, or until bread pulls away from edges of the pans. Remove from pans and let cool on wire racks.

APPROXIMATE NUTRITIONAL CONTENT PER SLICE OF OLD-FASHIONED WHEAT BREAD (20 SLICES PER LOAF)

Total calories: 92
Protein: 2 g
Carbohydrates: 16 g
Cholesterol: Tr
Fat: 1 g
Sodium: 338 mg

Percentage of calories from:
  Protein: 11%
  Carbohydrates: 74%
  Fat: 15%

OAT-BRAN BREAD

2 loaves

     3 cups unbleached white flour
     2 cups whole-wheat flour
     1 cup rolled oats
    ⅓ cup wheat germ
    ½ cup oat bran
     1 tablespoon salt
     2 packages active dry yeast
    ½ cup warm water
  1½ cups water
    ½ cup molasses
     2 tablespoons safflower oil
        tub safflower margarine

In a large mixing bowl, combine flours, oats, wheat germ, oat bran and salt. Dissolve yeast in ½ cup warm water; add to flour mixture. Add 1½ cups water, molasses and safflower oil. Stir with a wooden spoon to form a soft dough.

(continued on next page)

Knead on lightly floured surface until smooth and elastic. Place in mixing bowl greased with tub safflower margarine. Cover and let rise in a warm place 2 hours. Punch down; knead slightly. Cover and let rise 1½ hours. Punch down.

Divide dough in half. Roll each half into a rectangle and place in a loaf pan greased with tub safflower margarine. Cover and let rise in a warm place 1½–2 hours.

Bake at 375°F. 30 minutes, or until bread pulls away from edges of the pans. Remove from pan and let cool on wire racks.

VARIATION: To make rolls, divide dough into 4 dozen equal-size balls. Grease muffin pans with tub safflower margarine. Place 3 balls into each cup; brush tops with safflower margarine. Bake at 375°F. 30 minutes. Rolls will have approximately 120 calories each.

APPROXIMATE NUTRITIONAL CONTENT PER SLICE OF OAT-BRAN BREAD (20 SLICES PER LOAF)

Total calories: 81

Percentage of calories from:

Protein: 2 g — Protein: 12%

Carbohydrates: 15 g — Carbohydrates: 75%

Cholesterol: 0 mg — Fat: 13%

Fat: 1 g

Sodium: 163 mg

OATMEAL BREAD

2 loaves

> 1 cup rolled oats
> 2 cups hot water
> ½ cup molasses
> 2 teaspoons olive oil
> 2 teaspoons safflower oil
> 1½ teaspoons salt
> 1 package active dry yeast
> ¼ cup warm water
> 6 cups unbleached white flour
>   tub safflower margarine

Pour rolled oats into a mixing bowl; add 2 cups hot water. Stir slightly. Let stand 10 minutes. Stir in molasses, olive oil, safflower oil and salt.

Dissolve yeast in ¼ cup warm water; add to oat mixture. Add flour and mix with a wooden spoon to form a soft dough. Remove to a heavily floured surface. Knead 3–4 minutes, or until smooth and elastic.

Place dough in a mixing bowl greased with tub safflower margarine. Cover with a kitchen towel. Let dough rise in a warm place until double in size, about 2 hours. Punch down. Divide in half. Turn into 2 loaf pans greased with tub safflower margarine. Cover and let rise until double in size, about 1½ hours.

Bake at 350°F. oven 45 minutes, or until bread pulls away from edges of the pans. Remove from pans and let cool on wire racks.

APPROXIMATE NUTRITIONAL CONTENT PER SLICE
(20 SLICES PER LOAF)

Total calories: 90
Protein: 2 g
Carbohydrates: 18 g
Cholesterol: 0 mg
Fat: Tr
Sodium: 86 mg

Percentage of calories from:
  Protein: 11%
  Carbohydrates: 80%
  Fat: 9%

CRANBERRY BREAD

1 loaf

1¼ cups unbleached white flour
¾ cup whole-wheat flour
⅔ cup granulated sugar
1½ teaspoons baking powder
½ teaspoon baking soda
1 teaspoon salt
2 tablespoons safflower oil
¾ cup freshly squeezed orange juice
1 tablespoon grated orange peel
1 egg, beaten
1 12-ounce package fresh cranberries,
    coarsely chopped
tub safflower margarine

In a mixing bowl, combine flours, sugar, baking powder, baking soda and salt. Stir in safflower oil, orange juice, orange peel and egg, mixing just to moisten. Fold in cranberries. Pour into a loaf pan greased with tub safflower margarine.

Bake at 350°F. 50 minutes, or until toothpick inserted into center comes out clean. Cool on wire rack for 15 minutes. Remove bread from pan and continue cooling on wire rack.

APPROXIMATE NUTRITIONAL CONTENT PER SLICE
(20 SLICES PER LOAF)

Total calories: 100
Protein: 2 g
Carbohydrates: 19 g
Cholesterol: 14 mg
Fat: 2 g
Sodium: 161 mg

Percentage of calories from:
Protein: 7%
Carbohydrates: 75%
Fat: 18%

SHALLOT-BASIL BREAD

1 loaf

1 loaf French bread
3 tablespoons tub safflower margarine
3 shallots, thinly sliced
3 tablespoons chopped fresh basil
2 tablespoons grated Parmesan cheese

Slice French bread in half lengthwise. Spread with tub safflower margarine. Sprinkle with shallots and basil, then with Parmesan. Place bread on a foil-lined pan in a preheated broiler 2–3 inches from heat 3–4 minutes, or until bread begins to brown and cheese melts.

SERVING SUGGESTION: This bread is great for dipping into Seafood Stew (page 365).

APPROXIMATE NUTRITIONAL CONTENT PER SLICE (15 SLICES PER LOAF)

Total calories: 127
Protein: 4 g
Carbohydrates: 18 g
Cholesterol: Tr
Fat: 3 g
Sodium: 247 mg

Percentage of calories from:
Protein: 12%
Carbohydrates: 60%
Fat: 28%

GRILLED GARLIC BREAD

1 loaf

1 loaf French bread
8 teaspoons tub safflower margarine
  garlic powder
  chopped fresh parsley

Slice French bread in half lengthwise. Spread with tub safflower margarine. Sprinkle generously with garlic powder
and lightly with chopped parsley. Place bread on a foil-
lined pan in a preheated broiler 2–3 inches from heat for
2–3 minutes, or until lightly browned.

APPROXIMATE NUTRITIONAL CONTENT PER SLICE
(15 SLICES PER LOAF)

Total calories: 124
Protein: 3 g
Carbohydrates: 20 g
Cholesterol: 0 mg
Fat: 3 g
Sodium: 244 mg

Percentage of calories from:
  Protein: 11%
  Carbohydrates: 66%
  Fat: 23%

POPOVERS

8 popovers

2 eggs, room temperature
1 egg white, room temperature
1¼ cups skim milk
1¼ cups unbleached white flour
¼ teaspoon salt
  tub safflower margarine

In a mixing bowl, beat eggs and egg white with a rotary beater until lemon colored and frothy; add milk. Beat 1 minute. Add flour and salt; beat 1-2 minutes, or until batter is smooth and foamy on top.

Generously grease popover pans, individual custard cups or standard muffin pans with tub safflower margarine. Fill each cup ⅔ full with batter. (If using standard muffin pans, grease and fill alternating cups to prevent sides of popovers from touching.)

Bake at 450°F. 15 minutes (do not open oven). Reduce heat to 350°F.; bake 20-25 minutes, or until high, hollow and golden brown. Remove from oven. Insert a sharp knife into each popover to allow steam to escape. Remove from pan. Serve hot.

NOTE: The eggs and milk must be at room temperature or the popovers will not rise. It is also essential that the custard cups or the muffin pans (including the tops) be very well greased or the popovers will stick.

SERVING SUGGESTION: Serve with warm Apple Butter (page 407).

APPROXIMATE NUTRITIONAL CONTENT PER POPOVER

Total calories: 106
Protein: 5 g
Carbohydrates: 17 g
Cholesterol: 55 mg
Fat: 2 g
Sodium: 110 mg

Percentage of calories from:
Protein: 20%
Carbohydrates: 65%
Fat: 14%

BLUEBERRY MUFFINS

16 muffins

¼ cup safflower oil
¾ cup brown sugar
1 cup unbleached white flour
2 teaspoons baking powder
1 teaspoon baking soda
¼ teaspoon salt
1 cup 1% buttermilk
1 egg
⅓ cup oat bran
⅓ cup oatmeal
⅓ cup wheat germ
1⅓ cups blueberries

In a mixing bowl, combine safflower oil, brown sugar, flour, baking powder, baking soda and salt. Add buttermilk, egg, oat bran, oatmeal and wheat germ; mix lightly with a wooden spoon to moisten. Stir in blueberries. Fill paper-lined muffin tins ¾ full with batter. Bake at 400°F. 20 minutes, or until toothpick inserted into center comes out dry. Remove muffins from tins and cool on wire racks.
VARIATION: Substitute raisins for blueberries.

APPROXIMATE NUTRITIONAL CONTENT PER MUFFIN

Total calories: 138
Protein: 3 g
Carbohydrates: 23 g
Cholesterol: 16 mg
Fat: 4 g
Sodium: 141 mg

Percentage of calories from:
Protein: 9%
Carbohydrates: 63%
Fat: 28%

BANANA CURRANT MUFFINS

18 muffins

1	cup unbleached white flour
1¼	cups whole-wheat flour
⅓	cup granulated sugar
2	teaspoons baking powder
½	teaspoon baking soda
2	teaspoons cinnamon
½	teaspoon nutmeg
½	cup 1% buttermilk
½	cup safflower oil
2	ripe bananas, mashed
1	egg
1	cup currants

In a mixing bowl, combine flours, sugar, baking powder, baking soda, cinnamon and nutmeg. In a smaller bowl, combine buttermilk, oil, bananas and egg; add to dry ingredients. Stir with a wire whisk just until all ingredients are moistened. Fold in currants. Fill paper-lined muffin cups ¾ full with batter. Bake at 375°F. 15–20 minutes, or until toothpick inserted into center comes out dry. Remove muffins from tins and cool on wire racks.

APPROXIMATE NUTRITIONAL CONTENT PER MUFFIN

Total calories: 146
Protein: 3 g
Carbohydrates: 20 g
Cholesterol: 15 mg
Fat: 7 g
Sodium: 61 mg

Percentage of calories from:
 Protein: 7%
 Carbohydrates: 53%
 Fat: 40%

Reducing the safflower oil to ⅓ cup lowers the calories to 128 and the calories from fat to 32%. The muffins are still very good, only not quite as moist.

OVERNIGHT OATMEAL MUFFINS

14 muffins

½ cup unbleached white flour
½ cup whole-wheat flour
¼ cup oat bran
1 cup rolled oats
⅓ cup brown sugar
½ teaspoon baking powder
½ teaspoon baking soda
½ teaspoon cinnamon
¼ teaspoon salt
¾ cup 1% buttermilk
¼ cup safflower oil
1 egg
½ cup puréed apricots*
½ cup raisins

In a mixing bowl, combine flours, oat bran, rolled oats, brown sugar, baking powder, baking soda, cinnamon, salt, buttermilk, safflower oil, egg and apricots. Stir in raisins. Cover and refrigerate overnight or bake at once. Fill paper-lined muffin cups ¾ full with batter. Bake at 400°F. 20–25 minutes, or until toothpick inserted into center comes out dry. Remove muffins from tins and cool on wire racks.

*If using canned apricots, use unsweetened. Three apricots yield ½ cup puréed apricots. If using fresh, wash, halve and seed 3 whole apricots. Simmer, covered, in a saucepan, with 3 tablespoons water 5–10 minutes, or until apricots soften. Purée in blender or food processor.

APPROXIMATE NUTRITIONAL CONTENT PER MUFFIN

Total calories: 151
Protein: 4 g
Carbohydrates: 25 g
Cholesterol: 19 mg
Fat: 5 g
Sodium: 100 mg

Percentage of calories from:
Protein: 9%
Carbohydrates: 62%
Fat: 29%

OAT-BRAN MUFFINS

18 muffins

- ¼ cup safflower oil
- ¾ cup brown sugar
- 1 cup unbleached white flour
- 2 teaspoons baking powder
- ¼ teaspoon salt
- 1 cup 1% buttermilk
- 1 egg
- 1 teaspoon baking soda
- 1 cup oat bran
- 1 cup raisins

In a mixing bowl and with a wire whisk, combine safflower oil, brown sugar, flour, baking powder and salt. Add remaining ingredients and stir just until moistened. Fill paper-lined muffin cups ¾ full with batter. Bake at 400°F. 20 minutes, or until toothpick inserted into center comes out dry. Remove muffins from tins and cool on wire racks.

APPROXIMATE NUTRITIONAL CONTENT PER MUFFIN

Total calories: 137
Protein: 3 g
Carbohydrates: 24 g
Cholesterol: 15 mg
Fat: 4 g
Sodium: 125 mg

Percentage of calories from:
Protein: 8%
Carbohydrates: 68%
Fat: 25%

APPLE COFFEE CAKE

12 slices

  2½ cups peeled and coarsely chopped apples
  1¼ cups unbleached white flour
  ¾ cup whole-wheat flour
  ½ cup plus 1 tablespoon brown sugar
  2 teaspoons baking powder
  ¼ teaspoon salt
  ½ teaspoon cinnamon
  ¼ cup safflower oil
  ½ cup skim milk
  1 egg

In a small bowl, toss apples with ½ cup of the unbleached white flour; set aside. In a mixing bowl, combine remaining unbleached white flour, whole-wheat flour, ½ cup brown sugar, baking powder, salt and ¼ teaspoon of the cinnamon. Add safflower oil, milk and egg; stir with a wire whisk until dry ingredients are moistened. Stir in apples. Pour batter into a 10-inch round, nonstick baking pan. Combine remaining 1 tablespoon brown sugar and ¼ teaspoon cinnamon; sprinkle over coffee cake. Bake at 400°F. 30 minutes, or until toothpick inserted into center comes out clean.

APPROXIMATE NUTRITIONAL CONTENT PER SLICE

Total calories: 181

Protein: 3 g

Carbohydrates: 31 g

Cholesterol: 23 mg

Fat: 5 g

Sodium: 122 mg

Percentage of calories from:

Protein: 7%

Carbohydrates: 67%

Fat: 26%

STEAMED TORTILLAS

2 cups hot water
1–2 flour or stone-ground corn tortillas* per person

In a wok, bring water to a boil. Insert a vegetable steamer basket or a bamboo steamer basket into the wok, making sure water is kept below basket level. Put tortillas into basket. Cover wok with lid. Steam 3–5 minutes, or until tortillas are warm and limp. Fold each tortilla into thirds. Arrange in napkin-lined basket. Serve piping-hot.

For Pan-fried Tortillas: Preheat a nonstick 10-inch skillet over medium heat. Add tortillas and cook, one at a time, 1–2 minutes on each side, or just until tortillas are warm and limp.

*When buying flour tortillas, look for ones that are made with soy bean oil, not with lard. Corn tortillas generally do not contain any oil or shortening so are more heart-healthy and lower in calories.

APPROXIMATE NUTRITIONAL CONTENT PER 1.5-OUNCE FLOUR TORTILLA

Total calories: 95
Protein: 3 g
Carbohydrates: 17 g
Cholesterol: 0 mg
Fat: 2 g
Sodium: 147 mg

Percentage of calories from:
Protein: 10%
Carbohydrates: 73%
Fat: 17%

APPROXIMATE NUTRITIONAL CONTENT PER 1.5-OUNCE STONE-GROUND CORN TORTILLA

Total calories: 67
Protein: 2 g
Carbohydrates: 13 g
Cholesterol: 0 mg
Fat: 1 g
Sodium: 53 mg

Percentage of calories from:
Protein: 12%
Carbohydrates: 74%
Fat: 14%

SANDWICHES

POACHED CHICKEN ON DILL RYE

1 sandwich

- ½ poached chicken breast (see page 433)
- 2 slices dill rye bread
- ½ teaspoon safflower mayonnaise
  Bibb lettuce

Tear chicken into strings. Spread bread with mayonnaise. Layer with chicken. Top with lettuce and second slice of bread.

SERVING SUGGESTION: Good on a picnic with Pasta Salad (page 380) or White Bean Salad (page 378), fresh fruit and Oatmeal Raisin Cookies (page 532).

APPROXIMATE NUTRITIONAL CONTENT PER SANDWICH

Total calories: 224
Protein: 18 g
Carbohydrates: 28 g
Cholesterol: 34 mg
Fat: 4 g
Sodium: 330 mg

Percentage of calories from:
  Protein: 33%
  Carbohydrates: 50%
  Fat: 17%

ROAST TURKEY IN PITA

1 sandwich

- 1 pita (pocket bread)
- ½ teaspoon safflower mayonnaise
- 2 ounces roast turkey breast (see page 436)
  Bibb lettuce
- 2 ripe tomato slices
- 1 thin slice red onion

Spread pita pocket with mayonnaise. Stuff with turkey, lettuce, tomato and onion.

SERVING SUGGESTION: Good with White Bean Salad (page 378).

APPROXIMATE NUTRITIONAL CONTENT PER SANDWICH

Total calories: 318
Protein: 25 g
Carbohydrates: 42 g
Cholesterol: 41 mg
Fat: 5 g
Sodium: 335 mg

Percentage of calories from:
Protein: 32%
Carbohydrates: 54%
Fat: 14%

TURKEY, TOMATO AND CUCUMBER

2 open-faced sandwiches

2	slices black bread or pumpernickel rye
¼	teaspoon safflower mayonnaise mixed with ⅛ teaspoon fresh lemon juice
2	ounces turkey breast, roasted (see page 436) or poached in broth (see page 433)
1	ripe tomato, thinly sliced
½	cucumber, thinly sliced black pepper
½	cup alfalfa sprouts

Spread bread with mayonnaise. Layer each slice with turkey, tomato and cucumber. Sprinkle with black pepper. Top with sprouts.

SERVING SUGGESTION: Serve with fresh seasonal fruit.

APPROXIMATE NUTRITIONAL CONTENT PER OPEN-FACED SANDWICH

Total calories: 111
Protein: 7 g
Carbohydrates: 18 g
Cholesterol: 20 mg
Fat: 1 g
Sodium: 196 mg

Percentage of calories from:
Protein: 26%
Carbohydrates: 63%
Fat: 11%

VEGGIE

1 sandwich

2 slices sour dough French bread
½ teaspoon safflower mayonnaise
¼ teaspoon Dijon mustard
2 slices ripe tomato
¼ zucchini, thinly sliced
  leaf lettuce

Spread bread with mayonnaise and mustard. Layer with tomatoes, zucchini and lettuce. Top with second slice of bread.

VARIATION: Add 1 ounce thinly sliced part-skim mozzarella or hoop cheese.

APPROXIMATE NUTRITIONAL CONTENT PER SANDWICH

Total calories: 236
Protein: 8 g
Carbohydrates: 42 g
Cholesterol: 0 mg
Fat: 4 g
Sodium: 322 mg

Percentage of calories from:
  Protein: 12%
  Carbohydrates: 71%
  Fat: 16%

APPROXIMATE NUTRITIONAL CONTENT PER SANDWICH WITH CHEESE

Total calories: 318
Protein: 14 g
Carbohydrates: 42 g
Cholesterol: 18 mg
Fat: 8 g
Sodium: 520 mg

Percentage of calories from:
  Protein: 19%
  Carbohydrates: 55%
  Fat: 25%

BEEF WITH MUSHROOMS AND TOMATOES

2 open-faced sandwiches

2   slices pumpernickel rye bread
    Dijon mustard
2   ounces roast beef (lean only), thinly sliced
3   fresh mushrooms, sliced
1   ripe tomato, sliced

Spread bread with mustard. Layer each bread slice with beef, mushrooms and tomato.
NOTE: Rump roast is the leanest cut of beef.

APPROXIMATE NUTRITIONAL CONTENT PER OPEN-FACED SANDWICH

Total calories: 142
Protein: 11 g
Carbohydrates: 18 g
Cholesterol: 24 mg
Fat: 3 g
Sodium: 208 mg

Percentage of calories from:
Protein: 31%
Carbohydrates: 48%
Fat: 21%

ROAST VEAL WITH RED ONION

1 open-faced sandwich

1   slice black bread or pumpernickel rye
¼   teaspoon safflower mayonnaise mixed with
     a touch of garlic powder and a dab of
     fresh lemon juice
2   ounces roast veal (lean only), thinly sliced
2   slices red onion
     red leaf lettuce

Spread bread with mayonnaise. Layer with roast veal. Top with red onion and leaf lettuce.

APPROXIMATE NUTRITIONAL CONTENT PER
ROAST VEAL WITH RED ONION
OPEN-FACED SANDWICH

Total calories: 159
Protein: 11 g
Carbohydrates: 18 g
Cholesterol: 28 mg
Fat: 5 g
Sodium: 210 mg

Percentage of calories from:
Protein: 28%
Carbohydrates: 45%
Fat: 27%

LETTUCE, TOMATO AND SPROUTS

1 open-faced sandwich

1 slice toasted whole-grain bread
¼ teaspoon Creamy Dijon Vinaigrette
(page 398)
Bibb lettuce
sliced ripe tomatoes
black pepper
alfalfa sprouts

Spread toast with Dijon Vinaigrette. Layer with lettuce and tomatoes. Season generously with black pepper. Top with sprouts.

APPROXIMATE NUTRITIONAL CONTENT PER
LETTUCE, TOMATO AND SPROUTS SANDWICH

Total calories: 107
Protein: 5 g
Carbohydrates: 20 g
Cholesterol: 0 mg
Fat: 2 g
Sodium: 197 mg

Percentage of calories from:
Protein: 16%
Carbohydrates: 70%
Fat: 15%

TUNA, RED ONION AND TOMATO

6 open-faced sandwiches

1   6½-ounce can water-packed tuna
¼   cup safflower mayonnaise*
6   slices black bread or pumpernickel rye
1   red onion, thinly sliced
1   large ripe tomato, thinly sliced
   Bibb lettuce

Mix tuna with mayonnaise. Spread over bread. Top with onion, tomato and lettuce.

*To further reduce the fat content of this recipe, use less mayonnaise.

APPROXIMATE NUTRITIONAL CONTENT PER SANDWICH

Total calories: 180
Protein: 11 g
Carbohydrates: 21 g
Cholesterol: 19 mg
Fat: 6 g
Sodium: 277 mg

Percentage of calories from:
Protein: 25%
Carbohydrates: 45%
Fat: 30%

CRABMEAT AND TOMATO

1 sandwich

> 1/4 cup crabmeat
>   2 teaspoons safflower mayonnaise mixed
>   with 1/4 teaspoon fresh lemon juice
>   2 thick slices crusty French bread
>   2 ripe tomato slices
>   red leaf lettuce

Mix crabmeat with mayonnaise. Spread on bread. Top with tomato slices, lettuce and second slice of bread.

APPROXIMATE NUTRITIONAL CONTENT PER SANDWICH

Total calories: 306
Protein: 12 g
Carbohydrates: 40 g
Cholesterol: 36 mg
Fat: 10 g
Sodium: 419 mg

Percentage of calories from:
Protein: 17%
Carbohydrates: 54%
Fat: 29%

SOUPS

CHICKEN STOCK

4¹/₂ quarts

2   pounds meaty chicken pieces*
3   pounds chicken trimmings (carcass,
        bones, backs)**
4   quarts cold water
3   leeks, roots and green stems removed
3   carrots, peeled
3   stalks celery with leaves
1   large yellow onion, quartered
2   cloves garlic, peeled
2   teaspoons salt
1   tablespoon white peppercorns

In a shallow baking dish, combine meaty chicken pieces; bake at 350°F. 20–25 minutes. Remove to stock pot; add chicken trimmings and water. Bring slowly to a boil, removing scum (and fat) as it floats to the top. Add remaining ingredients and simmer 3¹/₂ hours. (Do not boil or fat will be reabsorbed into the broth, making it cloudy.) Cover only partially with lid so that steam can escape. Strain stock. Refrigerate overnight. Skim and discard fat that floats to the top.
    Return broth to stock pot. Simmer, uncovered, 3 hours,

or until broth is reduced by one-third. Test seasoning. Sparingly add salt, if needed. Use broth at once, or store in refrigerator or freezer for later use. (You may want to freeze some stock in ice-cube trays to use for stir-frying or sautéing vegetables.)

*Remove breasts and other meaty pieces from stock as soon as they are cooked (about 45–60 minutes). Reserve for stews, soups, salads and sandwiches. Return any bones, scraps and skin to stock pot for remainder of cooking.

**Do not use the liver and the giblets when making stock as they impart a bitter taste.

VARIATION: For Turkey Stock, substitute turkey pieces for chicken.

APPROXIMATE NUTRITIONAL CONTENT PER CUP
OF CHICKEN STOCK

Total calories: 27   *Percentage of calories from:*
Protein: 4 g   Protein: 62%
Carbohydrates: Tr   Carbohydrates: 8%
Cholesterol: 2 mg   Fat: 30%
Fat: 1 g
Sodium: 275 mg

Don't be too concerned with the high percentage of calories from fat in this recipe. The calories of the stock are so low that even a trace of fat elevates the percentage.

BEEF STOCK

7¹/₂ quarts

4	pounds beef chuck, cut into 2-inch cubes*
4	pounds beef marrow bones
7	quarts cold water
3	cloves garlic, peeled
3	leeks, roots and green stems removed
1	large yellow onion, quartered
3	stalks celery with leaves
3	carrots, peeled
3	ripe tomatoes, quartered
2	bay leaves
¹/₄	cup chopped fresh parsley
1	teaspoon thyme
1	tablespoon salt
3	black peppercorns
4	white peppercorns

In a stock pot, combine beef chuck, marrow bones and water; bring slowly to a boil, removing scum (and fat) as it floats to the top. Add remaining ingredients and simmer 3¹/₂ hours. (Do not boil or fat will be reabsorbed into the broth, making it cloudy.) Cover only partially with lid so that steam can escape. Strain broth. Refrigerate overnight. Skim and discard fat that floats to the top.

Return broth to stock pot. Simmer, uncovered, 3 hours, or until broth is reduced by one-third. Test seasoning. Sparingly add salt, if needed. Use broth at once, or store in refrigerator or freezer for later use. (You may want to freeze some stock in ice-cube trays to use for stir-frying or sautéing vegetables.)

*Remove choice pieces of meat from stock as soon as they are cooked (about 1¹/₂–2 hours). Serve for dinner with Steamed Red Potatoes (page 487) and stir-fried snow peas.

APPROXIMATE NUTRITIONAL CONTENT PER CUP
OF BEEF STOCK

Total calories: 37
Protein: 5 g
Carbohydrates: Tr
Cholesterol: 2 mg
Fat: 1 g
Sodium: 275 mg

Percentage of calories from:
  Protein: 59%
  Carbohydrates: 11%
  Fat: 30%

Don't be too concerned with the high percentage of calories from fat in this recipe. The calories of the stock are so low that even a trace of fat elevates the percentage.

VEAL STOCK

3¹/₂ quarts

  1 pound veal chuck, cut into 2-inch pieces*
  3 pounds veal bones
  2 carrots, peeled
  1 large yellow onion, quartered
  3 quarts cold water
  2 stalks celery with leaves
  2 cloves garlic, peeled
  1 bay leaf
  2 teaspoons white peppercorns
  ¹/₂ teaspoon thyme
  2 teaspoons salt
  2 tablespoons tomato paste
  ¹/₂ cup white wine

In a shallow baking dish, combine veal chuck, veal bones, carrots and onion; bake at 350°F. 15–20 minutes. Remove to stock pot; add water. Bring slowly to a boil, removing scum (and fat) as it floats to the top. Add remaining ingredients and simmer 5 hours. (Do not boil or fat will be

(continued on next page)

reabsorbed into the broth, making it cloudy.) Cover only partially with lid so that steam can escape. Strain stock. Refrigerate overnight. Skim and discard fat that floats to the top.

Return broth to stock pot. Simmer, uncovered, 3 hours, or until broth is reduced by one-third. Test seasoning. Sparingly add salt, if needed. Use broth at once, or store in refrigerator or freezer for later use. (You may want to freeze some stock in ice-cube trays to use for stir-frying or sautéing vegetables.)

*Remove choice pieces of meat from stock as soon as they are cooked (about 1–1½ hours). Serve for dinner with fresh asparagus and a heavy-type pasta, such as penne, with Marina Sauce (page 404).

APPROXIMATE NUTRITIONAL CONTENT PER CUP OF VEAL STOCK

Total calories: 27
Protein: 3 g
Carbohydrates: Tr
Cholesterol: 3 mg
Fat: Tr
Sodium: 258 mg

Percentage of calories from:
  Protein: 62%
  Carbohydrates: 8%
  Fat: 30%

Don't be too concerned with the high percentage of calories from fat in this recipe. The calories of the stock are so low that even a trace of fat will elevate the percentage.

CHICKEN-AND-BEEF STOCK

7¹/₂ quarts

1½ pounds beef chuck, cut into 2-inch
   pieces*
2¼ pounds chicken parts
2 pounds beef soupbones
7 quarts cold water
3 cloves garlic, peeled
3 leeks, roots and green stems removed
1 large yellow onion, quartered
3 stalks celery with leaves
3 carrots, peeled
3 ripe tomatoes, quartered
2 bay leaves
¼ cup chopped fresh parsley
1 teaspoon thyme
1 tablespoon salt
3 black peppercorns
4 white peppercorns

In a stock pot, combine beef, chicken parts, soupbones and water; bring slowly to a boil, removing scum (and fat) as it floats to the top. Add remaining ingredients and simmer 3½ hours. (Do not boil or fat will be reabsorbed into the broth, making it cloudy.) Cover only partially with lid so that steam can escape. Strain broth. Refrigerate overnight. Skim and discard fat that floats to the top.

Return broth to stock pot. Simmer, uncovered, 3 hours, or until broth is reduced by one-third. Test seasoning. Sparingly add additional salt, if needed. Use at once, or store in refrigerator or freezer for later use. (It's a good idea to freeze some stock in ice-cube trays to use for stir-frying or sautéing vegetables).

*Remove meaty chicken breasts and beef chuck from stock as soon as they are cooked (about 45–90 minutes).

(continued on next page)

Reserve for stews, soups, salads and sandwiches. Return any bones, scraps and skin to stock pot for remainder of cooking.

APPROXIMATE NUTRITIONAL CONTENT PER CUP OF CHICKEN-AND-BEEF STOCK

Total calories: 37
Protein: 5 g
Carbohydrates: Tr
Cholesterol: 2 mg
Fat: 1 g
Sodium: 275 mg

Percentage of calories from:
  Protein: 59%
  Carbohydrates: 11%
  Fat: 30%

Don't be too concerned with the high percentage of calories from fat in this recipe. The calories of the stock are so low that even a trace of fat will elevate the percentage.

BEAN SOUP STOCK

3 quarts

>   2   tablespoons dried parsley
>   1   tablespoon thyme
>   1   tablespoon marjoram
>   2   bay leaves
>   2   tablespoons celery seed
>   1   meaty ham hock, about 2½–3 pounds
>   3   quarts water
>   1   tablespoon salt

Measure parsley, thyme, marjoram, bay leaves and celery seed into a square of cheesecloth and tie cloth securely at the top with a string. Combine with ham hock, water and salt in a stock pot. Bring slowly to a boil, removing scum (and fat) as it floats to the top. Cover and simmer 2½–3 hours. (Do not boil or fat will be reabsorbed into the broth, making it cloudy.) Refrigerate overnight. Skim and discard fat that floats to the top. Cut ham off bone, reserving only very lean meat. Dice and return to stock pot with seasoning pouch. Discard ham bones and ham fat. Use stock at once, or store in refrigerator or freezer for later use.

APPROXIMATE NUTRITIONAL CONTENT PER CUP

Total calories: 16
Protein: 3 g
Carbohydrates: Tr
Cholesterol: 5 mg
Fat: Tr
Sodium: 240 mg

Percentage of calories from:
  Protein: 50%
  Carbohydrates: 19%
  Fat: 31%

Don't be too concerned with the high percentage of calories from fat in this recipe. The calories of the stock are so low that even a trace of fat will elevate the percentage.

FRENCH MARKET SOUP

8 quarts (32 cups)

1	recipe Bean Soup Stock (page 357)
3	tablespoons dry yellow split peas
¼	cup dry black-eyed peas
2½	tablespoons dry green split peas
¼	cup dry pearl barley
2½	tablespoons dry pinto beans
2½	tablespoons dry pink beans or small red beans
2½	tablespoons dry garbanzo beans
2½	tablespoons dry lentil beans
2½	tablespoons dry lima beans
1½	tablespoons dry mung beans
⅓	cup dried black beans
1	28-ounce can plum tomatoes, diced
2	medium yellow onions, chopped
6	stalks celery, chopped
2	cloves garlic, minced
1–2	chicken breasts, skinned, boned and diced

In a stock pot, heat stock just to boiling (do not boil); reduce heat to simmer. Thoroughly wash peas, barley and beans; add to stock. Add tomatoes, onions, celery and garlic; simmer, covered, 3 hours, or until beans are tender. Add chicken; cook 30 minutes, or until chicken is cooked.

NOTE: This soup is sensational and well worth the effort. Finding all these types of beans may require shopping in more than one supermarket. The dry beans will keep for months. As a timesaver, measure out the beans for several recipes and store them in plastic bags.

SERVING SUGGESTION: Good with homemade bread and fresh seasonal fruit.

APPROXIMATE NUTRITIONAL CONTENT PER CUP
OF FRENCH MARKET SOUP

Total calories: 68

Percentage of calories from:

Protein: 6 g

Protein: 33%

Carbohydrates: 10 g

Carbohydrates: 59%

Cholesterol: 8 mg

Fat: 8%

Fat: Tr

Sodium: 240 mg

SPINACH SOUP AU GRATIN

8 cups

1   large bunch fresh spinach
3   cups Chicken Stock (page 350)
2   slices French bread
1   ounce part-skim mozzarella cheese, sliced
¼   teaspoon nutmeg

Wash and trim spinach; shake off excess moisture. In a saucepan, cook spinach, covered, just until leaves begin to wilt. (It is not necessary to add additional cooking liquid as the moisture on the leaves is sufficient.) Add stock. Heat just to boiling. Reduce heat; simmer 5 minutes. Toast bread, turning once, in a 350°F. oven 5 minutes, or until crisp; cut each slice into quarters. Layer toast with cheese and return to oven until cheese melts. Stir nutmeg into soup. Ladle soup into bowls. Top with toasted cheese bread.

APPROXIMATE NUTRITIONAL CONTENT PER CUP

Total calories: 70

Percentage of calories from:

Protein: 6 g

Protein: 34%

Carbohydrates: 8 g

Carbohydrates: 47%

Cholesterol: 3 mg

Fat: 19%

Fat: 2 g

Sodium: 217 mg

MINESTRONE

3¹/₂ quarts (14 cups)

4 cups Chicken Stock (page 350)
1 medium white onion, chopped
3 stalks celery, chopped
2 cloves garlic, chopped
1 leek, chopped, roots and green stems removed
1 28-ounce can plum tomatoes,* diced
1 teaspoon basil
¹/₂ teaspoon oregano
¹/₄ teaspoon black pepper
3 cups Chinese (Napa) cabbage, shredded
1 medium zucchini, thinly sliced
2 carrots, grated
1 8-ounce can garbanzo beans
1 15-ounce can red kidney beans, with liquid*
3 cups cooked elbow macaroni

In a stock pot, heat stock just to boiling (do not boil); add onion, celery, garlic and leek. Reduce heat to simmer; cook 1 hour. Add tomatoes, basil, oregano and pepper; simmer 30 minutes. Return stock just to boiling (do not boil). Add cabbage, zucchini and carrots; reduce heat and simmer 20 minutes. Add remaining ingredients and heat.

*To further decrease the sodium level of this recipe, use low-sodium canned tomatoes and/or kidney beans. Also look for brands of kidney beans canned without fat.

NOTE: This soup tastes even better the second day.

APPROXIMATE NUTRITIONAL CONTENT PER CUP OF MINESTRONE

Total calories: 124
Protein: 7 g
Carbohydrates: 22 g
Cholesterol: Tr
Fat: 1 g
Sodium: 304 mg

Percentage of calories from:
Protein: 22%
Carbohydrates: 69%
Fat: 8%

PASTINA IN BRODO

8 cups

2   quarts Chicken Stock (page 350)
1   cup egg or spinach pastina
¼   cup chopped fresh parsley

In a stock pot, heat stock just to boiling (do not boil). Stir in pastina. Reduce heat; simmer 6–7 minutes. Ladle into soup bowls. Sprinkle with parsley.

SERVING SUGGESTION: Good choice for light lunch or first dinner course.

APPROXIMATE NUTRITIONAL CONTENT PER CUP

Total calories: 81
Protein: 7 g
Carbohydrates: 10 g
Cholesterol: 1 mg
Fat: 1 g
Sodium: 276 mg

Percentage of calories from:
Protein: 34%
Carbohydrates: 51%
Fat: 15%

TORTELLINI IN BRODO

6 cups

6   cups Chicken Stock (page 350)
1   dozen uncooked Spinach Tortellini
      (page 460) or Chicken Tortellini
      (page 462)
½   cup chopped fresh parsley

In a medium saucepan, bring stock just to boiling (do not boil). Add tortellini; simmer 10–15 minutes, or until tortellini are cooked. Ladle into soup bowls. Sprinkle with parsley.

SERVING SUGGESTION: This soup can be a hearty main meal or a suitable first course with a chicken or veal entrée.

APPROXIMATE NUTRITIONAL CONTENT PER CUP

Total calories: 107
Protein: 10 g
Carbohydrates: 8 g
Cholesterol: 19 mg
Fat: 3 g
Sodium: 336 mg

Percentage of calories from:
  Protein: 38%
  Carbohydrates: 31%
  Fat: 30%

HEARTY TORTELLINI SOUP

2½ quarts (10 cups)

10 cups Chicken Stock (page 350)
1 chicken breast, skinned and boned
2 carrots
½ medium yellow onion
1 stalk celery
1½ dozen uncooked Spinach Tortellini
　　(page 460)
¼ bunch fresh parsley, chopped

In a stock pot, combine stock, chicken breast, carrots, onion and celery; bring just to boiling (do not boil). Reduce heat; simmer 20–25 minutes. Remove from heat. Allow chicken and vegetables to cool in broth. When cool, remove chicken and vegetables. Dice carrots and set aside. Reserve chicken, onion and celery for later use. Return broth just to boiling. Add tortellini; cook over medium heat 5–10 minutes, or until tortellini are cooked. Remove from heat. Add carrots. Ladle into bowls. Sprinkle with parsley.

SERVING SUGGESTION: This soup makes a delightful main meal with a simple tossed salad and crusty French rolls.

APPROXIMATE NUTRITIONAL CONTENT PER CUP

Total calories: 129
Protein: 14 g
Carbohydrates: 11 g
Cholesterol: 26 mg
Fat: 3 g
Sodium: 410 mg

Percentage of calories from:
　Protein: 44%
　Carbohydrates: 37%
　Fat: 19%

FISHERMAN'S SOUP *

3 quarts (12 cups)

½ pound clams
½ pound mussels
8 cups Chicken Stock (page 350)
½ chicken breast, skinned, boned and cut
    into 1-inch cubes
¼ pound orange roughy or other whitefish,
    cut into 1-inch cubes
1¼ teaspoons arrowroot dissolved in ¼ cup
    water
¼ pound scallops, quartered and poached
    (see page 417)
3 cups cooked Saffron Rice (page 500)
¼ red pepper, diced
¼ green pepper, diced

Clean and soak clams and mussels in salt water to remove sand (page 409). In a covered vegetable steamer basket over boiling water, steam clams and mussels until shells open. Remove half of the clams and half of the mussels from their shells; leave the other half in their shells for garnish. Set aside.

In a stock pot, heat stock to boiling; add chicken. Reduce heat; cook 15 minutes. Add orange roughy; cook 2 minutes. Gradually add arrowroot, stirring constantly, until stock thickens slightly. Add scallops, rice, shelled clams and mussels. Heat. Ladle into soup bowls. Garnish with unshelled clams and mussels. Top with peppers.

APPROXIMATE NUTRITIONAL CONTENT PER CUP

Total calories: 152
Protein: 15 g
Carbohydrates: 16 g
Cholesterol: 34 mg
Fat: 2 g
Sodium: 301 mg

Percentage of calories from:
Protein: 43%
Carbohydrates: 43%
Fat: 15%

SEAFOOD STEW

8 servings

  1   2-pound can plum tomatoes, diced
  1   tablespoon fresh basil or ½ teaspoon dried
 ½   teaspoon saffron
  1   white onion, chopped
  1   large fennel bulb, chopped
  6   cloves garlic, peeled
 ½   cup dry white wine
  1   pound mussels, soaked and cleaned
        (see page 409)
  1   pound clams, soaked and cleaned
        (see page 409)
 ½   pound scallops
 ½   pound black cod fillets, cut into 2-inch
        squares
 ½   pound squid tubes, cleaned and cut into
        rings
  2   tablespoons chopped fresh parsley

In a medium stock pot, combine tomatoes, basil and saffron. Simmer 30 minutes. In a nonstick skillet, sauté onion, fennel and garlic in white wine 5–10 minutes, or until softened. Add to stock pot. Simmer 20 minutes. Raise heat and bring just to a boil (do not boil). Add mussels and clams. Reduce heat to medium. When mussels and clams begin to open, add scallops, cod and squid. Cook 5 minutes, or until most shells have opened and fish is cooked. Ladle into bowls. Sprinkle with parsley.

SERVING SUGGESTION: Serve with Shallot-basil Bread (page 333) for dipping.

(continued on next page)

APPROXIMATE NUTRITIONAL CONTENT PER SERVING OF SEAFOOD STEW

Total calories: 157
Protein: 23 g
Carbohydrates: 10 g
Cholesterol: 114 mg
Fat: 2 g
Sodium: 310 mg

Percentage of calories from:
  Protein: 61%
  Carbohydrates: 28%
  Fat: 12%

SWISS BARLEY SOUP

10 quarts (40 cups)

1½ cups dry pearl barley
2   cups water
4   quarts Chicken or Turkey Stock
      (page 350)
1   large yellow onion, chopped
½   cup dry yellow split peas
¼   cup dry egg pastina
1   tablespoon salt
¼   teaspoon black pepper

Soak barley in 2 cups water overnight. In a stock pot, heat stock just to boiling (do not boil). Add barley with soaking liquid and onion. Simmer, uncovered, 1½ hours. Add split peas; simmer 1–1½ hours, or until barley and split peas are tender. Stir in pastina, salt and pepper. Simmer 5–10 minutes, or until pastina is cooked.

APPROXIMATE NUTRITIONAL CONTENT PER CUP

Total calories: 51
Protein: 3 g
Carbohydrates: 8 g
Cholesterol: Tr
Fat: Tr
Sodium: 276 mg

Percentage of calories from:
  Protein: 25%
  Carbohydrates: 65%
  Fat: 10%

LENTIL-AND-BARLEY SOUP

9 cups

- ³/₄ cup dry pearl barley
- 4 cups hot water
- 6 cups Veal Stock (page 353) or Beef Stock (page 352)
- ¹/₂ cup dry lentil beans
- 1 medium white onion, chopped
- 2 stalks celery, chopped
- ¹/₂ pound fresh mushrooms, sliced
- 1 ripe tomato, diced
- ¹/₂ teaspoon salt
- ¹/₄ teaspoon black pepper
- ¹/₂ pound extra-lean ground round or ground veal, browned and drained

Soak barley in 4 cups hot water for 1 hour. In a stock pot, heat stock just to boiling (do not boil); reduce heat to simmer. Add barley with soaking liquid to stock. Add lentils, onion and celery; simmer 2–2¹/₂ hours, or until barley is tender and lentils are cooked. Stir in mushrooms, tomatoes, salt, pepper and ground round or veal; simmer 10–15 minutes.

SERVING SUGGESTION: Serve with low-sodium accompaniments such as Steamed Tortillas (page 341) and fresh seasonal fruit.

APPROXIMATE NUTRITIONAL CONTENT PER CUP

Total calories: 159
Protein: 13 g
Carbohydrates: 22 g
Cholesterol: 24 mg
Fat: 2 g
Sodium: 408 mg

Percentage of calories from:
Protein: 32%
Carbohydrates: 55%
Fat: 13%

BLACK BEAN SOUP

4¹/₂ quarts

1   recipe Bean Soup Stock (page 357)
1   28-ounce can plum tomatoes,* diced
1   large white onion, diced
3   stalks celery, diced
4   cloves garlic, peeled
1¹/₂   cups dry black beans
¹/₂   cup dry black-eyed peas
¹/₂   cup dry pearl barley
2   cups cooked heavy-type pasta, such as penne

In a stock pot, bring stock to a boil. Add tomatoes, onion, celery and garlic. Thoroughly wash beans, peas and barley; add to stock pot. Simmer, covered, 3–4 hours, or until beans are tender. Stir in pasta.

*To further decrease the sodium level in this recipe, use salt-free or low-sodium canned tomatoes.

NOTE: Black Bean Soup is high in sodium. Keep this in mind and allow for it when planning your daily sodium intake.

APPROXIMATE NUTRITIONAL CONTENT PER CUP

Total calories: 108
Protein: 5 g
Carbohydrates: 21 g
Cholesterol: 0 mg
Fat: Tr
Sodium: 451 mg

Percentage of calories from:
  Protein: 19%
  Carbohydrates: 77%
  Fat: 4%

PASTA-AND-BEAN SOUP

4¹/₂ quarts (18 cups)

1 pound dry cannellini beans or small
  California white beans
1 large, meaty ham hock
3 quarts water
1 tablespoon salt
2 cloves garlic, peeled
2 bay leaves
2 tablespoons dried parsley
2 teaspoons thyme
2 teaspoons marjoram
2 cups Chicken Stock (page 350)
2 carrots, diced
2 stalks celery, thinly sliced
1 small white onion, diced
1 1-pound package fusilli,* cooked *al dente*
  black pepper

Wash and drain beans. In a stock pot, combine beans, ham hock, water, salt, garlic, bay leaves, parsley, thyme and marjoram; bring to a boil. Reduce heat; simmer 2½ hours. Refrigerate overnight. Skim and discard fat that floats to the top.

In a blender or food processor, purée ½ of the beans from the stock; set aside. Remove and discard bones, fat and skin from the ham hock. Dice lean ham and return to stock.

Add puréed beans and stock to broth; bring to a boil. Reduce heat. Add carrots, celery and onion; simmer 1 hour.

Put pasta in soup bowls and ladle soup over pasta. Sprinkle with black pepper.

*Fusilli can be found in Italian markets and supermarkets that carry a wide variety of pastas.

(continued on next page)

NOTE: Pasta-and-bean Soup is high in sodium. Keep this in mind and allow for it when planning your daily sodium intake.

To further reduce the sodium level of this recipe, omit or reduce the added salt.

APPROXIMATE NUTRITIONAL CONTENT PER CUP OF PASTA-AND-BEAN SOUP

Total calories: 157
Protein: 8 g
Carbohydrates: 29 g
Cholesterol: 2 mg
Fat: Tr
Sodium: 447 mg

Percentage of calories from:
Protein: 21%
Carbohydrates: 74%
Fat: 5%

SALADS

ENGLISH CUCUMBER SALAD

4 servings

1 English cucumber, unpeeled
2 teaspoons salt (to be rinsed off)*
⅓ cup tomato salsa

Cut cucumber lengthwise into ⅛-inch flat strips about ½ inch wide. Arrange in a bowl and sprinkle with salt. Let stand 10 minutes. Arrange in a colander and rinse thoroughly. Drain and pat dry. Chill. Just before serving, toss lightly with salsa.

*To further decrease the sodium level of this recipe, reduce the amount of salt and be sure to rinse the cucumbers thoroughly.

APPROXIMATE NUTRITIONAL CONTENT PER SERVING

Total calories: 12
Protein: 1 g
Carbohydrates: 3 g
Cholesterol: 0 mg
Fat: Tr
Sodium: 396 mg

Percentage of calories from:
Protein: 18%
Carbohydrates: 70%
Fat: 12%

ENGLISH CUCUMBER AND CRABMEAT SALAD

40 slices

1 English cucumber, sliced
2 tablespoons plain non-fat yogurt
1 tablespoon safflower mayonnaise
2 tablespoons tomato salsa
¼ pound crabmeat
1 bunch watercress, for garnish

Arrange cucumber slices on a serving tray. Blend yogurt and mayonnaise, and put a small dollop in center of each cucumber slice. Top with a dab of salsa and a small piece of crabmeat. Garnish with watercress.

SERVING SUGGESTION: Also good as an hors d'oeuvre.

APPROXIMATE NUTRITIONAL CONTENT PER CUCUMBER SLICE

Total calories: 7
Protein: Tr
Carbohydrates: Tr
Cholesterol: 1 mg
Fat: Tr
Sodium: 42 mg

Percentage of calories from:
Protein: 35%
Carbohydrates: 31%
Fat: 33%

Do not be too concerned about the calories from fat. They are high primarily because the cucumber has so few calories.

SPINACH SALAD

4 servings

2 bunches fresh spinach
1 bunch radishes, sliced
8 fresh mushrooms, sliced
   Mustard-and-lemon Vinaigrette (page 395)
      or Oil-free Lemon Vinaigrette (page 391)

Wash and trim spinach. Chill. Tear into bite-size pieces. Put in a bowl and toss with radishes and mushrooms. Pour dressing into cruet; pass with salad.

APPROXIMATE NUTRITIONAL CONTENT PER SERVING WITHOUT DRESSING

Total calories: 27
Protein: 3 g
Carbohydrates: 5 g
Cholesterol: 0 mg
Fat: Tr
Sodium: 67 mg

Percentage of calories from:
   Protein: 31%
   Carbohydrates: 61%
   Fat: 9%

Add 108 calories per tablespoon of Mustard and Lemon Vinaigrette.
Add 2 calories per tablespoon of Oil-free Lemon Vinaigrette.

BEAN SPROUT SALAD

8 servings

1 pound bean sprouts
¾ cup sliced water chestnuts
3 stalks celery, thinly sliced
1 bunch green onions, thinly sliced into
    strings
2 tablespoons rice vinegar
¼ cup reduced-sodium soy sauce

In a bowl, combine bean sprouts, water chestnuts, celery and green onions. Blend vinegar and soy sauce. Toss with vegetables.

APPROXIMATE NUTRITIONAL CONTENT PER SERVING

Total calories: 41
Protein: 3 g
Carbohydrates: 6 g
Cholesterol: 0 mg
Fat: Tr
Sodium: 330 mg

Percentage of calories from:
  Protein: 28%
  Carbohydrates: 67%
  Fat: 4%

FARM SALAD

6 servings

½ head Bibb lettuce
½ head Boston lettuce
½ head red leaf lettuce
1 English cucumber, unpeeled and cut into
    julienne strips
  Szechuan Vinaigrette or Oil-free Szechuan
    Vinaigrette (pages 392–393)

Wash lettuces and tear into bite-size pieces. Combine in a bowl. Garnish with cucumber. Pour dressing into cruet; pass with salad.

APPROXIMATE NUTRITIONAL CONTENT PER SERVING OF FARM SALAD WITHOUT DRESSING

Total calories: 30
Protein: 2 g
Carbohydrates: 5 g
Cholesterol: 0 mg
Fat: Tr
Sodium: 13 mg

Percentage of calories from:
Protein: 27%
Carbohydrates: 56%
Fat: 17%

Add 75 calories per tablespoon of Szechuan Vinaigrette. Add 5 calories per tablespoon of Oil-free Szechuan Vinaigrette.

FRESH BASIL AND TOMATO SALAD

4 servings

1 bunch fresh basil
4 ripe tomatoes, quartered
black pepper to taste

Wash and trim basil. Spread over chilled salad plates. Arrange tomatoes over basil. Sprinkle with black pepper.

VARIATIONS: Squeeze lemon or lime juice over tomatoes and basil for a wonderful flavor.

Drizzle ¾ teaspoon of olive oil over each salad. Sprinkle with black pepper. (Add 30 calories per salad.)

APPROXIMATE NUTRITIONAL CONTENT PER SERVING

Total calories: 31
Protein: 1 g
Carbohydrates: 8 g
Cholesterol: 0 mg
Fat: Tr
Sodium: 16 mg

Percentage of calories from:
Protein: 14%
Carbohydrates: 79%
Fat: 7%

COLD SCALLOP AND NOODLE SALAD

6 servings

> 1   pound scallops
> ½   cup thinly sliced celery
> 1   8-ounce can sliced water chestnuts
> 4   green onions, cut into strings
> 1   8-ounce package buckwheat (Soba)
>   noodles,* cooked and drained
> 1   head red leaf lettuce, shredded
> ¼   cup reduced-sodium soy sauce
> 2   tablespoons rice vinegar

In a nonstick skillet, sauté scallops 2–3 minutes, or until cooked. Chill scallops, celery, water chestnuts, onions, noodles and lettuce. Just before serving, arrange lettuce over chilled salad plates. Top with noodles, then with scallops, celery, water chestnuts and green onions. Combine soy sauce and vinegar; drizzle over salads.

*Soba noodles are available in Oriental markets, if not in your supermarket.

SERVING SUGGESTION: Dishes made with soy sauce, even reduced-sodium soy sauce, are high in sodium. Keep this in mind and serve with low-sodium accompaniments.

APPROXIMATE NUTRITIONAL CONTENT PER SERVING

Total calories: 255

Protein: 24 g

Carbohydrates: 37 g

Cholesterol: 40 mg

Fat: 2 g

Sodium: 614 mg

Percentage of calories from:

Protein: 36%

Carbohydrates: 56%

Fat: 8%

MUSSEL AND TOMATO SALAD

4 servings

1½ pounds mussels, in their shells
2   heads Bibb lettuce
¼   cup diced ripe tomatoes
    Creamy Dijon Vinaigrette (page 398) or
    Oil-free Lemon Vinaigrette (page 391)

Wash and clean mussels. Steam just until shells open. Chill.
Arrange lettuce leaves over chilled salad plates. Garnish
with mussels and tomatoes. Pour dressing into cruet; pass
with salad.

APPROXIMATE NUTRITIONAL CONTENT PER SERVING WITHOUT DRESSING

Total calories: 68
Protein: 9 g
Carbohydrates: 7 g
Cholesterol: 55 mg
Fat: 1 g
Sodium: 12 mg

Percentage of calories from:
  Protein: 46%
  Carbohydrates: 36%
  Fat: 18%

*Add 24 calories per tablespoon of creamy Dijon Vinaigrette. Add 4
calories per tablespoon of Oil-free Lemon Vinaigrette.*

WHITE BEAN SALAD

3¹/₂ quarts (14 cups)

1   pound small dry white beans
2   stalks celery
2   teaspoons salt
1   red onion, diced
2   ripe tomatoes, diced
2   stalks celery, diced
      Olive Oil-and-lemon Vinaigrette (page 390)
¹/₂   cup fresh parsley, chopped
      black pepper to taste
1   bunch fresh spinach, washed and trimmed
1   lemon, sliced into rounds

Wash beans and put into a stock pot. Add 2 quarts water; cover and bring to a boil. Remove from heat and let soak 1 hour. Drain. Return beans to stock pot with 2 quarts fresh water; bring to a boil. Add 2 stalks celery and salt; reduce heat to medium. Cook 35–40 minutes, or until beans are tender. Drain. Discard celery stalks. Rinse beans with cold water and chill. Just before serving, toss beans with onion, tomato, diced celery and just enough vinaigrette to moisten. Sprinkle with parsley and season generously with black pepper. Line a shallow salad bowl with spinach greens. Spoon beans into center. Ring beans with lemon rounds.

VARIATION: Steam fresh asparagus tips and fresh mushrooms 1–2 minutes. Chill. Toss with beans; add sliced cucumbers and toss again.

SERVING SUGGESTION: Especially good with barbecued chicken.

APPROXIMATE NUTRITIONAL CONTENT PER ½ CUP OF WHITE BEAN SALAD WITHOUT DRESSING

Total calories: 125
Protein: 8 g
Carbohydrates: 23 g
Cholesterol: 0 mg
Fat: Tr
Sodium: 356 mg

Percentage of calories from:
Protein: 25%
Carbohydrates: 70%
Fat: 4%

Add 61 calories per tablespoon of dressing.

TIJUANA SALAD

4 servings

  1   head iceberg lettuce, shredded
 10   fresh mushrooms, sliced and steamed
         1–2 minutes
 ¼   cup chopped white onion
 ¼   cup grated part-skim Cheddar cheese
  2   tablespoons sunflower seeds
  2   ripe tomatoes, quartered
        tomato salsa

Arrange lettuce on chilled salad plates. Top with mushrooms and onions. Sprinkle with cheese. Garnish with sunflower seeds. Ring with tomatoes. Pass with salsa.

SERVING SUGGESTION: Good for lunch or light supper.

APPROXIMATE NUTRITIONAL CONTENT PER SERVING WITHOUT SALSA

Total calories: 117
Protein: 7 g
Carbohydrates: 26 g
Cholesterol: 14 mg
Fat: 7 g
Sodium: 108 mg

Percentage of calories from:
Protein: 15%
Carbohydrates: 54%
Fat: 31%

Add 4 calories per tablespoon of salsa.

PASTA, BASIL AND TOMATO SALAD

2 quarts (8 cups)

  1   pound package rotini, cooked *al dente*
  2   cups fresh basil
  2   cups diced ripe tomatoes
 ¼   pound part-skim mozzarella cheese, cubed
     Italian Vinaigrette or Oil-free Italian
       Vinaigrette (pages 388–389)
     black pepper

In a salad bowl, combine rotini, basil, tomatoes and cheese. Pour dressing into cruet; pass with salads. Accompany with black pepper.
SERVING SUGGESTION: Serve hot or cold.

APPROXIMATE NUTRITIONAL CONTENT PER ½ CUP WITHOUT DRESSING

Total calories: 123
Protein: 6 g
Carbohydrates: 22 g
Cholesterol: 4 mg
Fat: 2 g
Sodium: 42 mg

Percentage of calories from:
  Protein: 18%
  Carbohydrates: 70%
  Fat: 12%

Add 90 calories per tablespoon of Italian Vinaigrette. Add 1 calorie per tablespoon of Oil-free Italian Vinaigrette.

PASTA SALAD

2½ quarts (10 cups)

  1   pound package rotini, cooked *al dente*
  1   6-ounce jar marinated artichoke hearts*
  1   green pepper, diced
  1   red pepper, diced

1 15-ounce can whole baby corn spears
1 8-ounce can mushrooms, stems and pieces
8 cherry tomatoes
   Italian Vinaigrette or Oil-free Italian
      Vinaigrette (pages 388–389)
   salt and pepper to taste

In a bowl, while rotini are still warm, toss with artichoke hearts and their marinade. Chill. One hour before serving, toss pasta and artichokes with peppers, baby corn and mushrooms. Garnish with tomatoes. If using Italian Vinaigrette, toss with just enough vinaigrette to moisten; season with salt and pepper. If using Oil-free Italian Vinaigrette, pour dressing into cruet and pass with salad; accompany with salt, if desired, and black pepper.

*The most heart-healthy brands of marinated artichoke hearts, available so far, are those in which the oil is a nonhydrogenated soybean oil.

VARIATION: Just before serving, sprinkle with ⅓ cup freshly grated Parmesan cheese.

SERVING SUGGESTION: Serve with chicken sandwiches on dill rye bread. This is a wonderful salad for picnics or big family dinners.

APPROXIMATE NUTRITIONAL CONTENT PER CUP OF PASTA SALAD WITHOUT DRESSING

Total calories: 122
Protein: 4 g
Carbohydrates: 24 g
Cholesterol: 0 mg
Fat: 1 g
Sodium: 129 mg

Percentage of calories from:
Protein: 13%
Carbohydrates: 77%
Fat: 10%

Add 90 calories per tablespoon of Italian Vinaigrette. Add 1 calorie per tablespoon of Oil-free Italian Vinaigrette.

PAELLA SALAD

6 servings

- ½ pound clams, steamed (see page 409)
- ½ pound mussels, steamed (see page 409)
- ½ pound scallops, poached (see page 417)
- 3 cups cooked Saffron Rice (page 500)
- ½ red pepper, diced
- ½ green pepper, diced
- 2 ripe tomatoes, quartered
- 1 head romaine lettuce, torn into bite-size pieces
- 1 bunch watercress
- 2 fresh lemons, quartered
  black pepper to taste

Chill seafood, rice and vegetables. Line a large serving platter with romaine and watercress. Mound rice in center. Arrange clams, mussels and scallops around rice. Garnish with red and green peppers. Ring with tomatoes and lemons. Season with black pepper.

APPROXIMATE NUTRITIONAL CONTENT PER SERVING

Total calories: 227
Protein: 18 g
Carbohydrates: 36 g
Cholesterol: 41 mg
Fat: 2 g
Sodium: 217 mg

Percentage of calories from:
  Protein: 31%
  Carbohydrates: 61%
  Fat: 8%

COUNTRY CHICKEN SALAD

6 servings

2 whole chicken breasts, skinned, boned
1 tablespoon peanut oil
1 small head cauliflower, florets only
3 stalks celery, cut on the diagonal into
   1½-inch pieces
12 fresh mushrooms, sliced
1 6½-ounce can whole water chestnuts,
   drained
½ red pepper, cut into julienne strips
½ green pepper, cut into julienne strips
1 head Chinese (Napa) cabbage, shredded
1½ cups bean sprouts
¼ cup reduced-sodium soy sauce
2 tablespoons rice vinegar

Cut chicken into julienne strips and sauté in a nonstick skillet 10–15 minutes, or until cooked; chill. Heat oil in a wok. Add cauliflower; stir-fry 4 minutes. Add celery; stir-fry 2 minutes. Add mushrooms, water chestnuts, and red and green pepper; stir-fry 3–4 minutes, or until all vegetables are crisp-tender. Chill. Before serving, toss vegetables with chicken, cabbage and bean sprouts. Combine soy sauce and vinegar; pour over vegetables.

SERVING SUGGESTION: To compensate for the sodium in the soy sauce, serve with low-sodium accompaniments.

APPROXIMATE NUTRITIONAL CONTENT PER SERVING

Total calories: 190
Protein: 24 g
Carbohydrates: 14 g
Cholesterol: 47 mg
Fat: 5 g
Sodium: 518 mg

Percentage of calories from:
Protein: 50%
Carbohydrates: 28%
Fat: 22%

PASTA WITH CHICKEN SALAD

4¹/₂ quarts (18 cups)

 1 1-pound package rotini, cooked *al dente*
    Italian Vinaigrette or Oil-free Italian
       Vinaigrette (pages 388–389)
 2 cups Chicken Stock (page 350)
 2 whole chicken breasts, skinned and boned
 ¹/₂ bunch broccoli, florets only
 ¹/₂ head cauliflower, florets only
 12 fresh mushrooms, thinly sliced
 1 red pepper, diced
 1 green pepper, diced
 1 15-ounce can artichoke hearts, quartered
 1 15-ounce can whole baby corn spears
 12 cherry tomatoes
    salt and black pepper to taste

In a bowl, while rotini are still warm, toss with just enough vinaigrette to moisten. (If using oil-free dressing, omit this step). Chill. Bring stock to a boil; add chicken and cook over medium heat 20 minutes, or until chicken is done. Drain chicken. Cool. Cut into 1-inch cubes. Chill. Reserve broth for another use. In a covered vegetable steamer basket over boiling water, steam broccoli and cauliflower 1–2 minutes, or until crisp-tender. Chill.

Just before serving, combine the pasta, chicken and vegetables. Toss with additional Italian Vinaigrette; season with salt and pepper. If using oil-free dressing, pour dressing into cruet; pass with salad.

VARIATION: Just before serving, sprinkle with ¹/₃ cup freshly grated Parmesan cheese.

APPROXIMATE NUTRITIONAL CONTENT PER CUP OF PASTA WITH CHICKEN SALAD WITHOUT DRESSING

Total calories: 183
Protein: 17 g
Carbohydrates: 24 g
Cholesterol: 32 mg
Fat: 2 g
Sodium: 140 mg

Percentage of calories from:
Protein: 37%
Carbohydrates: 53%
Fat: 10%

Add 90 calories per tablespoon of Italian Vinaigrette. Add 1 calorie per tablespoon of Oil-free Italian Vinaigrette.

COLD NOODLE SALAD

6 servings

3   cups Chicken Stock (page 350)
1   8-ounce package buckwheat (Soba)
     noodles*
¾   pound snow peas
6   carrots, thinly sliced on the diagonal
1   head Chinese (Napa) cabbage, shredded
1   6½-ounce can whole water chestnuts
     Szechuan Vinaigrette or Oil-free Szechuan
     Vinaigrette (pages 392–393)

In bottom of a double boiler, bring stock to a boil. Add noodles; cook 5–6 minutes, or until noodles are tender. Remove noodles from broth to a colander, using salad tongs so that the broth remains in the double boiler. Rinse noodles; set aside. Bring broth back to boiling. Snap ends from snow peas. In a covered vegetable steamer basket over boiling broth, steam snow peas 1–2 minutes, or just until color begins to deepen; plunge into ice water. Drain snow peas and carrots, and chill with noodles.

Arrange shredded cabbage over salad plates. Top with

(continued on next page)

noodles. Mound snow peas, carrots and water chestnuts in sections over noodles. Serve with dressing.

*Soba noodles are available in Oriental markets, if not in your supermarket.

APPROXIMATE NUTRITIONAL CONTENT PER SERVING OF COLD NOODLE SALAD WITHOUT DRESSING

Total calories: 235
Protein: 11 g
Carbohydrates: 45 g
Cholesterol: Tr
Fat: 2 g
Sodium: 177 mg

Percentage of calories from:
Protein: 18%
Carbohydrates: 75%
Fat: 7%

Add 75 calories per tablespoon of Szechuan Vinaigrette. Add 5 calories per tablespoon of Oil-free Szechuan Vinaigrette.

CHINESE TOSSED SALAD

6 servings

    1   2-inch piece ginger root, peeled
    2   whole chicken breasts, skinned, boned
          and halved
    4   cups Chicken Stock (page 350)
    1   6½-ounce package Maifun rice sticks*
   10   black forest (Shiitake) mushrooms,* cut
          into strings**
    1   English cucumber, thinly sliced
  3–4   green onions, cut into strings
          Szechuan Vinaigrette or Oil-free Szechuan
            Vinaigrette (pages 392–393)

Grate ginger root; squeeze pulp to make juice. Pour ginger juice over chicken breasts. Let stand 30 minutes. In a medium saucepan, bring stock to a boil. Add chicken and cook over medium heat 20 minutes, or until chicken is done. Remove chicken from broth (reserve broth). As soon as chicken is cool, tear into strings.

Bring broth to a second boil. Add rice sticks and mushrooms, and cook 5–7 minutes, or until rice sticks are tender. Drain any excess moisture (the rice sticks will soak up most of the broth in cooking).

Toss rice sticks with chicken, mushrooms and cucumber. Top with green onions. Pour dressing into cruet; pass with salad.

*Rice sticks and Shiitake mushrooms are available in Oriental markets, if not in your supermarket.

**If fresh black forest mushrooms are not available, use dried Shiitake mushrooms. Reconstitute by soaking them in water 30 minutes, or until soft (save the soaking water for soup).

VARIATIONS: Substitute buckwheat (Soba) noodles for Maifun rice sticks. Substitute 1 cup snow peas, steamed 1–2 minutes, for green onions.

APPROXIMATE NUTRITIONAL CONTENT PER SERVING OF CHINESE TOSSED SALAD

Total calories: 255
Protein: 19 g
Carbohydrates: 36 g
Cholesterol: 24 mg
Fat: 4 g
Sodium: 217 mg

Percentage of calories from:
Protein: 30%
Carbohydrates: 56%
Fat: 14%

DRESSINGS, SAUCES & SPREADS

ITALIAN VINAIGRETTE

1 cup

¼   cup cider vinegar
¾   cup olive oil
¾   teaspoon salt
¼   teaspoon black pepper

Combine ingredients in a covered jar and shake well.

VARIATIONS: Substitute fresh lemon juice for vinegar. Or, for a creamy dressing, combine lemon juice or vinegar, salt and pepper in a blender or food processor. With machine running, gradually add olive oil, one tablespoon at a time. With a wire whisk, beat 1 egg white until frothy; whisk into dressing.

APPROXIMATE NUTRITIONAL CONTENT PER TABLESPOON OF ITALIAN VINAIGRETTE

Total calories: 90
Protein: Tr
Carbohydrates: Tr
Cholesterol: 0 mg
Fat: 10 g
Sodium: 103 mg

Percentage of calories from:
Protein: 0%
Carbohydrates: 1%
Fat: 99%

Oil-based dressings are high in calories and fat. Use them judiciously.

OIL-FREE ITALIAN VINAIGRETTE

1 cup

- ¼ cup cider vinegar
- ¾ cup cold water
- ¾ teaspoon salt
- ¼ teaspoon black pepper

Combine ingredients in a covered jar and shake well.

APPROXIMATE NUTRITIONAL CONTENT PER TABLESPOON

Total calories: 1
Protein: Tr
Carbohydrates: Tr
Cholesterol: 0 mg
Fat: Tr
Sodium: 137 mg

Percentage of calories from:
Protein: 1%
Carbohydrates: 98%
Fat: 1%

OLIVE OIL-AND-LEMON VINAIGRETTE

¹/₂ cup

¼ cup fresh lemon juice
¼ cup olive oil
½ teaspoon salt
¼ teaspoon black pepper

Combine ingredients in a covered jar and shake well.

**APPROXIMATE NUTRITIONAL CONTENT PER
TABLESPOON**

Total calories: 61
Protein: Tr
Carbohydrates: Tr
Cholesterol: 0 mg
Fat: 7 g
Sodium: 137 mg

Percentage of calories from:
Protein: 0%
Carbohydrates: 4%
Fat: 95%

Oil-based dressings are high in calories and fat. Use them judiciously.

OIL-FREE LEMON VINAIGRETTE

¹/₃ cup

¹/₃ cup fresh lemon juice
¹/₂ teaspoon salt
¹/₄ teaspoon black pepper

Combine ingredients in a covered jar and shake well.

APPROXIMATE NUTRITIONAL CONTENT PER TABLESPOON

Total calories: 2
Protein: Tr
Carbohydrates: Tr
Cholesterol: 0 mg
Fat: 0
Sodium: 109 mg

Percentage of calories from:
Protein: 5%
Carbohydrates: 95%
Fat: 1%

SZECHUAN VINAIGRETTE

2/3 cup

1	tablespoon rice vinegar
1	tablespoon lemon juice
1	tablespoon sesame oil
1/2	teaspoon salt
1/8	teaspoon black pepper
2 1/2	tablespoons olive oil
2 1/2	tablespoons safflower oil
3–4	drops hot chili oil (LaYu)*
1	egg white, beaten until frothy

Combine vinegar, lemon juice, sesame oil, salt and pepper in a blender or food processor. With machine running, gradually add olive oil and safflower oil, 1 tablespoon at a time. Add chili oil. Whisk in egg white.

*Hot chili oil is available in Oriental markets, if not in your supermarket.

APPROXIMATE NUTRITIONAL CONTENT PER TABLESPOON

Total calories: 75
Protein: Tr
Carbohydrates: Tr
Cholesterol: 0 mg
Fat: 8 g
Sodium: 114 mg

Percentage of calories from:
Protein: 2%
Carbohydrates: 1%
Fat: 97%

Oil-based dressings are high in calories and fat. Use them judiciously.

OIL-FREE SZECHUAN VINAIGRETTE

½ cup

¼ cup reduced-sodium soy sauce
2 tablespoons rice vinegar

Combine ingredients in a covered jar and shake well.

APPROXIMATE NUTRITIONAL CONTENT PER TABLESPOON

Total calories: 5
Protein: Tr
Carbohydrates: Tr
Cholesterol: 0 mg
Fat: 0 g
Sodium: 411 mg

Percentage of calories from:
Protein: 40%
Carbohydrates: 60%
Fat: 0%

Dressings made with soy sauce, even reduced-sodium soy sauce, are high in sodium. Be judicious in their use.

CREAMY CHAMPAGNE VINAIGRETTE

2 cups

 1 egg
 2 egg whites
 1 tablespoon Dijon mustard
 ⅓ cup champagne vinegar
 ¾ teaspoon salt
 ¼ teaspoon pepper
 1 teaspoon fresh lemon juice
1¼ cups safflower oil
 ¼ cup olive oil

Combine eggs, mustard, vinegar, salt, pepper and lemon juice in a blender or food processor. With machine running, gradually add oils 1 tablespoon at a time. Chill.

APPROXIMATE NUTRITIONAL CONTENT PER TABLESPOON

Total calories: 80
Protein: Tr
Carbohydrates: Tr
Cholesterol: 0 mg
Fat: 9 g
Sodium: 183 mg

Percentage of calories from:
Protein: 0%
Carbohydrates: 2%
Fat: 98%

Oil-based dressings are high in calories and fat. Use them judiciously.

MUSTARD-AND-LEMON VINAIGRETTE

³/₄ cup

2   cloves garlic, peeled
2   tablespoons fresh lemon juice
½   teaspoon Dijon mustard
¾   teaspoon salt
⅓   cup safflower oil
⅓   cup olive oil

Combine garlic, lemon juice, mustard and salt in a blender or food processor. With machine running, gradually add oils, 1 tablespoon at a time.

SERVING SUGGESTION: Especially good on Spinach Salad (page 373).

APPROXIMATE NUTRITIONAL CONTENT PER TABLESPOON

Total calories: 108
Protein: Tr
Carbohydrates: Tr
Cholesterol: 0 mg
Fat: 12 g
Sodium: 140 mg

Percentage of calories from:
Protein: 0%
Carbohydrates: 1%
Fat: 98%

Oil-based dressings are high in calories and fat. Use them judiciously.

GARLIC VINAIGRETTE

³/₄ cup

3   cloves garlic, peeled
1   tablespoon white wine vinegar
1   tablespoon red wine vinegar
2   tablespoons Dijon mustard
¼   teaspoon salt
¼   teaspoon black pepper
½   cup olive oil
1   egg white, beaten until very frothy

Combine garlic, vinegars, mustard, salt and pepper in a blender or food processor. With machine running, gradually add oil, 1 tablespoon at a time. Whisk in beaten egg white.

SERVING SUGGESTION: Good on salads and vegetables; especially good over warm asparagus.

APPROXIMATE NUTRITIONAL CONTENT PER TABLESPOON

Total calories: 67
Protein: Tr
Carbohydrates: Tr
Cholesterol: 0 mg
Fat: 8 g
Sodium: 66 mg

Percentage of calories from:
Protein: 2%
Carbohydrates: 3%
Fat: 95%

Oil-based dressings are high in calories and fat. Use them judiciously.

MUSTARD-AND-GARLIC VINAIGRETTE

1 cup

¼ cup cider vinegar
2 cloves garlic, peeled
1 tablespoon Dijon mustard
¼ teaspoon black pepper
½ teaspoon salt
¼ cup olive oil
½ cup safflower oil
1 egg white, beaten until very frothy

Combine all ingredients in a covered jar. Shake.

VARIATION: Combine vinegar, garlic, mustard, pepper and salt in a blender or food processor. With machine running, gradually add oils, 1 tablespoon at a time. Whisk in beaten egg white just before serving.

APPROXIMATE NUTRITIONAL CONTENT PER TABLESPOON

Total calories: 86
Protein: Tr
Carbohydrates: Tr
Cholesterol: 0 mg
Fat: 10 g
Sodium: 76 mg

Percentage of calories from:
Protein: 0%
Carbohydrates: 2%
Fat: 98%

Oil-based dressings are high in calories and fat. Use them judiciously.

CREAMY DIJON VINAIGRETTE

1³/₄ cups

 ¼ small white onion
 ¼ cup Dijon mustard
 3 tablespoons red wine vinegar
 1 tablespoon white wine vinegar
 2 cloves garlic, peeled
 ¼ teaspoon salt
 ½ teaspoon dried basil
 ⅛ teaspoon black pepper
 ½ cup soft tofu
 ¼ cup plain non-fat yogurt
 2 tablespoons safflower oil
 2 tablespoons olive oil
 2 drops hot chili oil (LaYu)*

Combine onion, mustard, vinegars, garlic, salt, basil and pepper in a blender or food processor. Add tofu and yogurt. With machine running, gradually add oils, 1 tablespoon at a time.

*Hot chili oil is available in Oriental markets, if not in your supermarket.

SERVING SUGGESTIONS: Serve as a dip with crudités, as a salad dressing and as a sauce on vegetables, seafood, poultry and veal.

APPROXIMATE NUTRITIONAL CONTENT PER TABLESPOON

Total calories: 24   *Percentage of calories from:*
Protein: Tr   Protein: 9%
Carbohydrates: Tr   Carbohydrates: 11%
Cholesterol: Tr   Fat: 80%
Fat: 2 g
Sodium: 49 mg

Oil-based dressings are high in calories and fat. Use them judiciously.

AIOLI SAUCE

1¹/₂ cups

2 tablespoons raspberry vinegar
3 tablespoons skim milk
5 cloves garlic, peeled
1 egg
1 egg yolk
¹/₄ teaspoon salt
¹/₄ teaspoon white pepper
¹/₄ cup safflower oil
³/₄ cup olive oil
2 tablespoons fresh lemon juice
2 tablespoons plain non-fat yogurt

Combine vinegar, milk, garlic, egg, egg yolk, salt and white pepper in a blender or food processor. Process 3–4 minutes, or until mixture begins to thicken. With machine running, add safflower oil and olive oil in a steady stream, 1 tablespoon at a time. When oil is absorbed, add lemon juice and yogurt.

SERVING SUGGESTIONS: Serve as a dip with crudités or as a sauce on potatoes, vegetables and seafood.

APPROXIMATE NUTRITIONAL CONTENT PER TABLESPOON

Total calories: 26
Protein: 2 g
Carbohydrates: 2 g
Cholesterol: 9 mg
Fat: 1 g
Sodium: 50 mg

Percentage of calories from:
Protein: 36%
Carbohydrates: 30%
Fat: 35%

Oil-based dressings are high in calories and fat. Use them judiciously.

MUSTARD SAUCE

¹/₂ cup

> ¹/₃ cup Dijon mustard
> 1   teaspoon rice vinegar
> 2   teaspoons sesame oil

Combine mustard, vinegar and sesame oil in a bowl or covered jar. Stir until smooth.

SERVING SUGGESTION: Good on warm vegetables, especially broccoli, cauliflower and fresh green beans.

APPROXIMATE NUTRITIONAL CONTENT PER TABLESPOON

Total calories: 28
Protein: Tr
Carbohydrates: 1 g
Cholesterol: 0 mg
Fat: 2 g
Sodium: 208 mg

Percentage of calories from:
  Protein: 10%
  Carbohydrates: 15%
  Fat: 75%

BARBECUE SAUCE

5 cups

2   15-ounce cans tomato sauce
⅓   cup cider vinegar
⅔   cup white wine vinegar
¼   cup liquid smoke
1½ teaspoons Tabasco
1½ teaspoons Dijon mustard
3   cloves garlic, peeled
⅓   cup brown sugar

In a medium stock pot, combine ingredients. Bring to a boil over high heat, stirring frequently. Reduce heat and simmer, uncovered, 1½ hours.

NOTE: Sauce will keep 4–5 weeks in the refrigerator and may be frozen. The flavor is superior to that of commercial barbecue sauce.

SERVING SUGGESTIONS: Excellent on chicken, salmon, scallops and oysters—especially oysters on the half shell.

APPROXIMATE NUTRITIONAL CONTENT PER TABLESPOON

Total calories: 28
Protein: Tr
Carbohydrates: 7 g
Cholesterol: 0 mg
Fat: Tr
Sodium: 224 mg

Percentage of calories from:
Protein: 7%
Carbohydrates: 89%
Fat: 4%

HORSERADISH SAUCE

½ cup

⅓ cup plain non-fat yogurt
2 tablespoons prepared horseradish

Combine yogurt with horseradish. Stir until smooth.

VARIATION: For an even hotter flavor, use prepared horseradish that is labeled "hot" or "extra-hot."

SERVING SUGGESTIONS: Good as a dip with crudités and grilled vegetables and as a sauce with red meats.

APPROXIMATE NUTRITIONAL CONTENT PER TABLESPOON

Total calories: 7
Protein: Tr
Carbohydrates: 1 g
Cholesterol: Tr
Fat: Tr
Sodium: 11 mg

Percentage of calories from:
Protein: 32%
Carbohydrates: 64%
Fat: 3%

PESTO

2⅔ cups

5 cups fresh basil*
8 cloves garlic
1 teaspoon salt
½ cup pine nuts
¾ cup olive oil

Combine basil, garlic, salt and pine nuts in a blender or food processor and purée. With machine running, add olive oil 1 tablespoon at a time. Blend until smooth and oil is absorbed.

*To freeze fresh basil, place the basil on baking sheets

and freeze 1–2 hours. Remove to plastic freezer bags. Store in freezer. The leaves will turn black, but when used in cooking and sauces the flavor remains.

NOTE: Never double the pesto recipe as the oil will not absorb properly. To make several consecutive batches (25 half-pints), you'll need the following quantities of ingredients: 11 bunches fresh basil, 10 whole bulbs fresh garlic, 1⅔ pounds pine nuts, 3½ quarts olive oil, and salt per batch as in above recipe. Fill half-pint jars ¾ full with pesto. Spoon 1 tablespoon olive oil over pesto to seal. Screw lids tightly onto jars. Store jars in freezer.

SERVING SUGGESTIONS: Pesto is delicious on pasta, chicken, seafood, vegetables and potatoes.

APPROXIMATE NUTRITIONAL CONTENT PER TABLESPOON OF PESTO

Total calories: 63
Protein: 2 g
Carbohydrates: 5 g
Cholesterol: 0 mg
Fat: 5 g
Sodium: 55 mg

Percentage of calories from:
  Protein: 9%
  Carbohydrates: 30%
  Fat: 60%

Oil-based dressings are high in calories and fat. Use them judiciously.

MARINARA SAUCE

4¹/₄ cups

1   28-ounce can plum tomatoes, diced
2   tablespoons tomato paste
¹/₂   teaspoon oregano
¹/₂   teaspoon dried basil or ¹/₄ cup fresh
¹/₂   teaspoon black pepper
1   tablespoon olive oil
¹/₄   teaspoon cider vinegar

In a medium saucepan, combine tomatoes, tomato paste, oregano, basil and black pepper. Simmer 20 minutes (do not allow to boil). Stir in olive oil and vinegar. Simmer 10 minutes.

SERVING SUGGESTIONS: For a quick last-minute meal, serve over pasta. Accompany with a green salad and Grilled Garlic Bread (page 334).

This is also an excellent sauce to use on pizza or on grilled or baked eggplant.

APPROXIMATE NUTRITIONAL CONTENT PER ¹/₄ CUP

Total calories: 22
Protein: Tr
Carbohydrates: 3 g
Cholesterol: 0 mg
Fat: Tr
Sodium: 60 mg

Percentage of calories from:
Protein: 12%
Carbohydrates: 55%
Fat: 33%

TOMATO SALSA

2¹/₄ cups

1	16-ounce can plum tomatoes, diced
1¹/₂	tablespoons tomato paste
2¹/₂	teaspoons pure ground mild chili powder*
¹/₄	teaspoon ground cumin
¹/₄	teaspoon salt
¹/₄	teaspoon black pepper
¹/₄	teaspoon cayenne pepper
¹/₂	teaspoon olive oil
2	tablespoons diced green chilies

Combine ingredients in a covered jar. For best flavor, chill at least 2 hours.

*Take the time to search for a Spanish or Mexican market or a supermarket that carries pure ground chili powder. Pure ground chili powder is made by grinding dried chilies; its flavor is far superior to commercial chili powder, which is most often 40% salt and 20% additives.

APPROXIMATE NUTRITIONAL CONTENT PER TABLESPOON

Total calories: 4
Protein: Tr
Carbohydrates: Tr
Cholesterol: 0 mg
Fat: Tr
Sodium: 38 mg

Percentage of calories from:
Protein: 13%
Carbohydrates: 65%
Fat: 22%

BEAN DIP

4 cups

> 4   cups cooked Red Kidney Beans
>   (page 504)
> ¼   small white onion
> 2   cloves garlic, peeled
> 1   teaspoon pure ground mild red chili
>   powder*
> ½   teaspoon cumin
> ⅛   teaspoon oregano
> ¼   teaspoon salt

In a blender or food processor, purée beans, onion and garlic. Add seasonings and process 1 minute. Chill.

*Take the time to search for a Spanish or Mexican market or a supermarket that carries pure ground chili powder. Pure ground chili powder is made by grinding dried chilies; its flavor is far superior to that of commercial chili powder, which is most often 40% salt and 20% additives.

For a hotter flavor, substitute pure ground hot red chili powder.

APPROXIMATE NUTRITIONAL CONTENT PER ¼ CUP

Total calories: 67
Protein: 4 g
Carbohydrates: 12 g
Cholesterol: 0 mg
Fat: Tr
Sodium: 43 mg

Percentage of calories from:
  Protein: 25%
  Carbohydrates: 71%
  Fat: 4%

APPLE BUTTER

1¹/₂ pints

4 large Granny Smith apples, peeled, cored
 and quartered
¹/₂ cup apple juice
3 tablespoons brown sugar
1¹/₂ teaspoons cinnamon
¹/₄ teaspoon allspice
¹/₈ teaspoon ground cloves

In a stock pot, combine apples and juice. Cover and cook over low heat 45–60 minutes, or until apples are soft and sauce-like. Stir in sugar, cinnamon, allspice and cloves; cook, uncovered, 5–10 minutes, stirring often. Store in covered jar in refrigerator.

SERVING SUGGESTION: Serve warm over whole-wheat toast, English muffins or popovers.

APPROXIMATE NUTRITIONAL CONTENT PER TABLESPOON

Total calories: 20
Protein: Tr
Carbohydrates: 5 g
Cholesterol: 0 mg
Fat: Tr
Sodium: Tr

Percentage of calories from:
 Protein: 1%
 Carbohydrates: 95%
 Fat: 4%

STRAWBERRY PRESERVES

¹/₂ pint

    3   cups strawberries, sliced
    1   tablespoon granulated sugar
    2   teaspoons cornstarch combined with
         1 tablespoon water
  ¹/₄ teaspoon almond extract
  ¹/₄ teaspoon fresh lemon juice

In a saucepan over low heat, bring berries to a boil, stirring frequently. Add sugar and reduce heat; simmer 25–30 minutes. Gradually add cornstarch mixture; simmer 10 minutes. Stir in almond extract and lemon juice; simmer 10–15 minutes. Cool. Preserves may be frozen.

APPROXIMATE NUTRITIONAL CONTENT PER TABLESPOON

Total calories: 13
Protein: Tr
Carbohydrates: 3 g
Cholesterol: 0 mg
Fat: Tr
Sodium: Tr

Percentage of calories from:
  Protein: 5%
  Carbohydrates: 88%
  Fat: 7%

SEAFOOD

STEAMED CLAMS AND MUSSELS

Thoroughly wash clams and mussels.* Cover with salt water (⅓ cup salt to 1 gallon of cold water). Let stand 30 minutes. Rinse. Repeat cleaning process 2 times.

Place clams and mussels on rack in stock pot with 2 cups hot water. Cover tightly and steam 5–10 minutes, or just until shells open.

*For mussels, use a stiff wire brush to remove the tough outer beard that clings to the shells.

APPROXIMATE NUTRITIONAL CONTENT PER POUND OF CLAMS AND MUSSELS IN SHELLS

Total calories: 122
Protein: 18 g
Carbohydrates: 3 g
Cholesterol: 80 mg
Fat: 2 g
Sodium: 133 mg

Percentage of calories from:
Protein: 68%
Carbohydrates: 13%
Fat: 19%

GARLIC STEAMED CLAMS

4 servings

4	pounds clams
½	cup dry white wine
10	cloves garlic, peeled
4	fresh lemons, cut into wedges

Clean clams (see page 409). In a stock pot, combine clams, wine and garlic. Cover and steam 5-10 minutes, or just until shells open. Accompany with fresh lemons.

SERVING SUGGESTION: Serve with Steamed Red Potatoes (page 487).

APPROXIMATE NUTRITIONAL CONTENT PER SERVING

Total calories: 168
Protein: 19 g
Carbohydrates: 11 g
Cholesterol: 80 mg
Fat: 2 g
Sodium: 137 mg

Percentage of calories from:
Protein: 53%
Carbohydrates: 31%
Fat: 15%

STEAMED CLAMS WITH LEMON VINAIGRETTE

4 servings

Prepare Garlic Steamed Clams as directed above. Just before serving, drizzle clams with 3 tablespoons Olive Oil-and-lemon Vinaigrette (page 390).

SERVING SUGGESTION: The vinaigrette adds calories and fat to the recipe. Keep this in mind and plan to use low-fat accompaniments.

APPROXIMATE NUTRITIONAL CONTENT PER SERVING
OF STEAMED CLAMS WITH LEMON VINAIGRETTE

Total calories: 214
Protein: 19 g
Carbohydrates: 12 g
Cholesterol: 80 mg
Fat: 7 g
Sodium: 239 mg

Percentage of calories from:
Protein: 40%
Carbohydrates: 25%
Fat: 35%

STEAMED SHELLFISH WITH AIOLI SAUCE

6 servings

2 pounds mussels
2 pounds clams
1½ cups dry vermouth
¾ cup water
¾ teaspoon or less salt
1 leek, including greens, chopped
4 cloves garlic, peeled
1 pound scallops
1 whole crab, cracked and cleaned
1 bunch fresh parsley
Aioli Sauce (page 399)

Wash and soak clams and mussels (see page 409). Remove beards from mussels, if necessary. In a stock pot, combine vermouth, water, salt, leeks and garlic. Bring to a boil. Add clams and mussels. Cover and steam 6–8 minutes, or until shells begin to open. Add scallops. Cook 2–3 minutes, or until scallops are cooked and most clams and mussels have opened. Remove seafood from liquid. Arrange mussels, clams, scallops and crab on a parsley-lined tray. Serve with Aioli Sauce on the side.

SERVING SUGGESTIONS: This dish is good served hot or

(continued on next page)

cold. It is suitable as an appetizer, light lunch or main meal.

APPROXIMATE NUTRITIONAL CONTENT PER SERVING OF STEAMED SHELLFISH WITHOUT AIOLI SAUCE

Total calories: 250
Protein: 30 g
Carbohydrates: 9 g
Cholesterol: 125 mg
Fat: 2 g
Sodium: 466 mg

Percentage of calories from:
  Protein: 68%
  Carbohydrates: 20%
  Fat: 12%

Add 70 calories per tablespoon of Aioli Sauce. For fewer calories, serve with fresh lemon juice or tomato salsa.

MIXED SEAFOOD GRILL

4 servings

½	pound fresh tuna fillets
1	tablespoon olive oil
1	clove garlic, peeled
¼	teaspoon black pepper
½	pound fresh swordfish fillets
½	pound fresh scallops
1	bulb fresh fennel, chopped
1	bunch fresh fennel greens
1	cup skim milk
8	cherry or small plum tomatoes
1½	lemons, cut into wedges
1½	limes, cut into wedges

Rub tuna with olive oil, garlic and black pepper. Set aside. Arrange swordfish and scallops in a shallow baking dish. Layer chopped fennel bulb and some of the fennel greens over and under swordfish and scallops. Pour milk over top (milk gives moisture to the fish without having a milk taste). Let stand 1 hour at room temperature. Drain milk.

Prepare coals. Cover the grill grid with foil. Grill tuna, swordfish, scallops and tomatoes over hot coals 2–3 minutes on each side, or until fish flakes easily when tested with a fork (do not overcook).

Layer remaining fennel greens on a serving platter (this looks sensational in a large copper skillet or on an oval fish platter). Arrange seafood and tomatoes over fennel. Garnish with lemons and limes.

VARIATION: If fresh fennel is not available, use fresh dill.

SERVING SUGGESTION: Serve with Ala Pilaf with Tomatoes and Parsley (page 503) and Broccoli with Lemon Mustard Sauce (page 481).

APPROXIMATE NUTRITIONAL CONTENT PER SERVING OF MIXED SEAFOOD GRILL

Total calories: 279

Percentage of calories from:

Protein: 39 g   Protein: 53%

Carbohydrates: 15 g   Carbohydrates: 20%

Cholesterol: 83 mg   Fat: 27%

Fat: 9 g

Sodium: 234 mg

Fish oil, rich in cholesterol-lowering Omega 3's, provides almost all the fat in this recipe. For this reason, don't be too concerned with the relatively high fat content.

CALAMARI SEVICHE

4 servings

1 pound squid tubes
1 teaspoon olive oil
2 large beefsteak tomatoes, cut into 3-inch
   cubes
¾ medium red onion, coarsely chopped
2 tablespoons diced jalapeño peppers
3 cloves garlic, peeled
¼ cup rice vinegar
¼ cup fresh lime juice

Clean squid tubes. Slice into ⅓-inch rings. Toss with olive oil. In a nonstick skillet, sauté squid 3–4 minutes, or until color changes and squid are cooked. Plunge into ice water. Drain. Pat dry. Combine squid, tomatoes, onion, jalapeño peppers and garlic. Toss with rice vinegar and fresh lime juice. Chill 2–3 hours.

SERVING SUGGESTION: Good as an appetizer or served as a salad over red and green leaf lettuce.

APPROXIMATE NUTRITIONAL CONTENT PER SERVING

Total calories: 146
Protein: 19 g
Carbohydrates: 11 g
Cholesterol: 202 mg
Fat: 3 g
Sodium: 9 mg

Percentage of calories from:
Protein: 51%
Carbohydrates: 30%
Fat: 19%

STIR-FRIED CALAMARI

4 servings

1½ pounds squid tubes
½ teaspoon plus 1 tablespoon rice vinegar

1½ teaspoons cornstarch
1 egg white
¼ teaspoon salt
¼ teaspoon granulated sugar
¼ teaspoon black pepper
3 tablespoons Chicken Stock (page 350)
¾ pound snow peas
1 piece ginger root, peeled and thinly sliced
⅔ cup julienne bamboo shoots
1 teaspoon sesame oil

Clean squid tubes, cut into ½-inch rings and place in a bowl. In another bowl, combine ½ teaspoon of rice vinegar, ½ teaspoon of cornstarch and egg white with wire whisk; pour over squid. Let stand 20 minutes. Combine the remaining tablespoon rice vinegar, salt, sugar, pepper and remaining ½ teaspoon cornstarch; set sauce aside.

In a nonstick skillet over medium heat, stir-fry squid 3–5 minutes, or just until color changes. Set aside.

In a covered vegetable steamer basket over boiling water, steam snow peas, ginger root and bamboo shoots 2–3 minutes, or until snow peas are just crisp-tender. Drain any excess moisture. Remove ginger root.

Add steamed vegetables and sauce to squid and stir-fry 2–3 minutes, or until sauce thickens. Stir in sesame oil.

APPROXIMATE NUTRITIONAL CONTENT PER SERVING OF STIR-FRIED CALAMARI

Total calories: 220
Protein: 31 g
Carbohydrates: 15 g
Cholesterol: 303 mg
Fat: 4 g
Sodium: 168 mg

Percentage of calories from:
Protein: 57%
Carbohydrates: 27%
Fat: 16%

PAN-FRIED SCALLOPS

4 servings

1 pound scallops

Preheat a nonstick skillet; add scallops. Cook, turning frequently, 4–6 minutes, or just until scallops are tender.

SERVING SUGGESTION: Serve with Fettuccine with Vegetables and Pesto (page 509).

APPROXIMATE NUTRITIONAL CONTENT PER SERVING

Total calories: 90
Protein: 27 g
Carbohydrates: 3 g
Cholesterol: 42 mg
Fat: 1 g
Sodium: 289 mg

Percentage of calories from:
 Protein: 81%
 Carbohydrates: 13%
 Fat: 6%

SCALLOPS DIJONNAISE

4 servings

1 pound scallops
¼ cup Dijon mustard

In a bowl, toss scallops with mustard until coated. Preheat a nonstick skillet; add scallops and stir-fry 5 minutes, or until scallops are tender.

VARIATION: Substitute Creamy Dijon Vinaigrette (page 398) for Dijon mustard.

SERVING SUGGESTION: A perfect quick-to-fix entrée. Serve with Cold Noodle Salad (page 385) and fresh seasonal fruit.

APPROXIMATE NUTRITIONAL CONTENT PER SERVING OF SCALLOPS DIJONNAISE

Total calories: 134
Protein: 26 g
Carbohydrates: 5 g
Cholesterol: 60 mg
Fat: 2 g
Sodium: 496 mg

Percentage of calories from:
Protein: 72%
Carbohydrates: 14%
Fat: 14%

POACHED SCALLOPS

4 servings

3 tablespoons dry white wine, vermouth or
  fresh lemon juice
1 pound scallops

In a nonstick skillet, heat wine, vermouth or lemon juice. Add scallops. Cover and poach 4–6 minutes, or just until scallops are tender. (Do not overcook.)

APPROXIMATE NUTRITIONAL CONTENT PER SERVING

Total calories: 98
Protein: 17 g
Carbohydrates: 3 g
Cholesterol: 41 mg
Fat: 1 g
Sodium: 290 mg

Percentage of calories from:
Protein: 80%
Carbohydrates: 13%
Fat: 6%

SCALLOPS WITH TOMATOES AND ARTICHOKES

4 servings

    1   pound scallops
    ½   cup skim milk
    1   white onion
    1   green pepper
    1   red pepper
   12   cherry tomatoes
   12   fresh mushrooms
    1   15-ounce can artichoke hearts
    ½   pound fresh pineapple, cut into 2-inch
        cubes (optional)

Soak scallops in milk 30–40 minutes (milk gives moisture to the scallops without leaving a milk taste). Drain. Cook onion and peppers in boiling water to cover, 1–2 minutes; cut into 2-inch cubes. On skewers, alternate scallops with vegetables and pineapple.

Prepare coals. Cover the grill grid with foil. Grill over hot coals, turning frequently, 8–10 minutes, or until scallops are tender.

SERVING SUGGESTION: Accompany with Saffron Rice (page 500) and Cold Lemon Soufflé (page 525) or lemon ice for dessert.

APPROXIMATE NUTRITIONAL CONTENT PER SERVING

Total calories: 232
Protein: 25 g
Carbohydrates: 34 g
Cholesterol: 42 mg
Fat: 2 g
Sodium: 399 mg

Percentage of calories from:
  Protein: 39%
  Carbohydrates: 54%
  Fat: 7%

SKEWERED SCALLOPS WITH GARLIC AND TOMATOES

4 servings

  1 pound fresh scallops
     juice of 2 limes
 10 cloves garlic, peeled
 10 cherry tomatoes
  1 bunch fresh spinach
  1 fresh lemon, cut into wedges
  1 fresh lime, cut into wedges

Marinate scallops in lime juice for 3 hours. On skewers, alternate scallops, garlic and tomatoes.

Prepare coals. Cover the grill grid with foil. Grill scallop brochettes over hot coals, turning frequently, 8–10 minutes, or until scallops are tender.

While seafood is grilling, wash and trim spinach; shake off excess moisture. Cook, covered, in a nonstick skillet 1–2 minutes, or just until leaves begin to wilt (no additional moisture is necessary because of the moisture in the spinach and on the leaves).

Arrange spinach on a heated serving plate. Layer brochettes over spinach. Garnish with lemon and lime wedges.

SERVING SUGGESTION: Accompany with Pasta Salad (page 380).

APPROXIMATE NUTRITIONAL CONTENT PER SERVING

Total calories: 167
Protein: 24 g
Carbohydrates: 19 g
Cholesterol: 42 mg
Fat: 1 g
Sodium: 392 mg

Percentage of calories from:
  Protein: 52%
  Carbohydrates: 42%
  Fat: 6%

BLACKENED HALIBUT

4 servings

1   pound halibut fillets, sliced ½-inch thick
2   tablespoons olive oil
1   tablespoon garlic powder
1   tablespoon onion powder
½ teaspoon salt
2   teaspoons white pepper
2   teaspoons black pepper
2   teaspoons cayenne pepper
2   teaspoons thyme
2   teaspoons oregano
1   teaspoon paprika

Place halibut in a bowl with olive oil and let stand 30 minutes. Combine spices in a 9-inch pie plate. Heat a cast-iron skillet upside down over high heat 5–10 minutes, or until very hot. Using a hot pad, turn pan right side up. Remove halibut from olive oil and drain. Dip fillets into seasonings and coat each side evenly. Put fillets into hot skillet and cook 2–3 minutes on each side, turning only once.

VARIATIONS: Substitute bass, snapper or red fish for halibut.

APPROXIMATE NUTRITIONAL CONTENT PER SERVING

Total calories: 258

Protein: 30 g

Carbohydrates: 6 g

Cholesterol: 62 mg

Fat: 12 g

Sodium: 328 mg

Percentage of calories from:

  Protein: 48%

  Carbohydrates: 10%

  Fat: 43%

By draining the fish, most of the olive oil is left behind. Fish oil, rich in cholesterol-lowering Omega 3's, provides almost all the fat in this recipe (the halibut by itself is 38% fat). For this reason, don't be concerned with the relatively high fat content.

GRILLED HALIBUT STEAKS WITH ROSEMARY AND MUSTARD

4 servings

¼ cup Dijon mustard*
¾ teaspoon powdered rosemary
1 pound halibut steaks or fillets

Combine mustard and rosemary to make a sauce. Rub sauce into fillets; let stand 20 minutes.

Cover the grill grid with foil and prepare coals. Grill halibut over hot coals 5–6 minutes. Turn; cook 2–3 minutes, or until fish flakes easily when tested with a fork.

*To further reduce the sodium level of this recipe, use less Dijon mustard.

VARIATIONS: Substitute red snapper, cod or salmon for halibut.

APPROXIMATE NUTRITIONAL CONTENT PER SERVING

Total calories: 206
Protein: 29 g
Carbohydrates: 1 g
Cholesterol: 62 mg
Fat: 9 g
Sodium: 348 mg

Percentage of calories from:
Protein: 59%
Carbohydrates: 2%
Fat: 39%

Fish oil, rich in cholesterol-lowering Omega 3's, provides almost all the fat in this recipe. For this reason, don't be concerned with the relatively high fat content.

FILLET OF SOLE WITH CHEESE

4 servings

1   medium white onion, chopped
²/₃ pound fresh mushrooms, sliced
1   cup grated part-skim mozzarella cheese
1   pound fillet of sole

In a covered vegetable steamer basket over boiling water, steam onions 3 minutes. Add mushrooms and steam 2 minutes. In a shallow baking dish, layer half the onions, then half the mushrooms, then half the cheese. Arrange the sole over the cheese. Top sole with remaining onions, then mushrooms, then cheese. Bake at 400°F. 20–25 minutes, or until cheese is melted and fish flakes easily when tested with a fork.

APPROXIMATE NUTRITIONAL CONTENT PER SERVING

Total calories: 211
Protein: 33 g
Carbohydrates: 8 g
Cholesterol: 86 mg
Fat: 6 g
Sodium: 280 mg

Percentage of calories from:
Protein: 61%
Carbohydrates: 14%
Fat: 25%

STEAMED SEA BASS

4 servings

1 pound sea bass fillets
1 tablespoon rice vinegar
2 shallots, peeled
1 small ginger root, peeled
1 tablespoon peanut oil
2 tablespoons reduced-sodium soy sauce
1 cup dry white wine
1 bunch fresh cilantro

Marinate bass in rice vinegar 20 minutes. In a blender or food processor, chop shallots and ginger root (do not purée). In a medium saucepan, heat peanut oil. Add ginger root and shallots, and stir-fry 3–4 minutes. Reduce heat to simmer. Add soy sauce and keep warm over low heat.

Pour wine into a fish poacher or saucepan. Insert a rack or a vegetable steamer basket. Arrange bass on top of rack or in basket. Cover and steam 5–10 minutes, or until bass flakes easily when tested with a fork. (If additional moisture is needed during cooking, add more wine or hot water.)

Line a heated platter with cilantro. Layer bass over cilantro. Pour sauce over fish.

APPROXIMATE NUTRITIONAL CONTENT PER SERVING

Total calories: 296
Protein: 25 g
Carbohydrates: 9 g
Cholesterol: 83 mg
Fat: 8 g
Sodium: 330 mg

Percentage of calories from:
   Protein: 48%
   Carbohydrates: 17%
   Fat: 35%

Fish oil, rich in cholesterol-lowering Omega 3's, provides almost all the fat in this recipe. For this reason, don't be concerned with the relatively high fat content.

GRILLED BLACK COD

4 servings

1   pound black cod fillets
1   bunch fresh parsley
2   fresh lemons, cut into wedges

Prepare coals. Cover the grill grid with foil. Grill cod over hot coals 5–6 minutes. Turn; grill 2–3 minutes, or until fish flakes easily when tested with a fork. Serve on a bed of parsley with lemon wedges.

APPROXIMATE NUTRITIONAL CONTENT PER SERVING

Total calories: 159
Protein: 28 g
Carbohydrates: 3 g
Cholesterol: 68 mg
Fat: 4 g
Sodium: 125 mg

Percentage of calories from:
  Protein: 71%
  Carbohydrates: 7%
  Fat: 22%

GRILLED FRESH TUNA

4 servings

1   pound tuna fillets
1   tablespoon olive oil
1   large clove garlic, halved
¼   teaspoon black pepper

Arrange tuna in a shallow baking dish. Brush both sides with olive oil. Rub with cut garlic; sprinkle with black pepper. Let stand 1 hour.

Prepare coals. Cover the grill grid with foil. Grill tuna over hot coals 3–4 minutes on each side, or just until fish flakes easily when tested with a fork.

APPROXIMATE NUTRITIONAL CONTENT PER SERVING OF GRILLED FRESH TUNA

Total calories: 182
Protein: 28 g
Carbohydrates: Tr
Cholesterol: 65 mg
Fat: 8 g
Sodium: Tr

Percentage of calories from:
Protein: 59%
Carbohydrates: 1%
Fat: 40%

Fish oil, rich in cholesterol-lowering Omega 3's, provides almost all the fat in this recipe. For this reason, don't be concerned with the relatively high fat content.

BAKED RED SNAPPER

4 servings

1   pound red snapper fillets, cut into 3-inch cubes
2   teaspoons powdered rosemary
$\frac{1}{2}$ teaspoon black pepper
2   fresh lemons, peeled and finely diced
$\frac{1}{4}$ cup chopped fresh parsley

Sprinkle fish generously with powdered rosemary and black pepper. Arrange in a nonstick baking pan. Bake at 325°F. 15–20 minutes, or until fish flakes easily when tested with a fork. Remove to serving plate. Cover with lemons. Sprinkle with parsley.

VARIATIONS: Substitute black cod or monkfish for red snapper.

APPROXIMATE NUTRITIONAL CONTENT PER SERVING

Total calories: 135
Protein: 28 g
Carbohydrates: 3 g
Cholesterol: 68 mg
Fat: 2 g
Sodium: 62 mg

Percentage of calories from:
Protein: 80%
Carbohydrates: 10%
Fat: 11%

POACHED ORANGE ROUGHY

4 servings

juice of 1 lemon
1 pound orange roughy fillets
1 fresh lemon, quartered
black pepper to taste

In a large skillet, heat lemon juice. Add orange roughy. Cover and poach 3–8 minutes, or until fish flakes easily when tested with a fork. Serve with fresh lemon and black pepper.

SERVING SUGGESTION: Accompany with Vermicelli-stuffed Tomatoes (page 492).

APPROXIMATE NUTRITIONAL CONTENT PER SERVING

Total calories: 111
Protein: 23 g
Carbohydrates: 2 g
Cholesterol: 74 mg
Fat: 2 g
Sodium: 136 mg

Percentage of calories from:
Protein: 79%
Carbohydrates: 8%
Fat: 13%

CAJUN-STYLE WHITEFISH

4 servings

1½ cups fresh orange juice
2 tablespoons fresh lemon juice
3 tablespoons fresh lime juice
1 tablespoon rice vinegar
3 cloves garlic, peeled
2 tablespoons diced jalapeño peppers
2 tablespoons hot chili powder

2   tablespoons mild chili powder
2   teaspoons or less salt
¼   teaspoon black pepper
1   pound black cod, halibut, red snapper,
       monkfish, sole or perch

In a bowl, combine orange juice, lemon juice, lime juice, rice vinegar, garlic, jalapeño peppers, chili powders, salt and black pepper. Let sauce stand at room temperature 3 hours.

Arrange each fillet on a sheet of aluminum foil. Bring edges of foil upwards to form a bowl. Spoon 2 tablespoons of sauce over each fillet. Pinch top edges of foil together to seal (leave a small amount of space for steam between top of fish and top of foil).

Arrange foil packets in a baking dish. Steam at 450°F. 8–10 minutes, or until fish flakes easily when tested with a fork. Heat remaining sauce. Serve with fish.

APPROXIMATE NUTRITIONAL CONTENT PER SERVING OF CAJUN-STYLE WHITEFISH WITH 2 TABLESPOONS SAUCE

Total calories: 131
Protein: 23 g
Carbohydrates: 4 g
Cholesterol: 57 mg
Fat: 3 g
Sodium: 250 mg

Percentage of calories from:
   Protein: 70%
   Carbohydrates: 13%
   Fat: 18%

Add 9 calories per each additional tablespoon of sauce.

GRILLED SWORDFISH

4 servings

1 pound fresh swordfish fillets
1 fresh fennel bulb, cut into ½-inch cubes
½ cup chopped fresh fennel greens
¾ cup skim milk
½ fresh lime, cut into wedges
½ fresh lemon, cut into wedges

Arrange swordfish in a shallow dish. Layer cubed fennel bulb and half the chopped fennel greens over and around swordfish. Pour milk over top (milk gives moisture to the fish without leaving a milk taste). Let stand 1 hour at room temperature. Drain.

Prepare coals. Cover the grill grid with foil. Grill swordfish over hot coals 3–4 minutes on each side, or just until fish flakes easily when tested with a fork. Serve on a bed of remaining fresh fennel greens. Garnish with lemon and lime wedges.

APPROXIMATE NUTRITIONAL CONTENT PER SERVING

Total calories: 154
Protein: 25 g
Carbohydrates: 5 g
Cholesterol: 58 mg
Fat: 5 g
Sodium: 113 mg

Percentage of calories from:
  Protein: 61%
  Carbohydrates: 13%
  Fat: 26%

GRILLED SALMON WITH FRESH FENNEL

4 servings

> 1   pound salmon fillets
> 1   cup skim milk
> ½   pound fresh fennel greens
> ½   fresh lemon
> ½   fresh lime
>   black pepper to taste

Arrange salmon in a 9″ × 13″ × 2″ pan. Cover with milk (milk gives moisture to the fish without leaving a milk taste). Layer some of the fennel greens over and under the fish. Let stand 30 minutes.

Cover the grill grid with foil and prepare coals. Cover foil generously with some of the remaining fennel. Arrange salmon over fennel. Cover with additional fennel. Grill salmon 6–7 minutes, depending on the freshness and thickness of the salmon. Turn. Grill 2–3 minutes, or until fish flakes easily when tested with a fork.

Line a heated serving platter with fennel. Arrange salmon over fennel. Squeeze lemon and lime juice over fish. Sprinkle with black pepper.

VARIATIONS: Substitute fresh dill for fennel. Substitute scallops for salmon.

APPROXIMATE NUTRITIONAL CONTENT PER SERVING

Total calories: 242   *Percentage of calories from:*
Protein: 34 g   Protein: 56%
Carbohydrates: 8 g   Carbohydrates: 13%
Cholesterol: 54 mg   Fat: 32%
Fat: 9 g
Sodium: 164 mg

Fish oil, rich in cholesterol-lowering Omega 3's, provides almost all the fat in this recipe. For this reason, don't be concerned with the relatively high fat content.

POACHED SALMON WITH LEMON

4 servings

> 1   pound salmon fillets
> 1   cup white wine
>   juice of 2 fresh lemons

In a fish poacher or saucepan, combine salmon with wine and lemon juice. Cover. Bring to a boil (do not boil). Reduce heat and simmer 5–10 minutes, or just until fish flakes easily when tested with a fork. (If more moisture is needed, add additional wine or lemon juice.)

SERVING SUGGESTION: Serve with Chinese Vegetable Stir-fry (page 510).

APPROXIMATE NUTRITIONAL CONTENT PER SERVING

Total calories: 250
Protein: 30 g
Carbohydrates: 4 g
Cholesterol: 53 mg
Fat: 8 g
Sodium: 134 mg

Percentage of calories from:
   Protein: 57%
   Carbohydrates: 8%
   Fat: 35%

Fish oil, rich in cholesterol-lowering Omega 3's, provides almost all the fat in this recipe. For this reason, don't be concerned with the relatively high fat content.

GREEN PEPPERCORN SALMON

4 servings

2 tablespoons fresh lime juice
2 tablespoons green peppercorns
1 pound fresh salmon fillets
2 fresh limes, sliced into rounds

In a blender or food processor, combine lime juice and peppercorns. Process 2–3 minutes, or until peppercorns are crushed. Place salmon in a dish and arrange lime slices over and under it. Marinate 30 minutes.

Prepare coals. Cover the grill grid with foil. Layer ½ of the lime slices on top of foil. Arrange salmon with skin side up over limes. Cover salmon with remaining lime slices. Grill 5–6 minutes. Turn. Grill 2–3 minutes, or until salmon flakes easily when tested with a fork.

APPROXIMATE NUTRITIONAL CONTENT PER SERVING

Total calories: 220
Protein: 31 g
Carbohydrates: 6 g
Cholesterol: 53 mg
Fat: 9 g
Sodium: 135 mg

Percentage of calories from:
Protein: 55%
Carbohydrates: 11%
Fat: 34%

Fish oil, rich in cholesterol-lowering Omega 3's, provides almost all the fat in this recipe. For this reason, don't be concerned with the relatively high fat content.

TERIYAKI SALMON

4 servings

¼ cup Beef Stock (page 352)
¼ cup bourbon
1   tablespoon reduced-sodium soy sauce
1   pound salmon fillets

In a bowl, combine stock, bourbon and soy sauce. Place salmon in a dish and pour marinade over it. Marinate 45–60 minutes. Pour off marinade into small saucepan. Keep warm.

Prepare coals. Cover the grid grill with foil. Grill salmon skin side up 5–6 minutes. Turn. Cook 2–3 minutes, or until salmon flakes easily when tested with a fork. Serve with marinade.

APPROXIMATE NUTRITIONAL CONTENT PER SERVING

Total calories: 238
Protein: 31 g
Carbohydrates: Tr
Cholesterol: 54 mg
Fat: 8 g
Sodium: 295 mg

Percentage of calories from:
Protein: 62%
Carbohydrates: 0%
Fat: 38%

Fish oil, rich in cholesterol-lowering Omega 3's, provides almost all the fat in this recipe. For this reason, don't be concerned with the relatively high fat content.

POULTRY

POACHED CHICKEN

4 servings

4 cups Chicken Stock (page 350)
2 whole chicken breasts, skinned, boned
   and halved

In a saucepan, bring stock to a boil; add chicken breasts and bring to a second boil. Reduce heat to medium; cook 20 minutes, or until chicken is done. Remove chicken and reserve stock for later use. If chicken is to be used for sandwiches, cool 10 minutes and tear into strings or slice diagonally across top.

VARIATION: Substitute turkey breasts for chicken breasts.

SERVING SUGGESTION: Chicken poached in stock is excellent for sandwiches, salads and stir-fries, as well as for an entrée.

APPROXIMATE NUTRITIONAL CONTENT PER SERVING

Total calories: 142
Protein: 27 g
Carbohydrates: 0 g
Cholesterol: 70 mg
Fat: 3 g
Sodium: 64 mg

Percentage of calories from:
   Protein: 79%
   Carbohydrates: 0%
   Fat: 21%

PAN-FRIED CHICKEN

4 servings

> 2   whole chicken breasts, skinned, boned
>   and halved

Preheat a nonstick skillet over medium-high heat. Add chicken breasts and brown 10 minutes on each side. Reduce heat. Cook 15–20 minutes, turning occasionally.

VARIATION: Rub chicken breasts with powdered rosemary, garlic powder and black pepper before cooking.

SERVING SUGGESTION: Serve with Roast Potatoes with Rosemary (page 485) and Pan-steamed Asparagus (page 476).

APPROXIMATE NUTRITIONAL CONTENT PER SERVING

Total calories: 142
Protein: 27 g
Carbohydrates: 0 g
Cholesterol: 70 mg
Fat: 3 g
Sodium: 64 mg

Percentage of calories from:
Protein: 79%
Carbohydrates: 0%
Fat: 21%

ROAST CHICKEN WITH ROSEMARY

4 servings

1 roasting chicken, about 3–4 pounds
powdered rosemary
black pepper
1 large yellow onion, quartered
3 cloves garlic

Wipe inside of chicken with a damp paper towel; wash outside with cold water. Rub outside of bird and inside cavity with generous amounts of rosemary and black pepper. Put onions and garlic inside cavity. Skewer neck skin to back; tuck wing tips behind shoulder joints. Place chicken breast side up in a shallow roasting pan. Roast at 375°F. 60–75 minutes. Let stand 10 minutes before slicing.

VARIATION: Rub a skinned and boned chicken breast with rosemary, black pepper and garlic powder. Prepare as directed in Pan-fried Chicken (page 434). (Note the difference in calories and fat from using the white meat of the chicken and eliminating its skin.)

SERVING SUGGESTION: To reduce total percentage of calories from fat in the meal, serve with low-fat accompaniments.

APPROXIMATE NUTRITIONAL CONTENT PER SERVING

Total calories: 285
Protein: 41 g
Carbohydrates: 4 g
Cholesterol: 123 mg
Fat: 10 g
Sodium: 124 mg

Percentage of calories from:
Protein: 60%
Carbohydrates: 6%
Fat: 34%

ROAST TURKEY BREAST

4 servings

1   fresh turkey breast, about 2–3 pounds
powdered rosemary
garlic powder
black pepper

Remove and discard ¾ of the skin from the turkey breast. Leave on remaining skin for moisture. Rub breast on both sides with generous amounts of rosemary, garlic powder and black pepper. Roast at 325°F. 60–90 minutes, or grill over hot coals (allow approximately 35 minutes' cooking time per pound). Discard remaining skin after cooking.

APPROXIMATE NUTRITIONAL CONTENT PER SERVING

Total calories: 181
Protein: 34 g
Carbohydrates: 1 g
Cholesterol: 83 mg
Fat: 4 g
Sodium: 73 mg

Percentage of calories from:
Protein: 79%
Carbohydrates: 2%
Fat: 19%

TURKEY LUMPIA

12 servings

2   cups Chicken Stock (page 350)
1   turkey breast, about 2½–3 pounds
1   package spring roll (Lumpia) wrappers*
1   head Bibb lettuce, shredded
6   green onions, cut lengthwise into strings
½   cup hot Chinese mustard*
2   tablespoons toasted sesame seeds
¼   cup reduced-sodium soy sauce
2   tablespoons rice vinegar

In a large pot, bring stock and turkey to a boil. Reduce heat to medium. Cook 20 minutes, or until turkey is done. Remove turkey. Reserve stock for soup. Let turkey cool 10 minutes; tear into strings.

In a covered bamboo steamer basket or a vegetable steamer basket over boiling water, steam the wrappers 5–7 minutes, or until wrappers are hot. Remove from basket.

Lay wrappers flat. Mound some turkey, some lettuce and some green onion in center of each wrapper. Fold bottom edge up, top edge down, and left and right sides over (work quickly so wrappers are still hot when served).

Mound Chinese mustard and sesame seeds in center of serving tray. Ring with Turkey Lumpia. In a small bowl, combine soy sauce and vinegar; pass with Lumpia.

*Spring roll wrappers and hot Chinese mustard are available in Oriental markets, if not in your supermarket.

SERVING SUGGESTIONS: Serve with Steamed Oriental Rice (page 499) and fresh seasonal fruit. Also good as an appetizer.

APPROXIMATE NUTRITIONAL CONTENT PER TURKEY LUMPIA

Total calories: 162
Protein: 19 g
Carbohydrates: 13 g
Cholesterol: 36 mg
Fat: 3 g
Sodium: 326 mg

Percentage of calories from:
Protein: 48%
Carbohydrates: 34%
Fat: 18%

GARLIC CHICKEN

4 servings

2	whole chicken breasts, skinned and boned
1	teaspoon sake
2	teaspoons sesame oil
1	egg white
2	teaspoons safflower oil
¼	cup chopped garlic
2	carrots, sliced diagonally into thirds
½	cup bamboo shoots
½	cup water chestnuts
1	cup Chicken Stock (page 350)
1	tablespoon rice vinegar
1	tablespoon arrowroot

Cut chicken into 2-inch pieces. Combine sake, sesame oil and egg white; pour over chicken. Marinate 30 minutes.

In a wok or nonstick skillet, heat safflower oil. Add chicken and garlic, and sauté 15 minutes, stirring frequently. Add carrots and bamboo shoots; stir-fry 5 minutes, or until carrots are crisp-tender. Add water chestnuts; stir-fry 2–3 minutes.

In a saucepan, heat ¾ cup of stock to boiling. Add rice vinegar. Combine remaining ¼ cup stock with arrowroot and gradually add to boiling broth, stirring constantly 2–3 minutes, or until broth begins to thicken. Pour over chicken. Cook 1–2 minutes.

SERVING SUGGESTION: To reduce the total fat content of the meal, serve with low-fat accompaniments.

APPROXIMATE NUTRITIONAL CONTENT PER SERVING

Total calories: 230

Protein: 30 g

Carbohydrates: 9 g

Cholesterol: 70 mg

Fat: 7 g

Sodium: 167 mg

Percentage of calories from:

  Protein: 54%

  Carbohydrates: 16%

  Fat: 30%

STIR-FRIED CHICKEN

6 servings

2	whole chicken breasts, skinned, boned and cut into julienne strips
1	tablespoon peanut oil
1	small head cauliflower, florets only
3	stalks celery, cut on the diagonal into 1½-inch pieces
12	fresh mushrooms, sliced
1	6½-ounce can water chestnuts, drained
½	red pepper, cut into julienne strips
½	green pepper, cut into julienne strips
1½	cups bean sprouts
¼	cup reduced-sodium soy sauce
2	tablespoons rice vinegar

In a nonstick skillet, sauté chicken 10–15 minutes, or until nearly done. Reduce heat.

Meanwhile, in a wok, heat peanut oil. Add cauliflower; stir-fry 4 minutes. Add celery; stir-fry 2 minutes. Add mushrooms, water chestnuts and peppers; stir-fry 3–4 minutes, or until all vegetables are bright in color and crisp-tender. Add bean sprouts and chicken. Set aside.

Combine soy sauce and vinegar. Pour over vegetables.

APPROXIMATE NUTRITIONAL CONTENT PER SERVING

Total calories: 171
Protein: 22 g
Carbohydrates: 10 g
Cholesterol: 47 mg
Fat: 5 g
Sodium: 493 mg

Percentage of calories from:
  Protein: 52%
  Carbohydrates: 24%
  Fat: 24%

SAFFRON CHICKEN

4 servings

2	teaspoons olive oil
¼	teaspoon saffron powder
½	teaspoon thyme
2	whole chicken breasts, skinned, boned and halved

In a bowl, combine oil, saffron powder and thyme; brush over chicken breasts.

Prepare coals. Grill chicken over hot coals 10 minutes. Turn. Baste with sauce. Cook 5–10 minutes, or until chicken is tender.

SERVING SUGGESTION: The olive oil raises the calories from fat. To reduce the total fat content of the meal, serve with low-fat accompaniments such as Pan-steamed Asparagus (page 476), Wild Rice (page 497) and fresh pineapple and papaya.

APPROXIMATE NUTRITIONAL CONTENT PER SERVING

Total calories: 162
Protein: 27 g
Carbohydrates: 0 g
Cholesterol: 70 mg
Fat: 5 g
Sodium: 64 mg

Percentage of calories from:
Protein: 69%
Carbohydrates: 0%
Fat: 31%

SZECHUAN CHICKEN

6 servings

juice of ½ lemon
1 tablespoon green peppercorns
1 tablespoon olive oil
1 teaspoon hot chili oil (LaYu)*
1 teaspoon reduced-sodium soy sauce
1½ pounds chicken breast, skinned and boned

In a blender or food processor, combine lemon juice, peppercorns, olive oil, chili oil and soy sauce. Process until peppercorns are crushed. Pour over chicken. Marinate several hours or overnight.

Prepare coals. Grill chicken over hot coals 10 minutes. Turn. Baste with marinade. Cook 5–10 minutes, or until chicken is done.

*Hot chili oil is available in Oriental markets, if not in your supermarket.

VARIATION: Serve as a salad over lettuce. Garnish with sliced English cucumber. For a dressing, try Szechuan Vinaigrette (page 392) or Oil-free Szechuan Vinaigrette (page 393).

SERVING SUGGESTIONS: Serve with Chinese Vegetable Stir-fry (page 510) and fresh pineapple and papaya.

The leftover chicken makes great sandwiches.

APPROXIMATE NUTRITIONAL CONTENT PER SERVING

Total calories: 211
Protein: 35 g
Carbohydrates: 1 g
Cholesterol: 93 mg
Fat: 6 g
Sodium: 150 mg

Percentage of calories from:
Protein: 70%
Carbohydrates: 2%
Fat: 28%

CHICKEN CHOW MEIN

6 servings

1 whole chicken breast, skinned, boned and
    cut into julienne strips
2 cups Chicken Stock (page 350)
1 tablespoon reduced-sodium soy sauce
2 tablespoons cornstarch dissolved in ¼ cup
    cold water
½ white onion, thinly sliced
3 stalks celery, cut on the diagonal into
    1-inch pieces
1 red pepper, cut into julienne strips
10 fresh mushrooms, sliced
2 cups bean sprouts
1 8-ounce can water chestnuts
1 8-ounce package buckwheat (Soba)
    noodles, cooked and drained*

In a nonstick skillet, sauté chicken over medium-high heat
5 minutes, or until nearly cooked. Reduce heat; simmer.

In a saucepan, combine 1½ cups of stock with soy sauce;
bring to a boil. Gradually add cornstarch, stirring constantly, 2–3 minutes, or until sauce thickens. Reduce heat
to simmer.

In a wok, heat remaining ½ cup stock. Add onions and
celery; stir-fry 2–3 minutes. Add red pepper and mushrooms; stir-fry 2–3 minutes. Add bean sprouts and water
chestnuts. Remove from heat. Pour sauce over vegetables
and toss. Add chicken and noodles. Toss.

*Soba noodles are available in Oriental markets, if not
in your supermarket.

VARIATIONS: Substitute pork for chicken or use ½ pork
and ½ chicken.

APPROXIMATE NUTRITIONAL CONTENT PER SERVING OF CHICKEN CHOW MEIN

Total calories: 303
Protein: 26 g
Carbohydrates: 41 g
Cholesterol: 36 mg
Fat: 3 g
Sodium: 252 mg

Percentage of calories from:
  Protein: 35%
  Carbohydrates: 54%
  Fat: 11%

CHICKEN PICCATA

4 servings

> 1 tablespoon olive oil
> 2 very thin whole chicken breasts, skinned, boned and halved
> juice of 1 lemon
> ¼ cup dry white wine*
> 1 lemon, thinly sliced
> black pepper

In a nonstick skillet, heat oil. Add chicken and sauté over medium-high heat 10 minutes. Turn and cook 10 minutes. Reduce heat to simmer. Cook 5 minutes longer on each side, or until chicken is nearly done. Pour lemon juice over chicken. Cook 5 minutes. Remove chicken to heated plates. Add wine to the pan and deglaze over high heat 2–3 minutes, stirring constantly. Pour wine over chicken. Top each piece of chicken with lemon slices. Sprinkle with black pepper.

*Try Bollo Trebbiano for the cooking wine.

SERVING SUGGESTION: The calories from fat are high in this dish. Serve with low-fat accompaniments such as orzo (a type of pasta), Steamed Snow Peas (page 490) and

(continued on next page)

Grilled Tomatoes (page 491) to reduce the total fat content of the meal.

APPROXIMATE NUTRITIONAL CONTENT PER SERVING OF CHICKEN PICCATA

Total calories: 190
Protein: 27 g
Carbohydrates: 3 g
Cholesterol: 70 mg
Fat: 6 g
Sodium: 65 mg

Percentage of calories from:
  Protein: 61%
  Carbohydrates: 6%
  Fat: 33%

SOFT CHICKEN TACOS

4 servings

  4   cups Chicken Stock (page 350)
1½   chicken breasts, skinned and boned
  4   10-inch flour tortillas*
  2   ripe tomatoes, diced
 ½   white onion, diced
 ½   head leaf lettuce, shredded
 ½   cup alfalfa sprouts (optional)
 ½   cup grated part-skim Cheddar cheese
 ½   cup tomato salsa

In a medium saucepan, bring stock to a boil. Add chicken. Reduce heat to medium-high and cook 20–25 minutes, or until chicken is tender. Cool. Tear into strings.

In a covered vegetable steamer basket or bamboo steamer basket over boiling water, steam tortillas 3–5 minutes, or until steaming hot.

Lay each tortilla flat. Fill centers with chicken, tomatoes, onions, lettuce, sprouts and cheese. Drizzle with salsa. Fold sides of tortillas over center.

*The most heart-healthy flour tortillas are those made

with an unsaturated oil such as soy. Do not buy flour tortillas made with lard.

NOTE: Tacos are high in sodium and calories. Even with simple accompaniments such as steamed rice and fresh fruit, the total calories for the meal can be high. Keep this in mind and allow for it when you do your daily meal plan.

APPROXIMATE NUTRITIONAL CONTENT PER SERVING OF SOFT CHICKEN TACOS

Total calories: 358
Protein: 34 g
Carbohydrates: 53 g
Cholesterol: 75 mg
Fat: 12 g
Sodium: 690 mg

Percentage of calories from:
Protein: 30%
Carbohydrates: 46%
Fat: 23%

CHICKEN TOSTADOS

4 servings

4   10-inch corn or flour tortillas*
⅓   cup Refried Beans (page 505)
1½ chicken breasts, poached in broth and torn
      into strings (see page 433)
1   ripe tomato, diced
¾   cup grated part-skim Cheddar or
      mozzarella cheese
⅔   head leaf lettuce, chopped
½   cup tomato salsa

Lay tortillas flat. Spread with beans. Sprinkle with chicken and tomato. Top with cheese. Bake at 350°F. 5–6 minutes, or until cheese melts. Remove to heated plates. Top with lettuce. Drizzle with salsa.

*The most heart-healthy flour tortillas are those made with an unsaturated oil such as soy. Do not buy flour tortillas made with lard. Corn tortillas do not contain any oil or shortening and are more heart-healthy than flour tortillas. They also have 28 fewer calories.

NOTE: Tostados are high in sodium and calories. Keep this in mind and allow for it when you do your daily meal plan.

APPROXIMATE NUTRITIONAL CONTENT PER SERVING

Total calories: 376
Protein: 29 g
Carbohydrates: 39 g
Cholesterol: 54 mg
Fat: 12 g
Sodium: 460 mg

Percentage of calories from:
Protein: 30%
Carbohydrates: 41%
Fat: 28%

MEAT

GRILLED VEAL WITH MUSTARD SAUCE

4 servings

    4   very thin veal scallops*
    1   tablespoon Creamy Dijon Vinaigrette
        (page 398)

Prepare coals. Grill veal over hot coals 3–4 minutes on each side. Brush with vinaigrette last 1 minute of cooking.

*The fat content of veal differs markedly with the cut. We recommend veal scallops cut from the rump roast, which is 13% fat. By comparison, veal cutlets are 48% fat and rib roast is 58% fat.

SERVING SUGGESTION: The vinaigrette increases the calories from fat. Serve with low-fat accompaniments to reduce the total fat content of the meal.

APPROXIMATE NUTRITIONAL CONTENT PER SERVING

Total calories: 189
Protein: 30 g
Carbohydrates: Tr
Cholesterol: 76 mg
Fat: 7 g
Sodium: 75 mg

Percentage of calories from:
Protein: 56%
Carbohydrates: 10%
Fat: 34%

VEAL PICCATA

4 servings

- ½ teaspoon olive oil
- ¾ pound veal scallops,* very thinly sliced
  juice of 1 lemon
- ¼ cup dry white wine
- ½ lemon, thinly sliced
  black pepper

In a nonstick skillet, heat oil. Add veal and sauté 5–6 minutes. Turn. Add lemon juice. Cook 2–3 minutes, or to desired doneness. Remove veal to heated plates. Add wine to the skillet and deglaze over high heat, stirring constantly. Pour wine over veal. Top each scallop with a slice of lemon. Sprinkle with black pepper.

*The fat content of veal differs markedly with the cut. We recommend veal scallops cut from the rump roast, which is 13% fat. By comparison, veal cutlets are 48% fat and rib roast is 58% fat.

APPROXIMATE NUTRITIONAL CONTENT PER SERVING

Total calories: 152
Protein: 27 g
Carbohydrates: 1 g
Cholesterol: 0 mg
Fat: 2 g
Sodium: 112 mg

Percentage of calories from:
Protein: 80%
Carbohydrates: 4%
Fat: 16%

VEAL CHOPS WITH LEMON AND PEPPER

4 servings

> 4   small veal chops*
> 2   tablespoons fresh lemon juice
> 1/4 teaspoon black pepper
> 1   tablespoon chopped fresh parsley
> 1/2 fresh lemon, cut into wedges

Arrange veal chops in a shallow dish. Sprinkle with lemon juice, black pepper and parsley. Marinate 2 hours.

In a nonstick skillet over high heat, cook veal chops 2–3 minutes on each side. Remove veal to a platter. Squeeze a lemon wedge over each chop.

*The fat content of veal differs markedly with the cut. We recommend veal chops cut from the rump, which is 13% fat. By comparison, veal cutlets are 48% fat and rib roast is 58% fat.

SERVING SUGGESTION: Serve with Ala Pilaf with Tomatoes and Parsley (page 503).

APPROXIMATE NUTRITIONAL CONTENT PER SERVING

Total calories: 182
Protein: 29 g
Carbohydrates: 2 g
Cholesterol: 75 mg
Fat: 6 g
Sodium: 55 mg

Percentage of calories from:
  Protein: 67%
  Carbohydrates: 4%
  Fat: 29%

GRILLED VEAL WITH TOMATOES AND ARTICHOKES

4 servings

1   pound veal chops*
2   tablespoons fresh lemon juice
½   teaspoon black pepper
1   tablespoon chopped fresh parsley
1   16-ounce can plum tomatoes
½   red onion, diced
1   carrot, diced
1   stalk celery, diced
1   teaspoon fresh basil
⅓   pound fresh mushrooms, sliced
1   8-ounce can artichoke hearts, quartered
½   fresh lime

Arrange veal chops in a shallow dish. Sprinkle with lemon juice, ¼ teaspoon of black pepper and parsley. Marinate 2 hours.

Drain tomatoes and dice. Reserve juice. In a nonstick skillet, sauté onions, carrots and celery in reserved juice until vegetables are barely tender. Add diced tomatoes, remaining ¼ teaspoon black pepper, basil and mushrooms; simmer 15–20 minutes. Add artichoke hearts and cook 5–10 minutes. Set tomato sauce aside.

Prepare coals. Grill veal chops over hot coals 2–3 minutes on each side. Remove to shallow serving dish. Squeeze lime juice over chops. Cover with tomato sauce.

*The fat content of veal differs markedly with the cut. We recommend veal chops cut from the rump, which is 13% fat. By comparison, veal cutlets are 48% fat and rib roast is 58% fat.

SERVING SUGGESTION: Serve with a heavy-type pasta such as penne or rigatoni.

APPROXIMATE NUTRITIONAL CONTENT PER SERVING
OF GRILLED VEAL WITH TOMATOES AND ARTICHOKES

Total calories: 315   *Percentage of calories from:*
Protein: 43 g   Protein: 55%
Carbohydrates: 17 g   Carbohydrates: 21%
Cholesterol: 101 mg   Fat: 24%
Fat: 8 g
Sodium: 322 mg

GRILLED LAMB CHOPS
WITH ROSEMARY AND GARLIC

4 servings

> 4   extra-lean lamb chops
>   garlic powder
>   black pepper
>   powdered rosemary

Trim chops of all visible fat; score edges. Rub each chop with generous amounts of garlic powder, black pepper and rosemary.

Prepare coals. Grill over hot coals 8–10 minutes. Turn. Grill 5–8 minutes.

SERVING SUGGESTION: Accompany with Steamed Oriental Rice (page 499) and skewered, grilled artichoke hearts, mushrooms, zucchini and cherry tomatoes. These low-fat foods will help reduce the total fat content of the meal.

APPROXIMATE NUTRITIONAL CONTENT PER SERVING

Total calories: 222   *Percentage of calories from:*
Protein: 31 g   Protein: 58%
Carbohydrates: 1 g   Carbohydrates: 2%
Cholesterol: 101 mg   Fat: 40%
Fat: 9 g
Sodium: 78 mg

BUTTERFLIED LEG OF LAMB

4 servings

1   leg of lamb, about 3–4 pounds
    powdered oregano
    powdered basil
    powdered rosemary
    garlic powder
    black pepper
2   tablespoons olive oil
2   tablespoons red wine vinegar
1   tablespoon fresh lemon juice
3   cloves garlic, peeled
1   tablespoon Dijon mustard
1   teaspoon or less salt*

Have butcher remove bone from lamb and cut meat into butterfly shape. (Keep bones and scraps for soup stock.)

Place lamb in a dish. Rub on both sides with generous amounts of oregano, basil, rosemary, garlic powder and black pepper. In a bowl, combine oil, vinegar, lemon juice, garlic, mustard and salt. Pour over lamb. Marinate several hours or overnight, turning frequently. Remove lamb from marinade.

Prepare coals. Grill lamb over hot coals 10 minutes; turn. Baste; grill 10 minutes, or to desired doneness.

*To further decrease the sodium level of this recipe, omit or reduce the added salt to the marinade.

APPROXIMATE NUTRITIONAL CONTENT PER SERVING

Total calories: 238
Protein: 34 g
Carbohydrates: 2 g
Cholesterol: 119 mg
Fat: 10 g
Sodium: 404 mg

Percentage of calories from:
  Protein: 56%
  Carbohydrates: 4%
  Fat: 40%

ROAST LAMB WITH JUNIPER BERRIES

6 servings

1	leg of lamb, about 2½ pounds
	garlic powder
	black pepper
	powdered rosemary
½	cup dry white wine
15	whole juniper berries*

Rub lamb generously with garlic powder, black pepper and rosemary. Place roast on wire rack in roasting pan. Pour wine into bottom of pan. Add berries. Roast at 350°F. 1½ hours, or until meat is roasted to desired doneness.

*Juniper berries are available in the gourmet or spice section of most supermarkets.

SERVING SUGGESTION: Lamb is not a low-fat food. If accompanied by low-fat foods, the total fat content of the meal can drop. For example, served with ½ Grilled Tomato (page 491), Broccoli with Lemon Mustard Sauce (page 481) and Roast Potatoes with Rosemary (page 485), the fat content of the meal drops from 37% to 24%.

APPROXIMATE NUTRITIONAL CONTENT PER SERVING

Total calories: 229

Percentage of calories from:

Protein: 33 g   Protein: 62%

Carbohydrates: Tr   Carbohydrates: 1%

Cholesterol: 119 mg   Fat: 37%

Fat: 9 g

Sodium: 81 mg

ROAST PORK TENDERLOIN

6 servings

   1   extra-lean pork tenderloin roast, about
       1½ pounds
       garlic powder
       black pepper
       powdered rosemary

Rub roast generously with garlic powder, black pepper and rosemary. Place roast on wire rack in roasting pan. Roast at 350°F. 1 hour, or until meat is roasted to desired doneness.

SERVING SUGGESTION: Pork is not a low-fat food. Serve it with low-fat accompaniments to reduce the total fat content of the meal. For example, if served with Brown Rice with Mushrooms (page 500), Steamed Snow Peas (page 490), Grilled Tomatoes (page 491) and Apple-pear Sauce (page 523), the total fat content of the meal drops to 25%.

APPROXIMATE NUTRITIONAL CONTENT PER SERVING

Total calories: 290
Protein: 33 g
Carbohydrates: Tr
Cholesterol: 112 mg
Fat: 16 g
Sodium: 70 mg

Percentage of calories from:
  Protein: 48%
  Carbohydrates: 1%
  Fat: 52%

BARBECUED PORK

6 servings

1 extra-lean pork tenderloin roast, about
    1½ pounds
2 cups Barbecue Sauce (page 401)

Place the roast in a dish and pour 1 cup of the Barbecue Sauce over it; marinate 3 hours. Remove meat to wire rack in roasting pan. Roast at 350°F. 1 hour, or until meat is roasted to desired doneness. Heat remaining cup of Barbecue Sauce; pass with roast.

SERVING SUGGESTION: Pork is not a low-fat food. Serve it with low-fat accompaniments to reduce the total fat content of the meal. We suggest warming miniature crusty French rolls sliced lengthwise to make individual barbecued pork sandwiches. Accompanied with Pasta Salad (oil-free dressing, page 380) and fresh fruit, the total fat content of the meal is only 26%.

APPROXIMATE NUTRITIONAL CONTENT PER SERVING

Total calories: 303
Protein: 34 g
Carbohydrates: 4 g
Cholesterol: 112 mg
Fat: 16 g
Sodium: 166 mg

Percentage of calories from:
  Protein: 46%
  Carbohydrates: 5%
  Fat: 49%

BRAISED MEAT LOAF

6 servings

10–12	dried forest (Shiitake) mushrooms*
2	cups water
1	slice white bread, crust removed
1	tablespoon skim milk
1	pound extra-lean ground round
½	teaspoon Bakon torula yeast* (optional)
½	teaspoon garlic powder
½	teaspoon black pepper
3	tablespoons chopped white onion
2	egg whites
½	cup bread crumbs
⅓	cup dry white wine
2	tablespoons tomato paste

In a small bowl, soak mushrooms in 2 cups water 20–30 minutes, or until soft. Drain, reserving soaking liquid. Coarsely chop mushrooms, discarding the tough bottom stems. In a small saucepan, combine bread with milk. Simmer 3–5 minutes, or until milk is absorbed and bread is soft. Dice. In a mixing bowl, combine ground round, yeast, garlic powder and pepper. Knead in onions and diced bread, then egg whites. Shape into a firmly packed ball. Roll into a baguette-type loaf, about 2½ inches thick. Roll loaf in bread crumbs.

In a nonstick skillet over medium heat, brown the meat loaf on all sides, turning carefully so the loaf will not break. When meat is browned, add wine and cook over medium-high heat 5–10 minutes, or until wine is reduced by ½ (do not allow wine to boil).

In a small saucepan, warm reserved mushroom liquid. Stir in tomato paste. Simmer 5 minutes. Add to skillet along with chopped mushrooms. Cover and simmer 30 minutes, turning loaf twice. Adjust lid so it is slightly ajar and simmer 15 minutes longer.

Remove loaf to cutting board and let stand 5 minutes before cutting. Place on serving platter. Ring with mushrooms. Pour remaining sauce over top.

*Shiitake mushrooms are available in Oriental markets and Bakon torula yeast in health food stores, if not found in your supermarket.

VARIATION: For increased fiber, substitute oat bran for bread crumbs.

SERVING SUGGESTION: The leftovers make great sandwiches.

APPROXIMATE NUTRITIONAL CONTENT PER SERVING OF BRAISED MEAT LOAF

Total calories: 194
Protein: 25 g
Carbohydrates: 8 g
Cholesterol: 65 mg
Fat: 5 g
Sodium: 141 mg

Percentage of calories from:
Protein: 58%
Carbohydrates: 16%
Fat: 25%

CABBAGE ROLLS

20 rolls

1   cup dry pearl barley
4   cups water
1   cup Beef Stock (page 352)
1   pound extra-lean ground round
¼   teaspoon black pepper
½   teaspoon or less salt
⅛   teaspoon marjoram
¼   teaspoon garlic powder
1   egg, beaten
¾   cup skim evaporated milk
1   head cabbage

Soak barley several hours or overnight in 4 cups water. Pour barley with soaking liquid and stock into a medium saucepan; bring to a boil. Reduce heat. Cover and simmer 45 minutes, or until barley is tender and liquid is absorbed.

In a nonstick skillet, brown ground round. Drain on paper towels. Season with pepper, salt, marjoram and garlic powder. Toss with barley, egg and milk. Cool to room temperature.

Carefully separate cabbage leaves from head. Cut off tough stem ends. In a covered steamer basket over boiling water, steam cabbage leaves 2–3 minutes, or until leaves just begin to soften. Drain. Pat dry.

Fill each cabbage leaf with 1–2 tablespoons meat-and-barley mixture. Fold top and bottom ends of leaves toward center. Fold each side toward center, as if wrapping a square package. Secure with a toothpick.

In a covered vegetable steamer basket or a bamboo steamer basket over boiling water (make sure water level is below rack), steam cabbage rolls 2–3 minutes, or just until meat-and-barley mixture is hot.

NOTE: Cabbage rolls may be prepared ahead and steamed just before serving.

APPROXIMATE NUTRITIONAL CONTENT PER
CABBAGE ROLL

Total calories: 101
Protein: 9 g
Carbohydrates: 10 g
Cholesterol: 33 mg
Fat: 3 g
Sodium: 94 mg

Percentage of calories from:
  Protein: 34%
  Carbohydrates: 38%
  Fat: 28%

PASTA & BEAN ENTRÉES

SPINACH TORTELLINI

36 tortellini

2   bunches fresh spinach, washed and
    trimmed
1   egg, beaten
1   clove garlic, chopped
2   cups part-skim ricotta cheese
¼   teaspoon black pepper
¼   teaspoon nutmeg
3   tablespoons grated part-skim mozzarella
    cheese
1   1-pound package won-ton wrappers
    (3½″ × 3½″)*

In a covered vegetable steamer basket over boiling water, steam spinach 1–2 minutes, or just until leaves begin to wilt. Cool. Wring several times to extract as much moisture as possible. In blender or food processor, purée spinach with egg and garlic. Add ricotta cheese and process 1 minute, or until creamy. Add pepper, nutmeg and mozzarella, and process 1 minute, or until mixed.

Cut won-ton wrappers in half. Lay each wrapper flat. Spread with 1/3 teaspoon filling. Roll wrapper lengthwise (like a cigar). Then roll shape around finger to make a ring. Twist ends together and squeeze so that they are firmly locked.

Drop tortellini into 3½ quarts boiling water. Bring to a second boil; boil 2 minutes. Add 2 cups cold water and bring to a third boil; boil 2–3 minutes. Drain.

*Won-ton wrappers are available in Oriental markets, if not in your supermarket.

NOTE: Using prepared won-ton wrappers is a quick and easy way to prepare tortellini and ravioli. I think the quality is equal to those made with fresh homemade pasta.

VARIATION: To make Spinach Ravioli in the same amount, spread each half wrapper with ½ teaspoon filling. Fold wrapper in half. Crimp edges firmly with a fork or a ravioli wheel.

SERVING SUGGESTIONS: Serve in chicken broth with chopped fresh parsley (see Tortellini in Brodo, page 362); serve with Marinara Sauce (page 404) or Bolognese Sauce (page 465); or skewer with tomatoes and serve as an hors d'oeuvre (page 464).

APPROXIMATE NUTRITIONAL CONTENT PER SPINACH TORTELLINI OR RAVIOLI

Total calories: 50
Protein: 4 g
Carbohydrates: 5 g
Cholesterol: 13 mg
Fat: 2 g
Sodium: 43 mg

Percentage of calories from:
  Protein: 28%
  Carbohydrates: 41%
  Fat: 31%

CHICKEN TORTELLINI

36 tortellini

  1   whole chicken breast, skinned and boned
  3   cups Chicken Stock (page 350)
  1   celery stalk with leaves
  ½   yellow onion
  1   carrot, peeled
  1   bay leaf
  2   sprigs fresh parsley
  1½ bunches fresh spinach, washed and
         trimmed
  2   cloves garlic, peeled
  1   egg, lightly beaten
  3   tablespoons grated part-skim mozzarella
         cheese
  ¼   teaspoon nutmeg
  ¼   teaspoon salt
  ¼   teaspoon black pepper
  2   tablespoons plain non-fat yogurt
  1   1-pound package won-ton wrappers
         (3½″ × 3½″)*

In a medium saucepan, combine chicken, stock, celery, onion, carrot, bay leaf and parsley. Bring just to boiling (do not boil). Reduce heat and simmer 20–25 minutes. Remove from heat. Allow chicken to cool in broth. Drain (reserve broth and vegetables for soup). Coarsely grind chicken.

In a covered vegetable steamer basket over boiling water, steam spinach 1–2 minutes, or just until leaves begin to wilt. Cool. Wring several times to extract as much moisture as possible. In a blender or food processor, purée spinach with garlic and egg. Add cheese, nutmeg, salt, pepper and chicken. Process 1 minute. Moisten with yogurt.

Cut won-ton wrappers in half. Lay each wrapper flat.

Spread with ¹/₃ teaspoon filling. Roll wrapper lengthwise (like a cigar). Then roll shape around finger to make a ring. Twist ends together and squeeze so that they are firmly locked.

Drop tortellini into 3¹/₂ quarts boiling water. Bring to a second boil; boil 2 minutes. Add 2 cups cold water and bring to a third boil; boil 2–3 minutes. Drain.

*Won-ton wrappers are available in Oriental markets, if not in your supermarket.

VARIATION: To make Chicken Ravioli in the same amount, spread each half wrapper with ¹/₂ teaspoon filling. Fold wrapper in half. Crimp edges firmly with a fork or a ravioli wheel.

SERVING SUGGESTION: Serve with Bolognese Sauce (page 465), Marinara Sauce (page 404) or Pesto (page 402). Accompany with green salad tossed with Oil-free Italian Vinaigrette (page 389), crusty French bread and fresh fruit.

APPROXIMATE NUTRITIONAL CONTENT PER CHICKEN TORTELLINI OR RAVIOLI WITHOUT SAUCE

Total calories: 35
Protein: 3 g
Carbohydrates: 5 g
Cholesterol: 10 mg
Fat: Tr
Sodium: 58 mg

Percentage of calories from:
  Protein: 31%
  Carbohydrates: 53%
  Fat: 15%

TORTELLINI AND TOMATOES

1   recipe Spinach Tortellini (page 460) or
        Chicken Tortellini (page 462)
1   recipe Pesto (page 402) or Garlic
        Vinaigrette (page 396)
1   box cherry tomatoes
½   cup freshly grated Parmesan cheese

Prepare and cook the tortellini; while still hot, toss with
pesto or vinaigrette. Wash the tomatoes; pat dry and remove stems. Toss tomatoes with pasta and pesto or vinaigrette and Parmesan cheese.

VARIATION: Cut ¾ pound part-skim mozzarella cheese
into 1-inch cubes. Toss with tortellini, tomatoes and pesto
while tortellini are still hot.

SERVING SUGGESTION: The calories from fat are high in
this dish. Keep this in mind and serve with low-fat accompaniments such as watermelon or cantaloupe or whatever
fresh fruit is in season and crusty French bread.

This is a sensational hors d'oeuvre. To serve, alternate
tortellini and tomatoes on long skewers and arrange in a
low pasta bowl or on individual bread-and-butter plates with
cocktail forks.

APPROXIMATE NUTRITIONAL CONTENT PER
TORTELLINI WITHOUT DRESSING

Total calories: 52   *Percentage of calories from:*
Protein: 3 g   Protein: 27%
Carbohydrates: 6 g   Carbohydrates: 43%
Cholesterol: 78 mg   Fat: 30%
Fat: 2 g
Sodium: 44 mg

*The Pesto or Garlic Vinaigrette will each add 68–70 calories per
tablespoon. A less spectacular but low-calorie alternative is to use
Marinara Sauce (page 404) at about 7 calories per tablespoon.*

PASTA BOLOGNESE

12 servings

1 pound extra-lean ground round
3 tablespoons chopped onion
2 tablespoons chopped carrot
2 tablespoons chopped celery
1 cup dry white wine
½ cup skim milk
⅛ teaspoon nutmeg
1 28-ounce can plum tomatoes, chopped
1 1-pound package spaghetti, rotini, rotelle
   or penne, cooked *al dente*

In a nonstick skillet, sauté ground round, onion, carrot and celery. When meat is nearly cooked, add wine. Cook over medium heat, stirring frequently, until the wine has evaporated. Reduce heat slightly; add milk and nutmeg. Cook, stirring frequently, until the milk has evaporated. Add tomatoes. Reduce heat and simmer 2 hours, stirring occasionally. Serve pasta into bowls. Ladle sauce over pasta.

SERVING SUGGESTION: Serve with green salad tossed with Oil-free Italian Vinaigrette (page 389), Grilled Garlic Bread (page 334) and fresh seasonal fruit.

APPROXIMATE NUTRITIONAL CONTENT PER
¾-CUP SERVING

Total calories: 214
Protein: 17 g
Carbohydrates: 27 g
Cholesterol: 33 mg
Fat: 3 g
Sodium: 40 mg

Percentage of calories from:
Protein: 33%
Carbohydrates: 53%
Fat: 13%

PASTA WITH MARINARA SAUCE

15 servings

1 2-pound can plum tomatoes, diced
2 tablespoons tomato paste
½ teaspoon oregano
½ teaspoon dried basil
½ teaspoon black pepper
1 tablespoon olive oil
¼ teaspoon cider vinegar
1 1-pound package spaghetti, rigatoni, rotini
    or penne pasta, cooked *al dente*

In a medium saucepan, combine tomatoes, tomato paste, oregano, basil and black pepper. Simmer 20 minutes (do not allow to boil). Stir in olive oil and vinegar. Simmer 10 minutes. Serve over pasta.

VARIATION: Add one 8-ounce can drained mushroom stems and pieces and one 15-ounce can drained artichoke hearts.

SERVING SUGGESTION: This is perfect for a quick-to-fix, last-minute meal.

APPROXIMATE NUTRITIONAL CONTENT PER
½ CUP PASTA WITH ⅓ CUP SAUCE

Total calories: 120
Protein: 4 g
Carbohydrates: 23 g
Cholesterol: 0 mg
Fat: 1 g
Sodium: 87 mg

Percentage of calories from:
Protein: 13%
Carbohydrates: 76%
Fat: 10%

ITALIAN MACARONI AND CHEESE

6 servings

   2   cups cubed low-fat Cheddar cheese*
   1   cup skim evaporated milk
   1   tablespoon Dijon mustard
   2½ cups elbow macaroni, cooked *al dente*
   ½   teaspoon dried basil
   1   16-ounce can plum tomatoes with liquid,
         diced
   1   tablespoon bread crumbs

In a medium saucepan, combine cheese, milk and mustard. Cook over low heat, stirring constantly, until cheese melts. Add pasta and mix well. Add basil to tomatoes.

   In an ovenproof baking dish, layer ⅓ of the macaroni and cheese; top with ⅓ of the tomato mixture. Repeat layers, ending with macaroni and cheese but reserving a generous dollop of the tomatoes to put in center of the top layer. Sprinkle with bread crumbs. Bake, covered, at 350°F. 30 minutes, or until mixture is hot and bubbly.

   *To further decrease the sodium level of this recipe, use low-sodium, low-fat Cheddar cheese.

APPROXIMATE NUTRITIONAL CONTENT PER SERVING

Total calories: 285
Protein: 16 g
Carbohydrates: 73 g
Cholesterol: 39 mg
Fat: 11 g
Sodium: 447 mg

Percentage of calories from:
   Protein: 14%
   Carbohydrates: 64%
   Fat: 22%

LINGUINE WITH CLAMS AND ARTICHOKE HEARTS

8 servings

1 2-pound can plum tomatoes, diced
1 tablespoon tomato paste
½ teaspoon oregano
½ teaspoon dried basil or ¼ cup fresh
½ teaspoon black pepper
1 tablespoon olive oil
¼ teaspoon cider vinegar
¾ pound fresh mushrooms, thinly sliced
2 15-ounce cans artichoke hearts, drained
3 pounds clams, soaked, cleaned and
  steamed (see page 409)*
1 1-pound package linguine, cooked *al
  dente*
¼ cup finely chopped fresh parsley

In a stock pot, combine tomatoes, tomato paste, oregano, basil, black pepper, olive oil and vinegar. Heat just to boiling (do not boil). Reduce heat and simmer, uncovered, 30 minutes. Add mushrooms and simmer 10 minutes. Add artichoke hearts and clams. Heat. Divide pasta into bowls. Ladle sauce over pasta. Sprinkle with parsley.

*For a quick-to-fix meal, substitute three 6½-ounce cans chopped clams for the fresh clams. Remember that using canned clams instead of fresh will increase the sodium substantially.

APPROXIMATE NUTRITIONAL CONTENT PER SERVING

Total calories: 329	*Percentage of calories from:*
Protein: 19 g	Protein: 23%
Carbohydrates: 53 g	Carbohydrates: 63%
Cholesterol: 77 mg	Fat: 14%
Fat: 5 g	
Sodium: 315 mg	

SEAFOOD FETTUCCINE

8 servings

½ pound clams in shells, soaked and cleaned (see page 409)
½ pound mussels in shells, soaked and cleaned (see page 409)
½ pound scallops
½ pound orange roughy or other whitefish
½ pound squid tubes, cut into ⅓-inch rings
4 cups Chicken Stock (page 350)
¼ cup arrowroot dissolved in ½ cup water
1 pound fettuccine, cooked *al dente*
¼ pound crab legs for garnish

Place clams and mussels on rack in steamer with 2 cups water. Cover tightly and steam 5–10 minutes, or just until first shells begin to open. Add scallops and orange roughy. Cover and steam 2 minutes. Add squid tubes and steam 2–3 minutes, or just until scallops, orange roughy and squid are cooked and most clams and mussels have opened. Remove from steamer and set aside.

Bring chicken stock to a boil. Gradually add arrowroot to stock, stirring constantly until stock thickens, about 2–3 minutes. Toss fettuccine with ½ of the stock. Arrange in shallow pasta bowl. Arrange clams, mussels, scallops, orange roughy and squid over fettuccine. Garnish with crablegs. Pour remaining stock over top.

APPROXIMATE NUTRITIONAL CONTENT PER SERVING

Total calories: 298
Protein: 25 g
Carbohydrates: 41 g
Cholesterol: 24 mg
Fat: 3 g
Sodium: 363 mg

Percentage of calories from:
Protein: 34%
Carbohydrates: 57%
Fat: 10%

SEAFOOD LINGUINE WITH PESTO

8 servings

1   pound linguine
¼   cup dry white wine, vermouth or broth
½   pound orange roughy, halibut, red snapper
     or other whitefish, cut into 2-inch pieces
½   pound scallops, poached (see page 417)
1   cup Pesto (page 402)
½   pound clams in shells, steamed
     (see page 409)
½   pound mussels in shells, steamed
     (see page 409)
⅓   cup freshly grated Parmesan cheese

Cook linguine; set aside. In a nonstick skillet, heat wine, vermouth or broth. Add whitefish and scallops. Cover and poach 4–6 minutes, or until done.

Toss linguine with pesto. Arrange in a shallow paella-type dish. Garnish with seafood and sprinkle with Parmesan cheese.

APPROXIMATE NUTRITIONAL CONTENT PER SERVING

Total calories: 379
Protein: 24 g
Carbohydrates: 46 g
Cholesterol: 44 mg
Fat: 13 g
Sodium: 277 mg

Percentage of calories from:
  Protein: 24%
  Carbohydrates: 47%
  Fat: 29%

SCALLOP-AND-PESTO FETTUCCINE

8 servings

> 3   tablespoons dry white wine
> 1   pound fresh scallops
> 1   pound fettuccine, cooked *al dente*
> 1   cup Pesto (page 402)
> 2   ripe tomatoes, diced
> ½   cup freshly grated Parmesan cheese

In a nonstick skillet, heat wine. Add scallops. Cover and poach 5–6 minutes, or until scallops are tender. Turn fettuccine into a shallow pasta bowl. Toss with pesto. Add scallops, tomatoes and cheese. Toss.

SERVING SUGGESTION: Serve with crudités, hearts of romaine with fresh lemon juice, crusty French bread and fresh fruit.

APPROXIMATE NUTRITIONAL CONTENT PER SERVING

Total calories: 383
Protein: 24 g
Carbohydrates: 48 g
Cholesterol: 34 mg
Fat: 12 g
Sodium: 360 mg

Percentage of calories from:
  Protein: 24%
  Carbohydrates: 48%
  Fat: 28%

CHILI CON CARNE

2 quarts

1   28-ounce can plum tomatoes,* diced
2   tablespoons cider vinegar
1   tablespoon pure ground mild chili
      powder**
1/8 teaspoon ground cumin
1/8 teaspoon cayenne pepper
1/8 teaspoon black pepper
1/8 teaspoon oregano
1/2 teaspoon paprika
1/2 teaspoon salt
1   pound extra-lean ground round, browned
      and drained
2   15-ounce cans red kidney beans with
      liquid*

In a saucepan, combine tomatoes, vinegar and seasonings. Heat to boiling (do not boil). Add ground beef. Simmer, uncovered, 45 minutes. Add kidney beans. Heat.

*To further decrease the sodium level of this recipe, use salt-free or low-sodium canned tomatoes and substitute homemade Red Kidney Beans (see page 504).

**Take the time to search for a Spanish or Mexican market or a supermarket that carries pure ground chili powder. Pure ground chili powder is made by grinding dried chilies, and the flavor is far superior to that of commercial chili powder—which is most often 40% salt and 20% additives.

SERVING SUGGESTION: Double the recipe and serve the leftovers in Pasta e Fagioli (below).

Chili tends to be high in sodium. Keep this in mind and serve with low-sodium accompaniments.

Serve chili with zucchini, carrots, celery and cucumber

crudités for dipping in the chili. Accompany with Steamed Tortillas (page 341) and chilled watermelon or fresh seasonal fruit.

APPROXIMATE NUTRITIONAL CONTENT PER CUP OF CHILI CON CARNE

Total calories: 247
Protein: 23 g
Carbohydrates: 23 g
Cholesterol: 49 mg
Fat: 7 g
Sodium: 720 mg

Percentage of calories from:
Protein: 37%
Carbohydrates: 37%
Fat: 26%

PASTA E FAGIOLI

2 servings

⅓   1-pound package shell-shaped pasta, cooked *al dente*
4   cups Chili con Carne (above), warmed

Divide pasta into bowls. Ladle chili over top.

APPROXIMATE NUTRITIONAL CONTENT PER CUP

Total calories: 298
Protein: 18 g
Carbohydrates: 40 g
Cholesterol: 33 mg
Fat: 8 g
Sodium: 338 mg

Percentage of calories from:
Protein: 24%
Carbohydrates: 52%
Fat: 24%

VEGETABLES

ARTICHOKE FRITTATA

8 servings

2   eggs
3   egg whites
1   15-ounce can artichoke hearts, drained
      and cut into quarters
¾   cup grated part-skim Cheddar cheese

In a bowl, lightly beat eggs and egg whites. Stir in artichokes and cheese. Pour into a 9-inch quiche or pie plate.
Bake at 350°F. 45–60 minutes, or until eggs are set and
cheese is melted. Cut into wedges. Serve hot.

APPROXIMATE NUTRITIONAL CONTENT PER SERVING

Total calories: 91   *Percentage of calories from:*
Protein: 7 g   Protein: 20%
Carbohydrates: 18 g   Carbohydrates: 51%
Cholesterol: 79 mg   Fat: 29%
Fat: 7 g
Sodium: 128 mg

VERMICELLI-STUFFED ARTICHOKES

4 servings

> 4   fresh artichokes, cooked
> ½   pound vermicelli, cooked *al dente*
> 1   ripe tomato, diced
> ⅓   cup Pesto (page 402)

Remove small center leaves of each artichoke, leaving a cup; carefully remove choke. In a bowl, toss vermicelli with tomato and pesto; stuff artichokes.

SERVING SUGGESTION: The calories are high. Serve with a low-calorie entrée such as Pan-fried or Poached Scallops (pages 416–417). Accompany with sliced or grilled tomatoes and fresh fruit.

APPROXIMATE NUTRITIONAL CONTENT PER SERVING

Total calories: 265
Protein: 9 g
Carbohydrates: 47 g
Cholesterol: 0 mg
Fat: 7 g
Sodium: 92 mg

Percentage of calories from:
  Protein: 13%
  Carbohydrates: 65%
  Fat: 22%

PAN-STEAMED ASPARAGUS

4 servings

½ pound fresh asparagus, trimmed
2 tablespoons water
1 fresh lemon, cut into wedges

Wash and trim asparagus. In a nonstick skillet, heat water to boiling. Add asparagus spears. Cover tightly and steam over medium-high heat 3–5 minutes, or until asparagus is crisp-tender. Shake occasionally. Serve with lemon.

APPROXIMATE NUTRITIONAL CONTENT PER SERVING

Total calories: 16
Protein: 1 g
Carbohydrates: 3 g
Cholesterol: 0 mg
Fat: Tr
Sodium: 2 g

Percentage of calories from:
Protein: 30%
Carbohydrates: 61%
Fat: 9%

GREEN BEANS WITH LEMON

4 servings

1 pound fresh green beans
¼ cup fresh lemon juice
¼ teaspoon black pepper
½ teaspoon or less salt (optional)

Wash beans; remove ends and strings. In a covered vegetable steamer basket over boiling water, steam beans 5–15 minutes (depending on freshness of beans), or until just tender (do not overcook). Combine lemon juice, black pepper and salt, and pour over beans while beans are still hot.

APPROXIMATE NUTRITIONAL CONTENT PER SERVING
OF GREEN BEANS WITH LEMON

Total calories: 40
Protein: 2 g
Carbohydrates: 9 g
Cholesterol: 0 mg
Fat: Tr
Sodium: 280 mg

Percentage of calories from:
Protein: 18%
Carbohydrates: 77%
Fat: 4%

GREEN BEANS WITH TOMATOES AND PEPPERS

8 servings

1 pound fresh green beans
1 red pepper, cut into ¹/₂-inch julienne strips
¹/₂ cup chopped red onion
1 16-ounce can plum tomatoes, chopped
¹/₄ teaspoon black pepper

Wash green beans; remove ends and strings. In a medium saucepan, combine ingredients and heat to boiling (do not boil). Cover. Reduce heat and simmer 10–30 minutes, or until beans are tender.

APPROXIMATE NUTRITIONAL CONTENT PER SERVING

Total calories: 41
Protein: 3 g
Carbohydrates: 6 g
Cholesterol: 0 mg
Fat: Tr
Sodium: 15 mg

Percentage of calories from:
Protein: 20%
Carbohydrates: 74%
Fat: 7%

RED BEETS VINAIGRETTE

4 servings

4 medium-to-large beets
⅓ cup raspberry vinegar
   black pepper to taste

Wash beets; trim stems and roots. Cut into julienne strips. In a covered vegetable steamer basket over boiling water, steam beets 10-20 minutes, or until barely tender. Remove to serving bowl. While beets are still hot, toss with raspberry vinegar. Season with pepper.

VARIATION: While beets are still hot, toss with raspberry vinegar and 2 tablespoons walnut oil. (Walnut oil will increase the calories by 125 per tablespoon.)

APPROXIMATE NUTRITIONAL CONTENT PER SERVING

Total calories: 25
Protein: Tr
Carbohydrates: 6 g
Cholesterol: 0 mg
Fat: Tr
Sodium: 28 mg

Percentage of calories from:
  Protein: 14%
  Carbohydrates: 83%
  Fat: 3%

BABY CARROTS VINAIGRETTE

4 servings

12 baby carrots
2 tablespoons raspberry vinegar
black pepper

Select the smallest, bite-size carrots available. (If necessary, ask your greengrocer to special order them.) In a covered vegetable steamer basket over boiling water, steam carrots 3–4 minutes, or just until crisp-tender. Remove to serving bowl. While carrots are still hot, toss with raspberry vinegar. Season generously with black pepper.

VARIATION: Serve cold as part of an antipasto tray.

APPROXIMATE NUTRITIONAL CONTENT PER SERVING

Total calories: 25
Protein: Tr
Carbohydrates: 6 g
Cholesterol: 0 mg
Fat: Tr
Sodium: 28 mg

Percentage of calories from:
Protein: 14%
Carbohydrates: 83%
Fat: 3%

STIR-FRIED BROCCOLI

4 servings

1 bunch broccoli
1 tablespoon olive oil
  juice of 1 lemon
2 drops hot chili oil (LaYu)*
  black pepper to taste

Cut broccoli into florets. Peel stalks; cut into 1-inch pieces. In a covered vegetable steamer basket over boiling water, steam broccoli 1 minute.

In a nonstick skillet, heat olive oil. Add broccoli and stir-fry 2–3 minutes, or until crisp-tender. Squeeze lemon juice over broccoli. Toss with chili oil and black pepper.

*Hot chili oil is available in Oriental markets, if not in your supermarket.

VARIATION: Substitute cauliflower for broccoli.

SERVING SUGGESTION: The olive oil increases calories and fat. Keep this in mind when planning the remainder of the meal.

APPROXIMATE NUTRITIONAL CONTENT PER SERVING

Total calories: 71
Protein: 6 g
Carbohydrates: 7 g
Cholesterol: 0 mg
Fat: 3 g
Sodium: 35 mg

Percentage of calories from:
Protein: 29%
Carbohydrates: 35%
Fat: 36%

BROCCOLI WITH LEMON MUSTARD SAUCE

4 servings

1 bunch fresh broccoli, florets only
1 cup fresh lemon juice
1 tablespoon Dijon mustard

In a covered vegetable steamer basket over boiling water, steam broccoli 2–3 minutes, or until crisp-tender. Combine lemon juice with Dijon mustard and warm over low heat. Pour over broccoli. Toss and serve at once.

VARIATIONS: Substitute fresh asparagus or cauliflower for broccoli.

APPROXIMATE NUTRITIONAL CONTENT PER SERVING

Total calories: 35
Protein: 3 g
Carbohydrates: 8 g
Cholesterol: 0 mg
Fat: Tr
Sodium: 59 mg

Percentage of calories from:
Protein: 20%
Carbohydrates: 62%
Fat: 18%

PASTA WITH EGGPLANT

15 servings

1	large eggplant
½	teaspoon olive oil
8–10	fresh mushrooms, sliced
4	cups warm Marinara Sauce (page 403)
1	1-pound package heavy-type pasta (such as penne or rigatoni), cooked *al dente*
	dash salt (optional)
	black pepper to taste
1	teaspoon crushed red pepper (optional)

Slice unpeeled eggplant lengthwise into strips, French-fry style. In a nonstick skillet over medium heat, heat olive oil. Add eggplant and sauté 15 minutes. Add mushrooms and sauté 10 minutes, or until eggplant is done. Pour sauce over pasta. Toss with eggplant and mushrooms. Season. Sprinkle with crushed red pepper, if desired.

VARIATION: Omit crushed red pepper. Toss with ½ cup freshly grated Parmesan cheese.

SERVING SUGGESTION: This is a good side dish with roast lamb or chicken.

APPROXIMATE NUTRITIONAL CONTENT PER ½-CUP SERVING

Total calories: 120
Protein: 4 g
Carbohydrates: 23 g
Cholesterol: 0 mg
Fat: 1 g
Sodium: 230 mg

Percentage of calories from:
Protein: 14%
Carbohydrates: 74%
Fat: 12%

MARINATED MUSHROOMS

6 cups

  1½ pounds fresh mushrooms
   2   cups Chicken Stock (page 350)
   1   cup rice vinegar

Wipe mushrooms with a damp paper towel. Trim stems. In a small stock pot, combine mushrooms with stock. Cook over medium heat, stirring frequently, 20–30 minutes. Remove from heat. Allow mushrooms to cool in the broth. Drain. Toss with rice vinegar. Serve or refrigerate for later use.

VARIATION: Substitute 1 head of cauliflower (florets only) for mushrooms. Cook 3–4 minutes.

SERVING SUGGESTION: Marinated mushrooms, cauliflower and artichoke hearts are nice additions to an antipasto or vegetable platter.

APPROXIMATE NUTRITIONAL CONTENT PER ½-CUP SERVING

Total calories: 21
Protein: 2 g
Carbohydrates: 4 g
Cholesterol: Tr
Fat: Tr
Sodium: 51 mg

Percentage of calories from:
  Protein: 31%
  Carbohydrates: 54%
  Fat: 14%

MARINATED MUSHROOMS WITH ARTICHOKE HEARTS

10 cups

1½ pounds fresh mushrooms
2½ cups Chicken Stock (page 350)
1–2 15-ounce cans artichoke hearts, drained
1½ cups rice vinegar

Wipe mushrooms with a damp paper towel. Trim stems. In a small stock pot, combine mushrooms with stock. Cook over medium heat, stirring frequently, 20–30 minutes. Add artichoke hearts. Cook 10 minutes. Remove from heat. Allow mushrooms and artichokes to cool in broth. Drain. Toss with rice vinegar. Serve or refrigerate for later use.

SERVING SUGGESTION: Good as an antipasto or salad course, as part of a dinner buffet or with sandwiches on a picnic.

APPROXIMATE NUTRITIONAL CONTENT PER CUP

Total calories: 45
Protein: 4 g
Carbohydrates: 9 g
Cholesterol: Tr
Fat: 1 g
Sodium: 103 mg

Percentage of calories from:
Protein: 27%
Carbohydrates: 62%
Fat: 11%

ROAST POTATOES WITH ROSEMARY

4 servings

4   new potatoes, scrubbed and halved
2   teaspoons olive oil
    garlic powder
    powdered rosemary
    black pepper
¼   cup water

Brush potatoes with olive oil. Sprinkle with garlic powder, rosemary and black pepper. Arrange cut side up in shallow roasting pan. Pour ¼ cup water in bottom of pan. Roast at 375°F. 40–60 minutes, or until tender.

APPROXIMATE NUTRITIONAL CONTENT PER POTATO

Total calories: 129
Protein: 3 g
Carbohydrates: 25 g
Cholesterol: 0 mg
Fat: 2 g
Sodium: 4 mg

Percentage of calories from:
  Protein: 9%
  Carbohydrates: 74%
  Fat: 16%

PAN-FRIED POTATOES

4 servings

1 ½ tablespoons olive oil
3 large baking potatoes, unpeeled and diced
    or thinly sliced
    black pepper to taste

In a nonstick skillet, heat oil. Add potatoes. Cook over medium heat, stirring frequently, 10–15 minutes. Cover and cook 20–30 minutes, turning frequently. Remove lid. Cook 10–15 minutes, or until nicely browned. Sprinkle with black pepper.

SERVING SUGGESTION: The olive oil increases calories from fat. Keep this in mind and allow for it when planning the remainder of the meal.

APPROXIMATE NUTRITIONAL CONTENT PER
1-CUP SERVING

Total calories: 122
Protein: Tr
Carbohydrates: 23 g
Cholesterol: 0 mg
Fat: Tr
Sodium: Tr

Percentage of calories from:
Protein: 8%
Carbohydrates: 63%
Fat: 30%

STEAMED RED POTATOES

4 servings

8   bite-size red potatoes*

Select the smallest, most uniform bite-size (not dinner-size) red potatoes available. Scrub. In a covered vegetable steamer basket over boiling water, steam potatoes 15–20 minutes, or until just tender.

*You may want to phone your greengrocer and order potatoes in advance; many produce departments do not stock the tiny variety.

VARIATION: Chill. Toss with 1 red pepper that has been cut into julienne strips. Serve as a salad.

APPROXIMATE NUTRITIONAL CONTENT PER
2 BITE-SIZE POTATOES

Total calories: 99
Protein: 2 g
Carbohydrates: 23 g
Cholesterol: 0 mg
Fat: Tr
Sodium: 5 mg

Percentage of calories from:
Protein: 8%
Carbohydrates: 91%
Fat: 1%

STEAMED RED POTATOES VINAIGRETTE

4 servings

8	bite-size red potatoes
1½	tablespoons olive oil
¼	cup fresh lemon juice
¼	teaspoon black pepper
½	teaspoon or less salt (optional)

Select the smallest, most uniform bite-size (not dinner-size) red potatoes available. Scrub. In a covered vegetable steamer basket over boiling water, steam potatoes 15–20 minutes, or until just tender. Remove potatoes to serving bowl. Combine oil, lemon juice, pepper and salt. Pour over potatoes while potatoes are still hot.

VARIATION: Chill. Serve as a salad garnished with 1 red pepper that has been cut into julienne strips.

SERVING SUGGESTION: The olive oil increases calories from fat. Keep this in mind and allow for it when planning the remainder of the meal.

APPROXIMATE NUTRITIONAL CONTENT PER 2 BITE-SIZE POTATOES

Total calories: 122
Protein: Tr
Carbohydrates: 23 g
Cholesterol: 0 mg
Fat: Tr
Sodium: 290 mg

Percentage of calories from:
Protein: 8%
Carbohydrates: 63%
Fat: 30%

LEMON-STEAMED SPINACH

4 servings

    juice of ½ lemon
2 bunches fresh spinach, washed and
    trimmed

In a wok or heavy skillet, warm lemon juice. Add spinach. Cover and cook 3–5 minutes, or just until spinach begins to wilt. Serve at once.

APPROXIMATE NUTRITIONAL CONTENT PER ½-CUP SERVING

Total calories: 21
Protein: 2 g
Carbohydrates: 3 g
Cholesterol: 0 mg
Fat: Tr
Sodium: 47 mg

Percentage of calories from:
  Protein: 38%
  Carbohydrates: 53%
  Fat: 9%

STEAMED SNOW PEAS

4 servings

>   1   pound snow peas
> ¼   cup Chicken Stock (page 350)

Snap ends of snow peas and remove strings. Heat stock in a wok; stir in snow peas. Cover and cook 2–3 minutes, or until peas are deep green and crisp-tender.

VARIATION: In a covered vegetable steamer basket over boiling water, steam snow peas 2–3 minutes, or until crisp-tender.

APPROXIMATE NUTRITIONAL CONTENT PER SERVING

Total calories: 51
Protein: 3 g
Carbohydrates: 19 g
Cholesterol: Tr
Fat: Tr
Sodium: 18 mg

Percentage of calories from:
Protein: 24%
Carbohydrates: 72%
Fat: 4%

TOMATOES STUFFED WITH SNOW PEAS

4 servings

>   4   ripe tomatoes
> ¾   pound snow peas

Cut tops from tomatoes. Using a curved grapefruit knife, hollow centers. Stand tomatoes upside down to drain.

In a covered vegetable steamer basket over boiling water, steam snow peas 1–2 minutes, or until crisp-tender. Drain. Arrange vertically in tomato shells.

VARIATIONS: Hollow cherry tomatoes from each end.

Thread 3–4 snow peas through center of each tomato.
Substitute steamed green beans for snow peas.

**APPROXIMATE NUTRITIONAL CONTENT PER SERVING
OF TOMATOES STUFFED WITH SNOW PEAS**

Total calories: 61

Protein: 3 g

Carbohydrates: 14 g

Cholesterol: 0 mg

Fat: Tr

Sodium: 15 mg

Percentage of calories from:

Protein: 19%

Carbohydrates: 77%

Fat: 5%

GRILLED TOMATOES

4 servings

2   ripe tomatoes

Cook tomatoes in microwave or in boiling water 30 seconds. Slice in half, lengthwise.

Prepare coals. Cover grill grid with foil. Grill tomatoes,
cut side down, over hot coals, 4–5 minutes.

**APPROXIMATE NUTRITIONAL CONTENT PER
½ TOMATO**

Total calories: 15

Protein: 1 g

Carbohydrates: 7 g

Cholesterol: 0 mg

Fat: 0 g

Sodium: 5 mg

Percentage of calories from:

Protein: 18%

Carbohydrates: 76%

Fat: 4%

VERMICELLI-STUFFED TOMATOES

4 servings

8   large ripe tomatoes
½   pound vermicelli, cooked *al dente*
½   cup Pesto (page 402)
     fresh basil, for garnish

Cut tops from tomatoes. Using a curved knife, hollow centers. Stand tomatoes upside down to drain. Toss vermicelli with pesto and spoon into centers of tomatoes. Garnish with fresh basil.

SERVING SUGGESTION: The calories and fat are high in this dish. Keep the remainder of the menu low in calories and fat.

APPROXIMATE NUTRITIONAL CONTENT PER SERVING

Total calories: 170
Protein: 6 g
Carbohydrates: 29 g
Cholesterol: 0 mg
Fat: 5 g
Sodium: 71 mg

Percentage of calories from:
Protein: 12%
Carbohydrates: 62%
Fat: 26%

GRILLED ZUCCHINI

4 servings

4   small zucchini

Cook zucchini in microwave or in boiling water 2 minutes. Slice in half lengthwise.

Prepare coals. Cover grill grid with foil. Grill zucchini skin side up over hot coals, 4–5 minutes.

APPROXIMATE NUTRITIONAL CONTENT PER SERVING OF GRILLED ZUCCHINI

Total calories: 16
Protein: 1 g
Carbohydrates: 3 g
Cholesterol: 0 mg
Fat: Tr
Sodium: 3 mg

Percentage of calories from:
Protein: 21%
Carbohydrates: 73%
Fat: 5%

ZUCCHINI WITH GARLIC AND TOMATOES

6 servings

  1 16-ounce can plum tomatoes, diced
  ½ medium yellow onion, chopped
  2 cloves garlic, minced
  3 small zucchini, sliced ½ inch thick
  2 tablespoons chopped fresh parsley
  ½ teaspoon dried basil or 4–6 leaves fresh

In a medium saucepan, simmer tomatoes, onion and garlic 30–45 minutes. Add sliced zucchini; simmer 15–20 minutes, or just until zucchini begin to soften but are still crisp-tender. Sprinkle with parsley and basil.

APPROXIMATE NUTRITIONAL CONTENT PER ½-CUP SERVING

Total calories: 38
Protein: 2 g
Carbohydrates: 8 g
Cholesterol: 0 mg
Fat: 0 g
Sodium: 127 mg

Percentage of calories from:
Protein: 19%
Carbohydrates: 75%
Fat: 6%

ZUCCHINI WITH ONIONS AND TOMATOES

10 servings

1   large white onion, chopped
3   cloves garlic, peeled
¾   cup white wine
1   16-ounce can plum tomatoes, diced
1   cup Chicken Stock (page 350)
⅛   teaspoon thyme
⅛   teaspoon oregano
⅛   teaspoon marjoram
¼   teaspoon dried basil
¼   teaspoon black pepper
3   medium zucchini, thinly sliced

In a nonstick skillet, sauté onion and garlic in ½ cup white wine, just until onions begin to soften.

In a saucepan, combine remaining ¼ cup wine with tomatoes, stock, thyme, oregano, marjoram, basil and black pepper. Bring to a boil; reduce heat to simmer. Add onions, garlic and zucchini. Cover partially with lid. Simmer 30 minutes.

APPROXIMATE NUTRITIONAL CONTENT PER
½-CUP SERVING

Total calories: 40
Protein: 2 g
Carbohydrates: 6 g
Cholesterol: Tr
Fat: Tr
Sodium: 105 mg

Percentage of calories from:
Protein: 21%
Carbohydrates: 71%
Fat: 8%

GRILLED VEGETABLES

8 servings

1   large white onion
2   small pattypan squash or zucchini
1   summer squash
8   bite-size (not dinner-size) red potatoes
8   large fresh mushrooms
1   Japanese eggplant
1   zucchini
1   red pepper
1   green pepper
4   hot peppers
8   cherry tomatoes
    Horseradish Sauce (page 402)

In a 6-quart stock pot, bring 4 quarts water to a boil. Add onion, squash and potatoes. Cook 5–6 minutes. Add mushrooms, eggplant, zucchini and peppers. Cook 2–3 minutes. Remove vegetables to colander to drain as they are cooked.

Cut onion, squash, eggplant and peppers into 2-inch cubes. Alternate on skewers with whole mushrooms and cherry tomatoes.

Prepare coals. Grill vegetables over hot coals 12–15 minutes. Arrange on serving platter. Serve with Horseradish Sauce.

APPROXIMATE NUTRITIONAL CONTENT PER SERVING WITHOUT SAUCE

Total calories: 83
Protein: 3 g
Carbohydrates: 18 g
Cholesterol: 0 mg
Fat: Tr
Sodium: 13 mg

Percentage of calories from:
Protein: 15%
Carbohydrates: 81%
Fat: 4%

Add 7 calories per tablespoon of Horseradish Sauce.

CHINESE VEGETABLE STIR-FRY

6 servings

2   cups Chicken Stock (page 350)
1   8-ounce package buckwheat (Soba) noodles
1/2 teaspoon sesame oil
2–3 drops hot chili oil (LaYu)*
8–10 fresh black forest (Shiitake) mushrooms*
1   8-ounce can sliced water chestnuts
1   green pepper, cut into julienne strips
1   bunch fresh asparagus, steamed until crisp-tender
10   cherry tomatoes, halved
1/4 cup reduced-sodium soy sauce
2   tablespoons rice vinegar

In a saucepan, heat stock just to boiling (do not boil). Add noodles and cook 3–4 minutes, or until tender. Drain. Set aside. (Reserve broth for soup or later use.)

In a wok or heavy skillet, heat sesame oil and chili oil. Add Shiitake mushrooms and stir-fry 4–5 minutes. Add water chestnuts and green pepper and stir-fry 2–3 minutes. Toss with noodles, asparagus and tomatoes. Combine soy sauce with rice vinegar. Pour over noodles and vegetables. Toss.

APPROXIMATE NUTRITIONAL CONTENT PER SERVING

Total calories: 98
Protein: 6 g
Carbohydrates: 18 g
Cholesterol: Tr
Fat: 1 g
Sodium: 320 mg

Percentage of calories from:
Protein: 25%
Carbohydrates: 67%
Fat: 9%

GRAIN, BEAN & PASTA SIDE DISHES

WILD RICE

5 servings

- 1 cup uncooked wild rice
- 4 cups Chicken Stock (page 350)
- 7 large fresh mushrooms, thinly sliced
- 2 tablespoons finely chopped fresh parsley
- 1/2 ripe tomato, diced

Pour rice into a 6-quart saucepan. Cover with hot water; soak 1/2 hour. Drain. Add stock and heat to boiling (do not boil). Reduce heat. Cover and simmer 45 minutes. Stir in mushrooms. Remove from heat. Let stand 15 minutes. Stir in parsley and tomatoes.

APPROXIMATE NUTRITIONAL CONTENT PER
2/3-CUP SERVING

Total calories: 131
Protein: 7 g
Carbohydrates: 23 g
Cholesterol: 1 mg
Fat: 1 g
Sodium: 162 mg

Percentage of calories from:
Protein: 23%
Carbohydrates: 71%
Fat: 6%

WILD RICE STUFFING

6 servings

½   medium yellow onion, chopped
3   stalks celery, chopped
½–¾   cup Chicken Stock (page 350)
8   fresh mushrooms, thinly sliced
2   cups bread cubes
¾   teaspoon sage
¾   teaspoon black pepper
¼   teaspoon salt
¾   cup precooked Wild Rice (page 497)
1   6½-ounce can sliced water chestnuts

In a skillet, sauté onion and celery in small amount of stock until tender. Add mushrooms. Sauté 3 minutes. Add bread cubes. Toss. Gradually add remaining stock, a little less or a little more as needed to moisten. Season with sage, pepper and salt. Add rice and water chestnuts. Toss. Bake, covered, at 350°F. 30–35 minutes, or until hot.

APPROXIMATE NUTRITIONAL CONTENT PER SERVING

Total calories: 104
Protein: 5 g
Carbohydrates: 10 g
Cholesterol: Tr
Fat: 1 g
Sodium: 288 mg

Percentage of calories from:
Protein: 17%
Carbohydrates: 72%
Fat: 11%

STEAMED ORIENTAL RICE

4 servings

> 1   cup uncooked Oriental-style white rice*
> 1½ cups water

Pour rice into a medium saucepan. Rinse with fresh water 2–3 times, or until water runs clear. After the final rinse, drain as much water as possible (it is not necessary to drain every drop). Cover with 1½ cups fresh water. Bring to a boil uncovered. Reduce heat to low. Cover and cook 15–20 minutes, or until moisture is absorbed and rice is fluffy. Remove from heat. Let stand 5 minutes.

*We like the sticky rice served in Chinese restaurants. Our favorite brand is available in Oriental markets and some supermarkets. It is called Kokuho Rose No Talc Extra Fancy Rice.

APPROXIMATE NUTRITIONAL CONTENT PER ⅔-CUP SERVING

Total calories: 120
Protein: 3 g
Carbohydrates: 37 g
Cholesterol: 0 mg
Fat: Tr
Sodium: 2 mg

Percentage of calories from:
  Protein: 8%
  Carbohydrates: 91%
  Fat: 1%

SAFFRON RICE

4 servings

   1   cup uncooked Oriental-style white rice
1½   cups Chicken Stock (page 350)
  ½   white onion, diced
  ¼   teaspoon saffron powder

Pour rice into a medium saucepan. Rinse with fresh water 2–3 times, or until water runs clear. After the final rinse, drain as much water as possible (it is not necessary to drain every drop). Bring rice, stock and onion to a boil. Reduce heat to low. Add saffron powder. Cover and cook 15–10 minutes, or until moisture is absorbed and rice is fluffy. Remove from heat. Let stand 5 minutes.

APPROXIMATE NUTRITIONAL CONTENT PER ⅔-CUP SERVING

Total calories: 127
Protein: 3 g
Carbohydrates: 39 g
Cholesterol: Tr
Fat: 1 g
Sodium: 89 mg

Percentage of calories from:
  Protein: 11%
  Carbohydrates: 86%
  Fat: 3%

BROWN RICE WITH MUSHROOMS

5 servings

   1   cup uncooked short-grain California
       brown rice
2½   cups water
 10   fresh mushrooms, thinly sliced
       salt and black pepper to taste

In a medium saucepan, bring rice and water to a boil. Reduce heat to low. Cover and cook 30–40 minutes, or until most of the water has evaporated. Quickly lift lid and sprinkle mushrooms over top of rice (do not stir). Replace lid. Cook 10–15 minutes, or until rice is tender and moisture is absorbed. Remove from heat. Let stand 5–10 minutes. Toss mushrooms with rice. Season.

APPROXIMATE NUTRITIONAL CONTENT PER
²/₃-CUP SERVING OF BROWN RICE WITH MUSHROOMS

Total calories: 139
Protein: 3 g
Carbohydrates: 30 g
Cholesterol: 0 mg
Fat: Tr
Sodium: 116 mg

Percentage of calories from:
  Protein: 10%
  Carbohydrates: 84%
  Fat: 6%

COUSCOUS

4 servings

     2   cups Chicken Stock (page 350)
    ¹/₂ cup chopped yellow onion
     1   cup uncooked couscous

In a medium saucepan, bring stock to a boil. Add onion and couscous. Cover and remove from heat. Let stand 5 minutes.

APPROXIMATE NUTRITIONAL CONTENT PER
²/₃-CUP SERVING

Total calories: 112
Protein: 6 g
Carbohydrates: 20 g
Cholesterol: Tr
Fat: 1 g
Sodium: 140 mg

Percentage of calories from:
  Protein: 21%
  Carbohydrates: 72%
  Fat: 7%

ITALIAN RISOTTO

6 servings

>   1   tablespoon olive oil
>   4   cups Chicken Stock (page 350)
>   ½   cup chopped yellow onion
>   ½   cup chopped leek
>   ½   cup imported Italian rice (risotto)*
>   pinch saffron

In a nonstick skillet, heat olive oil and 2 tablespoons of the stock. Add onion and leek, and sauté over low heat until barely tender. Add rice. Brown, stirring often, until rice is toasted and begins to puff.

Warm remaining stock and gradually add to rice (about ½ cup at a time), stirring constantly. Add a pinch saffron. Simmer, uncovered, 20–30 minutes, or until moisture is absorbed and rice is tender.

*Italian rice (risotto) is available in Italian markets.

VARIATION: During the last 10 minutes of cooking, add asparagus tips or sliced mushrooms or ¼ cup grated part-skim mozzarella cheese.

APPROXIMATE NUTRITIONAL CONTENT PER
⅔-CUP SERVING

Total calories: 135
Protein: 7 g
Carbohydrates: 40 g
Cholesterol: 1 mg
Fat: 2 g
Sodium: 188 mg

Percentage of calories from:
  Protein: 12%
  Carbohydrates: 74%
  Fat: 14%

ALA PILAF WITH TOMATOES AND PARSLEY

6 servings

2½ cups Chicken Stock (page 350)
½ medium white onion, chopped
1 cup uncooked ala cracked wheat bulgur
1 teaspoon fresh lemon juice
¼ teaspoon salt
¼ teaspoon black pepper
½ teaspoon dried thyme or 1½ teaspoons finely chopped fresh
1 large ripe tomato, diced
½ cup coarsely chopped fresh parsley

In a heavy skillet, heat ½ cup of stock. Add onion and sauté 5 minutes. Stir in ala. Cook, stirring, 5 minutes, or until ala is browned. Add remaining stock. Cover and simmer 15 minutes, or until liquid is absorbed and ala is tender. Just before serving, stir in lemon juice, seasonings, tomatoes and parsley.

APPROXIMATE NUTRITIONAL CONTENT PER ⅔-CUP SERVING

Total calories: 126
Protein: 6 g
Carbohydrates: 24 g
Cholesterol: Tr
Fat: 1 g
Sodium: 213 mg

Percentage of calories from:
  Protein: 18%
  Carbohydrates: 75%
  Fat: 7%

RED KIDNEY BEANS

2³/₄ quarts (11¹/₂ cups)

- 1 pound dry red kidney or pinto beans
- 2 stalks celery
- 1 large yellow onion, quartered
- 2 cloves garlic, peeled
- 1 teaspoon salt

Thoroughly wash beans. Drain. In a small stock pot, combine beans with 2 quarts water. Cover and bring to a boil. Remove from heat. Set aside 1 hour. Drain.

Return beans to stock pot with 2 quarts fresh water, celery, onion and garlic. Cook 20 minutes. Add salt. Cook 15 minutes, or until beans are tender. Drain. Discard celery, onion and garlic.

VARIATION: Thoroughly wash beans. Drain. Cover beans and soak overnight in 2 quarts water. Drain. Cook according to instructions in preceding paragraph.

SERVING SUGGESTIONS: Serve as a vegetable side dish with onions or as a base for chili, refried beans or red bean dip.

APPROXIMATE NUTRITIONAL CONTENT PER
¹/₂-CUP SERVING

Total calories: 110
Protein: 7 g
Carbohydrates: 20 g
Cholesterol: 0 mg
Fat: Tr
Sodium: 213 mg

Percentage of calories from:
Protein: 25%
Carbohydrates: 71%
Fat: 4%

REFRIED BEANS

4 cups

> 2 15-ounce cans kidney or pinto beans,*
>   with liquid
> 2 cloves garlic, chopped
> ½ white onion, chopped
> ¼ teaspoon ground cumin
> ⅛ teaspoon oregano
> 1 teaspoon ground red chilies**
> ½ cup grated part-skim mozzarella cheese
> 1 tablespoon olive oil

In a blender or food processor, purée beans and garlic. Stir in onion, seasonings and cheese.

In a nonstick skillet over medium heat, heat olive oil. Add beans and cook, uncovered, 20–30 minutes, or until beans thicken; stir occasionally.

*To further reduce the sodium level of this recipe, use salt-free or reduced-sodium canned beans. When time permits, substitute homemade Red Kidney Beans (page 504) for canned beans.

**Ground red chilies are available in Spanish and Mexican markets, in gourmet kitchen stores and in the gourmet section of most supermarkets.

SERVING SUGGESTION: Refried beans are great in tacos, taco salad or as a dip with fresh vegetables.

APPROXIMATE NUTRITIONAL CONTENT PER ½-CUP SERVING

Total calories: 136
Protein: 8 g
Carbohydrates: 19 g
Cholesterol: 4 mg
Fat: 3 g
Sodium: 386 mg

Percentage of calories from:
  Protein: 24%
  Carbohydrates: 55%
  Fat: 22%

PEQUEÑO TOSTADOS

12 whole tortillas; 48 appetizer-size

1 package flour or corn tortillas*
½ cup Bean Dip (page 406)
½ pound extra-lean ground round, browned
　and drained
¼ pound fresh mushrooms, thinly sliced and
　steamed 2–3 minutes
⅓ pound part-skim mozzarella cheese,
　grated
1 cup tomato salsa

Lay tortillas flat. Spread with Bean Dip. Cut tortillas into fourths. Arrange on a nonstick baking sheet. Sprinkle with ground beef and mushrooms. Top with cheese. Bake at 400°F. 5–10 minutes, or until cheese melts. Serve with salsa.

*Corn tortillas have 30 fewer calories than flour tortillas.

VARIATION: Instead of cutting the tortillas into fourths, lay each tortilla flat. Using a 2-inch round-shape cookie cutter as a pattern, cut each full-size tortilla into several small tortillas. Make tortilla chips with the leftover scraps by baking them on a nonstick baking sheet at 350°F. 10 minutes, or until crisp. Season with chili powder, ground cumin, onion powder or garlic powder.

SERVING SUGGESTIONS: Serve with Steamed Oriental Rice (page 499), corn on the cob and fresh seasonal fruit. Also good as an appetizer.

APPROXIMATE NUTRITIONAL CONTENT PER SERVING OF 1 WHOLE-FLOUR TORTILLA WITH TOPPINGS

Total calories: 131
Protein: 8 g
Carbohydrates: 16 g
Cholesterol: 14 mg
Fat: 4 g
Sodium: 156 mg

Percentage of calories from:
　Protein: 25%
　Carbohydrates: 49%
　Fat: 27%

NACHOS GRANDES

9 servings

> ½ cup Bean Dip (page 406)
> ¾ pound extra-lean ground round, browned
>   and drained
> ½ white onion, diced
> ½ head leaf lettuce, chopped
> 2 tomatoes, diced
> ½ pound part-skim Cheddar cheese, grated
>   tomato salsa
> 1 package corn tortilla chips*

Spread a 10-inch platter or plate with Bean Dip. Sprinkle with ground round, then with onion, lettuce and tomato. Top with cheese. Drizzle with some of the salsa. Ring with chips.

*Choose unsalted tortilla or taco chips that have been baked, not fried, in a heart-healthy oil such as safflower oil. Then limit yourself to a designated amount of chips (6-8, for example) and concentrate on the vegetables. (See variation below.)

VARIATION: Thinly slice 4 carrots, 4 turnips and 4 stalks celery on the diagonal and arrange in a low bowl; pour salsa into a custard cup, and tuck cup among the vegetables. These crudités, somewhat like the chips in shape and consistency, are a low-calorie alternative. Tuck a small butter spreader next to the nacho platter so the toppings can be spread right onto the vegetables.

APPROXIMATE NUTRITIONAL CONTENT PER SERVING

Total calories: 201
Protein: 17 g
Carbohydrates: 43 g
Cholesterol: 46 mg
Fat: 9 g
Sodium: 323 mg

Percentage of calories from:
  Protein: 21%
  Carbohydrates: 53%
  Fat: 26%

FETTUCCINE PRIMAVERA

10 servings

4	cups Chicken Stock (page 350)
1	2-inch piece fresh ginger root, peeled
1	bunch fresh asparagus, cut diagonally into thirds
1	small zucchini, sliced
½	pound fresh mushrooms, sliced
½	pound snow peas
1	6½-ounce can sliced water chestnuts
¼	cup arrowroot dissolved in ½ cup water
1	1-pound package fettuccine, cooked *al dente*
	salt and pepper to taste
8–10	cherry tomatoes, halved

In a medium saucepan, heat stock just to boiling (do not boil). Reduce heat and simmer.

In a wok, bring ginger root and ½ cup of the stock to a boil. Add asparagus, zucchini, mushrooms, snow peas and water chestnuts. Cover and steam 3–5 minutes, or until vegetables are crisp-tender. Bring stock in the saucepan back to boiling. Gradually add arrowroot to stock, stirring constantly to thicken. Pour over vegetables. Pour vegetables and sauce over fettuccine. Season. Add tomatoes. Toss.

SERVING SUGGESTIONS: Serve as a side dish with chicken or fish, or serve larger portions as an entrée.

APPROXIMATE NUTRITIONAL CONTENT PER SERVING

Total calories: 191
Protein: 91 g
Carbohydrates: 37 g
Cholesterol: Tr
Fat: 1 g
Sodium: 122 mg

Percentage of calories from:
Protein: 18%
Carbohydrates: 76%
Fat: 6%

FETTUCCINE WITH VEGETABLES AND PESTO

8 servings

½	bunch fresh broccoli, florets only
⅓	head cauliflower, florets only
1	1-pound package fettuccine, cooked *al dente*
1	cup Pesto (page 402)
1	15-ounce can artichoke hearts, quartered
8–10	fresh mushrooms, sliced
10	cherry tomatoes, halved
⅓	cup freshly grated Parmesan cheese
	black pepper to taste

In a covered vegetable steamer basket over boiling water, steam broccoli and cauliflower 2–3 minutes.

In a bowl, toss fettuccine with pesto. Add artichoke hearts, mushrooms, tomatoes, broccoli and cauliflower. Toss. Sprinkle with Parmesan and toss again. Season with black pepper.

SERVING SUGGESTIONS: Good hot or cold as an accompaniment or as an entrée.

APPROXIMATE NUTRITIONAL CONTENT PER SERVING

Total calories: 348
Protein: 14 g
Carbohydrates: 53 g
Cholesterol: 2 mg
Fat: 11 g
Sodium: 222 mg

Percentage of calories from:
Protein: 15%
Carbohydrates: 57%
Fat: 28%

CHINESE VEGETABLE STIR-FRY

6 servings

2 cups Chicken Stock (page 350)
1 8-ounce package buckwheat (Soba) noodles
½ teaspoon sesame oil
2-3 drops hot chili oil (LaYu)*
8-10 fresh black forest (Shiitake) mushrooms*
1 8-ounce can sliced water chestnuts
1 green pepper, cut into julienne strips
1 bunch fresh asparagus, steamed until
    crisp-tender
10 cherry tomatoes, halved
¼ cup reduced-sodium soy sauce
2 tablespoons rice vinegar

In a saucepan, heat chicken stock just to boiling (do not boil). Add buckwheat noodles and cook 3–4 minutes, or until tender. Drain. Set aside. (Reserve broth for soup or later use.)

In a wok or heavy skillet, heat sesame oil and chili oil. Add Shiitake mushrooms and stir-fry 4–5 minutes. Add water chestnuts and green pepper and stir-fry 2–3 minutes. Toss with noodles, asparagus and tomatoes. Combine soy sauce with vinegar. Pour over noodles and vegetables. Toss.

*Chili oil and Shiitake mushrooms are available in Oriental markets. If fresh Shiitake mushrooms are not available, reconstitute dried by soaking them in water to cover 30 minutes, or until soft. Remove and discard hard center stems. (Be sure to save the soaking liquid for soup.)

APPROXIMATE NUTRITIONAL CONTENT PER SERVING

Total calories: 204
Protein: 9 g
Carbohydrates: 38 g
Cholesterol: Tr
Fat: 2 g
Sodium: 111 mg

Percentage of calories from:
Protein: 17%
Carbohydrates: 74%
Fat: 9%

DESSERTS

RASPBERRY PURÉE

4 cups

2 pints fresh or frozen raspberries
1 tablespoon fresh lemon juice
pinch granulated sugar
dash Kirsch liqueur (optional)

Wash and hull fresh berries. In a blender or food processor, combine ingredients and purée until smooth. Chill.

SERVING SUGGESTIONS: Serve fruit purées as a sauce with fresh berries, melons, apricots and peaches, as a sauce over ice cream and as a syrup over pancakes waffles or French toast.

APPROXIMATE NUTRITIONAL CONTENT PER ¼ CUP

Total calories: 12   *Percentage of calories from:*
Protein: Tr   Protein: 7%
Carbohydrates: 3 g   Carbohydrates: 84%
Cholesterol: 0 mg   Fat: 9%
Fat: Tr
Sodium: Tr

STRAWBERRY PURÉE

4 cups

 2 pints fresh or frozen strawberries
¼–½ teaspoon almond extract
¼–½ teaspoon vanilla extract
1–2 teaspoons granulated sugar (optional)

Wash and hull fresh berries. In a blender or food processor, purée the berries. Add almond and vanilla extracts. Sweeten with sugar.

NOTE: You may want to vary the amount of almond and/or vanilla extract, as well as the sugar, depending on the sweetness of the berries.

SERVING SUGGESTIONS: Serve fruit purées as a sauce with fresh berries, melons, apricots and peaches, as a sauce over ice cream and as a syrup over pancakes, waffles or French toast.

APPROXIMATE NUTRITIONAL CONTENT PER ¼ CUP

Total calories: 12
Protein: Tr
Carbohydrates: 3 g
Cholesterol: 0 mg
Fat: Tr
Sodium: Tr

Percentage of calories from:
Protein: 7%
Carbohydrates: 84%
Fat: 9%

CREAMY BANANA PURÉE

1¹/₂ cups

    3–4   ripe bananas, peeled

Wrap bananas in plastic wrap. Freeze. Just before serving, purée bananas in a blender or food processor.

APPROXIMATE NUTRITIONAL CONTENT PER ¹/₄ CUP

Total calories: 52
Protein: Tr
Carbohydrates: 13 g
Cholesterol: 0 mg
Fat: Tr
Sodium: Tr

Percentage of calories from:
Protein: 4%
Carbohydrates: 92%
Fat: 4%

FRESH PINEAPPLE PURÉE

2 cups

    1   fresh pineapple, peeled and
        cored

Cut pineapple into quarters. Purée in a blender or food processor.

APPROXIMATE NUTRITIONAL CONTENT PER ¹/₄ CUP

Total calories: 29
Protein: Tr
Carbohydrates: 14 g
Cholesterol: 0 mg
Fat: Tr
Sodium: Tr

Percentage of calories from:
Protein: 3%
Carbohydrates: 90%
Fat: 7%

RHUBARB PURÉE

6 cups

6 cups rhubarb, sliced into 1-inch pieces
½ cup orange juice
2 tablespoons granulated sugar

In a saucepan, combine rhubarb and orange juice. Cover and cook slowly 10 minutes. Add sugar. Cook 5–10 minutes, or until rhubarb is tender.

SERVING SUGGESTION: Serve warm over sliced bananas or fresh strawberries.

APPROXIMATE NUTRITIONAL CONTENT PER ½ CUP

Total calories: 25
Protein: Tr
Carbohydrates: Tr
Cholesterol: 0 mg
Fat: Tr
Sodium: Tr

Percentage of calories from:
Protein: 9%
Carbohydrates: 87%
Fat: 4%

PAPAYA PURÉE

1 cup

1 ripe papaya, peeled and
    seeded

Cut papaya into quarters. Wrap in plastic wrap and freeze. Just before serving, purée papaya in a blender or food processor.

APPROXIMATE NUTRITIONAL CONTENT PER ¼ CUP OF PAPAYA PURÉE

Total calories: 29
Protein: Tr
Carbohydrates: 7 g
Cholesterol: 0 mg
Fat: Tr
Sodium: 2 mg

Percentage of calories from:
Protein: 6%
Carbohydrates: 91%
Fat: 3%

FRESH PEACHES WITH STRAWBERRY AND CREAMY BANANA PURÉES

4 servings

½ cup Raspberry Purée (page 511)
½ cup Creamy Banana Purée (page 513)
4 ripe peaches, sliced
fresh blueberries for garnish

Chill 4 deep-lip dessert plates. Ladle 2 tablespoons Banana Purée and 2 tablespoons Raspberry Purée onto each plate. Arrange peaches symmetrically around sauces. Garnish with blueberries.

APPROXIMATE NUTRITIONAL CONTENT PER SERVING

Total calories: 94
Protein: 1 g
Carbohydrates: 23 g
Cholesterol: 0 mg
Fat: Tr
Sodium: 2 mg

Percentage of calories from:
Protein: 5%
Carbohydrates: 90%
Fat: 4%

FRESH FRUIT WITH RASPBERRY, BANANA AND PINEAPPLE PURÉES

8–10 servings

1   fresh pineapple
4   apricots, pitted and cut into quarters
4   peaches, pitted and cut into quarters
½   cantaloupe, peeled and cut into wedges
1   pint strawberries, hulled
1   papaya, peeled and cut into julienne strips
¼   watermelon, peeled and cut into wedges
1   cup Fresh Pineapple Purée (page 513)
¾   cup Creamy Banana Purée (page 513)
2   cups Raspberry or Strawberry Purée
       (pages 511–512)
       sprigs of fresh mint (optional)

Cut pineapple in half horizontally, leaving the stem end intact. Using a curved grapefruit knife, carefully remove pineapple from shell. Cut pineapple flesh into cubes and return to shell.

Arrange pineapple shell with pineapple cubes in center of a large platter. Ring with apricots, peaches, cantaloupe, and watermelon. Garnish with strawberries and papaya. Pour purées into small custard cups. Garnish with fresh mint, if desired. Tuck purées among fruits or arrange separately next to fruit platter.

VARIATION: During the winter months, use sliced pears and Granny Smith apples, fresh figs and Mandarin oranges. Accompany with Creamy Banana Purée, Papaya Purée and Rhubarb Purée (page 514).

SERVING SUGGESTION: This makes a spectacular dessert for any occasion. Serve with Meringue Cookies or Oatmeal Raisin Cookies (page 532).

APPROXIMATE NUTRITIONAL CONTENT PER CUP OF FRUIT WITHOUT PURÉES

Total calories: 50
Protein: Tr
Carbohydrates: 12 g
Cholesterol: 0 mg
Fat: Tr
Sodium: 3 mg

Percentage of calories from:
Protein: 6%
Carbohydrates: 86%
Fat: 8%

Add 13 calories per 1 tablespoon of Creamy Banana Purée. Add 3 calories per 1 tablespoon of Raspberry or Strawberry Purée. Add 7 calories per 1 tablespoon of Pineapple Purée.

FRESH RASPBERRIES WITH STRAWBERRY PURÉE

6 servings

1 cup Strawberry Purée (page 512)
3 pints fresh raspberries, washed and hulled

Chill 6 deep-lip dessert plates. Ladle ¼ cup of Strawberry Purée onto each plate. Arrange raspberries over sauce.

VARIATIONS: Substitute strawberries for raspberries, or use Raspberry Purée (page 511) in place of Strawberry Purée.

APPROXIMATE NUTRITIONAL CONTENT PER SERVING

Total calories: 69
Protein: 1 g
Carbohydrates: 16 g
Cholesterol: 0 mg
Fat: Tr
Sodium: 17 mg

Percentage of calories from:
Protein: 7%
Carbohydrates: 84%
Fat: 9%

STRAWBERRIES AND PAPAYA WITH RASPBERRY PURÉE

4 servings

1 cup Raspberry Purée (page 511)
2 pints fresh strawberries, washed and
    hulled
1 ripe papaya, peeled and cut into julienne
    strips

Chill 4 deep-lip dessert plates. Ladle ¼ cup of Raspberry Purée onto each plate. Arrange strawberries and papaya symmetrically over sauce.

VARIATION: Substitute cantaloupe for papaya.

APPROXIMATE NUTRITIONAL CONTENT PER SERVING

Total calories: 121
Protein: 2 g
Carbohydrates: 28 g
Cholesterol: 0 mg
Fat: 1 g
Sodium: 4 mg

Percentage of calories from:
  Protein: 6%
  Carbohydrates: 86%
  Fat: 8%

BANANAS AND FRESH STRAWBERRIES WITH RHUBARB PURÉE

4 servings

1 cup Rhubarb Purée (page 514)
1 pint fresh strawberries, washed and hulled
2 bananas, cut on the diagonal into 2-inch
    slices

Chill 4 deep-lip dessert plates. Ladle ¼ cup Rhubarb Purée onto each plate. Arrange strawberries and bananas symmetrically over the sauce.

SERVING SUGGESTION: Serve with Meringue Cookies (page 532).

APPROXIMATE NUTRITIONAL CONTENT PER SERVING

Total calories: 94
Protein: 2 g
Carbohydrates: 23 g
Cholesterol: 0 mg
Fat: Tr
Sodium: 3 mg

Percentage of calories from:
Protein: 6%
Carbohydrates: 89%
Fat: 6%

POACHED PEARS
WITH RASPBERRY PURÉE

4 servings

2 cups dry white wine
2½ cups water
1 cinnamon stick
1 vanilla bean
  zest of 1 lemon
4 firm, ripe pears
1 cup Raspberry Purée (page 511)

In a deep saucepan, combine wine, water, cinnamon stick, vanilla bean and lemon zest. Bring to a boil. Peel pears, leaving stems intact. Gently drop pears into poaching liquid, adding water or wine, if necessary, to completely cover the fruit. Cover and simmer 25–30 minutes, or until pears are tender. Remove from heat. Cool pears in the poaching liquid until ready to serve.

Serve pears on deep-lip dessert plates. Pour ¼ cup of Raspberry Purée over each pear.

NOTE: The poaching liquid will keep several weeks in the refrigerator and may be reused.

VARIATIONS: Substitute champagne for wine. Or use puréed strawberries or blueberries in place of Raspberry Purée.

APPROXIMATE NUTRITIONAL CONTENT PER SERVING

Total calories: 125
Protein: 2 g
Carbohydrates: 42 g
Cholesterol: 0 mg
Fat: 1 g
Sodium: 2 mg

Percentage of calories from:
  Protein: 4%
  Carbohydrates: 89%
  Fat: 7%

STRAWBERRY SHAKE

6 servings

	juice of 1 orange
2	pints strawberries, washed and hulled
½	teaspoon vanilla extract
1	cup plain non-fat yogurt
2–3	ice cubes

In a blender or food processor, purée orange juice and berries. Add vanilla extract and yogurt. Blend 1 minute. Add ice cubes, one at a time, and crush. Serve in old-fashioned soda glasses.

APPROXIMATE NUTRITIONAL CONTENT PER SERVING

Total calories: 58
Protein: 2 g
Carbohydrates: 12 g
Cholesterol: 1 mg
Fat: Tr
Sodium: 28 mg

Percentage of calories from:
Protein: 16%
Carbohydrates: 76%
Fat: 7%

PAPAYA SMOOTHIE

4 servings

1 ripe papaya, peeled and seeded
1 very small banana
3 ice cubes
$\frac{1}{2}$ cup plain non-fat yogurt

In a blender or food processor, purée papaya and banana. Add ice cubes, one at a time, and crush. Fold in yogurt. Pour into stemmed glasses.

APPROXIMATE NUTRITIONAL CONTENT PER SERVING

Total calories: 69
Protein: 2 g
Carbohydrates: 16 g
Cholesterol: 1 mg
Fat: Tr
Sodium: 22 mg

Percentage of calories from:
  Protein: 11%
  Carbohydrates: 85%
  Fat: 4%

PINEAPPLE SMOOTHIE

4 servings

1 fresh pineapple, peeled and cored
8 ice cubes
  whole orange slices, for garnish
  fresh mint sprigs, for garnish

In a blender or food processor, purée pineapple. Add ice cubes, one at a time, and crush. Pour into stemmed glasses. Cut a slit halfway through the orange slices and hook one over the edge of each glass. Garnish with fresh mint.

APPROXIMATE NUTRITIONAL CONTENT PER SERVING
OF PINEAPPLE SMOOTHIE

Total calories: 63
Protein: Tr
Carbohydrates: 11 g
Cholesterol: 0 mg
Fat: Tr
Sodium: Tr

Percentage of calories from:
Protein: 3%
Carbohydrates: 90%
Fat: 7%

APPLE-PEAR SAUCE

2 quarts

6 large Granny Smith apples, peeled and
   quartered
2 large pears, peeled and quartered
3/4 cup water
2 tablespoons brown sugar
1 teaspoon cinnamon

In a heavy saucepan, combine apples, pears and water. Cover and cook over low heat, stirring often, about 45–60 minutes, or until apples and pears soften and become saucy. Add sugar and cinnamon. Simmer 20–30 minutes.

**APPROXIMATE NUTRITIONAL CONTENT PER
1/2-CUP SERVING**

Total calories: 59
Protein: Tr
Carbohydrates: 15 g
Cholesterol: 0 mg
Fat: Tr
Sodium: 1 mg

Percentage of calories from:
Protein: 1%
Carbohydrates: 94%
Fat: 5%

COLD RASPBERRY SOUFFLÉ

10 servings

2   envelopes unflavored gelatin
½   cup fresh lemon juice
4   egg yolks
½   cup granulated sugar
2   cups raspberries, puréed
¼   cup Crème de Cassis liquor
8   egg whites
¼   teaspoon cream of tartar
2   cups plain non-fat yogurt

In a saucepan, soften gelatin in lemon juice. Simmer over low heat, stirring frequently, until gelatin is dissolved and liquid is clear. In a bowl, beat egg yolks with sugar about 5 minutes, or until light and fluffy.

In top of a double boiler, combine puréed raspberries and Crème de Cassis. Stir in egg yolks and gelatin. Cook over boiling water until mixture thickens, stirring constantly. Cool to room temperature, about 40–45 minutes.

Beat egg whites until soft peaks form. Add cream of tartar. Beat until stiff peaks form. Fold egg whites, then yogurt, into raspberry mixture. Pour into a 2-quart soufflé dish with a waxed-paper collar extending 2–3 inches above rim of dish. Chill 3 hours. Remove paper collar. Serve.

NOTE: Desserts using egg yolks tend to be high in cholesterol. Keep this in mind and allow for it when planning your daily food intake.

APPROXIMATE NUTRITIONAL CONTENT PER SERVING

Total calories: 132
Protein: 7 g
Carbohydrates: 19 g
Cholesterol: 106 mg
Fat: 2 g
Sodium: 77 mg

Percentage of calories from:
Protein: 23%
Carbohydrates: 60%
Fat: 17%

COLD LEMON SOUFFLÉ

8 servings

1	cup fresh lemon juice
3	egg yolks
¼	cup granulated sugar
2	tablespoons honey
3	envelopes unflavored gelatin
⅔	cup hot water
	grated peel of 1 lemon
1	tablespoon Grand Marnier
1¼	cups plain non-fat yogurt
5	egg whites
¼	teaspoon cream of tartar
⅛	teaspoon salt

In top of a double boiler, combine lemon juice, egg yolks, sugar and honey. Cook 5–7 minutes over hot (not boiling) water, beating constantly with electric mixer until thick and frothy. Remove from heat.

Dissolve gelatin in ⅔ cup hot water; gradually add to egg mixture. Stir in grated lemon. Place mixture over ice water and beat 5–10 minutes, or until mixture begins to jell. Add Grand Marnier. Beat 5–10 minutes. Set aside.

Combine remaining ingredients. Beat until egg whites form stiff peaks. Fold into egg mixture. Spoon into an 8-inch soufflé dish or individual parfait glasses. Chill 2–3 hours.

NOTE: Desserts using egg yolks tend to be high in cholesterol. Keep this in mind and allow for it when planning your daily food intake.

APPROXIMATE NUTRITIONAL CONTENT PER SERVING

Total calories: 112

Protein: 7 g

Carbohydrates: 16 g

Cholesterol: 99 mg

Fat: 2 g

Sodium: 98 mg

Percentage of calories from:

Protein: 26%

Carbohydrates: 57%

Fat: 18%

CRANBERRY CUSTARD

9 servings

1 cup orange juice
2 cups cranberries
2 egg whites
1 egg yolk
⅓ cup granulated sugar
¼ cup unbleached white flour
¾ cup skim milk
½ cup plain non-fat yogurt
½ teaspoon vanilla extract

In a saucepan, warm orange juice. Stir in cranberries. Cook 5–10 minutes, or until most berries have popped and juice begins to thicken. With a slotted spoon, remove cranberries from liquid and arrange in a 9-inch quiche pan or French pie plate. Set aside.

Boil remaining liquid 5–7 minutes, or until reduced to ½–⅓ cup. Cool. In a blender or food processor, combine reduced liquid, eggs, sugar, flour, milk, yogurt and vanilla extract. Process 3–4 minutes. Pour over cranberries. Bake at 400°F. 40 minutes, or until puffed and golden.

NOTE: Desserts using egg yolks tend to be high in cholesterol. Keep this in mind and allow for it when planning your daily food intake.

APPROXIMATE NUTRITIONAL CONTENT PER SERVING

Total calories: 88
Protein: 3 g
Carbohydrates: 17 g
Cholesterol: 30 mg
Fat: Tr
Sodium: 32 mg

Percentage of calories from:
Protein: 13%
Carbohydrates: 78%
Fat: 8%

PAVLOVA

6 servings

4 egg whites
½ cup granulated sugar
1 teaspoon white cider vinegar
1 teaspoon vanilla extract
1½ teaspoons cornstarch
1 recipe Whipped Cream Topping
  (page 534)
2 pints fresh raspberries

Beat egg whites to soft peaks. Gradually add sugar; beat until egg whites are thick and glossy. Add vinegar, vanilla extract and cornstarch; beat 1–2 minutes.

Cover a baking sheet with ungreased paper (such as brown mailing paper or a grocery sack cut to fit). Using a 4–5-inch salad plate or cereal bowl for a form, trace circles onto the paper. Mound about ½ cup of meringue over each circle, using the back of soup spoon to mold sides and indent center of meringue to a bowl-shaped shell.

Bake at 250°F. 1½ hours. Turn off oven. Leave meringue in oven (door closed) for 2 more hours, or until dry.

Mound Whipped Cream Topping in each meringue bowl. Top with raspberries.

APPROXIMATE NUTRITIONAL CONTENT PER SERVING WITH TOPPING

Total calories: 163
Protein: 5 g
Carbohydrates: 35 g
Cholesterol: 0 mg
Fat: Tr
Sodium: 59 mg

Percentage of calories from:
Protein: 12%
Carbohydrates: 86%
Fat: 2%

SPANISH CREAM

8 servings

1 egg yolk
2 cups skim milk
4 tablespoons granulated sugar
1 envelope unflavored gelatin
1 teaspoon vanilla extract
3 egg whites
1 fresh strawberry for garnish

In a saucepan, beat egg yolk; add milk. Beat 2–3 minutes. Combine 2 tablespoons of sugar with gelatin; add to egg mixture. Cook over low heat, stirring constantly, about 5 minutes, or until gelatin is completely dissolved. Add vanilla extract. Chill 1–1½ hours, or until partially set.

Beat egg whites to soft peaks. Gradually add remaining 2 tablespoons sugar; beat to stiff peaks. Fold into gelatin. Turn into 2-quart soufflé dish. Garnish with a strawberry.

VARIATION: Wash hull and slice 2 pints of strawberries. In individual parfait glasses, alternate layers of strawberries and Spanish Cream, beginning with a layer of strawberries and ending with a layer of Spanish Cream.

APPROXIMATE NUTRITIONAL CONTENT PER SERVING

Total calories: 64
Protein: 4 g
Carbohydrates: 10 g
Cholesterol: 34 mg
Fat: Tr
Sodium: 52 mg

Percentage of calories from:
Protein: 28%
Carbohydrates: 60%
Fat: 12%

APPROXIMATE NUTRITIONAL CONTENT PER SERVING OF SPANISH CREAM WITH STRAWBERRIES

Total calories: 87

Protein: 5 g

Carbohydrates: 15 g

Cholesterol: 34 mg

Fat: Tr

Sodium: 53 mg

Percentage of calories from:

Protein: 22%

Carbohydrates: 67%

Fat: 11%

BANANA CREAM PUDDING

10 servings

3 tablespoons unbleached white flour

3 cups skim milk

⅓ cup granulated sugar

1 egg white, slightly beaten

2 eggs, beaten

1 teaspoon vanilla extract

3 large bananas, sliced

fresh lemon juice

In a covered jar, shake flour and ½ cup of the skim milk; set aside. In top of double boiler, combine remaining milk, sugar and eggs. Place over boiling water. Gradually add floured milk. Cook, stirring frequently, 20–25 minutes, or until mixture thickens. Remove from heat. Stir in vanilla extract.

Line bottom and sides of a 9-inch pie plate with sliced bananas. Pour pudding over bananas. (To keep bananas from darkening, brush any that show with lemon juice.) Chill 2–3 hours.

VARIATION: Garnish with a strawberry or a sprinkle of raspberries or blueberries.

NOTE: Desserts using egg yolks tend to be high in cholesterol. Keep this in mind and allow for it when planning your daily food intake.

(continued on next page)

APPROXIMATE NUTRITIONAL CONTENT PER SERVING OF BANANA CREAM PUDDING

Total calories: 111
Protein: 5 g
Carbohydrates: 20 g
Cholesterol: 54 mg
Fat: 1 g
Sodium: 55 mg

Percentage of calories from:
Protein: 16%
Carbohydrates: 72%
Fat: 11%

STRAWBERRY PUDDING

9 servings

2 envelopes unflavored gelatin
½ cup apple–black cherry juice
1 cup skim milk, scalded
2 tablespoons granulated sugar
1 teaspoon almond extract
6 cups strawberries

In a blender or food processor, sprinkle gelatin with juice. Let stand 2–3 minutes, or until gelatin begins to gel. Heat milk just to boiling (do not boil); pour into blender or food processor. Add sugar and almond extract. Process 2–3 minutes. Add 3 cups berries and purée. Add 2 more cups berries. Process with 2–3 on/off motions to slice berries.

Pour into individual parfait glasses or 9-inch French pie plate. Slice remaining cup of berries. Arrange symmetrically over top. Chill until firm.

VARIATION: Use plain apple juice in place of apple–black cherry juice.

APPROXIMATE NUTRITIONAL CONTENT PER SERVING

Total calories: 62
Protein: 3 g
Carbohydrates: 13 g
Cholesterol: Tr
Fat: Tr
Sodium: 17 mg

Percentage of calories from:
Protein: 17%
Carbohydrates: 77%
Fat: 6%

EASY CHOCOLATE PUDDING

5 servings

- ¼ cup unsweetened cocoa powder
- ½ cup granulated sugar
- 2 tablespoons cornstarch
- ⅛ teaspoon salt
- 2 cups skim milk
- 1 egg, beaten
- ½ teaspoon vanilla extract

In a medium saucepan, blend cocoa, sugar, cornstarch, salt and milk. Cook over medium heat, stirring constantly, until mixture comes to a boil and begins to thicken. Remove from heat.

Mix ¼ cup of the mixture with beaten egg. Gradually stir egg mixture into hot mixture. Cook over low heat, stirring constantly, 5–10 minutes, or until mixture comes to a boil. Remove from heat. Stir in vanilla extract. Pour into custard cups. Chill.

NOTE: Desserts using egg yolks tend to be high in cholesterol. Keep this in mind and allow for it when planning your daily food intake.

APPROXIMATE NUTRITIONAL CONTENT PER ½-CUP SERVING

Total calories: 151
Protein: 5 g
Carbohydrates: 30 g
Cholesterol: 55 mg
Fat: 2 g
Sodium: 118 mg

Percentage of calories from:
Protein: 13%
Carbohydrates: 75%
Fat: 12%

MERINGUE COOKIES

12 cookies

3 egg whites
1/8 teaspoon salt
1/2 teaspoon cream of tartar
1/3 cup granulated sugar

In a mixing bowl, beat egg whites until foamy. Beat in salt and cream of tartar. Gradually add sugar and beat until stiff.

Cover a baking sheet with ungreased paper (such as brown mailing paper or a grocery bag cut to fit). Drop meringue by teaspoon onto paper. Bake at 200°F. 1½ hours.

NOTE: Meringue cookies are best when still warm from the oven.

APPROXIMATE NUTRITIONAL CONTENT PER COOKIE

Total calories: 28
Protein: Tr
Carbohydrates: 5 g
Cholesterol: 0 mg
Fat: Tr
Sodium: 40 mg

Percentage of calories from:
Protein: 12%
Carbohydrates: 78%
Fat: 10%

OATMEAL RAISIN COOKIES

48 cookies

1½ cups sifted, unbleached white flour
1/2 teaspoon baking powder
3/4 teaspoon baking soda
1/2 teaspoon salt
1 teaspoon cinnamon

½ teaspoon ginger
¼ cup brown sugar
¼ cup granulated sugar
⅓ cup safflower oil
½ cup molasses
2 eggs
1½ cups rolled oats
1 cup raisins

In a mixing bowl, combine flour, baking powder, baking soda, salt, cinnamon, ginger and sugars. Add safflower oil, molasses, eggs and rolled oats; mix with a wooden spoon until blended. Stir in raisins. (Dough will be soft.) Drop batter by heaping teaspoons onto nonstick baking sheet or, for giant-size cookies, drop by ¼ cup onto nonstick baking sheet. Bake at 350°F. 12–15 minutes. Remove from oven. Let stand 1 minute. Remove from baking sheet. Cool on wire racks.

NOTE: Desserts using egg yolks tend to be high in cholesterol. Keep this in mind and allow for it when planning your daily food intake.

APPROXIMATE NUTRITIONAL CONTENT PER REGULAR-SIZE OATMEAL RAISIN COOKIE

Total calories: 66
Protein: 1 g
Carbohydrates: 11 g
Cholesterol: 11 mg
Fat: 2 g
Sodium: 42 mg

Percentage of calories from:
Protein: 7%
Carbohydrates: 67%
Fat: 26%

Calories per jumbo cookie are 266 (12 cookies per recipe). Calories per medium cookie are 133 (24 cookies per recipe).

WHIPPED CREAM TOPPING

8 servings

- ½ teaspoon unflavored gelatin
- ¼ cup cold water
- ¼ cup granulated sugar
- 3 egg whites
- ¼ teaspoon cream of tartar
- 1 teaspoon vanilla extract

In a small saucepan, soften gelatin in cold water. Stir in sugar. Cook over low heat, stirring constantly, 2–3 minutes, or until mixture is hot (do not boil).

In top of a double boiler, using an electric mixer, beat egg whites to stiff peaks. Put pan over boiling water. Add cream of tartar; beat 2 minutes. Rewarm gelatin and pour in a steady stream into egg whites, beating at high speed to stiff peaks, about 1 minute.

Pour hot water out of the double-boiler bottom. Fill with ice water. Put top of double boiler over ice water. Add vanilla extract; beat 3 minutes. Serve.

NOTE: This sounds complicated, but it's easy once you have done it. The results are worth the effort.

APPROXIMATE NUTRITIONAL CONTENT PER SERVING

Total calories: 32
Protein: 1 g
Carbohydrates: 6 g
Cholesterol: 0 mg
Fat: 0 g
Sodium: 19 mg

Percentage of calories from:
Protein: 18%
Carbohydrates: 82%
Fat: 0%

SOURCE NOTES

Chapter One

The Cardiovascular Health Risk Self-Assessment: from *It's Your Choice* by Shirley Holder Hazlett, Zellerbach Family Fund, San Francisco, 1985. Used with permission.

Chapter Two

Statistics on what Americans eat in one day: from *In One Day* by Tom Parker, Houghton Mifflin Co., Boston, 1984. Used with permission.

Quote by Dr. George Sheehan on cholesterol levels: from a speech in Seattle, Wash., 1987.

Information on cholesterol risk levels: from a speech by Dr. William Castelli in Manchester, N.H., 1987.

Chapter Three

Tape Measure Test for calculating body fat percentage: adapted from research by Jack Wilmore, Ph.D., Physical and Health Education Dept., University of Texas at Austin. Used with permission.

Information on formula used to calculate calories needed daily: from a speech by Carol Caldwell, R.D., manager of Nutrition Services, Canyon Ranch, in Tucson, Ariz., 1985.

Chapter Four

Daily adult protein requirements: from a speech by author Jane Brody in Seattle, Wash., 1984.

Benefits of fish oil: from a speech by Dr. Basil Rifkind of the National Heart, Lung and Blood Institute, in Palo Alto, Calif., 1986.

Chapter Five

Influence of exercise vs. overeating on overweight: from a speech by Dr. Peter Wood of Stanford University, in Palo Alto, Calif., 1986.

Chart showing number of minutes to work off calories: prepared by the Bob Hope International Heart Research Institute, Seattle, Wash., 1985.

Concept of "overfat": from a speech by author Covert Bailey in Concord, Calif., 1985.

Exercise and blood flow: from a speech by Dr. Terry Kavanaugh of the Toronto Cardiac Rehabilitation Program, in Dearborn, Mich., 1986.

Information on exercise and HDLs: from a speech by Dr. William Haskell of Stanford University, in Palo Alto, Calif., 1986.

Minimum requirements for specific aerobic exercises: from a speech by Dr. Ken Cooper in South Bend, Ind., 1985.

Chapter Six

Dr. Thomas H. Holmes Social Readjustment Rating Scale: first published by Pergamon Journals Limited, Oxford, England, in *Journal of Psychosomatic Research,* Vol. 11, No. 2, Fall 1967. Used with permission.

Characteristics of Type A behavior: from a speech by Dr. Meyer Friedman in Dearborn, Mich., 1986.

Test for Type A personality: adapted from research by Drs. R. W. Bortner and Ray Rosenman published in *Journal of Chronic Diseases,* July 1967.

Information on "situation/belief/emotion" aspect of self-talk: from a speech by Dr. Carl Thoresen, Professor of

Education and Psychology at Stanford University, in Seattle, Wash., 1984.

Replacing negatives with positives in self-talk: from a speech by Dr. Wayne Dyer in Houston, Tex., 1987.

Information on dissipating stress through exercise: from a speech by Dr. William Haskell of the Stanford Heart Disease Prevention Clinic, in Palo Alto, Calif., 1986.

Chapter Seven

Quote by Dr. William Castelli regarding filter cigarettes: from a speech in Myrtle Beach, S.C., 1986.

Research on health articles and references to smoking in women's magazines: compiled by Dr. Rolf Holle, associate director of Respiratory Therapy, Providence Medical Center, Seattle, Wash., 1985.

Chapter Eight

Concept of "comfort zones": from a speech by Bob Moawad of Edge Learning Institute, in Tempe, Ariz., 1986.

"Spaceship test": from a speech by psychologist Dr. Jennifer James in Seattle, Wash., 1986.

Cliff Young story: from a speech by Lou Tice of the Pacific Institute, in Seattle, Wash., 1986.

Quote by Dr. Denis Waitley: from his book *The Double Win*, Berkeley Books, 1985.

BIBLIOGRAPHY

American Heart Association. "Dietary Fat and Its Relation to Heart Attack and Strokes." *Circulation* 23, 1961.

———. *Heartbook*. New York: E. P. Dutton, 1980.

———. *Heart Facts*. Dallas, Tex., 1985.

Anderson, James W. *Diabetes: A Practical Guide to Healthy Living*. New York: Arco Publishing, 1981.

Anderson, J. W., and Chen, W. L. "Plant Fiber: Carbohydrate and Lipid Metabolism." *American Journal of Clinical Nutrition*, Vol. 32, 1979.

Anderson, J. W., et al. "Hypocholesterolemic Effects of Oat-bran or Bean Intake for Hypercholesterolemic Men." *American Journal of Clinical Nutrition*, Vol. 40, 1984.

Anderson, Robert. *Stretching for Everyday Fitness and for Running, Tennis, Racquetball, Golf and Other Sports*. Bolinas, Calif.: Shelter Publications, 1980.

Armstrong, M. L., et al. "Regression of Coronary Atherosclerosis in Rhesus Monkeys." *Circulatory Research*, 1959.

Aronson, Virginia. "Effective Weight Control." *Runner's World*, March 1984.

Aykroyd, W. R. *The Story of Sugar*. Chicago: Quadrangle, 1967.

Bailey, Covert. *Fit or Fat?* Pleasant Hills, Calif.: Covert Bailey, 1977.

Barnett, Robert. "Why Fat Makes You Fatter." *American Health,* May 1986.

Benditt, E. P. "The Origin of Atherosclerosis." *Scientific American,* February 1977.

Bennett, William, and Gurin, Joel. *The Dieter's Dilemma: Eating Less and Weighing More.* New York: Basic Books, 1982

Benson, Herbert. *The Relaxation Response.* New York: William Morrow & Co., 1975.

Blackburn, Henry. "Progress in the Epidemiology and Prevention of Coronary Heart Disease." *Progress in Cardiology,* Vol. 3, edited by Paul N. Yu and John F. Goodwin, 1974.

Blondhein, S. H., et al. "Comparison of Weight Loss on Low-calorie (800–1200) and Very-low-calorie (300–600) Diets." *International Journal of Obesity,* Vol. 5, 1981.

Blumenfeld, Arthur. *Heart Attack: Are You a Candidate?* New York: Pyramid Books, 1971.

Bray, G. *Obesity in America.* U.S. Department of Health, Education and Welfare, NIH publication 79-359, 1979.

Brewster, L., and Jacobson, M. F. *The Changing American Diet.* Washington, D.C.: Center for Science in the Public Interest, 1978.

Brody, Jane E. "How Good Are Fast Foods." *New York Times,* September 19, 1970.

———. *Jane Brody's Good Food Book.* New York: W. W. Norton & Co., 1985.

———. *Jane Brody's Nutrition Book.* New York: W. W. Norton & Co., 1981.

Brown, M. S., and Goldstein, J. L. "Lowering Plasma Cholesterol by Raising LDL Receptors." *New England Journal of Medicine,* Vol. 305, No. 9, 1981.

Bruce, R. A. "Primary Intervention Against Coronary Atherosclerosis by Exercise Conditioning?" *New England Journal of Medicine,* Vol. 305, No. 25, 1981.

Burfoot, A. "The Pulse Rate Game." *Runner's World,* July 1981.

Burkitt, D. *Don't Forget Fiber in Your Diet.* New York:

Arco Publishing, 1984.

———. "Some Diseases Characteristic of Modern Western Civilization." *British Medical Journal*, 1973.

Burns, David. *Feeling Good: The New Mood Therapy.* New York: Institute for Rational-Emotive Therapy, 1980.

Caggiula, A. W., et al. "The Multiple Risk Intervention Trial (MRFIT). IV. Intervention on Blood Lipids." *Preventive Medicine,* Vol. 10, 1981.

"Carbohydrate-loading May Not Be Just for Athletes." New York *Daily News,* March 22, 1982.

"Cardiovascular Surgery." Public Health Service, Publication No. 1701, 1969.

Chiang, B. N., Perlman, L. V., and Epstein, F. H. "Overweight and Hypertension." *Circulation,* Vol. 39, No. 3, 1969.

Christen, A. G. "The Case Against Smokeless Tobacco: Five Facts for the Health Professional to Consider." *Journal of the American Dental Association,* Vol. 101, 1980.

"Cigarettes, Coronary Occlusions, and Myocardial Infarction." *Journal of the American Medical Association,* Vol. 246, No. 8, 1981.

"Composition of Foods in the United States—1909 to 1948." U.S. Department of Agriculture, 1949.

"Composition of Foods: Dairy and Egg Products, Raw, Processed, Prepared." U.S. Department of Agriculture, 1976.

"Composition of Foods: Fats and Oils, Raw, Processed, Prepared." U.S. Department of Agriculture, 1979.

"Composition of Foods: Poultry Products, Raw, Processed, Prepared." U.S. Department of Agriculture, 1979.

"Composition of Foods: Raw, Processed, Prepared." U.S. Department of Agriculture, 1975.

"Composition of Foods: Soups, Sauces and Gravies, Raw, Processed, Prepared." U.S. Department of Agriculture, 1977.

Connor, W. "The Interrelated Effects of Dietary Cholesterol on Serum Cholesterol in Man." *American Journal of Clinical Nutrition* 25, 1972.

———. "The Key Role of Nutritional Factors in the Prevention of Coronary Heart Disease." *Preventive Medicine* 1, 1972.

———. "Presidential Address: Too Little or Too Much, the Case for Preventive Nutrition." *American Journal of Clinical Nutrition,* 1979.

Cooper, Kenneth H. *Aerobics.* New York: M. Evans & Co., 1970.

———. *The Aerobics Program for Total Well-Being.* New York: M. Evans & Co., 1982.

———. *The New Aerobics.* New York: M. Evans & Co., 1970.

Cooper, R., et al. "Seventh-Day Adventist Adolescents— Life-Style Patterns and Cardiovascular Risk Factors." *Western Journal of Medicine,* Vol. 140, 1984.

Corbin, Cheryl. *Nutrition.* New York: Holt, Rinehart & Winston, 1980.

Cousins, Norman. *Anatomy of an Illness.* New York: W. W. Norton & Co., 1979.

———. *The Healing Heart: Antidotes to Panic and Helplessness.* New York: W. W. Norton & Co., 1983.

Clarke, N. E., Sr. "Atherosclerosis, Occlusive Vascular Disease and EDTA." *American Journal of Cardiology,* Vol. VI, 1960.

"Critical Review of Epidemiologic Studies of Physical Activity, A." *Annals of the New York Academy of Sciences,* Vol. 301, 1977.

"Critique of Low-carbohydrate Ketogenic Weight Reduction Regimens, A: A Review of Dr. Atkins' Diet Revolution," statement of the American Medical Association Council on Foods and Nutrition. *Journal of the American Medical Association* 224, 1973.

Daubar, R. R., and Kannel, W. B. "Some Factors Associated with the Development of Coronary Heart Disease. Six Years Follow-up Experience in the Framingham Study." *American Journal of Public Health* 49, 1959.

Dawber, T. "Eggs, Serum Cholesterol, and Coronary

Heart Disease." *American Journal of Clinical Nutrition* 36, 1982.

DeMoss, Virginia. "The Good, the Bad & the Edible." *Runner's World,* June 1980.

Deutsch, Ronald M. *Realities of Nutrition.* Palo Alto, Calif.: Bull Publishing Co., Inc., 1976.

"Dietary Goals for the United States." Washington, D.C.: Government Printing Office, Stock No. 052-070-03913-2.

"Diet, Cholesterol and Heart Disease." *New England Journal of Medicine,* Vol. 304, No. 19, 1981.

Duncan, K. "The Effects of High and Low Energy Density Diets on Satiety, Energy Intake, and Eating Time of Obese and Nonobese Subjects." *American Journal of Clinical Nutrition* 37, 1983.

Enos, W. F., et al. "Pathogenesis of Coronary Disease in American Soldiers Killed in Korea." *Journal of the American Medical Association,* 1955.

Falko, J. M., et al. "Improvements of High-Density Lipoprotein—Cholesterol Levels." *Journal of the American Medical Association,* Vol. 247, No. 1, 1982.

Farb, Peter, and Armelagos, George. *Consuming Passions: The Anthropology of Eating.* Boston: Houghton Mifflin Co., 1980.

Farquhar, John W. *The American Way of Life Need Not Be Hazardous to Your Health.* New York: W. W. Norton & Co., 1978.

Ferguson, J. M. *Habits, Not Diets: The Real Way to Weight Control.* Palo Alto, Calif.: Bull Publishing Co., 1976.

Fixx, James. *The Complete Book of Running.* New York: Random House, 1977.

Flippin, Royce. "Weight Control." *The Runner,* July 1985.

Flynn, M. "Effect of Dietary Egg on Human Serum Cholesterol and Triglycerides." *American Journal of Clinical Nutrition* 32, 1979.

Foote, E. "Advertising and Tobacco." *Journal of the American Medical Association,* Vol. 245, No. 16, 1981.

Friedman, G.D., et al. "Mortality in Cigarette Smokers and Quitters." *New England Journal of Medicine,* Vol. 304, No. 23, 1981.

Friedman, Meyer, and Rosenman, Ray H. *Type A Behavior and the Heart.* New York: Alfred A. Knopf, 1974.

Glass, C. David. *Behavior Patterns, Stress, and Coronary Heart Disease.* New York: Halsted Press, 1977.

Goulart, Francis Sheridan. "The Good—and Bad—of Diet Foods." *Consumer Digest,* September/October 1979.

Hamilton, E. M., and Whitney, E. N. *Nutrition: Concepts and Controversies.* St. Paul, Minn.: West Publishing Co., 1979.

Hanssen, Maurice. *Everything You Wanted to Know About Salt.* New York: Pyramid Books, 1968.

Hartung, G. H., et al. "Relation of Diet to High-density Lipoprotein Cholesterol in Middle-Aged Marathon Runners, Joggers, and Inactive Men." *New England Journal of Medicine,* Vol. 302, 1980.

Hausman, Patricia. *Jack Spratt's Legacy: The Science and Politics of Fat and Cholesterol.* New York: Richard Marek, 1981.

Hjermann, I., et al. "Effect of Diet and Smoking Intervention on the Incidence of Coronary Heart Disease." *The Lancet,* December 1981.

"How Bad Is Cholesterol?" *Newsweek,* June 9, 1980.

Hur, Robin. *Food Reform: Our Desperate Need.* Austin, Tex.: Heidelberg Publishers, 1975.

"Jogging Is as Beneficial to Heart as Marathon Running." *Internal Medicine News,* Vol. 11, No. 14, 1978.

Kannel, W. B., et al. "Is Serum Total Cholesterol an Anachronism?" *Lancet,* Vol. 2, 1979.

Katahn, Martin. *The 200 Calorie Solution.* New York: W. W. Norton & Co., 1982.

Keys, A. "Coronary Heart Disease Among Minnesota Business and Professional Men Followed After Fifteen Years." *Circulation* 27, 1963.

———. "Coronary Heart Disease in Seven Countries." *Circulation* 41, Supplement 1, 1970.

———. "The Diet and the Development of Coronary Heart Disease." *Journal of Chronic Diseases* 4, 1956.

Knowles, John. "The Responsibility of the Individual," in *Doing Better and Feeling Worse: Health in the United States,* edited by John Knowles. New York: W. W. Norton, 1977.

Kramsch, D. M., et al. "Reduction of Coronary Atherosclerosis by Moderate Conditioning Exercise in Monkeys on an Atherogenic Diet." *New England Journal of Medicine,* Vol. 305, No. 25, 1981.

Kraus, Barbara. *Calories and Carbohydrates.* New York: New American Library, 1981.

———. *The Dictionary of Sodium, Fats and Cholesterol.* New York: Grosset & Dunlap, 1974.

Kullman, Donald A. *ABC Milligram Cholesterol Diet Guide.* North Miami Beach, Fla.: Merit Publications, Inc., 1977.

Lappe, Francis Moore. *Diet for a Small Planet.* New York: Ballantine Books, 1971.

Lazarus, A., and Fay, A. *I Can if I Want to.* New York: William Morrow & Co., 1975.

Liebman, B. "Good Fats?" *Nutrition Action,* July/August 1986.

———. "Losing Streak, the Latest Diet Aids Deemed Dangerous to Your Health." *Nutrition Action,* September 1982.

Linde, S. M., and Finnerty, F., Jr. *High Blood Pressure.* New York: David McKay Co., 1975.

"Lipid Research Clinics Coronary Primary Prevention Trial Results. II. The Relationship of Reduction in Incidence of Coronary Heart Disease to Cholesterol Lowering." *Journal of the American Medical Association,* Vol. 251, No. 3, 1984.

Luna, David. *The Lean Machine.* Culver City, Calif.: Peace Press, 1980.

McDougall, J. A., and McDougall, M. A. *The McDougall Plan.* Piscataway, N.J.: New Century Publishers, 1983.

McNamara, J. J., et al. "Coronary Artery Disease in Viet

Nam Casualties." *Journal of the American Medical Association,* 1971.

Mahoney, Michael, and Mahoney, Kathryn. *Permanent Weight Control: A Total Solution to the Dieter's Dilemma.* New York: W. W. Norton, 1976.

Maultsby, Maxie C., Jr. *Help Yourself to Happiness Through Rational Self-Counseling.* New York: Institute for Rational-Emotive Therapy, 1975.

Mayer, Jean. *A Diet for Living.* New York: Pocket Books, 1976.

Midgley, W. "On the Fast Food Trail . . ." *Diabetes Forecast,* 1979.

Mirkin, Gabe. *Getting Thin.* Boston: Little, Brown & Co., 1983.

Mirkin, G. B., and Shore, R. N. "The Beverly Hills Diet—Dangers of the Newest Weight Loss Fad." *Journal of the American Medical Association,* Vol. 246, No. 19, 1981.

"Nutritive Value of American Foods in Common Units." U.S. Department of Agriculture, 1979.

O'Brien, B. "Human Plasma Lipid Responses to Red Meat, Poultry, Fish, and Eggs." *American Journal of Clinical Nutrition* 33, 1980.

Page, I. H., et al. "Prediction of Coronary Heart Disease Based on Clinical Suspicion, Age, Total Cholesterol, and Triglyceride." *Circulation* 42, 1970.

Piscatella, Joseph C. *Don't Eat Your Heart Out.* New York: Workman Publishing Co., 1983.

Pollock, Michael, Wilmore, Jack, and Fox, Samuel M., III. *Health and Fitness Through Physical Activity.* New York: Wiley Publishing Company, 1978.

Pomerleau, O. F., and Pomerleau, C. S. *Break the Smoking Habit.* Champaign, Ill.: Research Press, 1977.

Pritikin, N., Leonard, J., and Hofer, J. *Live Longer Now.* New York: Grosset & Dunlap, 1974.

Pritikin, N., and McGrady, P.M., Jr. *The Pritikin Program for Diet and Exercise.* New York: Grosset & Dunlap, 1979.

"Regression of Atherosclerosis: Preliminary but Encouraging News." *Journal of the American Medical Association,* Vol. 246, No. 20, 1981.

Remington, D. W., Fisher, A. G., and Parent, E. A. *How to Lower Your Fat Thermostat.* Provo, Utah: Vitality House International, Inc., 1983.

Revkin, Andrew. "Eat Like a Peasant, Feel Like a King." *American Health,* March 1986.

Rickman, F. "Changes in Serum Cholesterol During the Stillman Diet." *Journal of the American Medical Association,* Vol. 228, 1974.

Rifkind, B. M., and Segal, P. "Lipid Research Clinics Reference Values for Hyperlipidemia and Hypolipidemia." *Journal of the American Medical Association,* Vol. 250, No. 14, 1983.

Robinson, C. H. *Basic Nutrition and Diet Therapy.* New York: Macmillan Publishing Co., 1970.

Schaefer, E. J., et al. "The Effects of Low Cholesterol, High Polyunsaturated Fat, and Low Fat Diets on Plasma Lipid and Lipoprotein Cholesterol Levels in Normal and Hypercholesterolemic Subjects." *American Journal of Clinical Nutrition,* Vol. 34, 1981.

Schwartz, Robert M. *Diets Don't Work.* Las Vegas: Breakthru Publishing, 1982.

Selye, Hans. *Stress Without Distress.* Philadelphia: Lippincott Publishers, 1974.

Shealey, Tom. "The Good Fats." *Prevention,* December 1985.

Shekelle, R. B. "Western Electric Study." *New England Journal of Medicine,* 1981.

———, et al. "Diet, Serum Cholesterol, and Death from Coronary Heart Disease." *New England Journal of Medicine,* Vol. 304, No. 2, 1981.

Simonton, O. Carl, et al. *Getting Well Again.* Los Angeles: J. P. Tucker, 1978.

Sipple, H. L., and McNutt, K. *Sugars in Nutrition.* New York: Academic Press, 1974.

Smoking: Facts You Should Know. American Medical Association. Chicago: 1971.

Snider, Arthur J., and Oparil, Suzanne. *Hypertension*. Chicago: Budlong Press, 1976.

Sobey, E. "Aerobic Weight Training." *Runner's World,* August 1981.

Stamler, J. "Diet and Coronary Heart Disease." *Biometrics,* Vol. 38, Supplement, 1982.

———. "Lifestyle, Major Risk Factors, Proof, and Public Policy." *Circulation* 58, 1978.

Storer, T. W., and Ruhling, R. O. "Essential Hypertension and Exercise." *The Physician and Sportsmedicine,* Vol. 9, No. 6, 1981.

Streja, D., and Mylin, D. "Moderate Exercise and High-density Lipoprotein Cholesterol." *Journal of the American Medical Association,* 1979.

Stuart, R. *Act Thin, Stay Thin*. New York: W. W. Norton, 1978.

Stunkard, Albert J. *The Pain of Obesity*. Palo Alto, Calif.: Bull Publishing Co., 1976.

Sullivan, Steven. "Coping with Boredom, Rejection & Burnout." *Life Association News,* June 1986.

Swank, Roy L., and Pullen, Mary-Ellen. *The Multiple Sclerosis Diet Book*. Garden City, N.Y.: Doubleday & Co., 1977.

Thoresen, Carl, and Mahoney, Michael. *Behavioral Self-Control*. New York: Holt, Rinehart & Wintston, 1974.

Toufexis, Anastasia. "Dieting: The Losing Game." *Time,* January 20, 1986.

———. "Taming the No. 1 Killer." *Time,* June 1, 1981.

Trafford, Abigail. "America's Diet Wars." *U.S. News & World Report,* January 20, 1986.

"Two Studies Trace Role of Stress in Heart Disease." *Journal of the American Medical Association,* Vol. 232, No. 7, 1975.

Ulh, G. S., et al. "Relationship Between High Density Lipoprotein Cholesterol and Coronary Artery Disease in Asymptomatic Men." *American Journal of Cardiology,* Vol. 48, No. 5, 1981.

Walker, A. "The Human Requirement for Calcium: Should Low Intakes Be Supplemented?", *American Journal of Clinical Nutrition* 25, 1972.

Walker, C. E. *Learn to Relax: 13 Ways to Reduce Tension.* Englewood Cliffs, N.J.: Prentice-Hall, 1975.

Wallis, Claudia. "Salt: A New Villain?" *Time,* March 15, 1982.

Wisser, R. W., et al. "Atherosclerosis and the Influence of Diet: An Experimental Mode." *Journal of the American Medical Association,* 1965.

Woo, R. "Effect of Exercise on Spontaneous Calorie Intake in Obesity." *American Journal of Clinical Nutrition* 36, 1982.

Wood, Peter D. "The Cholesterol Controversy Is Over!" *Runner's World,* March 1984.

Yudkin, John. "Sugar and Coronary Heart Disease." *Food and Nutrition News,* Vol. 36, No. 6, 1965.

———. *Sweet and Dangerous.* New York: Bantam Books, 1972.

GENERAL INDEX

Butter, 118, 127
Buttermilk, low-fat, 111

C

Cabbage, Chinese, 316
Caffeine, 166–68
Calcium, 13, 200
  in dairy products, 90, 91 93,
    138
Calhoun, John B., 239
California, University of, 205,
    283
  at Los Angeles (UCLA),
    248, 265, 275
Calloway, Wayne, 177
Calories:
  in beverages, 139, 163–66
  burned at rest, 45, 61, 78–
    79, 84, 189–90, 215
  burned in exercise, 67, 182–
    83
  in carbohydrates, 88
  consumed by overweight vs.
    normal people, 180–81
  density of, 87, 132, 152
  digestive metabolism and,
    81, 118–19
  saved in easy recipe
    modifications, 308–9
  in fast foods, 122–23
  in fat, 87–89
  in fish vs. red meat, 105–6
  in gaining or losing a pound
    of body fat, 67–68
  needed for present and ideal
    weights, 77–83
  in oils and cooking fats, 118–
    19
  physical energy metabolism
    and, 79–80
  recorded in food diaries, 171
  timing intake of, 173–74
Cancer, 12, 33
Candy, 132, 133
  fat in, 134
Cannon, Walter B., 231

Carbohydrates, 67, 119
  calories in, 88
  in diets, 59–60
  See also Complex
    carbohydrates
Carbon monoxide, 21, 22,
    274–75, 276–77, 282
Cardiac risk factors, 4, 5
Cardiovascular Health Risk
    Self-Assessment, 27, 28–
    31
Cardiovascular system, 17–20
  exercise and, 193–94
  See also Coronary arteries;
    Heart
Castelli, William, 50–53, 107,
    318
Cellophane noodles, 318
Cellulite, 58, 187
Center for Science in the
    Public Interest, 95, 114
Cereals, breakfast, 125–26, 148
  fiber in, 146
  sugar in, 131, 134, 136
Cerebral hemorrhage, 53
Champagne vinegar, 321
Change, receptiveness to, 292–
    94
Cheese, 111–13
  Parmesan, 319
Chesney, Margaret, 249
Chew (smokeless tobacco), 284
Chicken:
  cooking methods for, 104
  defatted broth, vegetables
    sautéed in, 120–21
  fat content of, 103–4
Children:
  after-school snacks for, 312
  cigarette smoking by, 281–82
  coronary heart disease in,
    24–26, 54
  detrimental lifestyle of, 24–
    26, 202–3
  exercise by, 180, 202–3
  overweight in, 54–55
  passive smoking and, 282,

M

N

O

T

INDEX TO RECIPES

Note: Italic page numbers indicate variations within main recipes.

C

V

W

Z